HUMANKIND
SHARED PLANET
DIVIDED BY NORMS

A handbook for addressing diversity, equity, and inclusion through social responsibility.

Matthew Ajiake, PhD

SONIKA
PUBLISHING

San Francisco, Las Vegas, New York, London, Berlin

While the concepts, decision-making processes and practices discussed in this book are organization-focused, the models presented are also applicable to familial and other non-organization-based relationships. Since this is a handbook, not all the presentations are applicable to all readers as presented, but because we share one humankind and one planet, they are applicable in varying degrees by responsibility, association and/or impacts. They also provide actionable steps that we can each take to close the gaps in our divisive norms within our respective spheres of influence.

Publisher's cataloging-in-publication data

Names: Ajiake, Matthew, author.

Title: Humankind shared planet divided by norms: a handbook for addressing diversity, equity, and inclusion through social responsibility / Matthew Ajiake, PhD.

Description: San Francisco [and others]: Sonika Publishing, [2022] | Includes: bibliographical references.

Identifiers: ISBN: 978-1-60012-109-8 (hardback) | 978-1-60012-110-1 (eBook) | 978-1-60012-111-X (audiobook)

Subjects: LCSH: Diversity. | Equity. | Inclusion. | Social norms. | Belongingness. l Inequities. | Race relations. | Gender relations. | Social ethics. | Social problems. | Manners and customs. | Attitude change. | Cultural pluralism. | Fairness. | Social integration. | Sustainability. | Social systems. | Social institutions. | Attitude (Psychology) | Human behavior. | Social responsibility of business. | Diversity in the workplace. | Decision making. | Values.

Classification: LCC: HM676.A45 2022 | DDC: 306--dc23

Spanish: ISBN: 978-1-60012-112-8 (hardback) | 978-1-60012-113-6 (eBook) | 978-1-60012-114-4 (audiobook)

French: ISBN: 978-1-60012-115-2 (hardback) | 978-1-60012-116-0 (eBook) | 978-1-60012-117-9 (audiobook)

Portuguese: ISBN: 978-1-60012-121-7 (hardback) | 978-1-60012-122-5 (eBook) | 978-1-60012-123-3 (audiobook)

German: ISBN: 978-1-60012-118-7 (hardback) | 978-1-60012-119-5 (eBook) | 978-1-60012-120-9 (audiobook)

DEDICATION

To my children Olivia Ngozi Ajiake (husband Dana Farley), Jason Ozaoghena Ajiake (wife Rebeka), Austin Bawa Ajiake, (fiancé Rhonda Johnson) and granddaughter Eliana (Olere), Josiah Ayodele Ajiake, and Grace Anoke Ajiake—you have enriched my humanity and life beyond measure, and I am forever grateful for your love and support. Original manuscript was dedicated to Austin for his 20th birthday.

Acknowledgements

Very special thanks to my editor, Dr. Daniel DeCillis, who was very patient throughout the entire process of constant changes and who masterfully provided developmental editing and full fledge editing for the entire book. Very special thanks to Lisa Sanchez-Corea Simpson and husband Justin Simpson who also provided conceptual and editorial guidance and constant encouragement to press forward. Thanks for your friendship.

The making of this book was in a sense a global affair by professionals who were highly skilled in their crafts and who made our working together a pleasant experience. Very Special thanks to Oladimeji Alaka (Nigeria) who designed the book cover; Faisal Adeel (Pakistan) who designed the book interior, Jaylan McNealy (USA) who designed several of the graphics and charts. Very special thanks to the language translators: Annalie Smarry (Germany) who translated the book into French and German and Maria Semideyr (Venezuela) into Spanish.

Table of Contents

INTRODUCTION

Wе live on a shared planet that is shaking itself to pieces through biases; on this much we can all agree. Every organization, society, community, locale, country, and continent has its own norms and biases. Every human being alive today has their own biases. Norms and biases are the moderators that shape our decision-making because they are the intersection between our minds and our realities. Norms or biases affect the decisions that we make and the activities that we get involved in whether individually or collectively.

Norms live in our thoughts and manifest in everyday decisions and activities. Our successes in creating socially responsible organizations and meeting our sustainable development goals rest on how well we address them. In this book, I focus on addressing divisive norms that are discriminatory and have long plagued humankind. While racial discriminatory practices as we know them today are less than 500 years old, gender inequality and religious discriminations goes back to the beginning of recorded history. This is where diversity, equity and inclusion (referred to throughout this book as either DE&I or DEI) as an emerging social science becomes a very important tool for addressing organizational norms that are unfair and unjust, even if they are society-endorsed.

How do we define unfair or unjust norms? Unfairness, in its simplest definition, is any form of injustice, partiality, or deception that manifests in inequitable or unequal practices. According to the Federal Trade Commission and the US Dodd-Frank statutes, each unfair practice has three basic injury tests: *"It must be substantial; it must not be outweighed by any countervailing benefits to consumers or competition that the practice produces; and it must be an injury that consumers themselves could not reasonably have avoided (FTC 1980)."*

Discriminatory norms can cause personal, psychological, spiritual, mental, and generational injury to minority, marginalized, disadvantaged or vulnerable groups. They become rooted and amplified in social contracts—divisive norms that they cannot avoid because they are endorsed and enforced by society. These social contracts can be traditional (gender inequality), or they can be new, for example the segregation based on the European and American history of slavery. While much progress has been made since the 1960s to address discriminatory practices in America, systemic and structural racism have not gone away. Instead, they remain deeply rooted in housing, employment, consumer markets and credit markets.

There is abundant research in the Social Sciences on defining discrimination which is primarily focused on behavior. Some scholars and legal experts contend that discrimination by itself does not assume a specific cause but may be driven or motivated by racism (ideologies), prejudice (attitudes), or stereotype (beliefs)—(Pager and Shepherd 2008). These experts define racial discrimination as either having a disparate impact or manifesting as differential treatment. In differential treatment, a person is treated unequally because of their race; but in disparate impact, they are treated equally based on established norms or rules and procedures, which nonetheless generally favor one racial group over another (Pager and Shepherd 2008).

Contemporary literature on racial discrimination questions its relevance in the face of the progress that has occurred since the 1960s. But Dr. Martin Luther King's answer (part of his Washington DC "I have a dream" speech) remains true: *"There are those who are asking the devotees of civil rights, when will you be satisfied? We can never be satisfied as long as the Negro is the victim of the unspeakable horrors of police brutality...We cannot be satisfied as long as the Negro's basic mobility is from a smaller ghetto to a larger one...No, no, we are not satisfied, and we will not be satisfied until justice rolls down like waters, and righteousness like a mighty stream."*

The inequitable or unequal treatments of groups and persons based on ethnicity or race is the simplest form of racial discrimination. But racial discrimination goes beyond treatments due to race, because racial disparities go deeper; they manifest in divisive norms established over time through policies and privileges that deliberately accord one group privileges over another. For example, white privileges, established by policies and sustained by politics, continue to drive racial inequalities in America regardless of efforts to improve acceptance of our shared humanity and the quality of life for minorities, especially African Americans. Why?

Today's racial discriminatory norms in America were established not by the legacy of slavery alone, but by deliberate housing policies which began in the 1930s as the nation was coming out of the Great Depression. At the time, the government funded the establishment of white suburban neighborhoods with incentivized investment programs (including the GI Bill) while at the same time it disincentivized minority and black neighborhoods with disinvestment programs (including the later overrepresentation in subprime markets that led to the loss of black owned homes). These policies allowed white racial groups to prosper and pass down intergenerational wealth accrued through home ownership, provided a stronger and more sustainable tax base for schools, promoted quality of life through environmental and other life-enhancing ecosystems, supported healthcare access and affordability, etc. There's nothing wrong with these policies per se, but they deliberately marginalized and disenfranchised whole populations of minorities for generations.

Capitalism at the turn of the 20th century, amplified by a tremendous surge in economic prosperity after World War II, should have raised all peoples' "boats," but it did not because of white policies, politics, and practices. These decisions and activities economically pushed minorities back to the dark ages while enabling the white population to sail through generations of unchallenged prosperity.

Part of social responsibility involves not holding someone responsible for the actions of others from their identifying group when they were not involved in the decision-making process. White people living today cannot be blamed for the decisions and activities perpetrated against minorities by their forebears, but they are socially responsible for ensuring that those discriminatory norms and social contracts do not continue to marginalize and disadvantage minorities.

Racial discrimination in America and the systemic and structural decisions and activities that gave it sustenance were not level playing fields. A level playing field can't be considered fair and just when one group of runners begin a 100-yard race at the 50-yard mark while the rest of the runners are huddled back at the starting line. Understanding that at the end of slavery in 1865, the freed slaves were the most highly skilled workforce in America provides the illuminating context. What happened when the hopes and dreams of highly-skilled African Americans were systematically dashed and as a people group—for over 150 years—disenfranchised from the economic engine that capitalism birthed on their backs? The suggestion that the increased number of African Americans in the workforce is an indication that America has reached parity in race relations is a misnomer.

Are we supposed to forget that the plight of African Americans today is the result of engineered social change established and sustained by deliberate policies? If the Bible had not recorded the highs and lows of human beings who once lived out their lives in living colors, would Sunday school teachers or preachers have material to teach or preach about morality and how we can be better human beings because of their lived experiences? Right out the gate in human relations development, we learned that Adam and Eve's first offspring, Cain, killed his brother Abel; when asked the question, *"Where is your brother Abel?"* he responded with a question of his own: *"Am I my brother's keeper?"* Today, we answer this question in the affirmative, when we acknowledge the past unjust and unfair practices and create solutions to solve them together as our brothers and sisters' keepers by affirming the people and the impact of the human decisions and activities that adversely affected and continues to affect them as a people group. Therefore, applying DE&I as a moderator of human relationships within the social responsibility and sustainable development framework makes sense.

White policies, privileges, and politics kept America a racially divided nation in many ways, making them DE&I matters that cannot be resolved by wishing them away or by benevolent gestures or denial theatrics. We must study them as a social science so that current and future generations would learn from them and make our shared humankind better for it. If racial and gender inequalities could be wished away and we arrived at a utopian parity, we would have long been there. But systemic and structural racial and gender divisive norms require systemic and structural responses. There isn't an easy fix. Even when they work, ad hoc responses always have shelf lives.

As an emerging social science, DE&I impacts every single academic discipline and organization. Most college disciplines today do not include DE&I as a core competency alongside general education subjects such as western history, arts, literature, arithmetic, etc. This is a missed opportunity to create awareness and knowledge about our shared humankind's lived experiences through a DE&I lens. DE&I is so encompassing and penetrating because it involves the core of our humankind's norms—the good, the bad, and the ugly! Medical students need a good dose of DE&I awareness and training as much as practicing physicians do. Engineering students need lessons in DE&I as much as practicing engineers do in community planning, building bridges and widgets that make the human experience on planet earth more enjoyable. Arts and science students need DE&I competencies as much as practitioners who use knowledge from these disciplines to propose new ways of doing things or interacting with one another.

All school administrators, professors, and workers need working knowledge and understanding of the DE&I storylines of society because it is essential to moving forward. It's not a response to a social reckoning movement due to racial or gender tensions but rather a part of our human yearning for understanding, acceptance and belonging. From family interactions to organizational networks to national unity policies, DE&I is an invaluable tool in straightening the crooked edges of our current humankind's divisive norms. The irony is that we cannot fully realize the gains from social responsibility and sustainable development commitments without using DE&I as a moderator or currency for facilitating the conversations that lead to the development and implementations of these commitments. Ignoring the historical needs of sections of a population is not socially responsible, nor does it yield globally sustainable fruits like the wholesale adoption of climate change mitigation and adaptation for the good of our shared humanity.

Before we can address our divisive norms, we must first uncover how they were formed and how we process them. This is important because we cannot talk about DE&I without first understanding how our history and societal influences contribute to how we process everyday decisions that impact our workplace, workplans, and work-partners—our organizational eco-system. Ad hoc response to systemic problem is a Band-Aid at best.

The past is the lived experiences of human beings, a continuum that cannot be ignored, denied, or erased; it can provide us with lessons in healing our broken humanity for good. Humankind Shared Planet Divided by Norms looks at our past experiences on the DE&I questions and provides tools and structures for addressing them from a perspective of social responsibility and sustainable development. These tools and structures include the seven principles and seven core subjects as presented by International Standards Organization in its ISO 26000 Social Responsibility, supported by the United Nations' Sustainable Development Goals.

Since every country has its own DE&I issues, challenges, and opportunities, we need a systemic approach to evaluating, addressing, and reporting on them. How do we then collate these divisive norms and address them in a way that is applicable across families, organizations, countries, cultures, and societal proclivities?

I am introducing the Knowledge, Creativity, and Governance (KCG) framework as a model that is applicable in how we can close humankind's divisive norms through a deliberate systemic approach that is moderated by DE&I. The KCG model anchors two other models that we need to bring unfair and unjust societal practices into focus. The KCG framework provides a seamless flow between knowledge and responsibility driven by wholesome principles through (1) knowledge-informed diversity call to action, (2) creativity-driven 3-Step Equity Lens model (opportunity, reconciliation, and disruption) and (3) governance-centered inclusion actionable steps guided by a 3-Step racial and gender inclusion principles that are redemption-driven, restoration-focused and responsibility-centered.

By focusing on what we know about the history and impacts of divisive norms and biases, we can create fair and just solutions. These solutions must be centered with inclusion principles that allow our shared human desires for life, liberty and the pursuit of happiness in our generation to mirror the concerns and actions we take to preserve our shared planet for future generations so they too can live in a fair and just world. After all, fairness, and justice for all are not utopian thoughts but human yearnings that have been silenced for too long by what has become an unsustainable despotic system—unfair and unjust societal and organizational decision-making and activities that exalts some and marginalizes others, using artificial differentiators amplified by societal norms.

This may explain why organizational policies and procedures about DE&I matters are ignored in decision-making, even by those well-trained on why inclusivity is important to make our shared humankind whole. Yet, we know from experience that honor given in a place of dishonor—where our shared humanity is divided by norms—will always be out of order, just as a square peg is out of place in a round hole. Organizations can have the best-designed, most eloquent DE&I policies and procedures, but they are only as effective as the people who use them.

One thing we humans share with water is that we are full of it—water. It is estimated that our human bodies contain 65% to 90% water. Water always looks for a level playing field so it can do what it does best—flow! Humans likewise also pursue a level playing field to do what we do best—live! As water flows, it can become a lifegiving source or a destructive force even as it awaits another moderating force of nature—evaporation—and the return to earth as rain. In like manner, as humans live, we can choose to become a lifegiving source for reevaluating, reimagining, or reinventing ourselves from past unfair and unjust societal practices – or stifle growth with divisive norms and biases.

The question remains whether one generation can physically, mentally and spiritually cancel out or erase a previous generation's decisions—good, bad, and ugly—that contributed to our divisive norms and that marginalizes racial groups, denying them the rights and privileges of being human. Yet, the past never dies because it is a living classroom from which we can learn about broken divisive systems that enabled unjust and unfair practices to take root and thrive. We face the past to change for the better, not run from it, because we can only change what we face and running away from the past puts us in a constant holding pattern, useless motion that kicks the proverbial can down the generational road.

So, we come today to an era of higher purpose, beckoning us to a place of reckoning to become the change we want to see about the divisive norms birthed and administered untethered by previous generations. We still have norms established by people, for example, who believed women cannot be leaders over men–even though they play that role naturally in raising the next generation. We have men paying for the sins of other men in the way women have been treated in the past, becoming guilty today just by showing up male. We have white extremists everywhere afraid of becoming minorities (which tells you how they think minorities are generally treated) and blaming black and brown immigrants for the decisions of their own parents. We have women earning less than men for the same work—spurious inequities framed by gender-supremacist idealism. We even now have Millennials who think Gen Zs are weird and needing deliverance from their social media addictions—two generations that will be interacting in time for the foreseeable future while the older generations sunset. All this does not even scratch the surface of the plethora of humankind's divisive norms that we must face because pretending they don't exist is not a working plan.

My use of the term's "organization" and "organizational ecosystems" throughout this book is applicable to any family unit, association–groups, corporations/associations (for profit of not-for-profit), schools, institutions, small or large businesses, bodies, parties, clubs, etc. Every person works in or through any of these concerns to express their will or purpose or decision on some context or decision. Every human being alive today has norms or biases which they bring to the table. The key is recognizing them, understanding them, and ensuring that they don't negatively influence decision-making.

HOW HUMANS THINK AND MAKE DECISIONS

Before the 1980s airplane cockpits were becoming a challenge to pilots because the very instruments developed to better assist them navigate their aircrafts (norms) became onerously impersonal. Beginning in the 1980s, more attention was given to simplifying pilot decision processes through redesigned cockpit technologies (new norms) and how pilots interacted with them based on training and experience. Designers were engaged to assist instrumentation designers because they understood the nexus between the mind and context in decision-making. The results led to cockpit redesign that enabled pilots to use the technologies in a manner more consistent with how the human body uses its cognitive abilities (intellect, reasoning, thinking, cerebral, mental, etc.,) to make decisions (Wiener 1988).

DE&I and the approach used to address its challenges and opportunities generally take a cause-and-effect paradigm where cognitive solutions are heavily favored. We design DE&I policies, craft carefully curated procedures to address issues, and then make elaborate proclamations that often fall short at key moments. Why? By ignoring the social and psychological influences in our behavior, we create DE&I commitments that are like artificial intelligence coding for people instead of machines. Yet, humans are *"... malleable and emotional actors whose decision making is influenced by contextual cues, local social networks and social norms, and shared mental models. All of these play a role in determining what individuals perceive as desirable, possible, or even "thinkable" for their lives (World Bank 2015)."* We need systemic solutions for systemic problems not ad hoc responses that have shelf life and may buy time but not heal brokenness.

Our existence today is shaped by moderated social norms and biases that we need to understand if we hope to stop those DE&I divisive norms.

These divisive norms create or accentuate societal and organizational inequities and lack of inclusion and belonging by tossing into the social atmosphere the two-faced coin of favoritism and hostility. If, indeed, human identities are not fixed but malleable, then even a person's most entrenched and divisive habits can be reshaped to produce fair and just decisions. In designing effective DE&I plans and programs, consideration should be given to social norms as moderators of behavior and values.

In 2015, the World Bank produced a world development report titled "Mind, Society, and Behavior" that presented new research and practice from across many disciplines about the interrelatedness between mind and context in decision-making. The report integrates findings drawn from disciplines such as neuroscience, sociology, behavioral economics, political science, cognitive science, anthropology, and psychology to explain our understanding of social and psychological influences on how humans make decisions.

I am adapting the three thinking modes of human decision making in this report to explain how our thoughts play out in our DE&I decision paradox and how our biases impact them. These three thinking modes should serve as individual and organizational guides in relation to how the information presented in this book is understood, used as exchange currency for ongoing dialogue, and applied to create new healing norms to our current broken DE&I ecosystems. The three thinking modes of human decision making are: (1) automatic thinking, (2) social thinking, and (3) mental models thinking. This World Bank report captured the interplay between them:

> [T]he idea that paying attention to how humans think (the processes of mind) and how history and context shape thinking (the influence of society) can improve the design and implementation of development policies and interventions that target human choice and action (behavior)...In ongoing research, these findings help explain decisions that individuals make in many aspects of development, including savings, investment, energy consumption, health, and child rearing. The findings also enhance the understanding of how collective behaviors—such as widespread trust or widespread corruption—develop and become entrenched in a society (World Bank 2015).

As this report contends, humankind is not a victim of its own actions, and we always have the ability and capability to change course if we exercise our will:

> [W]hen failure affects the profit-making bottom line, product designers begin to pay close attention to how humans actually think and decide. Engineers, private firms, and marketers of all stripes have long paid attention to the inherent limits of human cognitive capacity, the role that social preferences and the context

play in our decision making, and the use of mental shortcuts and mental models for filtering and interpreting information (World Bank 2015).

For example, in the United States, there was a time when slavery was legal, and slaves were forced by law (and the barrel of a gun) to assume a less-than-human status in life. Both White slave owners and their slaves utilized automatic thinking to assign and exist by societal roles and responsibilities and the quality-of-life measures—opportunities, values, and behaviors. This was the norm in the Antebellum South, notwithstanding the constitutional declaration that all men were created equal and endowed with inalienable rights to life, liberty, and the pursuit of happiness. It was also a social norm in the North—where the champions of ending slavery were a majority—and where slavery was not prevalent, though a significant number of White people still believed innately and in everyday situations that they were a superior race to all others. For those to whom white supremacy was beneficial, it was easy to accept the interpretation that the constitutional reading of this declaration was color-and gender-blind and only meant for the perpetual benefit of White men.

Automatic thinking labeled blacks as inferior and whites as superior. Social thinking determined what roles or responsibilities blacks could assume in society and mental models of white supremacy in every aspect of society ruled the day. A century and half after slavery was abolished, racial injustice still dogs America with the same reinforcing three motifs—automatic, social and mental model thinking. Why?

Systemic and structural racism became the reinforcing social contract that replaced the law and spirit of slavery; it has proven to be a formidable foe to America's pursuit of racial reconciliation pursuit. The three thinking modes provides new scientific insights into how DE&I plans and programs can be made more effective social responsibility reinforcers when a systematic approach is used to drive fair and just organizational values and behaviors through the organization's consciousness. This type of DE&I-inspired systemic change requires individual buy-in to work. One-size-fits-all solutions will not get the job done, because each person must weigh what they must freely give up for the organization and society to move forward in fair and just practices. Exchanging old values and behaviors for new ones are not easy asks but necessary for humankind to progress collectively in an era of globalization and shared common interests including the saving of our planet for this and future generations.

The three thinking principles of decision-making are applicable to DE&I because every person alive have been labeled, have societal role models and mental models of what they can aspire or hope to achieve in the continuum of life, liberty and the pursuit of happiness. The difference is that depending on country, race, tribe, gender, sect, and other factors all contribute to shaping the narratives and the psychological and social influences that go into decision making.

In the twenty-first century, there are some White people in America who question why they should bear any responsibility for slavery when they never owned slaves. While this is a legitimate question to ask, it ignores the continuum of adverse impacts persisting through societal and organizational values, behaviors and culture because slavery and segregation laws once existed and are now comfortably embedded in systemic and structural racism and its many forms of manifestations.

Therefore, in addressing DE&I within the American context, ignoring the historical, psychological, and societal influences on behavior as causes for the enduring legacies of systemic and structural racism would be a mistake. This is because failing to connect the three principles of decision-making impact organizational behavior and to neglect them empowers the continuation of systemic and structural racism by those who deliberately or ignorantly make decisions that promote these values and behaviors. It is true that other nations have their own DE&I issues. But while the issues may be different, their systemic and structural strongholds and the determinations by those privileged by them to keep the status quo are eerily similar. It is the reason we need to understand how human thinking at the moment of decision-making affects the outcome.

AUTOMATIC THINKING

Psychologists broadly agree that human beings generally make decisions by simplifying problems and utilizing two different processing systems of thinking. The first is the automatic system, in which the individual frames a decision based on what immediately comes to mind. The second is the deliberative system, in which the individual is more reflective and considers a broad set of factors (World Bank 2015). According to this World Bank report,

> Most people think of themselves as primarily deliberative thinkers—but of course they tend to think about their own thinking processes automatically and under the influence of received mental models about who they are and how the mind works. In reality, the automatic system influences most of our judgments and decisions, often in powerful and even decisive ways. Most people, most of the time, are not aware of many of the influences on their decisions. People who engage in automatic thinking can make what they themselves believe to be large and systematic mistakes; that is, people can look back on the choices they made while engaging in automatic thinking and wish that they had decided otherwise. Automatic thinking causes us to simplify problems and see them through narrow frames. We fill in missing

information based on our assumptions about the world and evaluate situations based on associations that automatically come to mind and belief systems that we take for granted. In so doing, we may form a mistaken picture of a situation, just as looking through a small window overlooking an urban park could mislead someone into thinking he or she was in a more bucolic place (World Bank 2015).

Figure 0.1 Automatic thinking

Automatic thinking gives us a partial view of the world
To make most decisions and judgments, we think automatically. We use narrow framing and draw on default assumptions and associations, which can give us a misleading picture of a situation. Even seemingly irrelevant details about how a situation is presented can affect how we perceive it, since we tend to jump to conclusions based on limited information.
Humans are inherently social. In making decisions, we are often affected by what others are thinking and doing and what they expect from us. Others can pull us toward certain frames and patterns of collective behavior.

Source: World Bank 2015. This is an adaptation of an original work by The World Bank. Views and opinions expressed in the adaptation are the sole responsibility of the author and are not endorsed by The World Bank.

In the above picture, all four individuals made decisions from an automatic thinking mode because the view available to them provided a narrow framework. Water gushing out of a fire hydrant is misconstrued as rainfall and even the person with a direct view of the hydrant still unfurls an umbrella believing it was rain because of the actions of the other three. We tend to fill in additional information based on *"assumptions about the world and evaluate situations based on associations that automatically come to mind and belief systems that we take for granted."* Moreover, while it is true that we tend to jump to conclusions based on limited information, we also generally process the information that has the most meaning to us – which may not consider important consequences or omit key information from the decision-making process altogether. Sometimes, there is a significant gulf between our intentions and actions. Even with clear knowledge of the full consequences, people may choose to *"make decisions that favor the present at the expense of the future, so that they consistently fail to carry out plans that match their goals and fulfill their interests."*

This paradigm is also applicable when an individual has the authority and the responsibility to make decisions on behalf of a socially responsible organization but allows their own influences and preferences to dictate the decisions they make on behalf of the organization. We know from experience that other people do influence our decisions and choices by what they think, expect, and do. As the World Development Report suggests, in *"experimental situations, most people behave as conditional cooperators rather than free riders (World Bank 2015)."*

Organizational policies and procedures on DE&I matter that affect decision-making and activities face the added challenge of widespread adoption, because they must contend with belief systems that we take for granted, sometimes erroneously assuming that we have overcome these limitations. How many times have you heard someone say they do not see color, and yet their decisions are colored by societal racial divisive norms? Conversely, how many times has an individual had their decisions labeled as racist because they belong to the racial group whose predominant worldview and cultural inclinations historically is racist, though they may not be racist? The novelist Jane Austen reminds us that *"We each begin probably with a little bias and upon that bias build every circumstance in favor of it* (World Bank 2015)." As the World Bank report suggests:

> We normally think of ourselves in terms of the deliberative system—the conscious reasoning self—yet automatic operations generate complex patterns of ideas that influence nearly all our judgments and decisions...Confirmation bias contributes to overconfidence in personal beliefs. People may fail to recognize that they do not know what they claim to know, and they may fail to learn from new information...Persuasion and education must engage with the automatic system to overcome resistance to new points of view (World Bank 2015).

Work in the field of behavioral economics by psychologists such as Daniel Kahneman, Amos Tyversky and many others has expanded the knowledge base on the roles that psychology, social and cultural tendencies play in decision-making. These understandings have informed us that people rarely weigh decisions by comparing them to alternatives (World Bank 2015). This does not mean that people are not capable of considering alternatives, but rather that *"people are hard wired to use just a small part of the relevant information to reach conclusions* (World Bank 2015)." The World Bank report clarified these dichotomies:

> [O]ver the past few decades, evidence has mounted that automatic thinking cuts across wide swathes of human behavior to the point that it can no longer be ignored. The anomalies that behavioral economics is trying to explain are not minor and scattered. They are systematic regularities that can be of first-

order importance for health, child development, productivity, resource allocation, and the process of policy design itself...In standard economic theory, an important behavioral assumption is that people use information in an unbiased way and perform careful calculations. The calculations allow them to make choices based on an unbiased consideration of all possible outcomes of alternative choices that might be made. After people make a choice and observe the outcome, they use the information in an unbiased way to make the next decision, and so on......But confronted with the mounting empirical evidence on large and costly errors that people often make in critical choices—such as poor financial decisions and the failure to adhere to health regimens, take health precautions, and adopt income-increasing techniques after receiving new information—economists have come to recognize the importance of considering the possible impacts on behavior of our dual system of thinking, automatic and deliberative, in the design and testing of policy (World Bank 2015).

Research also indicates that people can switch from automatic to deliberative thinking within an automatic thinking framework. They describe these two thinking patterns as system 1, where decisions are fast, automatic, effortless and associative, and system 2, where they are slower and more reflective.

Figure 0.2 The two systems of automatic thinking

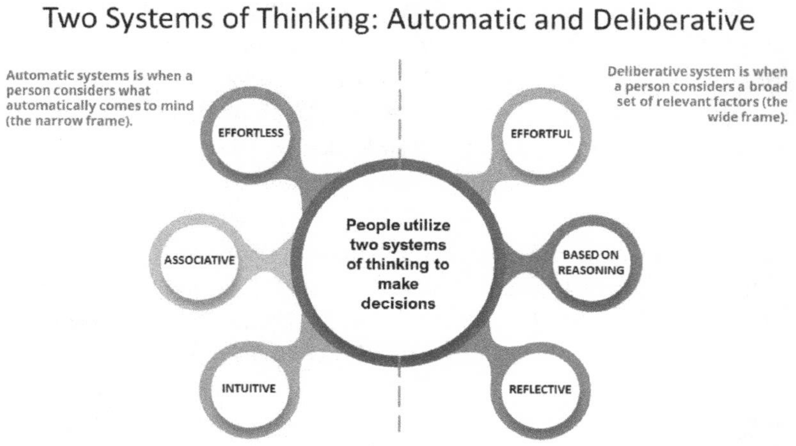

Two Systems of Thinking: Automatic and Deliberative

Automatic systems is when a person considers what automatically comes to mind (the narrow frame).

Deliberative system is when a person considers a broad set of relevant factors (the wide frame).

EFFORTLESS · EFFORTFUL · ASSOCIATIVE · BASED ON REASONING · INTUITIVE · REFLECTIVE

People utilize two systems of thinking to make decisions

Sources: Adapted by the author from: Evans, Jonathan St. B. T. 2008. "Dual-Processing Accounts of Reasoning, Judgment, and Social Cognition." Annual Review of Psychology 59 (January): 255–78.; Kahneman, Daniel. 2003. "Maps of Bounded Rationality: Psychology for Behavioral Economics." American Economic Review 93 (5): 1449–75.

When DE&I policies and procedures are written, organizations assume that people follow these guidelines in a lineal manner—observing every established cue and considering the consequences of their decisions on all people groups and environments impacted. Yet, even before the age of social media, people were already bombarded by race and gender norms in such quantities that organizing them in furtherance of socially responsible decision-making was near-impossible. In particular, the influence of social media far outweighs some of the motivation for socially responsible changes in decision-making at many organizations. While our understanding of social media and its influence on decision making is in its infancy, economic theory has evolved to more realistically align with how and why people make decisions the way they do. The World Development report made the case for how economics has evolved:

> After a respite of about 40 years, an economics based on a more realistic understanding of human beings is being reinvented. But this time, it builds on a large body of empirical evidence— microlevel evidence from across the behavioral and social sciences. The mind, unlike a computer, is psychological, not logical; malleable, not fixed. It is surely rational to treat identical problems identically, but often people do not; their choices change when the default option or the order of choices changes. People draw on mental models that depend on the situation and the culture to interpret experiences and make decisions (World Bank 2015).

This is instructive for leaders and policy makers who establish organizational DE&I frameworks. Just because DE&I policies and procedures are written down and explained in detail does not mean the message is internalized by the workforce and used in a socially responsible manner when making decisions. The role of automatic thinking at this moment of decision must be part of the curated DE&I design.

SOCIAL THINKING

By nature, humankind is a species that shares a common attribute—we are all social creatures. We are influenced by our social identities, networks, norms and preferences (World Bank 2015). Those we value provide the behavioral inference points that we emulate and preferentially identify with in our own decision making. According to the World Bank report:

> Many people have social preferences for fairness and reciprocity and possess a cooperative spirit. These traits can play into both good and bad collective outcomes; societies that are high in trust, as well as those that are high in corruption, require extensive amounts of cooperation... Human sociality (the tendency of people to be concerned with and associate with each other) adds a layer

of complexity and realism to the analysis of human decision making and behavior (World Bank 2015).

When it comes to DE&I, we assume people in general would make fair and just decisions based on our shared humanity when dealing with people from groups that are different from their own. We make this assumption believing that DE&I policies and procedures, driven by well-intentioned trainings and promoted by executive proclamations, are enough to overcome the powerful social narratives that reinforce decisions by social preferences. The World Bank report reminds us that assumptions and reality can actually be miles apart, because people tend to behave as conditional actors in these situations:

However, human sociality implies that behavior is also influenced by social expectations, social recognition, patterns of cooperation, care of in-group members, and social norms. Indeed, the design of institutions, and the ways in which they organize groups and use material incentives, can suppress or evoke motivation for cooperative tasks, such as community development and school monitoring. People often behave as conditional cooperators—that is, individuals who prefer to cooperate as long as others are cooperating (World Bank 2015).

A key reason why good and decent people belonging to dominant preference-driven groups remain complicit is because they enjoy the benefits of the privileges conferred on them by societal networks. This makes them conditional cooperators in the face of unfair and unjust treatments of groups on the receiving end. Preserving privilege becomes the clarion call that reinforces in-group membership and thinking and shows up prominently in decisions. This explains why any threat or perception of the loss of that privilege conjures up the worst norms and biases. Why? One explanation rest in the power of social networks. The World Bank report surmised as much:

All of us are embedded in networks of social relations that shape our preferences, beliefs, resources, and choices…Social networks are the sets of actors and relational ties that form the building blocks of human social experience. Networks provide scope for individuals to reinforce existing behaviors among one another, but they can also transmit novel information and normative pressures, sometimes sparking social change…The ability of social networks to both stabilize and shift patterns of behavior means that they may be able to play an important role in social settings where formal institutions are lacking (World Bank 2015).

The United States provides the context that explains how societal networks stabilize and shift patterns of behavior. In 1865, the Emancipation Proclamation ended slavery in all the Confederate states then at war with the United States through Executive Order. In 1865, the Thirteenth amendment ended all slavery and indentured servanthood in America. In 1868, the fourteenth amendment followed to grant citizenship and equal civil and legal rights to African Americans and other enslaved people. Then in 1870, the fifteenth amendment guaranteed the right to vote to all citizens regardless of race, color, or previous status as slaves. All these were intended to guarantee African Americans the rights to life, liberty and the pursuit of happiness, just like their White American counterparts. It's been more than a century and half since then; while much has changed, much remains the same in social preferences that shape everyday decisions framed by societal values and behaviors in America.

The fact that America still struggles with racial reckoning is perplexing considering it has done more work to correct its original sin of slavery through legislative means than most countries have done in addressing their own respective DE&I challenges. Yet, ingrained social preferences and networks are difficult to change even with very reasoned DE&I plans, as the World Bank report attests:

> Social preferences and social influences can lead societies into self-reinforcing collective patterns of behavior. In many cases, these patterns are highly desirable, representing patterns of trust and shared values. But when group behaviors influence individual preferences and individual preferences combine into group behaviors, societies can also end up coordinating activity around a common focal point that is ill-advised or even destructive for the community. Racial or ethnic segregation and corruption are just two examples (World Bank 2015).

After DE&I trainings are completed and DE&I policy and procedure documents the organization's order of how everyone should conduct themselves when making decisions, these well-intentioned interventions fall short of producing the expected values and behaviors because social preferences are strongholds not lightly discarded. These call for more intentional interventions to counter the stronger social narratives. The World Bank report provides this insight:

> When self-reinforcing "coordinated points" emerge in a society, they can be very resistant to change. Social meanings and norms, and the social networks that we are a part of, pull us toward certain frames and patterns of collective behavior. Conversely, taking the human factor of sociality into account can help in devising innovative policy interventions and making existing interventions more effective. In India, microfinance clients who were randomly assigned to meet weekly, rather than monthly, had more informal social contact with one another two years after the loan cycle ended, were more willing to pool risks, and were three times less likely to default on their second loan (World Bank 2015).

Having a systemically structured response to racial and gender inequalities is probably the only surefire way to establish new norms that can counter the deep-rooted systemic and structural systems upon which current societal social networks are based. Well-intentioned government policies and affirmative action initiatives have not sustainably worked because the pull towards racial and gender frames and patterns of discriminatory collective behaviors have been allowed to be a strong force with no counter-balancing equal and opposite force of change. We generally have DE&I mitigation meetings and corrective actions after a fiasco, but not in everyday encounters. DE&I commitments need just-in-time reinforcements through social contacts that contextualize the changes we want to see within routine interactions.

The workplace is generally functionally designed for people to work in specific disciplines or fields, and it is within these spheres that decisions are made by content matter experts who should be seen as allies on changing the organization's DE&I ecosystem because it is within these settings that the DE&I battles are won or lost. When individuals accept the benefits inherent in our shared humankind as a strength to be harnessed, they can be trusted to reimagine and reinvent their own ecosystems when DE&I moderates social responsibility and sustainable development goals to save our planet for future generations. It ensures that those living in this generation can achieve their purpose and dreams through a more inclusive drive. It begins by moderating social thinking actions to more just and fair patterns for all.

MENTAL MODELS THINKING

The adage that "nothing is new under the sun" is applicable to human mental models, as rarely does a person invent new ways of thinking other than the ones he or she was, is, and continues to be exposed to by others, society and even organizations. These mental models are programmed into our thinking patterns in the form of identities, concepts, categories, causal narratives, prototypes, worldviews, and stereotypes (World Bank 2015). In mental models, perceptions rule reality and interpretations; what individuals perceive to be true become manifested in values and behaviors which end up in decision-making. As the World Bank report notes:

> *The links between perception and automatic thinking are strong, as emphasized by Kahneman (2003)...While both involve the construction of meaning, in both cases the perceiver or thinker is not aware of constructing anything. He imagines that he is responding objectively to the stimulus or the situation...Individuals can also hold onto multiple and sometimes even contradictory mental models—drawing on one or another mental model when the context triggers a particular way of looking at the world.*

Mental models matter for development because they affect decision making (World Bank 2015).

Mental models aren't intrinsically bad; they make the world of decision making possible. Without them, we cannot make shared decisions or understand each other, build networks, take collective actions, or find common ground. They differ from social norms because there is no pressure to conform to values or behaviors that are socially enforced. Instead, mental models are broad themes of how an individual fits in a predefined understanding about how the world works (World Bank 2015). Mental models can also be enablers or exacerbators of divisive norms and biases. For example:

Evidence suggests that historical experience exerts a powerful influence on mental models and, consequently, on how individuals understand and react to the world. An example is the legacy of the Atlantic slave trade. Slavery was ubiquitous in many eras and in many societies, but the slavery associated with the Atlantic slave trade had some properties that made it especially destructive. The middlemen for the white slave traders included local Africans. To protect themselves from being captured and sold as slaves, individuals needed guns, but to buy guns they needed cash. The main way of obtaining cash was to kidnap someone and sell him into slavery. Thus the Atlantic slave trade turned brothers against each other, chiefs against subjects, and judges against defendants. Lower levels of trust in some parts of Africa today are related to the intensity of slave trading centuries ago. Regions that were more susceptible to slave raids due to accidental features of geography have lower levels of trust today—trust toward strangers, friends, relatives, and institutions (World Bank 2015).

Mental models about how the world works vary from one society to another and from one country to another; this makes them DE&I matters for all organizations, whether local or global in scope. If DE&I frames how fair and just decisions are made, it should also provide mental models of how social responsibility works the world over.

The twenty-first century has seen mass movements of people from one society or country to another. We have also seen global organizations exert direct influence as both employers and providers of products and services. Mental models are of particular interest in decision making because when individuals move from society to society, their mental models are called to question by the expectations in their new environments—workforce, workplace, and work-partners. The World Bank report contends that:

Institutions and mental models are closely related; sometimes a change in a mental model requires a change in an institution. But in some cases, exposure to alternative ways of thinking and to new role models—in real life, in fiction, and through public deliberation—can have a measurable influence on mental models and on behaviors, such as investment and education (World Bank 2015).

Consider, for example, a manager in a high-tech company in Silicon Valley, California who grew up in India where their mental models were framed by a caste system. While not every person who grew up in India subscribes to mental models framed by caste systems, this manager (within this context) would need to adjust their mental models to match the expectations in a country that has its different mental models—imperfect, but models, nonetheless. What if the Indian manager works in India and must make decisions impacting Americans with a mental model based in a caste system? How does an organization capture broad, socially responsible DE&I mental models? The World Bank report continued:

As studies of immigrants show, mental models can be passed down from generation to generation: mental models of trust, gender, fertility, and government, for instance, are typically learned from the culture one grows up in. Social learning processes allow for the intergenerational transfer of mental models. A society's past may affect the perceptions and evaluations of opportunities by current members of the society (World Bank 2015)...Since we are social animals, our mental models often incorporate the taken-for-granted beliefs and routines of the culture in which we were raised. One way of thinking about culture is as a set of widely shared tools for perception and construal. The tools may not be fully consistent with one another [and] a given person might exhibit different behaviors when the mental model that is most accessible to him or her changes (World Bank 2015).

Mental models are sometimes collectively referred to as "culture" because they originate from the cognitive side of our social relationships and play key roles in our individual decision making by providing links to the meanings, we use to justify the actions we take. The linkage therefore between culture and meaning serves as *"tools for enabling and guiding action; (World Bank 2015)"* the World Bank report affirmed that:

Mental models and social beliefs and practices often become deeply rooted in individuals. We tend to internalize aspects of society, taking them for granted as inevitable "social facts." People's mental models shape their understanding of what is right, what is natural, and what is possible in life. Social relations and structures, in turn, are the basis of socially constructed "common sense," which represents the evidence, ideologies, and aspirations that individuals take for granted and use to make decisions—and which in some cases increase social differences (World Bank 2015).

In the American classroom of social change, the Constitutional Amendments and Civil Rights Acts were tools to enable and guide Americans to choose a path towards racial reconciliation and build a more perfect union. Unfortunately, white supremacy and its quest for dominion has kept America racially polarized and conspiratorially imprisoned many within the White racial group. The Ku Klux Klan was formed in 1865 specifically to defend and reestablish Southern norms (continuing the automatic thinking about race relations). Jim Crow laws legalized these norms through separate but equal laws (continuing the social thinking). Movies like *Birth of a Nation* justified these norms, establishing mental models for generations of White Americans about their roles and responsibilities in society. Together, these three institutions framed the white entitlement mental models (privilege, politics, policies) that are at the heart of white supremacy which manifests as racial injustice, unfair equity practices and culturally exclusive America even today. About mental models, the World Bank report attests:

> *A body of writing by anthropologists and other social scientists points out that what people take to be hard evidence and common sense (their basic mental models of their world and how it works) is often shaped by economic relationships, religious affiliations, and social group Identities. Much of that work argues that achieving social change in a situation where mental models have been internalized may require influencing not only the cognitive decision making of particular individuals but also social practices and institutions. A canonical example of a mental model is a stereotype, which is a mental model of a social group. Stereotypes affect the opportunities available to people and shape processes of social inclusion and exclusion. As a result of stereotypes, people from disadvantaged groups tend to underestimate their abilities and may even perform worse in social situations when they are reminded of their group membership. In these and other ways, the stereotypes can be self-fulfilling and can reinforce economic differences among groups (World Bank 2015).*

When a ten-person corporate board, for example, is forced by law or stakeholder pressures to include minorities and women in their ranks, they typically include a single person of color and one woman to comply, and then celebrate these appointments as if they fully accomplished the intention of the ideals. It's not hard to see that even if the two newcomers vote in tandem on board decisions, they remain vastly outnumbered, and the old boy network can easily continue business as usual. When the person of color and the woman are made to feel as though they should be grateful to be allowed as part of the board, it reinforces the stereotypes, adding acrimonious feelings on all sides. The World Bank report states:

Since we are social animals, our mental models often incorporate the taken-for-granted beliefs and routines of the culture in which we were raised. One way of thinking about culture is as a set of widely shared tools for perception and construal. The tools may not be fully consistent with one another [and] a given person might exhibit different behaviors when the mental model that is most accessible to him or her changes (World Bank 2015).

In the above example, the minority male and female must find new ways to create a new normal within the context of cultural relationships in which they must exercise their roles and responsibilities as board members. Since human divisive norms are etched in the mind, policies and procedures by themselves—no matter how well curated or intentioned—are generally not enough to address DE&I matters of the heart. This is further exacerbated when the individuals that must carry out these decisions are unaware of the principles that frame their own decision-making processes.

Leaders, policy makers, and all those involved in carrying out decisions within an organization's eco-system should be aware of their own individual and institutional proclivities that impact these decisions and the three principles that frame them—automatic and social thinking and mental models. Even DE&I professionals, advocates and champions are not exempt from biased norms that can creep up in their decision-making. Awareness of these three decision-making principles along with the seven principles and seven core subjects in ISO 26000's social responsibility framework and the three models introduced in this book provide a systematic approach to implement in policies and procedures around organizations' DE&I commitments.

Knowing the principles that affect our decisions allows individuals and organizations to create procedures to mitigate their divisive and adverse impacts on minority and vulnerable groups. After all race, tribe, gender, caste, class and other forms of -isms used to divide humankind are themselves perpetuated by systemic and structural norms. Below are findings summarized in the World Bank report of 2015:

In India, low-caste boys were essentially just as good at solving puzzles as high-caste boys when caste identity was not revealed...However, in mixed-caste groups, revealing the boys' castes before puzzle-solving sessions created a significant "caste gap" in achievement in which low-caste boys underperformed the high-caste boys by 23 percent, controlling for other individual variables (Hoff and Pandey 2006, 2014). Making caste salient to the test takers invoked identities, which in turn affected performance. The performance of the stigmatized low-caste boys declined relative to the performance of the high-caste boys. When caste was revealed to the high-caste boys when they were not mixed with low-caste boys, the high-caste boys underperformed, perhaps because the revelation evoked a sense of entitlement and "Why try?" The simple presence of a stereotype can contribute to measured ability differences, which in turn can reinforce the stereotype and serve as a basis for distinction and exclusion, in a vicious cycle.

Finding ways to break this cycle could increase the well-being of marginalized individuals enormously. Evidence from a number of contexts suggests that invoking positive identities can counteract stereotypes and raise aspirations. Having individuals contemplate their own strengths has led to higher academic achievement among at-risk minorities in the United States, to greater interest in antipoverty programs among poor people, and to an increase in the probability of finding a job among the unemployed in the United Kingdom (Cohen and others 2009; Hall, Zhao, and Shafir 2014; Bennhold 2013).

The above findings are instructive when creating or developing DE&I-moderated solutions across sustainable development principles, because the goal is to break the cycle of divisive norms and not amplify or create new ones. Understanding the seven principles and seven core subjects of social responsibility moderated by DE&I gives an organization added tools to ensure DE&I commitments as decision-making frameworks are implemented across its eco-system with value-added, incentivized new norms that effectively supersede older, inequitable ones.

Furthermore, since our global divisive norms are interrelated—like gender and racial or ethnic inequalities—understanding where the rest of the world is aspiring to go in making our planet safer and the humans living in it reaching their full potential becomes very important. The United Nation's Sustainability Goals 2030 provide opportunities for organizations to make impacts through structured organizational actions that feed into and support global collective actions. Finally, the KCG, 3-Step Equity lens and 3-Step Inclusion actional principles provide a synergistic approach by bringing all the above-mentioned knowledge, principles, and tools together to address our divisive norms, laying out systematical counterbalancing measures to systemic and structural racism and gender inequalities.

WHY I CHOSE TO GET INVOLVED ON DE&I MATTERS

As a C-suite executive, I was often baffled by how some academically curated solutions to organizational challenges sometimes fail to include people that look and think like me. These solutions, in other words, do not identify or engage me as a stakeholder of interest and of influence.

So, in my 40s, I decided to go back to school and earn a PhD in Management with Leadership and Organizational Change specialization. Since the adage that, "if you cannot beat them, join them" is true, I decided to base my research and creation of new knowledge in the areas of change management and leadership with a global perspective, uninhibitedly energized by my African flair and the vitality of a global citizen. For my dissertation, I researched the application of a social responsibility construct on the triple bottom line of prosperity, people, and planet within the public sector. This research, titled "The Triple Bottom Line and Social Responsibility Framework in Public Sector Management," has been downloaded in 130 countries by individuals representing 517 institutions (education 43%, commercial 37%, government 13%, other 3%). Taking this research further, I am now applying it in this book to DE&I as a moderator for Social Responsibility and Sustainable Development frameworks from both academic and practice perspectives.

This book is part of my own journey to choose a path with a higher purpose so I may leave the world better than I found it. As an African American of Nigerian descent, I learned to appreciate my roots, particularly thanks to the self-esteem and self-worth that was infused in me through my family and through prevailing societal social thinking and mental models. Nowhere did this become clearer for me than when I heard the famous South African Archbishop Desmond Tutu recall how his self-esteem and self-worth was damaged because he was born and raised in then Apartheid South Africa.

Archbishop Desmond Tutu recalled a time in the 1970s when he visited Nigeria and boarded a local flight where the pilot and copilot were black. Tutu was thrilled to see this, because in his mental models from South Africa, such a sight would be considered an aberration. However, while the impact of this sight was real to Tutu because it shattered a false mental model of what black people could do, it did not free him from the damage already done to his psyche about his humanity, reinforced by societal divisive norms and applied to his everyday view of realities.

Once they were fully seated, Tutu went effortlessly into automatic thinking mode and became uneasy and scared, wondering whether that day was his last on Earth because black pilots were in the cockpit. Tutu then moved into deliberative thinking by giving meaning to his fear, because a White person was not in control in the cockpit which meant that they were likely going to crash and die. This false belief trap led Bishop Tutu to conclude later that discriminatory and divisive norm promoted within the apartheid system *"... can cause a child of God to doubt that he or she is a child of God... You come to believe what others have determined about you, filling you with self-disgust, self-contempt and self-hatred, accepting a negative self-image (Tutu 1986)."*

Divisive norms that marginalize minority groups and women do not stop at denial of rights but extend to damaging their self-worth and wellbeing—psychologically, socially, spiritually and even generationally. When a person's identity and capabilities are framed by societal norms that are so divisive and marginalizing, our collective humanity is diminished beyond what we can fully capture in research studies. Dreams never come to life, cures are never invented, and solutions to humankind's problems remain unsolved. Unfortunately, sometimes these decisions and the frames and patterns that moderate them are ingrained so deeply that they manifest in automatic, social and mental models thinking without the individuals even realizing what affected their decisions.

As a Nigerian studying in the United States, I faced the same historical automatic, social and mental models used to categorize and marginalize black people. But because I had a deeper infusion of self-esteem and self-worth moderated by my national pride in being a Nigerian, I struggled to understand the new social thinking and mental models used to identify and engage me as a person. It took me almost three years to wrap my brains around the extent of racism and its various manifestations as frames and patterns that shaped the values and behaviors that I confronted daily from both white and black and brown people groups—all expecting me to conform to their models of who I was and what I can and cannot achieve in life. But conformity to a divisive and marginalizing system was a slow death, and I wanted to live a life uninhibited by societal limitations based on the color of my skin. I learned to stop wasting time shadow boxing people who did not understand why I could not conform or buy into a white supremacy framework or allow it to define my humanity, even if I lived in America.

It all began for me innocuously in college after living with all racial and tribal groups in Nigeria. Yes, there were ethnic and cultural differences, but not superiority-inferiority dichotomies cemented by public policy and implemented in societal norms. I remember a White professor in college who felt they could not give a black person an "A" grade in a class where White students were earning lesser grades **(social thinking)**. It had nothing to do with work product, because in my case, the curriculum for this Sophomore class was equivalent to my high school third year curriculum in Nigeria. In a sense, I was repeating a class I received an "A" equivalent in Nigeria for, but because of racial profiling, I could not get more than a "B"—and that was "generous" from the professor's perspective.

Then I had another White professor who had experience with many Nigerian students who generally got "A's" in his classes. This professor was confused as to whether I was really from Nigeria because I was dribbling in circles between a B and a C+ in one of his classes **(mental model thinking)**. I quickly awoke from my lackadaisical slumber, sharpened my chops and scored A's in this professor's classes going forward. I was not going to be the exception or the asterisk in this professors' mental model of Nigerian students.

Finally, I had a professor who already established I was a "D" student just by showing up in his class black **(automatic thinking)**. I quickly figured out the situation and changed the class to an audited one, which meant no grade could be assigned. Two weeks before the end of class, I sat in front of this teacher as he regrettably explained how he was struggling not to give me an "F" for the class. I watched this professor just about explode when I informed him that I was auditing the class.

I had no concept then of the role automatic, social, and mental model thinking played in society let alone in academic environment—mostly driven by racial and gender stereotyping. The same thinking models followed me as I climbed the corporate ladder with an MBA, backed by work experiences. This did not spare me from the assumption by some that I was an affirmative action hire, my qualifications and merits explained away by stereotypical profiling. Today, I am using these experiences and those of others before me and my contemporaries to research and produce new knowledge on global leadership and DE&I from around the world.

The first version of this book was a 600-page titled *"Diversity, Equity and Inclusion, a Social Responsibility Currency"* but just before the release, I shared the book with some members of the Harvard Business School Community Partners who took special interest in both the topic and material. After reviewing the book and with input from my editor, Lisa Sanchez-Corea Simpson from the group reported that I actually had three books compressed into one. We agreed that a handbook for both academic and practice leaders on DE&I was needed as the subject was becoming an emerging social science and the implications were global not just relevant to one country. So, I did what humans do best: adapted. I:

1. reimagined a book series that can speak to most people around the world on the DE&I issues, challenges, and opportunities as a handbook for this emerging social science, thus **Humankind Shared Planet** became the new lifecycle title for the series,

2. reevaluated my existing material and how best to present and apply them in more manageable and consistent manner beginning with establishing the key principles and models introduced in this book for a wholesome social responsibility ecosystem moderated by DE&I, thus "...**Divided by Norms, a handbook for addressing diversity, equity, and inclusion through social responsibility"** became this first volume, and

3. reinvented or repurposed the exploration of each countries DE&I from its own unique DNA story (issues, challenges, and opportunities) using the key principles and models introduced in volume 1. I then shifted or repurposed my existing research and

writings on four countries, moving them into a second volume, thus, the **Global DE&I Stories…a handbook for exploration and navigation of the social science of diversity, equity and inclusion** became the focus and drive for each country to be examined each year.

Volume I establishes the structural tools, principles, and key understandings in utilizing DE&I as the moderator for social responsibility and sustainable development for addressing societal and organizational norms that are divisive and marginalizing of people groups on artificial differentiators. I also used them to research, examine, explore and share new understandings around DE&I issues, challenges, and opportunities from various countries.

Volume II of the Humankind Shared Planet book series looked at global DE&I stories from Brazil, India, Nigeria, and the United States. Together, these four countries will be home to 27% of the world's population by 2050. Their high proportion of the global population, their educational profiles, and the mobility of their citizens across nations makes these four countries a force to be reckoned with both as a source of DE&I inspiration and a classroom for understanding the issues, challenges and opportunities of our divisive humankind norms and biases, along with what we can do to address them collectively. By 2100, the world's population is expected to top 10.9 billion people; these same four countries will still be home to over 27% of the population. By then India is projected to rank #1 at 1.09 billion, Nigeria at #2 with 791 million, USA at #4 with 336 million and Brazil at #13 with 165 million (World Economic Forum 2020).

These four countries have their own DE&I storylines with unique DNAs that tell their stories from their beginning until the present day. Yet, these countries also have correlations that are extremely rich and outstanding— two immigrant-built nations on top of preexisting indigenous people groups and two colonized nations with their DNAs framed by both the colonizers and their own actions after independence. Together, they offer rich insight on the divisive norms that vexes and blesses our shared humankind—their DE&I stories. These stories reveal the origins of some of our divisive norms, as well as the keys to solving them together through the utilization of some basic socially responsible frameworks.

DE&I IS A LEADERSHIP AND CHANGE MANAGEMENT MATTER

Change in the world continues at an ever-increasing rate, and the advent of the internet has only accelerated this pace in recent years. The internet has emerged as a connecting force for negotiating relationships with all stakeholders—internal and external. Communications tools such as cellphones have leveled the global playing field and provided widespread access to products and services. Technological tools that would have left the developing world in the dark for decades are now seamlessly integrated and accessible by people in the remotest parts of our globe. Human demographics and the educational attainment of minority and vulnerable groups have also changed, no doubt due at least in part to the divide between communities which have ready access to high-speed internet connectivity and those which don't.

Whenever people of different races or genders interact, DE&I issues, challenges and opportunities always exist. But DE&I is not just an organizational or societal issue, it is also a family affair. The notion of a father and mother as a unit is the very definition of diversity. Family structures are increasingly diverse and have equity and inclusion challenges of their own. This book offers broad concepts that can be applied in family DE&I situations as well.

In the United States, it is projected that by 2045, no single race or ethnic group will be in the majority. This means that any organization serious about sustainability must embrace DE&I as core elements of its policies and procedures and do everything possible to create a culturally relevant environment. A diverse, inclusive, and equity-focused corporate ecosystem will be the differentiator between organizations today and in the future because the workforce will become even more selective about which corporate values appeal to their higher purpose.

Unfortunately, racism and deep-rooted hatred have become even more potent and aggravating, and organizations are paying the price in lawsuits for the actions of some of their employees. JPMorgan Chase Bank, for example, recently paid $24 million to settle a class action lawsuit with some of its African American employees who sued because of discriminatory practices by their supervisors and managers. There is no simple solution to this situation; racism in American businesses must be dealt with within each entity's ecosystem.

The triple bottom line of economy, environment and social conversations have gone mainstream as organizations now see the big picture and integrate them as part of their social responsibility and sustainable worldview. While sustainable development is being tackled in a discipled and structured way, systemic racism, sexism, tribalism, and sectionalism continue to confound attempts to weed them out. Without a clear and effectively implemented DE&I plan, organizations become environments where these stereotypes are perpetuated.

As people groups from around the world move away from their ancestral homes to new homelands, with mobility enabled by globalization, they also carry with them social mental models or contracts about human behavior that impacts their automatic, social, and mental models thinking. Studies of immigrants have shown that mental models are transferable from generation to generation because they *"are typically learned from the culture one grows up in (World Bank 2015)"* and as social creatures, *"our mental models often incorporate the taken-for-granted beliefs and routines of the culture in which we were raised (World Bank 2015)."* Since "culture" is a shared tool for human perception and construal, we also know that a person has the capability to demonstrate *"...different behaviors when the mental model that is most accessible to him or her changes (World Bank 2015)."* Little academic work has been done to study these dynamics in relation to DE&I.

For DE&I plans to be sustainably effective, they should be systemic and in direct response to systemic and structural racial, gender and other related issues. DE&I platitudes and promises to do better in the future are no longer enough unless they are backed by actionable steps that lead to an ecosystem of inclusivity and belonging for all.

The truth is that marginalized and vulnerable groups did not become disenfranchised overnight. The actions and policies that marginalized these groups took time to develop before they became established divisive norms that were normalized by social contracts. Therefore, we cannot resolve divisive norms if we fail to acknowledge they exist. The past never dies, and it is foolhardy to believe that a generation removed from it can erase or deny it ever existed.

Human experiences are part and parcel of humanity's lived continuum on planet earth and serve as lessons to be learned—either for good or evil. Today, discriminatory practices adversely impact minority and vulnerable groups, preventing them from achieving their potential and impeding access to institutional processes, credit facilities, employment opportunities and other benefits easily accorded their counterparts in the majority.

At issue for most organizations, at least those whose leaders are truly committed to a diverse and inclusive workforce, workplace, and work partners, is what to do about residual racism and other forms of societal discriminatory practices. These longstanding biases are often heart-deep; they are far more difficult to root out with executive memos or governmental decrees. Employees bring life-long learned biased values and behaviors to the workplace, many of which do not manifest in explicit behaviors but are present, nonetheless.

Explicit bias is in-your-face blatant, outwardly lived, and easily identifiable, but implicit bias manifests inwardly. Implicit bias is not as easy to spot or root out but releases gut-wrenching punches that have significant adverse implications for minority and vulnerable groups. This makes implicit bias far more dangerous than explicit bias. Implicit bias cannot be easily "unlearned;" it requires social dialogue, where people describe and confront the issues of implicit and explicit bias head-on with lived experiences stories to illuminate the pain and suffering caused by them.

These externally learned values and behaviors create a gap with the organizational codes aimed at creating and promoting an equitable, diverse, and inclusive work environment. Promoting and upholding fair and just decisions and practices is hard work, but the potential payoffs are substantial. With a new generation of workers not satisfied working just for paychecks and wanting to find higher purpose meaning in their work, the competition for a sustainable workforce is a challenging but competitive investment for all organizations. In America, a positive glimpse into the workforce suggests that there are more White people ready and willing to join the cause for fair and just sea change on the divisive norms that have long plagued the country. They should be encouraged and supported, not lumped with those in their demographic who clamor for a long-gone era, wishing for a return to an irreconcilable and unrealistic quest for a white supremacist status quo.

The world has changed in the last half a century, America is still changing, and much of the workforce no longer supports divisive behaviors, values and norms. For example, a World Bank survey report on *"closing the gender gap (World Bank 2022)"* contends that no country or community or economy can prosper to its fullest potential when it ignores the full and equal participation of men and women. According to this Energy Sector Management Assistance Program survey report, when women are equally engaged in the workforce, financial performance is enhanced, development outcomes are improved, innovation is stimulated, and safe work environments become normalized (World Bank 2022). Further, when women serve in executive and management positions, they can assist organizations achieve gender equality faster and transform it to become more innovative, profitable and even generous (World Bank 2022). Other benefits include:

1. Global GDP could rise by up to $28 trillion by 2025 if women participate in the economy at the same rate as men.
2. Access to quality jobs and assets are key levers of change for women, communities, businesses, and economies. They are also fundamental drivers of economic growth, poverty reduction, and shared prosperity.
3. Multiple studies show that women are 9 to 23 percentage points more likely to gain employment outside the home following electrification. Although in 2018, $1.9 trillion was invested, globally, interventions and investment to address gender gaps in the sector remain minimal
4. At least 30 percent of female leadership in firms is linked with profit margins up to six percentage points higher than firms with no women in the top ranks (World Bank 2022).

Although the above numbers were focused on the electrification industry, they are relevant to the overall impact women can have in the workforce when they are represented in equal numbers as men. Today, women are 50% or more of populations in most countries. They are graduating from college at higher numbers than men and increasingly moving into the workforce. All these positive steps are the keys to unlocking socially responsible organizational values, behaviors, and cultures. This is the hope that globalization can help enhance and sustain for humankind.

One leader in the twentieth century who gave us a good lesson on identifying, reconciling, and closing the gaps between aspirational DE&I goals and actual lived experiences was Dr. Martin Luther King, Jr. Dr. King taught us that we all share one humanity, and we live on one shared planet, and that our individual happiness is intrinsically tied to the freedoms we enjoy together. We are brothers and sisters, adorned in different hues. The color of a person's skin does not determine their character, qualifications, or experiences, and neither does the primary group he or she identifies with socially—certainly not in this new dawn. So, Dr. King prophetically painted a socially responsible and sustainable vision of what America as a country could become, while directly addressing the actual state of the nation's affairs on race relations during his time—hope captured by the renowned Sam Cooke song, "A Change is Gonna Come." Dr. King's words are inspirational, but they were also aspirational at that time. Using the models mentioned above, we could easily summarily categorize Dr. King's I have a Dream speech (King Institute) as follows:

- **Knowledge-informed diversity call to action**

  Five score years ago, a great American, in whose symbolic shadow we stand today, signed the Emancipation Proclamation. This momentous decree came as a great beacon light of hope to millions of Negro slaves who had been seared in the flames of withering injustice. It came as a joyous daybreak to end the long night of their captivity. But 100 years later, the Negro still is not free. One hundred years later, the life of the Negro is still sadly crippled by the manacles of segregation and the chains of discrimination. One hundred years later, the Negro lives on a lonely island of poverty in the midst of a vast ocean of material prosperity. One hundred years later the Negro is still languished in the corners of American society and finds himself in exile in his own land. And so we've come here today to dramatize a shameful condition. In a sense we've come to our nation's capital to cash a check.

- **Creativity-driven equity opportunity, reconciliation and disruption**

  Ajiake 3-Step Equity Lens model:

Equity Opportunity: *I have a dream that my four little children will one day live in a nation where they will not be judged by the color of their skin but by the content of their character. I have a dream today.*

Equity Reconciliation: *I have a dream that one day down in Alabama, with its vicious racists, with its governor having his lips dripping with the words of "interposition" and "nullification", one day right there in Alabama little black boys and black girls will be able to join hands with little white boys and white girls as sisters and brothers. I have a dream today.*

Equity Disruption: *I have a dream that one day every valley shall be exalted, every hill and mountain shall be made low, the rough places will be made plain, and the crooked places will be made straight, and the glory of the Lord shall be revealed, and all flesh shall see it together.*

- **Governance-centered inclusion actionable steps**
  Ajiake 3-Step Inclusion Principles

  Redemption-driven Principle 1: *This is our hope. This is the faith that I go back to the South with. With this faith we will be able to hew out of the mountain of despair a stone of hope.*

  Restoration-focused Principle 2: *With this faith we will be able to transform the jangling discords of our nation into a beautiful symphony of brotherhood.*

  Responsibility-centered Principle 3: *With this faith we will be able to work together, to pray together, to struggle together, to go to jail together, to stand up for freedom together, knowing that we will be free one day.*

The time *"...to transform the jangling discords of our nation into a beautiful symphony of brotherhood"* is upon us. America can and should take the lead in this era, because despite its deep-rooted racial problems, it has done the most work in DE&I. America continues to struggle with its racial reckoning because it has not fully resolved its racial divides. Yet, although deeply entrenched biases persist and still flare up in American policies and culture, America has not entirely abandoned the quest for a more racially equitable and inclusive nation. Today, the advent of globalization has made it a worldwide issue. It's actually disruptive to disregard DE&I these days.

While it's true that America is distracted and divided in unprecedented ways today, it is still a country that has demonstrated an ability to reinvent itself over and over, both in peaceful and chaotic times. History bears this out. America's racial reckoning and heightened discord are particularly heated today because a privileged group is dying out. After all, the heat from a dying sun is hottest not in the middle, but in the outer peripheries where embers flash themselves to oblivion. The middle of the sun is where new power comes to life and reinvigorates the sun's natural order. Racial rhetoric that flames white supremacy ideals may burn hot but are no longer sustainable. It's heated rhetoric, spewing hate, longing for a bygone era.

Dr. King's words are prophetic, poetic, and poignant, especially for those in authority today. A lot has changed since he gave that speech; few African Americans living in America today are facing and fighting the same racist systems that Dr. King and his generation fought. We are no longer denied access to restaurants and restrooms; we more rarely face the ugliness of the evil face of racism, and when we do, there is often public backlash against the racists. There are more African Americans rising to the top of business and civic life, like President Barack Hussein Obama — *"every valley is becoming exalted."*

All the exalted hills and mountains of institutional racism and their support infrastructures that stood against equal rights and freedom for gainful employment, to vote and to exercise our human rights have and continue to be made obsolete—*made low*, even amid today's stubborn opposition from those who want to revive the inglorious days of divided America through manipulating the ballot box.

The *"rough places"* in our courtrooms, where inconsistent application of the law has dealt great injustice to African Americans, are no longer hidden or recognized only by the victims. The pervasive injustices have become more widely recognized and, more importantly, rejected by people of all colors. The rough places have become and continue to become plain.

The *"crooked places,"* where police dogs were unleashed on peaceful civil rights protesters or where minority and vulnerable groups endured cruelties up to and including lynching, are no longer everyday realities. And when they do occur, these events invite backlash from all Americans, not just the affected minority groups. The crooked places have become and are becoming straight. While there are still distressingly high numbers of racists and hatemongers in America, most Americans have come to terms with our shared humanity in recognition of our shared origin—revealing the glory and wisdom of a Creator who created many hues in wholesome representation of Himself, personified in male and female genders. Globalization amplifies our interdependence and our singular humanity. This is why it threatens those who prefer America isolated for the ideological benefit of one group.

Some people point to recent progress, so hard-won, and erroneously claim that remedies for racism are a thing of the past, because we're living in a post-racial society. Are we living in a post-racism era? Far from it! The forms of racism and other forms of -isms today are in some ways even more lethal now because they are better hidden and more difficult to diagnose and address. Historically, the widespread fear of Black people by White people that sustained racism for so long has been fading, as stereotypes are dispelled when the two groups intermingle, especially in the workforce and at sporting events. Movies like *Birth of a Nation* amplified these stereotypes;

movies today, which generally feature far more diverse casts, are much more likely to amplify the truth about real Americans.

I was barely three months old when Dr. King made his transcendent speech and called on everyone now under 60 years old today to be part of the generation who would hold hands together – brothers and sisters of a shared humanity. Holding the hands of our brothers and sisters metaphorically challenges us to heal our broken human systems by disrupting discriminatory norms. This is a stark contrast to previous generations of Americans (collectively) who refused to or could not achieve an American dream that embraced people from all racial and gender groups. That dream is the quintessential meaning of One nation, under God, indivisible with liberty and justice for all! Therefore, America can set an example for addressing DE&I issues, challenges, and opportunities if for no other reason but for the fact that it is still the leader of the free world and the sons and daughters of every nation on earth lives within its borders. As the saying goes, as America goes so goes the rest of the world!

This also means that when anyone works in an organization that is not diverse, they have a social responsibility to make waves, to question when there will be a more diverse board of directors, management, and workforce. When one occupies a position of authority, making decisions and establishing practices, one needs to consider ways to bring healing. To do nothing is to be complicit. In the past, this was socially acceptable. Today, it's unconscionable.

Lived experiences are the key. They are as real to those who lived through them as their humanity. These lived experiences are meant to light the way for present-day humans, so they can make better, fairer, and more just decisions, and promote activities that narrow or eliminate divisive norms. Attempts to ignore, deny, or erase past unfair and unjust human DE&I experiences only highlight the reasons why they must be preserved, studied, and learned from. In a sense, the desire to erase what happened in the past is a desire to avoid change, both now and in the future. This is not a sustainable plan because it confirms the adage that when we forget the past, we repeat it.

Humankind Shared Planet, Divided by Norms invites you the reader to come explore what humans do best: reexamine, reimagine, and reinvent ourselves, our divisive human legacies, and our visions of what is possible, both for ourselves and our shared legacy. Guided by social responsibility principles and core subjects, we can create a fair and just world today and still ensure that future generations can do the same in their time—thus sustaining a humankind that exists in a shared planet with less divisive norms. WELCOME ABOARD!

Chapter One

INTRODUCING DIVERSITY, EQUITY AND INCLUSION, AND OTHER KEY CONCEPTS AND THEIR APPLICATIONS

Gone are the days when diversity, equity, and inclusion were a footnote in organizational reports. The issues have taken center stage in public and private institutions, including governments, business, and academia. There is a dynamic and growing dialogue about how these entities can adapt and improve their individual and organizational response to the changes demanded, as they seek to be more diverse, equitable, and inclusive.

Organizations are becoming more cognizant of their roles and responsibilities beyond profits for financial stakeholders. Their roles and responsibilities are becoming more clearly defined and expanded. Finally, we are beginning to see our planet as a communal asset that must be protected from the effects of climate change. While governments and private enterprises spend trillions of dollars to combat the damage already done to our planet, a more corrosive damage remains unresolved: our racial and gender divides. Just like our planet, our people are assets; not commodities to be used and abused, but something valuable to be nurtured, developed, and allowed to reach their full potential.

Organizations are like people; they have values and behaviors that amplify societal realities within their eco-systems. Businesses, from large corporations through small and microbusinesses, are in fact attempting to combat deep-rooted racism, gender inequalities and other forms of discriminatory practices that contradict and undermine their stated core values and desired operating practices. These ingrained biases are the weak links in an organization's commitment to social responsibility and its sustainable development pursuit. It does not mean however that these weak links are lost causes. That is what motivated the creation of this book. It is a handbook for organizations aspiring to go beyond abstract goals for a diverse, equitable and inclusive work environment, to tangible goals that implement practical working solutions which are based in the realities of the workplace.

Diversity, Equity and Inclusion Primer

Black Lives Matter (BLM) has become a global mantra chanted in nearly every language on Earth. It's been emblazoned on any surface imaginable and used as a rallying cry for a new generation, exhausted by the systemic and structural racism that has historically disadvantaged black, brown, and colored people. BLM exposes and challenges societal values concerning how we define our shared and equal humanity (diversity), how we participate individually and as groups in the shared resources of our shared planet (equity) and how we belong and find both our place and voice in the systems and structures that govern or regulate our everyday life experiences (inclusion). As Archbishop Desmond Tutu reminded us,

> When we see others as the enemy, we risk becoming what we hate. When we oppress others, we end up oppressing ourselves. All of our humanity is dependent upon recognizing the humanity in others (Tutu 2015).

Diversity, equity, and inclusion (DE&I) is not a fad or just another management strategy that the rank-and-file employee can wait out. On the contrary, DE&I represents core social responsibility norms or mores that both organizations and society ignore at their peril. It's essential and has tremendous impacts on the people, the planet and directly on the profit and on sustainable pursuits. By pursuing social responsibility objectives, organizations are tackling sustainable issues and challenges, whether they recognize it openly or not.

Understanding our human diversity

Human diversity refers to any characteristic differences between individuals and groups; it can manifest in race, gender, nationality, religion, sexual orientation, ethnicity, socio-economic status, physical and mental abilities differences, ideas, thoughts, perspectives, values, etc. The identification of "race" as a form of diversity is a social construct that we have generally accepted, though the word is a misnomer and perpetuates the divide of humanity in artificial terms. Does color establish differences in human "races" that are biologically distinct in such a way as to differentiate a person or group from humanity as a species? Has skin color ever defined gender or intellectual capacity in the womb?

Diversity around the world is characteristics-based, demographically measured and compliance-enforced, but it can mean different things in different places. While most of the characteristics apply universally, not all differences are measured in all jurisdictions or legally and equally enforced. For example, in a country where nearly everyone is predominantly of one skin color, racial equity may not be a major priority. The same is true if a nation does not have norms for honoring and providing for its veterans of war, or if it fails to affirm the roles of women in society outside the traditional domesticated ones. In general, diversity is defined by the following array of characteristics:

Table 1.1: General human diversity categorization

GENERAL DIVERSITY CATEGORIZATION			
Characteristics-based, demographically measured and legally enforced:			
☐ Race ☐ Gender or Gender Reassignment ☐ Ethnicity ☐ Tribe	☐ Religion or Belief ☐ Sex or Sexual Orientation ☐ Age	☐ Disability ☐ Veteran Status ☐ Pregnancy and Maternity	☐ National Origin ☐ Language ☐ Socio-economic Status ☐ Other

Diversity based on individual and/or group characteristics usually do not address any other diversity-related concerns above legal demographic categorizations, nor do they consider our shared humanity as its bedrock. Executing the Social Responsibility agenda extends our understanding of diversity and opens a dialogue that goes beyond legal definitions, helping us realize our shared humanity. The diversity of being human beacons us to appreciate our shared humanity and compels us to close the divisive norms in our generation so future generations can build upon our collective goodwill to humankind.

Understanding Equity vs Equality.

Philosophically, equality and equity are often perceived as two different thoughts: while equality refers to treating everyone the same without preference for their needs: equal rights; equity refers to treating everyone fairly based on their individual or group needs: equity rights.

Equity is about rights and justice embedded in equitable matters free from favoritism and bias—whether implicit or explicit. The state or quality of being equal is expressed through identical measurements, amount, quantity, or even identification (such as society, group, class, etc.). In the context of social justice equity is "fair" treatment of people that gives them access to opportunities and advancements while reducing or eliminating the barriers that prevent them from achieving their life's purpose or contributing their best at work, school, community, etc.

Historically, affirmative action steps have been taken to address inequalities in society. These measures are generally not popular; they're typically followed by strong backlash from majority racial groups that believe such actions takes things away from them. While affirmative action may have assisted the United States in pushing the needle forward on race relations, for example, its impact as a sustainable solution against the backdrop of often formidable opposition has reached some limits. The situation demands new or additional tools or measures to change societal inequities and inequalities.

The Independent Sector, a US-based membership organization that brings non-profits, foundations, and corporations together "to advance the common good," provides a comprehensive definition for equity:

> Equity is the fair treatment, access, opportunity, and advancement for all people, while at the same time striving to identify and eliminate barriers that have prevented the full participation of some groups. Improving equity involves increasing justice and fairness within the procedures and processes of institutions or systems, as well as in their distribution of resources. Tackling equity issues requires an understanding of the root causes of outcome disparities within our society (Kapila, Hines and Searby 2016).

All around the world, inequality has become a form of societal dysfunction requiring focused attention and responsiveness. In describing the magnitude of existing inequalities in our world, the United Nations' Transforming our world: the 2030 Agenda for Sustainable Development reported:

> Billions of our citizens continue to live in poverty and are denied a life of dignity. There are rising inequalities within and among countries. There are enormous disparities of opportunity, wealth and power. Gender inequality remains a key challenge. Unemployment, particularly youth unemployment, is a major concern. Global health threats, more frequent and intense natural disasters, spiralling conflict, violent extremism, terrorism and

related humanitarian crises and forced displacement of people threaten to reverse much of the development progress made in recent decades (United Nations n.d.).

Therefore, to achieve equity or equality, we must first understand inequality and its many faces. Some are obvious, but sometimes manifestations of inequality are so innocuous that we become insensitive to their long-term consequences. For example, inequality is using long-held beliefs, customs and associations imposed on a person by virtue of their belonging to a group regardless of how they differ from the stereotyping of that group.

Inequality even manifests in the very way we build our cities. Waste treatment plants, train tracks, freeways, and so forth tend to be in low-income or vulnerable communities that lack the social and political power to object to their placement. This has adverse impacts on those communities economically, environmentally, and socially. The community members aren't generally at the decision table because they were never invited, and they are not schooled in the art of stakeholder advocacy. And often, governments' decision to place these things in poor neighborhoods is a conscious one based on the increased ease of doing so and the lower economic and political costs of doing so.

Understanding Inclusion

The reality is that most organizations today—from schools to corporations to government agencies to NGOs—want to create an environment that is not only inclusive, but fair and comfortable. Where individuals can thrive, rising above their differences to give their organizations the best they have to offer. In return, they want to receive good education, fair wages and to derive meaning from their efforts, creating in the process organizational "wholeness." Transitioning from inequity-prone cultural and societal norms to the equity aspirations of the 21st century is the challenge. Aligning recognition, rewards, and other forms of positive reinforcement to induce behavior that results in life-giving ventures that bring meaning and the means and resources for living.

Inclusion is the intentional act to avoid excluding people or treating them in an unfair or unequal manner for any reason. At the root of inclusion is the ideal of fairness and equality for all within the spheres to which they belong, have historically belonged, or to which they have been adequately trained and prepared to belong. Inclusion is an important ideal for everyone to consider, because there are inequalities needing to be addressed in nearly every facet of modern life. While we cannot completely eradicate inequity in our world, we can become instruments of healing in the broken systems we confront in our respective spheres of influence.

The spirit of inclusion is our individual and collective capacity and commitment to embrace the equitable participation of our diverse humanity in all our endeavors. Several organizations today have their own definitions of "inclusion" within the context of diversity and equity, and most of these definitions speak to valuing our differences both individually and as groups where all involved in the enterprise achieve their full potential or higher purpose. The Independent Sector, for example, defines it as follows:

Inclusion is the act of creating environments in which any individual or group can be and feel welcomed, respected, supported, and valued to fully participate. An inclusive and welcoming climate embraces differences and offers respect in words and actions for all people. It's important to note that while an inclusive group is by definition diverse, a diverse group isn't always inclusive. Increasingly, recognition of unconscious or 'implicit bias' helps organizations to be deliberate about addressing issues of inclusivity (Kapila, Hines and Searby 2016).

The Ford Foundation provides another definition that captures the spirit of inclusion:

...a culture of belonging by actively inviting the contribution and participation of all people. We believe every person's voice adds value, and we strive to create balance in the face of power differences. We believe that no one person can or should be called upon to represent an entire community (Ford 2022).

Organizations, like human beings, are living organisms existing in an ecosystem that include unconscious and conscious biases, unexamined and preconceived assumptions, unspoken and unvetted differences that shape values, behaviors, and attitudes. These are all manifestations of deep-rooted societal and individual norms and biases that cannot be addressed solely through an organization's policies and procedures. An inclusive vision and mission encouraging a diverse and inclusive workforce, workplace and work partners is vital, but must be accompanied by actual examples and enforcement.

An organization may be limited in its power to change an employee whose worldview conflicts with its vision and mission statements. Personal values and behaviors are largely fixed in place before an employee comes to the employer. Every employee has deep-rooted conscious and unconscious biases exemplified through unexamined and preconceived assumptions. It takes intentional and consistent social dialogues on subject matters that build on each other for an organization to produce a diverse and inclusive workplace environment. These core subjects must cover issues that are real, have been vetted, and include workable solutions so that each employee is comfortable enough to want to embrace a vision of inclusion that brings about belonging.

THE TOOL BOX: ISO 26000 Framework, the 3-Equity Lens Model, and the 3-Step Inclusion Principles

In the twenty-first century, stakeholders have become increasingly savvy, and many require organizations to be socially responsible. This means that these stakeholders want organizations to commit to environmental and societal welfare issues and challenges even as they pursue profitable bottom lines. And they want these organizations to reflect this commitment in their performance reporting. Historically, DE&I was just a few numbers—check in the box—in the voluminous performance metrics that organizations used to define their "good citizens" profile. Today, DE&I is a well-established and growing movement that demands social equity and inclusion matters be more central to the organizational healthy eco-system mapping.

The world as we knew it changed dramatically after the September 11, 2001, attack on the World Trade Center in New York, and again in 2020 when the COVID-19 virus shut down country after country, taking the lives of millions around the world. Against the backdrop of the pandemic another profound event took place: the world watched the sacrifice of George Floyd on an American street corner. Along with the growing awareness and experience of climate change and the real dangers facing current and future humanity, these transformative events have redefined how we think about and protect humankind, pushing issues of DE&I squarely to center stage in the national narrative.

Socio-cultural and globalization upheaval calls for systemic responses to xenophobia, systemic racism, and other structural discriminatory practices that are at the root of the challenges facing individuals, families, business enterprises, and nations today. These challenges can generate or exacerbate gaps between policies and procedures and actual decision-making practices. These gaps present opportunities for us to explore solving the underlying issues through a holistic framework. In this book, I am presenting a vetted academic social responsibility framework and three models that serve as a toolkit focused on addressing these gaps: **(1) ISO 26000 Social Responsibility framework, (2) the Knowledge, Creativity and Governance (KCG) model, (3) the 3-Step Equity model, and (4) the 3-Step Inclusion model.**

1.   ISO 26000 Guidance on Social Responsibility Framework

This book was inspired by the International Organization for Standardization's ISO 26000 Guidance on Social Responsibility because it incorporates 7 principles and 7 core subjects that I used to integrate DE&I as currency for organizational social dialogues:

Table 1.2: The 7 principles and 7 core subjects listing

The Seven Principles	The Seven Core Subjects
1. Accountability	1. Organizational Governance
2. Transparency	2. Human Rights
3. Ethical Behavior	3. Labor Practices
4. Respect for Stakeholders' Interests	4. The Environment
5. Respect for The Rule of Law	5. Fair Operating Practices
6. Respect for International Norms of Behavior	6. Consumer Issues
7. Respect for Human Rights	7. Community Involvement and Development

Together, the 7 principles and 7 core subjects form an intentional framework for organizational social dialogue where DE&I serves as currency for social responsibility exchanges. This approach gives the organization a reasoned and intentional path to sustainable development of social responsibility and to organizational wholeness beyond just complying with existing laws. This path also leads to the implementation, promotion, and integration of socially responsible norms throughout an organization's ecosystem, beginning with its policies and procedures. While the ISO 26000 provides common understanding around social responsibility, it does not replace other existing tools and initiatives such as the triple bottom line. Rather, while remaining consistent with international behaviors and norms, this social responsibility construct allows us to develop synergies with frameworks such as DE&I through a lens of organizational diversity, socio-economic, cultural, political and legal conditions and ramifications (ISO 26000 2010).

2. Knowledge, Creativity and Governance Model

The knowledge, creativity and governance model or KCG model is based on the simple notion that **knowledge** invites **creativity** to the table of **governance**. We generally do not create things or systems in a vacuum. Background knowledge is necessary, and what we create needs a structure (governance) to establish the rules of the game, engagement, or participation. This is the essence of the KCG model:

AJIAKE KNOWLEDGE, CREATIVITY AND GOVERNANCE (KCG) FRAMEWORK

Knowledge prepares the groundwork for creative solutions to emerge from data-driven awareness and/or data-mined Knowledge-informed information
Creativity converts informed knowledge into just and fair socially responsible actions or results leading to sustainable development outcomes
Governance establishes just and fair decision-making and operational practices, rules of engagement, and paths to an inclusive organizational eco-system

3. Ajiake 3-Step Equity Lens Model

The 3-Step Equity lens model provide a framework for creatively developing solutions to diversity and inclusion issues by asking the tough questions as to how we got to where we are and what we must do to ensure we do not remain there. To bridge inequity gaps, we need three para-mediating focus areas: opportunity, reconciliation, and disruption. These three focus areas require the engagement of all appropriate stakeholders.

AJIAKE 3-STEP EQUITY LENS MODEL
Equity Opportunity (EO) focuses on opportunities to adjust or correct current inequitable or biased practices (racial, gender and others) with socially responsible fair and just ones.
Equity Reconciliation (ER) focuses on systemic biases (racial, gender and others) and equity norms (values, behaviors, traditions, and activities) that should be reconciled, improved upon, or replaced with socially responsible systemic fair and just ones.
Equity Disruption (ED) focuses on the unjust or unfair decision-making practices and discriminatory social contracts that must be stopped for socially responsible equity framework (racial, gender and others) to develop sustainable root.

4. Ajiake 3-Step Inclusion Principles Model

The Ajiake 3-Step Inclusion Principles provide a working framework to create actionable steps that lead to organizational inclusive environment both immediately and over time. The pursuit of inclusion should be: (1) **redemption-driven**, (2) **restoration-focused**, and (3) **responsibility-centered**. While these 3-Step Inclusion Principles have universal application, for the purposes of this book, I am using them within the context of racial, gender and other inclusion pursuits:

AJIAKE 3-STEP INCLUSION PRINCIPLES

Redemption-driven (RD) principle should guide steps or opportune actions taken to create visible, practical, and measurable socially responsible inclusive (racial, gender and others) organizational eco-system.
Restoration-focused (RF) principle should guide steps or on-going actions that identify entrenched inequitable inclusion barriers (racial, gender and others) and replaces them with socially responsible fair and just ones.
Responsibility-centered (RC) principle should guide steps or actions taken to stop or disrupt divisive norms (the status quo values, behaviors, traditions, and activities) that obstruct socially responsible inclusive (racial, gender and others) practices.

In short, the 7 principles and 7 core subjects of social responsibility can assist you and your organization to bring healing and meaning to your workforce, workplace, and work-partners. This book plays a symphony of different core subject issues that, when addressed at the individual and organizational level, enrich and enhance work and work life balance for all stakeholders—internal and external alike.

Most organizations can curtail explicit bias—outward demonstrations of discriminatory practices—to some extent by DE&I policies and procedures as well as organizational cultural practices. A far more difficult and sinister challenge for organizations pursuing social responsibility is the collection of adversarial, personally-held beliefs, entrenched values and behavioral strongholds that form the inner sanctum of implicit bias. Changing this deep-rooted culture and engaging in a constructive dialogue that will make a difference is the whole point of the frameworks explored in this book.

CASE STUDY 1:
JPMorgan Chase and its Internal Stakeholders

JPMorgan Chase (JPMorgan), a major banking organization, has taken significant and constructive steps to articulate its commitments to DE&I, and has shown some positive progress in its diversity and inclusion framework. This is captured by its commitment as follows:

> *Employees are our greatest asset, and we strive to attract talent from the broadest pool to foster innovation, creativity and productivity. There is tremendous power that results from this kind of diversity. In fact, creating a diverse and inclusive environment is critical to our success, and we are deeply committed to hiring and retaining employees from different backgrounds, experiences, and locations.*
>
> *Diversity brings together people with unique perspectives, and inclusion creates opportunities for all individuals to contribute and work together to achieve success. We believe working in an inclusive environment*

motivates exceptional effort, or—put more simply—it makes us all better at what we do.

Our diverse workforce helps our customers and business partners achieve their business goals. By recruiting the highest quality people who reflect the customers and communities that we serve, we increase our ability to deliver the best possible solutions (JPMorgan 2022).

The above are wholesome, socially responsible, life-breeding statements that earned the company accolades from those organizations monitoring such progress. From a stakeholder identification and engagement strategic view, the above commitment demonstrates a clear understanding of stakeholder relationships:

1. **Between the organization and its stakeholders:** Employees are our greatest asset, and we strive to attract talent from the broadest pool to foster innovation, creativity and productivity. There is tremendous power that results from this kind of diversity. In fact, creating a diverse and inclusive environment is critical to our success, and we are deeply committed to hiring and retaining employees from different backgrounds, experiences, and locations.

2. **Between the organization and society:** Diversity brings together people with unique perspectives, and inclusion creates opportunities for all individuals to contribute and work together to achieve holistic success. We believe working in an inclusive environment motivates exceptional effort, or—put more simply—it makes us all better at what we do.

3. **Between the stakeholders and society:** Our diverse workforce helps our customers and business partners achieve their business goals. By recruiting the highest-quality people who reflect the customers and communities that we serve, we increase our ability to deliver the best possible solutions.

A CNBC business report published April 26, 2016 applauded the company's stance and recognition for it, reporting:

JPMorgan Chase has gone above and beyond its peers in diversity and inclusion efforts, according to one measure released Tuesday. The banking giant was named the Diversity Corporation of the Year by the National Business Inclusion Consortium and National Gay & Lesbian Chamber of Commerce. The groups highlighted the Top 30 American companies for diversity.

"We're proud of this recognition by NBIC," JPMorgan Chairman and CEO Jamie Dimon said. "People are our most important asset and enable our long-term growth and success. Maintaining a diverse and inclusive

*workplace where everyone can thrive is not only the smart thing to do—
it's the right thing to do (Pramuk 2016). "*

However, despite apparently doing everything right in their mission statement, JPMorgan still experienced some high-profile DE&I problems. On December 11, 2019, a New York Times article written by Emily Flitter had the following caption: *"This Is What Racism Sounds Like in the Banking Industry."* In this article, Ms. Flitter described what could easily be classified as explicit and implicit racism that occurred within the bank – the same one that has made its diversity and inclusion and social responsibility commitments known in writing and emphasized by its leadership in various forums.

Implicit bias adversely impacted a former African American National Football League player who was denied the same "private client" status benefits normally accorded clients with over $250,000 in deposits, even after he gradually moved $800,000 to the bank. The manager behind this decision had access to all the diversity and inclusion material and positions advocated by the bank but just did not see the relationship between him (the bank's stakeholder) and the football player (stakeholder of interest and representative of society). Instead, this manager acted on his own implicit bias against the former football player. Yet, if this same football player was on the team that the manager supported, he might well have idolized the sports figure—even asking for an autograph and ignoring all his implicit bias.

The vexing thing about implicit bias is that this manager never shared them with his employers—when they hired or promoted him over the years or the football player. Yet, this manager had no problem letting his explicit bias hang out when it came to another situation. The same manager had no problem expressing his explicit bias against a woman he did not know personally but to whom he attributed the stereotypes of people who live in government-subsidized housing (Section 8). This manager denied the woman the "private client" status as well, saying:

> *You've got somebody who's coming from Section 8, never had a nickel to spend, and now she's got $400,000... What do you think's going to happen with that money? It's gone... You're not investing a dime for this lady... This is not money she respects... She didn't earn it (Pramuk 2016)."*

Yes, this woman received a sizeable amount of settlement money from the wrongful death of her son. No, the manager had no statistic or experiential support that he had that all Section 8 residents cannot save money. There are rich White people who are splashy with their money with little savings and those who hold tight to every dime and have large savings. The same is true for black and brown people too and the difference is opportunities not human proclivities.

This manager's beliefs and entrenched discriminatory values guided his behavior and decision-making towards minority and vulnerable groups regardless of their capacity and qualification to be granted the "private client" status. Having individuals pay for the perceived limitations or stereotyping of a group is a classic way that both implicit and explicit bias plays out every day in all sectors of society from churches to corporate offices, to governments offices to courtrooms, schools and even hospitals.

How many of JPMorgan's 256,105 (Statista 2022) employees share this manager's views—materially or even philosophically? If just 1% believed or agreed with such a discriminatory worldview, that would translate to 2,561 employees. Worse yet, if 50% were to agree, you would have over 128,052 employees whose views are adversarial to the corporate social responsibility wishes of its top leadership.

Let's take this even further: have any of these 256,105 JP Morgan employees attended separatist hate rallies? Or railed against minority groups or vulnerable people around the dinner table, or at the local bar, or online? How does an employee who attends these rallies on the weekend, come to work on Monday and not carry this hate into decisions and performance of routine activities? How can an organization ensure that this is not the case? how does an organization deal with the societal divisions that have dominated the political discourse and no doubt exist in its work ecosystem?

To answer these and many more questions like them, we need a reasoned social responsibility construct where DE&I serves as the currency for negotiating value-added decisions and performance monitoring activities. To his credit, the CEO and Chairman of JP Morgan expressed his disillusionment in the following letter to his employees:

> *Message from Jamie Dimon*
>
> *Dear colleagues,*
>
> *I am disgusted by racism and hate in any form. Any such behavior — explicit or veiled, deliberate or unconscious — is unacceptable and does not reflect who we are as a company and how we serve our clients and communities every day.*
>
> *We must make sure that the culture we aspire to reaches every corner of our company. We have done some great work on diversity and inclusion, but it's not enough. We must be absolutely relentless on doing more. I've instructed my management team to continually look into our policies, procedures, management practices and culture to set and achieve the highest possible standards. There is always more we can do.*
>
> *Racism has existed for too long — in our country, in our communities — and unfortunately, at times, even at our company. But this is not who we are. We want all of you to be active in making needed progress.*

Using the KCG model, we can break down Mr. Dimon's response as follows:

- **Knowledge:** "I am disgusted by racism and hate in any form. Any such behavior — explicit or veiled, deliberate or unconscious — is unacceptable and does not reflect who we are as a company and how we serve our clients and communities every day...Racism has existed for too long — in our country, in our communities — and unfortunately, at times, even at our company. But this is not who we are. We want all of you to be active in making needed progress."

- **Creativity:** "We will use this moment as an opportunity to do better — as leaders, as employees and as human beings...We must make sure that the culture we aspire to reaches every corner of our company. We have done some great work on diversity and inclusion, but it's not enough."

- **Governance:** "We must be absolutely relentless on doing more. I've instructed my management team to continually look into our policies, procedures, management practices and culture to set and achieve the highest possible standards. There is always more we can do."

It would be too optimistic for an organization's leadership to believe that the same people who go out on the weekends and advocate for separatist values or are sympathetic to their cause aren't represented among their employees or vendors. How realistic, then, is it to expect that these employees and vendors have the mental and emotional capacity to separate their personal views from the organization's pursuit of DE&I without mitigating measures?

To be sure, this separatist and hate-propagating culture is hardly a uniquely American phenomenon. It is a growing menace in Europe and takes many forms in other countries, as the impact of global warming and other climate change conditions forces people to migrate to more sustainable places for themselves and their families. Globally, racism, tribalism, sexism, regionalism, classism, political affiliation, sexual orientation, and religion continue to drive discriminatory practices. Further, as organizations become increasingly global or add products and services with a global reach and impact on diverse groups, their social responsibility grows and the need for DE&I increases.

One key to breaking the logjam between a person's personal values, beliefs, and divisive cultural orientation and the organization's pursuit for a more diverse and inclusive workforce, workplace and work partners, is **intentional social dialogue,** in which all stakeholders engage with each other in a non-judgmental forum. These forums, preferably in small groups like brown bag meetings, give the organization the opportunity to reinforce its diversity and inclusion commitments while communicating the real costs of lack of diversity and inequalities to the organization and society at large. To spark real conversations about DE&I, an organization needs social responsibility core subject issues which have been vetted, like ISO 26000 and the three models I am introducing as part of the response toolkits.

CASE STUDY 2:
Coca Cola and its External Law Firm Stakeholders

There are times when an organization also has the social responsibility to use its influence to cause DE&I changes in other organizations. This is the case with Coca Cola, a global brand that relies significantly on external attorneys to carry out its legal activities. Some of these external law firms were not as diverse and inclusive as Coca Cola's legal department. As a leader in this space, Coca Cola's legal department expected its external law firm partners to share in the same commitment to diversity, equity, and inclusion (belonging). So, in January 2021, Coca Cola's then Senior Vice President and General Counsel, Bradley M. Gayton, sent out an open letter to these firms:

January 28, 2021

To: U.S. Law Firms Supporting The Coca-Cola Company

Re: Commitment to Diversity, Belonging, and Outside Counsel Diversity

I write you with a heavy heart. For decades, our profession has had discussions about why diversity is important. We have developed score cards, held summits, established committees and written action plans. These efforts are not working. I'm reminded of this by the alarming number of new partner headshots that continue to be proudly published with an obvious lack of diversity and when I read that Black equity partners will not reach parity with the Black U.S. population until 2391.

The hard truth is that our profession is not treating the issue of diversity and inclusion as a business imperative. We are too quick to celebrate stagnant progress and reward intention. We have a crisis on our hands and we need to commit ourselves to specific actions that will accelerate the diversity of the legal profession. Our profession needs to be representative of the population it serves. All of us in leadership positions need to be the drivers of that change - and we will be better for it.

We know how to develop and implement clear timebound actionable plans that move organizations and industries to solve complex problems. In the grand scheme of things, the issue of the diversity of our profession *is not a complex problem. If we approach this like any other business imperative, we would allocate capital and invest in aspects of our business that move us forward to achieve our goal and grow profitably.*

As a consumer of legal services, we believe that diversity of talent on our legal matters is a critical factor to driving better business outcomes. We will no longer celebrate good intentions or highly unproductive efforts that haven't and aren't likely to produce better diverse staffing. Quite simply, we are no longer interested in discussing motivations, programs, or excuses for little to no progress– it's the results that we are demanding and will measure going forward.

The Coca-Cola Company's legal department has thought deeply about the design of our collective efforts and how we might change the present trajectory and bend the arch so that we are on a path to achieve parity. Our plan is far from perfect, but we believe that it offers greater promise than continuing down the current path hoping to reach a different destination. We encourage other law departments to join us in the initiatives outlined below or develop their own to further accelerate our progress... While the above actions focus on the United States for now, we intend for these initiatives to be customized and applied throughout our global organization.

Coca-Cola Company Actions – Over the past several months, the Global Legal team at The Coca-Cola Company as well as many across the organization has looked deeply into the meaning of our Company's purpose in relation to advancing Social Justice, Diversity, Inclusion and Belonging.

We believe our company should be representative of the markets that we serve. Within the U.S, 51% of our lawyers are ethnically diverse and 23% of that group is Black, 18% Asian, and 10% Hispanic. Additionally, 53% of our U.S. based lawyers are women. We are pushing ourselves to think boldly about the actions we take inside our company, within our areas of expertise and across the community to drive significant collective change.

As a function, we believe that pursuing diversity is not only the right thing to do, but it's a business imperative to do so quickly. We know firsthand that a diversity of thought, perspective and experience is critical to drive the best work and outcomes for our Company...I hope you will join us in this work and embrace these changes as an opportunity. While there is a long road ahead to effect systemic change around social justice, diversity, inclusion and belonging, we believe that the actions outlined above are steps in the right direction and look forward to working toward our shared goals with our law firm partners. As a legal community, we must use our collective power and knowledge of the law to enact meaningful change. Together, there is endless good we can do and I look forward to your partnership (Coca Cola n.d.).

This letter, and the Revised Outside Counsel Diversity Guidelines that accompanied it, addressed the key issues one would expect when there is entrenched resistance to racial reckoning changes, as Mr. Gayton put it. Why was there such a strong pushback from some of the stakeholder law firms? This letter provides several lessons, touching on issues such as whether America has gone beyond the point where Affirmative Action is constructive, whether the comfort of the wealthy shareholders in large corporations should dictate the pace of systemic and structural changes, and whether the time has come to make racial equity part and parcel of any social responsibility and sustainable discourse. Using the tools I introduced earlier, we will dissect the letter and the reactions it sparked.

Opposition to racial equity and inclusion within the American context

One of the biggest backlashes to Coca Cola's law firm diversity policy letter was that on April 21, 2021, less than 90 days after its release, Mr. Gayton unexpectedly resigned his position at Coca Cola. Between the time of the release of the letter and the resignation, several stakeholders—law firms, media, Coca Cola stock owners, etc.—had all weighed in both positively and negatively about the decisions inherent from the letter.

One stakeholder group that may not have been directly impacted by the new guidelines but had influence with the Coca Cola company was an advocacy group of shareholders represented by The American Civil Rights Project (ACR) (Morenoff 2021). According to ACR, this shareholder group felt the decision and the guidelines were illegal and placed the blame on Coca Cola' board members. They threatened that if the company did not rescind the new guidelines, they would demand access to its internal records to ascertain whether the board members were derelict with their fiduciary responsibilities. Lawsuits that demand access to a corporation's internal records are generally avoided by large corporations because they can become very costly, generate bad publicity, and take years to move through the court systems.

Now comes the question as to whether Coca Cola's legal department had the authority to demand the racial equity changes it wanted to see in external organizations that handle its legal matters and the punitive loss of revenues attached to non-compliance. From a legal perspective, a law firm—Boyden Gray & Associates, PLLC—representing stakeholders of firms directly affected by the law firm diversity policy declared it illegal and invoked the Civil Rights Act of 1866:

> *Such a policy of discrimination is illegal. Since the Civil Rights Act of 1866 (codified at 42 U.S.C. § 1981), federal law has prohibited all forms of racial discrimination in private contracting. As the late Justice Ginsburg noted just last year, § 1981 is a '"sweeping' law designed to 'break down all discrimination between black men and*

white men' regarding 'basic civil rights.'" And decades of case law have held that-no matter how well intentioned-policies that seek to impose permanent racial balancing are prohibited (Gray 2021).

This statement represents the tired excuses used to sustain systemic and structural racism; it has been in use for over 155 years (1866-Present). The letter and spirit of the law embedded in the Civil Rights Act of 1866 emboldened the United States to pursue an inclusive American agenda after the abolishment of slavery. Congress, led by White Republicans, believed back then that it was the social responsibility of the government through legislation to provide the mechanism for a racially integrated America.

This 39th Congress understood the landmines the Southern states were prepared to lay down to undermine any racial equity and inclusion path set forth on a national and state levels. These Republican legislators knew that the freed slaves would continue to be economically and politically enslaved, especially in the South, despite the Thirteenth Amendment, which abolished slavery in the United States. This reality necessitated the promulgation and enactment of a counter-measure, which was what the Civil Rights Act of 1866 was all about. Against the opposition of President Andrew Johnson, the Act passed *"with near unanimous Republican support, 122 to 41, marking the first time Congress legislated upon civil rights."* This law:

> *... mandated that "all persons born in the United States," with the exception of American Indians, were "hereby declared to be citizens of the United States." The legislation granted all citizens the "full and equal benefit of all laws and proceedings for the security of person and property." To Radical Republicans, who believed the federal government had a role in shaping a multiracial society in the postwar South, the measure seemed the next logical step after the ratification of the 13th Amendment on December 18, 1865 (which abolished slavery)...President Johnson disagreed with the level of federal intervention implied by the legislation, calling it "another step, or rather a stride, toward centralization and the concentration of all legislative power in the national Government" in his veto message. The Civil Rights Bill of 1866 proved to be the opening salvo of the showdown between the 39th Congress (1865–1867) and the President over the future of the former Confederacy and African-American civil rights (History 2022).*

President Johnson's veto of the Civil Rights bill was overturned by Congress. This was not the first time he'd vetoed a bill aimed at creating racial reconciliation in the American ecosystem. President Johnson who was responsible for setting America back from the path of racial equity and inclusion—a path begun by his predecessor, President Abraham Lincoln—maintained that no government support was needed for the freed slaves because at that time they were the most highly skilled workforce America had. In vetoing the Freedmen's Bureau Bill of February 1866, President Johnson described what probably represented the threat most poor whites felt about having freed slaves as labor competitors:

His [Black man] condition is not so exposed as may at first be imagined. He is in a portion of the country where his labor cannot be spared. Competition for his services from planters, from those who are constructing or repairing railroads, and from capitalists in his vicinage, or from other States, will enable him to command almost his own terms (History 2022). (Emphasis added)

Yes, it was indeed true that freed slaves did have some advantages, having worked for free in most of the then known infrastructure projects; in the process many of them had developed more advanced marketable and on-demand skillsets. But in the court of social justice, it was unjust to purposefully disadvantage them when they had no generational wealth or access to capital to actualize these knowledge assets without relying on the government for help. This was the whole reason Congress established the Freemen's Bureau Act of 1865 to begin with:

On March 3, 1865, Congress passed "An Act to establish a Bureau for the Relief of Freedmen and Refugees" to provide food, shelter, clothing, medical services, and land to displaced Southerners, including newly freed African Americans. The Freedmen's Bureau was to operate "during the present war of rebellion, and for one year thereafter," and also established schools, supervised contracts between freedmen and employers, and managed confiscated or abandoned lands (U.S. Senate 2017).

The Freedmen and Refugee Act addressed the critical issues of the day—issues that remain critical today: making the African American population and poor whites whole from systemic racism and bad economic policies to build a future for themselves and their posterity. A paramount issue at the time was land distribution or reallocation, which was an effective economic policy intended to give freed slaves more ownership of their destinies.

Another effective and necessary equity policy tool, both then and now, is the provision for governmental oversight over contracting and employment. The freed slaves were at a disadvantage following the Civil War because the white population still controlled contracting and employment systems and practices, including access to capital. The government providing oversight over these systems had the onerous responsibility for serving as a referee of social justice.

Senator Lyman Trumbull of Illinois, a White man, understood the implications of limiting the Freedmen and Refugee Act to a one-year time frame. He refused to allow America to pursue a gradual path for addressing racial equity and inclusion, and successfully worked the legislative process to pass a Bill that extended the timeframe and included a more focused agenda towards the healing of the nation's divisive norms

Unfortunately, President Johnson, who had assured Senator Trumbull that he was all in on the healing of the soul of America, vetoed the bill. Although the Legislature overrode the veto, President Johnson's opposition became a clarion call that emboldened White Supremacists to fight any social order that benefited black and brown people groups (U.S. Senate 2017).

It was no surprise that all the well-intentioned Acts—the Freedmen and Refugee Act of 1865 and the Civil Rights of 1866—benefited White people and continued to enable the disenfranchisement of the black and brown population. Agricultural and Mechanical Engineering, then part of Mechanic Art and Plantation Farming, were the very sectors where black slaves had established their expertise, to the envy of the poor White people who owned family farms trying to compete (U.S. Senate 2017).

President Johnson was intervening to gain support amongst the poor White population who were aggrieved by the rich White plantation owners and the growing expertise of black farmers and engineers responsible for the success and dominance of the larger plantations and the railroad constructions and repairs. The culture wars which continue to undermine humankind with its divisive norms, reverberate over the centuries stemming from this same complex.

President Johnson argued that the nation had never built schools for White people in 1865, when the Morrill Act was already three years old. In 1862, U.S. Congress had established the Morrill Act introduced by a Vermont congressman Justin S. Morrill, which created government-sponsored Agricultural and Mechanic Arts institutions.

Expectedly for the times, the new schools, publicly and privately held alike, disproportionately favored White students. Admission to the land-grant institutions was restricted to Whites, which by itself extended the societal disadvantages of black and brown people with significant multi-generational impacts. This imbalance led to the founding of schools like Howard University which admitted both black and White students, but this was the exception rather than the rule; there were hardly enough schools to take in all the African American students who needed access. This also began the rise of White generational prosperity at the expense of black prosperity and is one of the reasons why every generation of America has since faced racial reckoning.

When these land grant institutions were taking root, many freed slaves already had established skillsets and expertise in agriculture and mechanic arts. This was courtesy of two centuries of plantation farming, railroad construction and repair experiences from slavery and involuntary servitude.

The school-aged, freed slaves could have excelled in these land grant schools had they been allowed to attend. How do we know this? Largely because they grew up establishing and using the actual farming best practices of the day in the plantation farms as child laborers and were used as free labor for many of the very disciplines considered mechanic arts: hunting, agriculture, blacksmithing, weaving, navigation, war, and medicine).

Generations of African Americans were deliberately denied the education that would have enabled them to own property and grow generational wealth for themselves and for their posterity. The American dream could have included the success stories of African Americans just like German-, Irish-, Italian-Americans wrote their success stories – but it didn't. The legacy of inequity created by this decision is one of the fundamental reasons why there is unfinished business in American society.

In a 100m race, when one runner is placed at the 50m point and others are expected to begin at the starting point of 0m, it would take superhuman powers for them to catchup and this was and still is the kind of odds African Americans have and continue to face in America. The inequities that began to manifest in society because the Morrill Act (1862) became a White Affirmative Action booster led to the Morrill Act (1890) as a corrective measure. This second Morrill Act began an annual federal funding system where Congress appropriated funds for land-grant institutions because of their growing importance in transforming America into a global leader in varied academic disciplines: *"Acts in 1887 and 1914 appropriated funds to the land-grant colleges to promote the development of scientific methods of agriculture. Land-grant status was conferred on 30 Native American tribal colleges under the Improving America's Schools Act of 1994 (Britannica 2017)."*

The second Act also denied funding to states that refused admissions to students who were not White unless they also provided "separate but equal" facilities—a provision that led to the founding of 17 black colleges *(Britannica 2017)*. Some of these black colleges included North Carolina A&T (Greensboro), Alcorn State University in Mississippi, Tennessee State University (Nashville), Florida A&M University, just to name a few *(Britannica 2017)*. However, the abysmal facilities that black and brown people had access to was light years behind what their White counterparts enjoyed within the same community. This divisive norm was justified in some circles as product of tax base capitalism—the community that pays the most taxes get the best facilities—a petitio principii or circular argument considering who sacrificed first to make the access to wealth possible.

It took another 64 years before the Supreme Court would declare "separate but equal" institutions unconstitutional—enough time to give the White racial group an unprecedented advantage in the journey to manifest the constitutionally guaranteed human right to life, liberty and the pursuit of happiness. During this White Affirmative Action period, educational opportunities were made available to them wholesale, opportunities that were denied to the black and brown racial groups. The injustice galore embedded in the American system is vexing at best because African American free labor built the capitalist system that provided the nation with the wealth that was later appropriated to fund educational institutions that then pulled majority poor White people into the middle- and upper-class economic demographic over time:

> The influence of the land-grant schools on American higher education has been formidable. By the early 21st century a significant percentage of all students seeking degrees in the United States were enrolled in land-grant institutions. Pioneering research in physics, medicine, agricultural science, and other fields has been done at land-grant schools, which, over the years, were responsible for a large proportion of the doctoral degrees awarded in the United States. And, because their admissions policies have had a history of being more open than most other institutions, land-grant colleges and universities made it possible for women, working-class students, and students from remote areas to obtain undergraduate and professional education at low cost (Britannica 2017).

Since the first Morrill Act (1862) and over the century and a half that has followed, Blacks fought for greater equality; but every step forward resulted in vitriolic pushback. Under President Johnson, domestic terrorism in the name of white supremacy through the Ku Klux Klan ensured African Americans would remain marginalized and as a community restrained from creating their own generational wealth or sustainable participation in the economic engine of the country. Signs of African American affluence were taken as an affront by Whites, who, driven by biases and deep-seated insecurities, felt obligated to put down any successful venture. This is what happened in "Black Wall Street" in Tulsa City in 1921 when a burgeoning African American part of the city was burned to the ground and razed by a mob of angry White men.

Consider that less than sixty years from Emancipation (1865 to 1921), the African American community in Tulsa City against all odds and impossible mounds of divisive societal norms or barricades had established their own successful American dream reality alongside the White community. Yet, unsatisfied with their own success story, White extremists motivated by hate, fear and warmongering declared a mini-civil war on Black American citizens denying them of the rights to life, liberty, and the pursuit of happiness. How many countless and nameless "Black Wall Street" type communities over the years were razed down and African American citizens murdered in broad daylight and at night by White racist mobs gone amok.

Still, African Americans continued to find within themselves the strength to still believe and still love America and passed such deep love of God and country to their posterity.

The implementation of a White Affirmative Action plan in institutions of higher education transformed into all-out society-wide socio-cultural and socio-economic and political white advantages, collectively called white privilege. The Civil Rights Act of 1875 opened the Pandora's box for Jim Crow era laws, which continued the marginalization of African Americans. The GI Bill at the end of World War II accelerated the growth of white middle class, while Jim Crow laws boxed in the African American population, again cutting them off from any meaningful social, economic, or political progress.

Therefore, the braggadocious invocation of the Civil Rights Act of 1866 against Coca Cola's law firm diversity policy was a spurious argument because it assumed that America was fully racially reckoned both in equity and inclusion matters: *"full and equal benefit of all laws and proceedings for the security of person and property."* The fact that after 155 years, the racial equity and inclusion debate is still very relevant and the opposition is still using the same tired arguments, calls for a different corporate response in addressing this American nightmare.

Before the Civil War, the South was deeply segregated in what is sometimes called *de jure* segregation, or segregation by law. *De jure* segregation was also empowered by Black codes and Jim Crow laws. In places where there were no such laws, *de facto* segregation was the norm, which is generally segregation without law or sanction. For example, in the North, where Black codes did not exist, there were still church, school and residential segregations with blacks and whites divided on the basis of race.

By 1890—the same year that the second Morrill Act was enacted—a new set of segregation laws—Jim Crow Laws—took hold in the South, and they changed America into a government-sponsored, class-based democracy. Jim Crow laws, an extension of the more patchwork Black codes, restricted the rights and freedoms of African Americans in ways subtle and overt; they were used by Southern states to get around the Constitutional amendments and the Civil Rights Acts. Essentially Jim Crow laws were the institutionalization of pre-Emancipation Southern values, behaviors, and customs, all designed to keep African Americans as second-class citizens and promote white supremacy as an American norm. It was a deliberate attack on DE&I. While Black codes had been desperate ragtag responses to maintain political power in the South, Jim Crow laws were strategically meant to prevent African Americans from ever becoming a successful community in America.

Jim Crow Laws kept African Americans marginalized by denying them access to capital, voting, education, healthcare, jobs, churches, and more. The enforcement of these Jim Crow Laws was not only harsh for African

American offenders, but also punished any Whites who defied the statutes and attempted to help African Americans. As recorded in the Congressional archives:

> Beginning in the last quarter of the 19th century, African Americans—the vast majority of whom still lived in the South—experienced unique suffering and deprivation under the system of racial segregation known as Jim Crow. Enforced by legal and extralegal means, the laws and practices that constituted the Jim Crow system evolved over several decades and ultimately restricted civil and political rights, economic opportunities, and social mobility for African Americans until the 1960s...Beginning with Tennessee in 1870, every southern state adopted laws against interracial marriage. By the 1880s, most public places and many private businesses had "Whites Only" and "Colored" facilities. These included schools, seating areas, drinking fountains, workspaces, government buildings, train stations, hospitals, restaurants, hotels, theaters, barbershops, laundries, and even public restrooms (History 2008).

No one would argue that 100% integration has been achieved; for all the progress made, Blacks have not had *"full and equal benefit of all laws and proceedings for the security of person and property."* These were the structural imbalances in how legal work assignments on Coca Cola projects were impacted. But it's a fact that corporations even today reflect a de facto segregation, a lingering legacy of slavery through the impact of Jim Crow laws and all the other roadblocks placed in the way of Black progress for the last century and a half. From a social responsibility framework, ISO 26000 provides guidance on organizations' responsibility within their spheres of influence; it clearly supports the intent of Mr. Gayton and his team:

> **ISO** *An organization is responsible for the impacts of decisions and activities over which it has formal and/or de facto control. (de facto control refers to situations where one organization has the ability to dictate the decisions and activities of another party, even where it does not have the legal or formal authority to do so). Such impacts can be extensive. In addition to being responsible for its own decisions and activities, an organization may, in some situations, have the ability to affect the behaviour of organizations/parties with which it has relationships. Such situations are considered to fall within an organization's sphere of influence. This sphere of influence includes relationships within and beyond an organization's value chain. However, not all of an organization's value chain necessarily falls within its sphere of influence. It can include the formal and informal associations in which it participates, as well as peer organizations or competitors.*

Clearly, Coca Cola's external law partners fall under its value chain. Further, Coca Cola as a company has a rich history of promoting diversity, equity and inclusion. In fact, on its website, the company lauds itself as follows:

> *Diversity, equity and inclusion are at the heart of our values and our growth strategy and play an important part in our company's success. We leverage the remarkable diversity of people across the world to achieve our purpose of refreshing the world and making a difference. For The Coca-Cola Company, creating a diverse workforce and an inclusive workplace is a strategic business priority that fosters greater creativity, innovation and connection to the communities we serve. Our aspiration is not only to mirror the diversity of the communities where we operate, but also to lead and advocate for a better shared future (Coca Cola 2008).*

In the case of Coca Cola and its external law firm partners, both the legal and formal authority existed as posited in ISO 26000 because the former was contracting with the later to perform legal work for which it expected its racial equity values and behaviors to moderate the relationship. The work performed for the company, whether by internal staff or external partners, was expected to be guided by these values and behaviors:

> **ISO** *An organization does not always have a responsibility to exercise influence purely because it has the ability to do so. For instance, it cannot be held responsible for the impacts of other organizations over which it may have some influence if the impact is not a result of its decisions and activities. However, there will be situations where an organization will have a responsibility to exercise influence. These situations are determined by the extent to which an organization's relationship is contributing to negative impacts. There will also be situations where, though an organization does not have a responsibility to exercise influence, it may nevertheless wish, or be asked, to do so voluntarily. An organization may decide whether to have a relationship with another organization and the nature and extent of this relationship. There will be situations where an organization has the responsibility to be alert to the impacts created by the decisions and activities of other organizations and to take steps to avoid or to mitigate the negative impacts connected to its relationship with such organizations.*
>
> *ISO 26000:2010, page 26.*

Using the KCG model for social change

From a KCG model perspective, Mr. Gayton and his team demonstrated clear knowledge of the inequity in the employment of Black attorneys by the external law firm partners and for those that rise to partner level. The inequities were so audaciously repugnant that they supported Mr. Gayton's reason for why drastic change was unavoidable: *"...I read that Black equity partners will not reach parity with the Black U.S. population until 2391."*

Mr. Gayton knew very well that the change they were seeking from their external partner firms was necessary and achievable, and he was cognizant of Martin Luther King Jr.'s warning about gradualism as the bottleneck in any change movements. Dr. King elucidated: *"This is no time to engage in the luxury of cooling off or to take the tranquilizing drug of gradualism."* The change Coca Cola was seeking had already been achieved in its own legal department, judging by the numbers:

> *We believe our company should be representative of the markets that we serve. Within the U.S, 51% of our lawyers are ethnically diverse and 23% of that group is Black, 18% Asian, and 10% Hispanic. Additionally, 53% of our U.S. based lawyers are women. We are pushing ourselves to think boldly about the actions we take inside our company, within our areas of expertise and across the community to drive significant collective change. As a function, we believe that pursuing diversity is not only the right thing to do, but it's a business imperative to do so quickly. We know firsthand that a diversity of thought, perspective and experience is critical to drive the best work and outcomes for our Company.*

The intention was sound. Where Mr. Gayton's letter and its implementation fell short were in the creativity and the governance parts of the KCG model within a social responsibility construct.

1. The creativity gap in the Coca Cola design

On the creativity side, stakeholder involvement in decisions that affect them is a fundamental requirement in social responsibility-driven organizational change. From this letter, we can safely deduce that the creativity in finding the solutions that Coca Cola was seeking with its external partner law firms were internally developed with little participation from the firms directly affected by the diversity guidelines:

> *The Coca-Cola Company's legal department has thought deeply about the design of our collective efforts and how we might change the present trajectory and bend the arch so that we are on a path to achieve parity. Our plan is far from perfect, but we believe that it offers greater promise than continuing down the current path hoping to reach a different destination. We*

Coca Cola's legal department played into the hands of those opposed to any plan that gives opportunity to black and brown people as a corrective measure to past discriminatory practices beginning by not engaging all stakeholders, including the opposition. It is generally accepted knowledge that, particularly in the South, some Americans do not like to be told what to do and would even act against their own self-interest to uphold this ideal. Yet, these same Americans would blindly follow the dictate of preferred leaders. This is where stakeholder identification and engagement play a key role in social responsibility and sustainable idealism.

Coca Cola's legal department was the primary stakeholder in the need to have external law firms it contracted with to have fair representation of Black and minority attorneys working on their New Matters. But there were other stakeholders whose voices were not heard in the law firm policy as far as we can gather from the letter and the guidelines. The missed opportunity was not engaging the creative powers of Coca Cola's external law firm partners in coming up with solutions for the diversity problem outlined in the letter. Mr. Gayton acknowledged that these stakeholders also had the knowledge to help develop creative solutions that could lead to good governance:

We know how to develop and implement clear timebound actionable plans that move organizations and industries to solve complex problems. In the grand scheme of things, the issue of the diversity of our profession is not a complex problem. If we approach this like any other business imperative, we would allocate capital and invest in aspects of our business that move us forward to achieve our goal and grow profitably.

These external law firms were both stakeholders of interest (directly impacted) and society was also a stakeholder of influence. The society that has come to trust Coca Cola's leadership and commitments to diversity, equity and inclusion matters had a stake in knowing that the company exercised its influence to promote these values across its supply chain. The unique use of "our collective efforts" in the letter projects the participation of the external law firms in the decision Coca Cola was making, yet no such evidence was shared. ISO 26000 provides the following guidance on point:

ISO *Although an organization itself may believe it understands its social responsibility...it should nevertheless consider involving stakeholders in the identification process to broaden the perspective on* *the core subjects and issues. It is important to recognize, though, that issues may be relevant even if stakeholders fail to identify them. In some instances an organization might assume that because it operates in an area with laws that address core subjects of social responsibility, then compliance with the law will be sufficient to ensure that all the relevant issues of such core subjects are addressed. A careful review of the core subjects and issues [show] that some relevant issues are not regulated or are covered by regulations that are not adequately enforced or are not explicit or sufficiently detailed.*

ISO 26000:2010, page 71.

2. The shared governance imbalance in Coca Cola's policy design and implementation

On the governance side, the company made room for other firms to come up with their own diversity and belonging plan: *"We encourage other law departments to join us in the initiatives outlined below or develop their own to further accelerate our progress. "* However, it did not provide guidance on what it would or would not accept outside of its internally crafted solution. A 30% quantifiable number was used (without any explanation as to how the number was arrived at) to establish the billed time commitments, the quarterly evaluations and the relationship partner/succession planning performance criteria and metrics:

- On the **"Billed Time Commitments"** the following guideline was provided: "… you commit that at least 30% of each of billed associate and partner time will be from diverse attorneys, and of such amounts at least half will be from Black attorneys. Work performed by diverse attorneys is expected to be accretive to their development and advancement at the firm. These percentages are approximately linked to U.S. Census population data."
- On the **"Quarterly Evaluation"** the following guideline was provided: "The responsible KO attorney for each New Matter will review performance against your commitment for New Matters each quarter. For New Matters failing to meet the commitment, you will be required to provide a plan to meet your commitment. Failure to meet the commitment over two quarterly reviews will result in a non-refundable 30% reduction in the fees payable for such New Matter going forward until the commitment is met and, continued failure may result in your firm no longer being considered for KO work."
- On the **"Relationship Partner/Succession Planning"** the following guideline was provided: "You will identify two or more diverse attorneys, at least half of whom are Black, as candidates for

succeeding to the relationship partner role with KO. KO's goal is to have at least 30% diverse relationship partners at our highest-spend and preferred panel firms with at least half of these partners being Black."

A. *Applying the 3-Step Equity Model*

The central issue Coca Cola sought to address through its law firm diversity policy was diversity (equitable minority and Black attorney representation) and belonging (inclusion in the partner ranks for Black attorneys). The equity lens and inclusion principles could have provided a winning solution for all stakeholders. Since one size does not fit all, in the 3-Step equity lens model, Coca Cola would have had at its disposal three strategic options to address (1) the lack of diversity in the pool of external attorneys to work on its assignments (equity distribution), and (2) the lack of mobility into the partner ranks within these external law firms that use the Coca Cola assignments as career-enhancing projects. The New Matters assignment could also have provided the opportunity for black and brown attorneys to gain the experiences they need to become Partners over time:

- **Equity opportunity option** would have allowed the internal Coca Cola team to present "New Matters" opportunities as low-hanging fruit with the 30% requirement for firms who want to participate in the work to demonstrate how they would meet this billed time commitments before they are assigned the work. A corporation should be able to expect that its external partners perform their assignment based on the client's expectation(s). Any external law firm that cannot demonstrate that it has the current capacity or plan to ramp up its capacity to meet or exceed the client's expectations by de fault has created a potential performance gap—the very basis for not getting the assignment. In Coca Cola's case, if these external firms cannot show how they will meet the commitment with associate and partner time from diverse attorneys, their inability to perform the work to specifications created the gap not affirmative action system.

  Corporate management has the prerogative to ensure work is done in accordance with its terms, values, and behaviors and this carries over to the firms in which it has contracted or about to enter contract relationships or influence. This means both Coca Cola and the external law firms have the managerial prerogative to choose how work is performed in their respective organizations. The difference is that the "one who pays the piper calls the tune" and Coca Cola is the piper payer in this case.

  Alternatively, the external firms could be asked by Coca Cola to demonstrate how they have transitioned their respective firms to create the right environment for diverse attorneys to be assigned Coca Cola related work and the projected numbers should back such claims. External law firms interested in performing Coca Cola New Matters assignments should be able to demonstrate how they plan to meet the requirement for racial and equity staffing and how they plan to get more of these attorneys into the partner ranks because of the experiences gained from Coca Cola assignments.

- **Equity Reconciliation option** would have given the internal Coca Cola team a tool to require that its external partners conduct and report on their own internal assessments to (1) identify within their own eco-systems the systemic barriers that have hindered them historically from including diverse attorneys (including Black attorneys) in Coca Cola assignments, (2) what they plan to do to fix these barriers and (3) how long it would take them to implement their plans. This would give the Coca Cola internal team the leverage to assign work to firms that are in concert with their stated diversity and belonging goals and objectives today. A firm that would take ten years for instance to reconcile its diversity and belonging commitments with its own policies and procedures manual and decision-making practices should be in the back of the line for New Matters assignment. This is a socially responsible response to the "drug" of gradualism as Dr. King aptly posited. If a firm is unwilling to change its practices to be diverse and inclusive, it technically disqualified itself from working for an organization like Coca Cola that had already done the work in its own eco-system before requiring its partners to do the same.

  Firms who fail to reconcile their decision-making and operational practices with their commitment to diversity and inclusion, yet still expect to get Coca Cola's New Matters contracts, are driven by a sense of entitlement. It is noteworthy that the law firm that threatened to sue Coca Cola for the decision and guidelines actually invoked the Civil Rights Act of 1866. It's ironic that the Civil Rights Act, invoked here to protect the rights of firms to avoid conforming to Coca Cola's inclusivity guidelines, was passed by those who wanted a more inclusive America.

- **Equity disruption option** would have given the internal Coca Cola team a tool to require that its external partners identify and report on their own internal practices, things that they stopped doing because they contributed to the systemic barriers keeping minority attorneys from working on Coca Cola New Matters or becoming partners. If any firm does not have this problem and can adequately demonstrate this to be true, then it should be rewarded, not penalized along with the others. When a firm has identified its own bottlenecks which are adversarial to the goals of Coca Cola's diversity policy and has taken unilateral decisions to correct them, they should be rewarded for their efforts. But when a firm neither knows nor cares about its internal bottlenecks, it should not be rewarded with "New Matters" assignments because in doing so, Coca Cola would become complicit, and the firm would pollute the entire diversity stream that the policy was meant to bring alive and sustain.

This report would provide vital information to the internal Coca Cola team, which it could score as part of its decision-making process in selecting the firms to handle its New Matters business without running afoul with those who already complained that Coca Cola was practicing racial quota system within a private enterprise. Rather, as a private enterprise, Coca Cola reserves the right to do business with firms that are in concert with its own internal diversity and belonging commitments. For Coca Cola to do any different would be complicit.

Actualizing the 3-step equity lens model within the Coca Cola context could be as simple as developing a scoring mechanism to prioritize external law firms that are ready, willing and able to perform its "New Matters" assignments under the new framework. Just for the sake of simplicity, Mr. Gayton and his team could have assigned 10% scores for each of the three equity options:

- When a law firm seeking assignment in the New Matters category presents Black and minority attorneys who would be assigned the work, it should receive anywhere from 1-10%.
- When a firm demonstrates that it has assessed its recruitment, promotions and retention practices and reconciled them with its policies and procedures in support of becoming socially responsible on equity and inclusion goals for blacks and minorities, it should be scored from 1-10%.
- When the same organization also demonstrates that it has voluntarily assessed its own decision-making processes and practices in assigning work that intentionally or unintentionally excluded blacks and minority attorneys and has stopped or is planning to stop these practices (with verifiable timelines), it should score between 1-10%.

When the scores are tallied, firms with the highest scores should be assigned the "New Matters" work, when they demonstrate that they also have the capacity to complete the work within other criteria of course (such as coming in under budget and on-time). The company also has the flexibility to assign work based on where the firm is on its diversity, equity and inclusion journey utilizing any one of the options as a decision point. This approach guarantees that the work assignment and the attorneys assigned to do them reflect the same values and results that the Coca Cola legal department would have used and achieved respectively were they to do it in-house.

Figure 1.1: The equity score tally

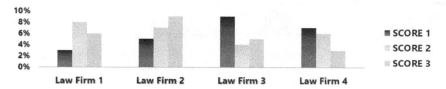

B. Applying the 3-Step Inclusion Principles

The 3-Step Inclusion Principles could have helped frame the solutions the Coca Cola legal team came up with. The hefty fine of a 30% loss in revenue from Coca Cola business was by itself troubling because no explanation was given as to why this percentage was selected. This type of arbitrarily set penalty is generally red meat for opponents of Affirmative Action policies, unless they are managerial decisions with justifiable and defendable rationales. it's no surprise that conservative Affirmative Action opponents backed the letter from the ACR and began recruiting other legal firms to join the opposition to the diversity policy. Their chief argument concerning the legal framework of Coca Cola's implementation plan highlighted the inconsistencies in the plan:

> *Coca-Cola's stated goal is that the legal teams it hires "be representative of the population it serves," and the policy's minimum racial quotas therefore roughly track the racial distribution of the American population at large, rather than the labor market for attorneys. Thus, for example, the letter requires that at least 15% of time be billed by black attorneys. Blacks make up approximately 13.4% of the U.S. population, but only 5.9% of attorneys. The policy also states that "these minimum commitments will be adjusted over time as U.S. Census data evolves (Gray 2021)."*

When predominantly white law firms stood to lose 30% of their Coca Cola business for not hiring Black attorneys, and possibly more business overall from the negative publicity, their quick and sharp response should come as no surprise. The strategies in this response should also be no surprise; invoking Affirmative Action and quota system have been a common rallying point against policies that benefit people of color going back to 1866.

However, since all white law firms that compete for Coca Cola assignments are not the same, a more nuanced approach should have been used to separate those that want the status quo to continue (where predominantly White attorneys get the prized Coca Cola assignments) from those that are willing to work with the diversity and inclusion policy envisioned—not the one promulgated. The 3-Step Inclusion principles presented in this book could have assisted the Coca Cola Company in avoiding these challenges altogether because they are based on fair social responsibility and a more sustainable framework:

- **Redemption-driven Inclusion Principle 1:** Coca Cola's legal department could have engaged its external stakeholder firms by showcasing how it met its own diversity and belonging commitments. This shared inclusion steps could have provided models of actions that these external law firms could emulate to create measurably inclusive environments and opportunities within their own eco-systems. Sometimes, it is easier for organizations that are not sure about racial equity matters to invoke racial quotas to cloud out any racial reckoning requirements of them. This does not mean that these external law firms are altogether opposed to the DE&I commitments Coca Cola was demanding for how its New Matters assignments were carried out. But sometimes, these firms are stunted by the requirements and expectations, which seemed daunting.

  Others who prefer the "good old boy" networking see it as an overreach by big brother—in this case Coca Cola. These firms don't prioritize diversity and inclusion but still want Coca Cola business gained the old fashion country club way. This is the entitlement club, and they are usually the group that invokes affirmative action and quota systems as the pariah panacea against their interests that have been historically exclusive of minority and black attorneys. If they were not, a policy like the one Coca Cola was imposing would not be necessary. These types of firms do not have redemptive unction by their lack of actionable steps towards meeting any racial reckoning goals and they should not be allowed to poison the stream of hope that Dr. King envisioned, and which the Coca Cola New Matters business strategy was meant to address. Dr. King said: *"This is our hope. This is the faith that I go back to the South with. With this faith we will be able to hew out of the mountain of despair a stone of hope. With this faith we will be able to transform the jangling discords of our nation into a beautiful symphony of brotherhood."* Unfortunately, there are firms who'd rather play requiem tunes in a racially divisive band than participate in an inclusive symphony of diversity.

This is where the experiences from companies like Coca Cola that have gone beyond legal compliance and now operating as socially responsible and live sustaining organizations throughout its internal eco-system can prove valuable to other companies and nations. These trailblazing examples could help companies struggling with diversity, equity and inclusion matters within their sphere of influence by engaging them as coach, advocate, and enforcer.

Tried and true DE&I models could also have far-reaching societal redemption values. Organizations that implement successful DE&I models can help America forge another path towards racial reconciliation, a path begun by President Abraham Lincoln but systematically derailed by his successor and other opponents. This is even more so because the very people that champion and implement these policies also live within the American society that is currently racially polarized after 155 years of trying to move forward through governmental processes.

- **Restoration-focused Inclusion Principle 2:** Coca Cola's legal team could have engaged its external stakeholder firms by demonstrating steps it has taken to identify and correct its own once entrenched equitable inclusion barriers. Where they still exist, it could have shown what steps it has implemented to end them. Coca Cola is one of the largest enterprises in the world and has been around a long time. Surely, it has barriers to DE&I that it has already corrected and ones that it is still working to correct. This gives Coca Cola the loudest microphone in the room to legitimately ask for these changes, guided by a restoration-focused principle. The authority for this restoration-focused inclusion principle is derived from "Justice and Liberty for All...We the people...Out of Many, One" because the American story has not lived up to the tenets of these ideals. While governmental programs have sought to move the country towards racial reconciliation with considerable success, corporations have a unique opportunity to take the country to its own mountaintop experience, wherein diversity policies may become a thing of the past because society at large is fully integrated. Dr. King envisioned such an America and closed out his last speech—"I've Been to the Mountaintop"—with this encouragement to all Americans—White, Black, Jew, Moslem, Atheist and all:

    Like anybody, I would like to live a long life. Longevity has its place. But I'm not concerned about that now. I just want to do God's will. And He's allowed me to go up to the mountain. And I've looked over. And I've seen the Promised Land. I may

not get there with you. But I want you to know tonight, that
we, as a people, will get to the promised land!

What promised land, you ask? America existing as a country where all its citizens are fully racially and equitably reconciled. Dr. King dreamed of a nation where little black boys and white boys and little white girls and black girls held hands and sang free at last, grown white men and black men and grown white women and black women clapped their hands in celebration of a country that got there—a racially reconciled nation. It's a powerful aspiration, and an important one, because as America goes, so does the rest of the world. Why? America is a "shining city on a hill" – its citizens mirror the world's varied communities.

This was hopefully the restoration-focused principle that drove the aspirational law firm diversity policy Mr. Gayton articulated: *"As a legal community, we must use our collective power and knowledge of the law to enact meaningful change. Together, there is endless good we can do and I look forward to your partnership."*

- **Responsibility-centered Inclusion Principle 3:** Coca Cola had every right to demand that its external law firm partners be socially responsible in their DE&I commitments going beyond the minimum required by law. In fact, ISO 26000 provides guidelines on why compliance with the law as a fundamental duty is and represents the organization's social responsibility. Going beyond the law and doing good for all stakeholders should be the ideal within a social responsibility and sustainable continuum, not the exception. Coca Cola had this principle right, as expressed in Mr. Gayton's letter:

    "As a function, we believe that pursuing diversity is not only the right thing to do, but it's a business imperative to do so quickly. We know firsthand that a diversity of thought, perspective and experience is critical to drive the best work and outcomes for our Company...I hope you will join us in this work and embrace these changes as an opportunity. While there is a long road ahead to effect systemic change around social justice, diversity, inclusion and belonging, we believe that the actions outlined above are steps in the right direction and look forward to working toward our shared goals with our law firm partners. As a legal community, we must use our collective power and knowledge of the law to enact meaningful change. Together, there is endless good we can do and I look forward to your partnership.

Mr. Gayton and his team knew the significant role the company plays not just within the American border but around the world and articulated well the far-reaching impact they were seeking with the policy: *"While the above actions focus on the United States for now, we intend for these initiatives to be customized and applied throughout our global organization."*

Unfortunately for Mr. Gayton and his team, the "actions" it outlined were built on only one stakeholder perspective—its own—and did not include input from the external stakeholders who were directly impacted. If Coca Cola had gone about things a little differently, these external stakeholders law firms could have contributed to the solution, made both the commitments and the steps to achieving them holistic with their strong buy-in because they were invited to the table of decision—the very firms Coca Cola needed to extend its *"systemic change around social justice, diversity, inclusion and belonging"* eco-system.

Summary or Food for Thought

The examples of JP Morgan and Coca Cola illustrate both the power and the challenges inherent in corporate-led movements towards implementing DE&I in society. On the one hand, companies such as this have a degree of power and influence that the government, for all its reach, does not. Corporations are not subject to the same stalling tactics so often employed to derail progressive policies by the federal government. However, that doesn't mean it's easy to change things with the stroke of a pen or a memo from the top office.

It's heartening to see two such major companies take such firm steps towards integrating DE&I into their own environments and the ways that they do business. Unfortunately, both experienced the gap between expectation and reality, and the challenges that come with trying to make changes not everyone is on board with. Good intentions are not enough for effective implementation of DE&I. The framework proposed here is exactly the sort of thing that both JP Morgan and Coca Cola could have benefited from, in different ways, to bridge the gap between aspiration and implementation.

Chapter Two

UNDERSTANDING ISO 26000 SOCIAL RESPONSIBILITY + SUSTAINABLE DEVELOPMENT

Sustainable development and social responsibility are terms that are sometimes used interchangeably, though they are not quite the same concept. Sustainable development covers the planet's ecosystem interdependently made whole by the economy, social and environmental intersection addressing humanity's generational responsibilities holistically, allowing the current generation to meet its needs without debilitating future generation's ability to do likewise. We cannot responsibly protect and preserve planet Earth for future generations while denying our current fellow earth dwellers the opportunities for lives well-lived anchored in liberty and the pursuit of happiness. This is where sustainable development (which is a conglomeration of society's expectations) connects with social responsibility (which is an organization's willingness to act in a socially responsible manner).

Social responsibility, on the other hand, is an organization's responsibility to both society and the environment because as it seeks to act in a responsible manner its decision making and activities touch on sustainable development's humanity common goals of economy, social and environment expectations. Whereas an organization's sustainable pursuits may or may not benefit all of society and the environment, its pursuit of sustainable resource use, sustainable livelihoods and sustainable consumption do contribute to sustainable development (ISO 26000 2010). Hence, an organization's socially responsible decision-making processes and activities when attained by addressing profit, people and planet contributes to sustainable development and DE&I serves as a good moderator.

Humankind is currently at a crossroads, with multiple major juxtaposition upheavals between our lifestyles and work routines. After things return to "normal," after the Black Lives Matter protests cease and COVID-19's threat subsides, will we return to business as usual? Or will we establish a new normal influenced by these events and their impacts? This is a question we are beginning to answer individually, corporately, and as a society—at the local, regional, national, and global levels.

These events have forced us as a society to reflect on ourselves. What the public murder of George Floyd stirred up around the world is our sense of shared humanity, shared response to senseless murders due to police brutality and shared responsibility as our brothers and sisters' keepers when we are faced with inequities and social injustices. COVID-19 has reminded us that life is fragile for all – here today, gone tomorrow—and that our responsibility to one another includes putting others first (in or out of pandemic crisis—getting the vaccine, wearing masks and social distancing). Together, we proactively right the wrongs perpetuated through societal and environmental forces. Together, these two events tuned most of our individual spirits to a common sound—our shared humanity.

The lasting consequences of these systemic discriminatory practices are the intentional and unintentional negative generational impacts on minorities and vulnerable groups, the result of which is the denial of "life well-lived" experiences. George Floyd was certainly denied a life well-lived; he will never be able to see his daughter grow up to be the woman she was born to become, and she in turn has been deprived of her father. There are communities around the United States and the world over suffering from environmental decisions that were made deliberately to harm communities of color, such as lead polluted waters piped into neighborhoods of Flint, Michigan or freeways placed strategically in neighborhoods where minority and vulnerable groups live (affecting their health and wellbeing for generations).

A "life well-lived" should not be dependent on skin color or what educational, economic or social status a person is born into, but rather on what a person brings to the human story because of the meaningful life experiences he or she was allowed to engage in. This is the spirit of the law that began with the singular American declaration of Independence, and which has served ever since as a clarion call to all humanity: *"We hold these truths to be self-evident: that all men are created equal; that they are endowed by their Creator with certain unalienable rights; that among these are life, liberty, and the pursuit of happiness."*

Life, liberty, and the pursuit of happiness should ring true for all Americans—citizens and non-citizens alike—in every street corner, legislative house, courthouse, and c-suite (where key decisions with reverberating societal and environmental impacts are made). Life, liberty, and the pursuit of happiness is not a single trait or event, but a continuum of life phenomenon. For example, as more and more baby boomers age into retirement, America needs more younger workers from every demographic to keep the social security system afloat. Without a sustainable workforce, it is conceivable that the level of social security benefits the baby boomers expect at retirement may not be sustainable. Regardless, it's irritating for the younger workers to know that their social security payments are benefiting those who don't value them as human beings.

Life, liberty, and the pursuit of happiness should also ring true for the rest of the world because it is a shared human ideal, now accentuated in sustainable development goals and objectives and in global organizational social responsibility decision making and best practices. These values should also be important to organizations because they have measurable impacts on profits, the environment, and people. To the extent that employees and customers believe their engagement with an organization both enhances their economic wellbeing and gives meaning to their lives, they are much more motivated to give their best to it.

The unrest we've seen these past few years demonstrates that society is ready for some deeper changes. The civil protest marches and advocacies in various forms and formats for Black Lives Matter are the start of a new generation of humanity's rise for righteousness in our institutions. However, the real work will begin as we return to life after COVID-19 and we are forced to reexamine our social contracts and organizational decision-making practices, hopefully with a new resolve to do something about our perennial systemic and structural racism and other forms of inequities. To do nothing and return to the old status quo would be complicit at best and duplicitous at worse.

The problems we face today with systemic racism are not new. They have been part of America's way of life for close to 400 hundred years. European Colonialism, which sowed the seeds of modern slavery, essentially began as government-sponsored global terrorism in the 1500s and created the systemic obfuscation about our shared humanity. We have come a long way since then, with positive milestones forward such as the Civil Rights Laws of 1965. Yet, the vestiges of discriminatory practices and laws have remained with us as systemic and structural racism and manifest in many forms of inequity. Generation after generation has tried to deal with these issues.

As has often been the case throughout history, progress towards DE&I has prompted a backlash from those opposed to losing what they perceive as their entitled positions (socially and economically). Today, there are white supremacists and sympathizers who argue that systemic racism is not only justified, but intrinsic to society, going back to the beginning of time. This attempt to bolster the legitimacy of the ideology is disingenuous; its roots are but 500 years deep at the most. The relatively shallow depth in years of systemic racism compared to thousands of years of human history gives us hope that one or two committed generations can make a meaningful change in the inequitable status quo.

The momentum of the positive actionable protests generated by the murder of George Floyd in our streets and airwaves by all people groups—white, black, brown, etc.—about black lives mattering gives us hope that perhaps this is the generation that Martin Luther King saw through "spirit eyes." This America will be the one where each person's inalienable rights do produce a "life well-lived" testimonial at death because he or she lived in the promised land of the free and the home of the brave, having experienced life, liberty, and the pursuit of happiness. This is how Martin Luther King described the certainty of the generation that brings America closer to a more perfect union.

To reach this goal, we must use the existing knowledgebase of economy, environment and social and enhance them with the trifecta knowledge-base of DE&I and together forge a new systemic and structural currency for negotiating change in our societal and organizational decision-making and activities. This calls for the creation of an enabling environment in all spheres that supports a living language, facilitating dialogues where we are comfortable enough to dig deep into our implicit bias and bold enough to uproot them.

We also need to address the real challenges exposed by COVID-19 in all its amplifying manifestations—lack of access to healthcare, capital, housing stability, food security, and education as described below by the United Nations:

> The COVID-19 pandemic represents a severe threat to city services, global health, and is radically transforming the societies in which we live. Physical distancing measures adopted around Latin America and the world directly impact the life and well-being of almost 4.1 billion people living in cities. The populations considered at high risk include persons with disabilities and older persons. Local governments need to plan and address the unprecedented political, economic and social implications that resulted from the limitations of mobility, participation, expression, and social interactions. Therefore, it is vital to document the experience lived by persons with disabilities and older persons, including the identification of the physical, health, and socioeconomic barriers that affect their fair, full, active participation and human rights in the cities in which they live (United Nations 2021).

The dangers posed by the pandemic are new; the inequities in healthcare availability and economic resilience are not. But the disease has thrown these perennial, generally underappreciated problems into the spotlight.

Sustainable Development + Social Responsibility Frameworks

Sustainable development and social responsibility are complementary systemic and structural guidance approaches intended to address societal and organizational issues, challenges, and practices. The United Nations Millennial Development Goals (MDGs), which ran from 2013 through 2015, comprised eight goals, agreed to by all countries of the world. They were aimed at addressing global issues such as poverty, HIV/AIDS, access to primary education and ensuring no one was left behind. The Sustainable Development Goals (SDGs) that succeeded MDGs has 17 goals and runs through 2030:

> *The Sustainable Development Goals are the blueprint to achieve a better and more sustainable future for all. They address the global challenges we face, including those related to poverty, inequality, climate change, environmental degradation, peace and justice. The 17 Goals are all interconnected, and in order to leave no one behind, it is important that we achieve them all by 2030.*

Figure 2.1: UN sustainable development goals (UN SGS)

Sustainable development is not a new concept for the UN. The 1987 "United Nation's World Commission on Environment and Development: Our Common Future" report describes sustainable development as having three interdependent facets: economic, environment and social. Sustainable

Development is about achieving holistic progress with each generation of humanity meeting its needs within the ecological limits of the planet, without sacrificing the ability of future generations to meet their own needs.

Since 1987, other international forums have amplified the sustainable development mantra, including the 1992 United Nations Conference on Environment and Development and the 2002 World Summit on Sustainable Development. The 2016 Sustainable Development Goals carry on this tradition of linking economic, environment and social factors by creating systemic and structured guidance, which is integral to dealing with local and global perennial systemic issues and challenges. While Sustainable Development deals with societal economic, environment and social issues and how to address them, Social Responsibility deals with organizational responses to these issues and provides a framework for how to address them responsibly in support of sustainable development. In acting responsibly on all three areas, organizations contribute to society's sustainable development efforts.

The notion of corporate social responsibility has evolved over recent decades. It's been a topic of conversation since the 19th century, when newly minted industrial magnates used ostentatious public spending as a way of self-aggrandizement and improving public acceptance of their newfound concentration of wealth (e.g. Andrew Carnegie). It's been in much more widespread use since the early 1970s when corporate social responsibility (CSR) became fashionable, with each focus area coming to light as societal needs changed and efforts made to address them. During the industrial revolution, many successful industry leaders used philanthropic contributions to charitable causes as a way of addressing the issues of their day. Early discourse on social responsibility focused on traditionally philanthropic activities (feeding the hungry, endowing university programs, funding social ventures, etc). A century later, labor practices and fair operating practices were added to the social responsibility umbrella. Over time, other subjects like the environment, human rights, countering corruption and consumer protection also became part of the definition of social responsibility.

The Four Sustainable Development and Social Responsibility Frameworks

THE UN GLOBAL COMPACT

The mental model of the United Nations having anything to do with an organization's decisions and activities when it is not a national entity is inexact at best. The image most organizational leaders have of the UN is more likely as champions of nation-state matters, not necessary how an organization can become sustainable through its initiatives. NGOs are more likely to be familiar with the principles and activities championed by the UN to improve managerial best practices on climate change, poverty eradication, water rights, etc., Nonetheless, since 2000 when it launched the UN Global Compact, the UN has been in the forefront of providing resources and support systems and promoting awareness about how business decisions and activities of organizations, small and large, contribute to humankind's shared prosperity and the sustainability of our shared planet.

This is evidenced by the UN Global Compact, which aims to support companies in becoming more sustainable and in engaging its stakeholders to work together toward a better and prosperous world through ten shared principles. While many multinational organizations have bought into the UN Global Compact, it is far from mainstream adoption by rank-and-file organizations around the world.

The UN Global Compact covers four ecosystems: human rights, labor, environment, and anti-corruption. These four ecosystems are guided by ten principles that an organization can—as appropriate—use to improve its decisions and activities in concert with sustaining its wellbeing in economic, social and environment, all while contributing to the UN's global sustainability goals.

Table 2.1: Ten principles of the UN global compact

Human Rights	
Principle 1:	Businesses should support and respect the protection of internationally proclaimed human rights; and
Principle 2:	[M]ake sure that they are not complicit in human rights abuses.
Labour	
Principle 3:	Businesses should uphold the freedom of association and the effective recognition of the right to collective bargaining;
Principle 4:	The elimination of all forms of forced and compulsory labour;
Principle 5:	The effective abolition of child labour; and
Principle 6:	The elimination of discrimination in respect of employment and occupation.
Environment	
Principle 7:	Businesses should support a precautionary approach to environmental challenges;
Principle 8:	Undertake initiatives to promote greater environmental responsibility; and
Principle 9:	Encourage the development and diffusion of environmentally friendly technologies.

Anti-Corruption	
Principle 10:	Businesses should work against corruption in all its forms, including extortion and bribery.

The overall focus of the UN Global Compact is corporate sustainability leading to the achievement of the 17 SDGs discussed earlier. To assist corporations with adopting the principles, the UN and Deloitte developed the UN Global Compact Management Model which consists of six steps. The six steps call business leadership team to:

1. **COMMIT** to Global Compact principles at the highest levels of the business by integrating them into decisions and activities as applicable.
2. **ASSESS** its business risks and opportunities utilizing financial terms tied to the principles on how its operational decisions and activities impact each applicable principle.
3. **DEFINE** its roadmap based on the results of its assessment in developing and refining its goals, policies and strategies.
4. **IMPLEMENT** the goals, policies and strategies throughout the business' ecosystem—internally and across its value chain.
5. **MEASURE** and monitor progress on a continual basis
6. **COMMUNICATE** its progress on applicable principles to its stakeholders with face-forwarding toward continuous improvement.

GRI REPORTING STANDARDS

On March 23, 1989, an Exxon oil tanker spilled 11 million gallons of crude oil into the water of Alaska's Prince William Sound. This was the largest single oil spill that had ever affected the U.S. coastline to date, covering over 1,300 miles (History 2021). This oil spill took a major toll on wildlife and responsible for the deaths of an "… estimated 250,000 sea birds, 3,000 otters, 300 seals, 250 bald eagles and 22 killer whales (History 2021)." The disaster "may have played a role in the collapse of salmon and herring fisheries in Prince William Sound in the early 1990s (History 2021)" and led to economic hardships for the poor whites and indigenous populations who live in many coastal fishing towns:

> *Fishermen went bankrupt, and the economies of small shoreline towns, including Valdez and Cordova, suffered in the following years. Some reports estimated the total economic loss from the Exxon Valdez oil spill to be as much as $2.8 billion (History 2021).*

In 1997, because of this disaster, a new guidelines organization—GRI—was founded in Boston to create new accountability principles for environmental responsibility. While the new guidelines initially focused on corporate environmental conduct, they expanded into social responsibility by including economic, social and governance matters into its guideline principles.

GRI transitioned in 2016 into a standards organization when it launched the first sustainability reporting standard, dubbed the GRI Standards. In 2017, GRI worked with the UN Global Compact to launch the Guidance for corporate reporting on SDGs. Since then, GRI has continued to refine its sustainability-driven tools and used them to devise both universal and industry-specific performance metrics. These tools are available for free and are a cornucopia of performance metrics that an organization can utilize to measure and monitor its sustainability commitments. Some of these measures are applicable to social responsibility principles.

Today, the GRI standards are divided into three impact cohorts designed for an organization to report its activities in a structured and transparent way to stakeholders and other interested entities: (1) universal standards, (2) sector standards which are industry or sector-specific and (3) topic standards which report on specific topics important to an organization.

THE ISO 26000 SOCIAL RESPONSIBILITY FRAMEWORK

The ISO 26000 social responsibility framework has a solid pedigree. It was vetted by over 500 experts from all sectors (private, public and Non-governmental Organizations), from 120 countries and has been used since its release in 2010 by over 80 countries (with more countries joining every year). The framework also served as the backbone for the United Nations' 17 Sustainable Development Goals (SDGs).

The incorporation of the 7 principles and 7 core subjects of social responsibility into a DE&I framework gives an organization a new order that enables difference makers who bring healing and meaning to their organization, personal interactions, and the global ecosystem, helping it to thrive and lead it towards a path to sustainable development.

Organizational wholeness is a novel concept that may be utopian, but it seems tantalizingly close considering that today's workforce is dominated by people who want to make a difference and find meaning in their work. The days of working just for a paycheck and earning a gold watch after 50 years have passed. Paycheck plus meaning and contribution to making the world a better place has become the higher purpose – the altruistic cry of today's young and vibrant workforce. Organizations that integrate sustainable social responsibility constructs together with DE&I can capitalize on these desires.

ISO 26000 identified three stakeholder relationships that are crucial to social responsibility and to DE&I as its moderator: (1) between the organization and its stakeholders, (2) between the organization and society, and (3) between the stakeholders and society. To integrate these principles and core subjects into DE&I as a social responsibility currency, I will be using three of my models to make the case for organizational wholeness as the higher purpose for 21st century organizations.

ISO 26000 as a model brings all these renditions of social responsibility together in a performance measurement and stakeholder engagement framework designed to be easily implemented in most organizations. A century ago, the predominant societal issues were fair operating practices and labor practices. Other societal focus areas followed suit, such as countering fraud and consumer protection, human rights, the environment, corruption, etc. Today, the predominant issues and challenges are racial and gender reckoning, while righting the wrongs of societal and corporate inequities and environmental justice. The International Standards Organization (ISO) produced its final version of the ISO 26000 in 2010 as a guide on how organizations can act ethically and transparently in ways that contribute to its health and welfare as well as that of society at large. ISO 26000 adds this guidance:

ISO *This International Standard was developed using a multi-stakeholder approach involving experts from more than 90 countries and 40 international or broadly-based regional organizations involved in different aspects of social responsibility. These experts were from six different stakeholder groups: consumers; government; industry; labour; non-governmental organizations (NGOs); and service, support, research, academics and others. In addition, specific provision was made to achieve a balance between developing and developed countries as well as a gender balance in drafting groups. Although efforts were made to ensure balanced participation of all the stakeholder groups, a full and equitable balance of stakeholders was constrained by various factors, including the availability of resources and the need for English language skills.*

ISO 26000:2010, page v.

This social responsibility framework provides guidance to organizations seeking to assess their past, present, and future decision-making, activities, and relationships with both internal and external stakeholders. ISO 26000 provided the following social responsibility benefits for an organization:

ISO *Social responsibility can provide numerous benefits for an organization. These include:*
☐ *encouraging more informed decision making based on an improved understanding of the expectations of society, the opportunities associated with social responsibility (including better management of legal risks) and the risks of not being socially responsible;*

- improving the organization's risk management practices;
- enhancing the reputation of the organization and fostering greater public trust;
- supporting an organization's social licence to operate;
- generating innovation;
- improving the competitiveness of the organization, including access to finance and preferred partner status;
- improving the organization's relationship with its stakeholders, thus exposing the organization to new perspectives and contact with a diverse range of stakeholders;
- enhancing employee loyalty, involvement, participation and morale;
- improving the safety and health of both female and male workers;
- impacting positively on an organization's ability to recruit, motivate and retain its employees;
- achieving savings associated with increased productivity and resource efficiency, lower energy and water consumption, decreased waste, and the recovery of valuable by-products;
- improving the reliability and fairness of transactions through responsible political involvement, fair competition, and the absence of corruption; and
- preventing or reducing potential conflicts with consumers about products or services.

ISO 26000:2010, pages 20-21.

No organization exists in isolation. Their effectiveness is guided by how they relate to the society and environment in which they exist. This means organizations were feasible should also consider engaging in the issues and challenges facing the society and environment, including perennial systemic and structural dysfunctions that put minority and vulnerable groups at a disadvantage while granting privileges to another group on the basis of skin pigmentation.

Organizations are well-positioned to join society in addressing societal systemic and structural dysfunctions because they provide the means for achieving sustainable development through the vast resources they control or have influence over—people, profit, and planet. The control and influence organizations exert comes with a degree of social responsibility, because organizational decisions and activities on an ongoing and regular basis have tremendous impacts on behaviors that affect the economy, environment and social matters. ISO 26000 provided the following guidance on the general characteristics of social responsibility:

ISO [It] is the willingness of an organization to incorporate social and environmental considerations in its decision making and be accountable

Black Lives Matter is about issues that all of humanity needs to resolve. We cannot address global warming and climate change matters without including racial equity matters, because people are at the core of why we want to save the planet in the first place. To save and preserve our beloved planet for future generations demands that we take racial and gender equity seriously and address them within a comprehensive and holistic framework of reform and growth.

To the extent that systemic and structural racism, prejudices against persons with disabilities, hate or other discriminatory practices are perpetuated in any society, they will find their way into organizational decision-making and activities. Organizations are made up of people, and people don't leave their biases at the door when they come to work. In the age of globalization, this puts enormous social responsibility on organizations to stand up and be counted in stemming the tides of these societal and global dysfunctions and not wait for society or governmental institutions alone to solve them. This makes the highway upon which socially responsible drivers can move from one issue to the other more sustainable, within cohesive networks of global and local challenges and opportunities.

The question of which comes first, the chicken or the egg, rings true when it comes to DE&I within an organizational or corporate context. Understanding first what _diversity_ is and why it is important to an organization's three bottom lines of profits, people, and planet opens the door to _equity_ issues, which in turn directly leads to the table of _inclusion_ where those seated have a say in the organization's decision making and activities—its very life blood. The concepts are interrelated and cannot be addressed in isolation and they begin by properly identifying the stakeholders and the stakes they represent. ISO 26000 provides the following guidance:

When the table of inclusion lacks diverse representations of people, groups, ideas, experiences, and knowledge, equity discourses are constrained and jaded at best. Furthermore, when inclusion decisions are made simply to address numerical abnormalities without first gaining and appreciating the values of diversity, they create unintended or even intended hills and mountains of inequalities that can sometimes be almost insurmountable.

The mountains of inequalities created by a lack of knowledge-based diversity and inclusion in our organizational life have direct impacts on our economic, environment, and social bottom lines. They perpetuate our broken humanity, accentuate our ongoing disunity, and elevate our self-imposed differences. Hence, understanding DE&I in their rightful order gives us the framework to seamlessly integrate them as a social responsibility currency, and in the process achieve some form of sustainable development while creating the path to wholeness within our organization's ecosystem.

ENVIRONMENTAL, SOCIAL AND GOVENANCE (ESG)

Environmental, social and governance (ESG) is an investment reporting mechanism investor can use to evaluate corporations' ethical, responsible and sustainable values and behaviors. Investors use ESG criteria to evaluate the future performance of corporations through the double lens of financial and social impact. While some experts argue that ESG focuses on non-financial performance indicators that may have adverse impacts on financial performance, others contend that social values actually enhance the corporation's performance in both financial and non-financial ways.

Today's social responsibility framework makes the separate consideration of financial and nonfinancial aspects of investments a mistake because globalization calls for more just and fair economic ecosystems overall. Both small and large investment firms are paying more attention to this trend. ESG criteria continue to evolve, but tend to focus around the following three areas:

Figure 2.2: Environmental, social & governance (ESG)

Environmental	Social	Governance
• climate change • greenhouse gas emission • waste and pollution • deforestation • resource depletion	• health and safety • employee relations & diversity • conflict • work conditions • minority, underserved, & vulnerable groups' impacts	• board structure and diversity • bribery and corruption • tax strategy • executive pay • philanthropy and political lobbying

Today, as investors focus on what modern ESG criteria should include, the reality is that wealth and income disparities around the world are becoming starker as the haves continue to disproportionately increase their net worth at the expense of the have-nots, who wander in a wilderness of lack and unfulfilled purpose. Further, misconceptions about ESG abound: social responsibility is not a call to embrace a socialist economic system, but rather for democratic capitalism to realign its values to lift every boat regardless of size or location. The UN Secretary-General Guterres (2022) echoed this reality: *"Between 1980 and 2016, the world's richest 1 per cent captured 27 per cent of the total cumulative growth in income. Low-skilled workers face an onslaught from new technologies, automation, the offshoring of manufacturing and the demise of labour organizations (Guterres 2022)."*

Figure 2.3: UN report on income inequality between 1980 and 2016

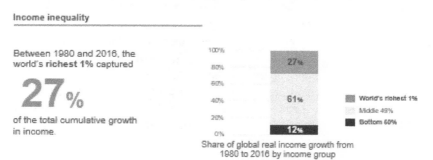

The value of democratic capitalism in unleashing and enhancing human creativity to support and sustain human existence on planet earth is not in question. The questions revolve around making corporate values assets to humanity, not divided by financial norms that continue the old system of divide and conquer—an enrich-and-impoverish dichotomic enterprise. This explains why shareholder democracy has been gathering momentum lately, because both small and large investment institutions are now seeking to address stakeholders' concerns through reformation of corporate management structures.

By exploring new and innovative ways to give stakeholders' voices a hearing in corporate decision-making, both investors and investment firms are examining varied approaches, including social media as moderator for investment decisions and performance monitoring. As social media becomes the preferred platform for billions of people to engage over common cause narratives, its impact can be increasingly positive and/or ominous for publicly-traded companies. Goetzmann (2022) of the Financial Analyst Journal posited:

> This empowerment of opinion and the rise of media influencers will almost certainly pose challenges for investment managers, especially those who are fiduciaries. Will companies become "memocracies" owned and governed by ideological social media communities? If so, is this good or bad for companies, shareholders and society (Goetzmann 2022)?

The idea that social media can be effectively deployed to influence stock values is becoming a reality that cannot be ignored within the confines of ESG. For example, the 2021 GameStop stock surge, where a group of online investors invested together on a common cause narrative—partly combative and partly aspirational (Goetzmann 2022)-demonstrated this phenomenon well. For socially conscious investors, financial and nonfinancial impacts are joined at the hip even if they are weighted separately. It is, however, also true that good corporate ESG-aligned intentions do not necessarily translate to socially conscious decision-making and practices.

ESG, like the Triple Bottom Line (TBL) phenom, may allow corporations to promote their "greatness" or simply check the boxes of intended goodwill - but may not necessarily tell the true story of their actual practices, including the good, the bad, and the ugly. Furthermore, ESG by its organic nature is driven by political and current affairs; outcries over issues of the day tend to subside as time matches on, a process that some companies cynically exploit. A broader social responsibility investment systemic structure that deepens the roots of ESG through consistent dedication to core subjects is needed, especially as it relates to DE&I.

Integrating DE&I as an Organization's Social Responsibility Currency

As the world today is increasingly attuned to the issues of DE&I, individuals and organizations want to join in the fight to change the tide on systemic and institutionalized racism. One question is what can be done and what solutions have worked previously. While each situation may be different, using a set of vetted guiding principles and core subjects that have been repurposed for addressing DE&I matters provides a valid path forward.

ISO 26000's seven principles and seven core subjects offer such a set of guiding principles which, when integrated into DE&I programs, provide a systemic and structured approach to addressing many of our societal issues and challenges from an organizational framework, along with issues pertinent to sustainable development.

Integrating ISO 26000's social responsibility principles, stakeholders engagement strategies and core subjects within a holistic management system enables an organization to strive towards organizational wholeness while achieving sustainable development goals. This framework must be genuinely supported by the organization, however, because there will always be those who oppose it. An organizational social responsibility framework that only tiptoes around DE&I matters and its translation into organization-wide communication language will have its policies and practices undermined by those within its own ranks who never bought into our shared humanity and shared planet construct.

The Minnesota Police Department, for example, is an organization that prided itself in its DE&I policies and practices. All its officers, like other Police officers around the country take the widely embraced International Association of Chiefs of Police oath: *"On my honor, I will never betray my badge, my integrity, my character or the public trust. I will always have the courage to hold myself and others accountable for our actions."* And for Officers in the United States, the following is generally part of the oath as well: *"I will always uphold the Constitution, my community, and the agency I serve."* Quite obviously, the policies, however aspirational, have not translated into practice for many members of the department – particularly the police officers who murdered George Floyd.

All members of the department are supposed to understand that all citizens in their respective jurisdictions are stakeholders both of interest (they pay the taxes, fines and fees that fund the police) and of expectations (they belong to society and to the human community which expects the police to uphold their oath). Yet, when it comes to Police brutality against citizens and non-citizens alike, some officers forget who pays for them to experience a "life well-lived." And when it comes to police brutality against black and brown people, the tradition is so deeply rooted in systemic and structural racism that are woven into the fabric of society that it is difficult to root out.

George Floyd, a Minneapolis resident and an American citizen was pinned down on a hard asphalt pavement by two officers, while the third officer put his knee on his neck. The officer killed him even as Floyd called out for his mom, who had died two years earlier. A fourth officer stood at the ready to block any interference from the public. These Officers had all sworn *"To Protect with Courage, To Serve with Compassion!"* Obviously, their actions against Mr. Floyd on that fateful day were not remotely courageous or compassionate.

All four officers failed to hear the pleading cry of Mr. Floyd as he used up his last oxygen in his lungs to wheeze out his now famous words, "I can't breathe." The same officers failed to heed the pleas of passersby to let him breathe. And when the paramedics arrived, they too failed to administer any first aid to try and resuscitate Mr. Floyd. Was Mr. Floyd already dead, or were they also complicit because Mr. Floyd was African American? Did they try to cover it up and put the death as an event that occurred in a different place— the hospital? In spite of the irrefutable video evidence that the officers' actions contradicted their own established code of conduct, the MPD initially declared Mr. Floyd's death a "medical incident." What went wrong?

In this case, *everything* went wrong, from the bankrupt immoral act, the official moves to initially conceal the truth from the public, and the complicity of institutional leaders who knew these systemic practices existed within their ranks but normalized it by allowing it to continue to fester. Obviously, just having good and well-reasoned policies on the books does not always translate to actions of the police officers on the street.

A Police Department's stakeholders—from the individual officers, their unions (current and retirement), their supervisors and management and the political and legal arm—must buy in to DE&I for it to actually work and be sustainable. Any weak link in this buy-in process leaves room for abuse, neglect and unenforceable norms that civil society expects from those who have sworn to protect it. This calls for both pre-emptively identifying and engaging all stakeholders for any police reform to be meaningful and have sustainable and social responsibility drivers.

PERTINENT QUESTIONS FOR POLICE DEPARTMENTS

The following guide has been adapted from ISO 26000 to pose the questions a Police Department needs to ask to fully identify and engage its stakeholders when it commits to a holistic sustainable and social responsibility change process:

- To whom does the police department have legal obligations?

- Who might be positively or negatively affected by the police department's decisions or activities?
- Who is likely to express concerns about the decisions and activities of the police department?
- Who has been involved in the past when similar concerns needed to be addressed?
- Who can help the police department address specific impacts?
- Who can affect the police department's ability to meet its responsibilities?
- Who would be disadvantaged if excluded from the engagement?
- Who or what in the value chain—community, people, environment—is affected?

Figure 2.1: A police department's stakeholder profile

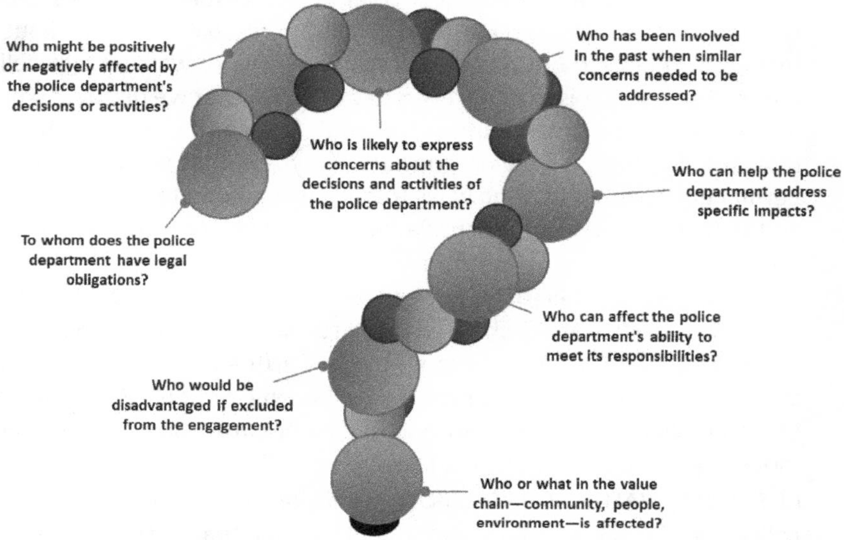

Who might be positively or negatively affected by the police department's decisions or activities?

Who has been involved in the past when similar concerns needed to be addressed?

Who is likely to express concerns about the decisions and activities of the police department?

Who can help the police department address specific impacts?

To whom does the police department have legal obligations?

Who can affect the police department's ability to meet its responsibilities?

Who would be disadvantaged if excluded from the engagement?

Who or what in the value chain—community, people, environment—is affected?

Answering these questions truthfully sheds light on blind spots that Police Departments generally ignore or avoid. While society may never have a cure for racists who refuse to be reformed by reason, organizations can protect the sanctity of their social responsibility commitment by translating their policies and practices into DE&I living language and medium or currency for negotiating decisions and activities. Currency is defined in Merriam-Webster as a *"medium of exchange...general use, acceptance or prevalence...a medium of verbal or intellectual expression."* It is in this vein that I use DE&I as a medium of verbal or intellectual expression for social responsibility.

By making DE&I an acceptable general-use currency for negotiating value-added decisions and performing routine activities, both society and organizations can institutionalize its policies and procedures. The diverse and inclusive culture it aspires to become can facilitate its sustainable development goals. The devil's in the details, however. To begin, we need streamlined working definitions of DE&I that are broad enough to be applicable to any organization worldwide by treating each one as a currency.

DE&I as Currency for moving organizations forward

- **CURRENCY VALUE 1 DIVERSITY**: Human diversity is all the individual and collective but unique ways we manifest, identify or celebrate our shared humanity within our shared planet Earth. Natural diversity is all the environmental—animate and inanimate—resources available on planet Earth to be shared and experienced by all humanity for all time. We need to normalize our discussion of race, gender, or disabilities so that issues related to them are not guarded or cause people to walk on eggshells around the topic. It is through everyday dialogue that we discover what people really believe about our shared humanity and our shared responsibility to it. A guiding principle should be that we do not have permanent enemies but find ways to bring even our hate-filled brothers and sisters to a place of reconciliation when they are ready to give up the hate.
- **CURRENCY VALUE 2 EQUITY:** Equity represents how we individually and collectively participate or share in all the resources available and utilized by our generation from our shared planet Earth and how we reconcile the differences when inequalities arise or become obvious. When we are able to discuss inequities freely and find common ground solutions, we move organizational wholeness forward.
- **CURRENCY VALUE 3 INCLUSION:** Inclusion is our individual and collective capacity and commitment to embrace the equitable participation of our diverse humanity in all our endeavors that utilizes resources from our shared planet.

When sustainable goals and social responsibility serve as the currency for DE&I exchanges, they empower and enable organizations to undo discriminatory practices from an institutional framework faster and more effectively than legally required or legislative mandates. Why? The combination of human "free will" applied to cause human "good" within an organization's eco-system affects profit, people, and planet. In essence it runs through the circle of life, liberty and the pursuit of happiness.

Figure 2.2: DE&I dialogue value trading cards

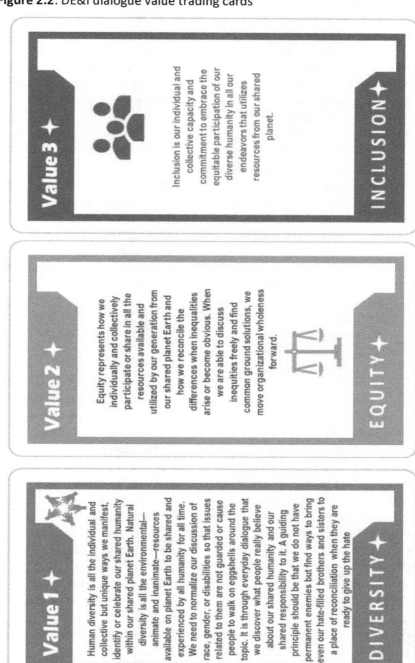

DE&I as a social responsibility must go beyond compliance-based diversity and include what is in the interest of the organization's desired outcomes, whatever that may be. For a school, it is ensuring that the environment is conducive for learning and knowledge exchange. Its student, faculty and administration reflect the community it serves and go beyond the legal requirements for minority and underserved communities. For Police Departments, it ensures that the decision-making processes and activities are consistent with serving and protecting the community in truth and not in name only. By integrating DE&I into social responsibility and sustainable development as a currency, we legitimize the free flow of imagined ways in which we can collectively move past systemic injustices.

George Floyd's case was hardly an isolated one. Daunte Wright was a twenty-year old African American young man who was stopped and killed by police in Brooklyn Center, Minnesota just as the George Floyd court hearings were ending. When the mayor of the city and acting police chief were asked by the media the next day about how many police officers were in the command, the answer was about 49. How many lived in Brooklyn Center? "None" was the answer, although they were not exactly sure. This brings up a fundamental question: why are Black neighborhoods policed by White officers who neither live in the neighborhood nor appear to be invested in it? While in most large cities or metropolis, it is understandable if a few officers policing a black neighborhood may live outside of it, this should be an exception, not the norm.

Stakeholder engagement is something that must be worked on from both sides. After decades of disenfranchisement thanks to white supremacy and the legacy of Jim Crow laws, Black leaders must demand that more officers who patrol their neighborhoods look like the people they serve. Taxation without representation should lead to a protest or demand for change. And yes, this means these communities must also proactively encourage their young men who do not want to follow the academic track to enroll in Police Academies. If the Academies make it impossible for minority candidates to get in, then stakeholders should use legal means to open the doors in the event that lobbying, and protests do not work. Corporations can become involved as well, investing in programs that would produce more police of color to stem the historical abuse.

The point is that police brutality in America has gone on for too long. It is likely that had two or more Black Police officers been present at the scene when George Floyd was slaughtered that they would have interfered. Better, their presence on the force might have caused reassessment of the department's DE&I practices in the first place.

DE&I as manifested through the ISO 26000 gives us the framework to ask the hard or taboo questions that we need to ask to get to the bottom of individual and organizational implicit bias. When senior executives, for example, talk about their commitment to DE&I, but 80% of them are white, the question becomes one of balance; one way to achieve it is to have a plan. This removes the distrust factor and makes the commitment achievable because people would rally around an imperfect management faster than they would a pretending to be perfect one.

The seven principles and seven core subjects of social responsibility are repurposed in this book to assist organizations of all sizes to systematically address the issues and challenges in organizational governance, human rights, labor practices, the environment, fair operating practices, consumer issues and community involvement and development. These core subjects follow an organization's review and commitment to be accountable, transparent, exemplify ethical behavior, respect stakeholder's interests, respect the rule of law, respect international norms of behavior, and respect human rights.

This integrative fundamental approach allows each organization's governance structure to be framed by its vision and mission but propelled or facilitated through DE&I as a social responsibility currency that drives everyday decisions and activities in pursuit of sustainable development goals. The rest of this book will use this integrative approach in making the case for diversity, equity, and inclusion as a social responsibility currency or moderator.

Figure 2.3: Diversity, equity and inclusion at work

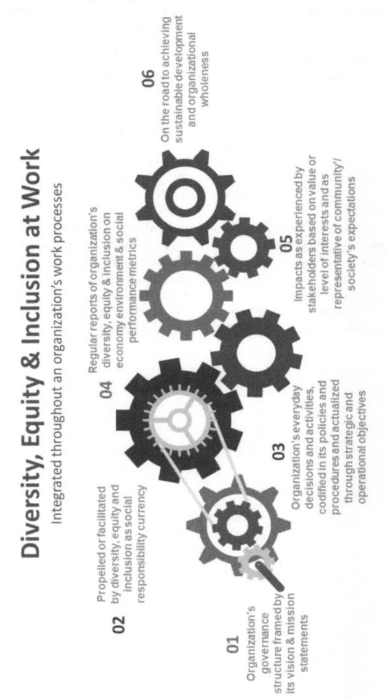

Diversity, Equity & Inclusion at Work

Integrated throughout an organization's work processes

01 Organization's governance structure framed by its vision & mission statements

02 Propelled or facilitated by diversity, equity and inclusion as social responsibility currency

03 Organization's everyday decisions and activities, codified in its policies and procedures and actualized through strategic and operational objectives

04 Regular reports of organization's diversity, equity & inclusion on economy environment & social performance metrics

05 Impacts as experienced by stakeholders based on value or level of interests and as representative of community'/ society's expectations

06 On the road to achieving sustainable development and organizational wholeness

Chapter Three

ESTABLISHING THE KNOWLEDGE, CREATIVITY AND GOVERNANCE (KCG) MODEL

E very human problem or challenge always begins with an identification process. What is the problem? Where did it originate from? How do we solve it? Until we acknowledge that a problem exists, we cannot begin to solve it. And without a framework of knowledge, we cannot organize things and devise a set of rules for how things should run.

The knowledge, creativity and governance model or KCG model is based on the simple notion that knowledge invites creativity to the table of governance. Once you know something (knowledge), you choose (creativity) how you act (governance) based on that knowledge. William Wilberforce rightly deduced that *"you may choose to look the other way, but you can never say again that you did not know."*

We generally do not create things or systems in a vacuum: Knowledge is necessary. What we create needs a structure to establish the rules of the game. This is the essence of the KCG model.

I developed the KCG model as a minimalist model to explain vast and varied human story from the beginning of time using knowledge, creativity and governance as simple parameters or predictors. As mortals, we enter the world with an empty slate: no preexisting knowledge to draw from, and dependent on the knowledge we acquire over time to shape our behaviors, values, and worldviews. How we use this knowledge depends on the boundaries, structures, and systems that govern or frame our individual and communal awareness, affinities, and acceptance—all prepackaged for us when we use automatic, social and mental model thinking.

I am further linking this KCG model to ISO 26000 in evaluating and creating socially responsible dialogues around DE&I as an ecosystem resting on three parameters: Knowledge-informed, creativity-driven, and governance-centered. Together, these tell the holistic story of where we came from, where we are, and where we are headed in our organizational continuum, which generally leads to sustainable development. This approach allows us to use the same nomenclature already prevalent in organizational discourses around corporate social responsibility, climate change, sustainable development, and the triple bottom line of economy, environment and social (or people, planet, and profit). In the KCG model:

- **Knowledge** prepares the groundwork for creative solutions to emerge from data-driven awareness and/or data-mined Knowledge-based information. We gain or acquire knowledge by experience or education based on facts or information that enter our cognitive or intellectual space. Knowledge is "...awareness, understanding, or information that has been obtained by experience or study, and that is either in a person's mind or possessed by people generally (Cambridge 2022)."

- **Creativity** converts informed knowledge into just and fair socially responsible actions or results leading to sustainable development outcomes. Creativity is synonymous with being imaginative, clever, ingenious, innovative, original, creative – or even stupid. Without prior knowledge, creativity cannot exist. A conductor of an orchestra cannot lead effectively unless they have knowledge of how music is scored, how to read notes, hear tones and read faces. This knowledge enables the conductor to direct the players, translating discombobulated sounds into pleasing musical masterpieces.

- **Governance** establishes just and fair decision-making policies and operational practices, rules of engagement, and paths to an inclusive organizational eco-system. Governance puts everything that is known into use by providing the structure and the space for activities to manifest. Governance is activity-focused and documents how organizations or countries have chosen to manage their affairs along with the systemic structure they use to make decisions, set priorities, and evaluate and monitor outcomes. Governance does not just occur at the highest level, but wherever products or services have been created by knowledge; creation and distribution need some form of structure to implement, regulate or enforce it. There is nothing to govern when nothing has been created through knowledge. It is only through knowledge that we create norms, products and services, and establish their use. Along this continuum is the inclusion of stakeholders whose diverse inputs and patronage make the products and services greater than originally envisioned.

Together, knowledge, creativity and governance set the stage upon which we see, interact, and are influenced by DE&I as social responsibility and sustainable development currency. For example, when you are aware of a broken system or unjust practices (knowledge), and you have developed answers and solutions (creativity), the next step is to establish how the new order of things will function or lead to wholeness (governance).

Figure 3.1: Ajiake Knowledge, creativity and governance (KCG) model loop

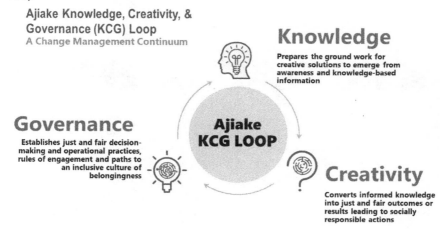

As the organization works towards perfecting its DE&I continuum, the gaps between aspiration and reality should narrow until a semblance of wholeness is reached. While the perfect union of DE&I in the decision-making processes and activities of an organization might be a little utopian, the more we aspire to this standard, the more likely our organizations will achieve a sustainable balance in profits, people, and planet. This balance can be viewed holistically as organizational wholeness.

We can achieve sustainable development by integrating a social responsibility construct in our organizations, society and politics, but this does not mean we achieve wholeness within our broken humanity. Employees might work for a socially responsible organization without experiencing an opportunity to bring their full potential or higher purpose to bear. This is a loss to the organization, the individual, and society at large considering that we spend more than fifty percent of our waking hours at work or school. These norms or limitations are often the result of bureaucratic, ineffective, and inefficient processes that do not include the diverse opinions, thoughts, and experiences of internal and external stakeholders. It is also often the result of historical stereotyping which forces us to view certain tasks from a gender-centric viewpoint. As Supreme Court Justice Ruth Bader Ginsburg observed:

> *Feminism...I think the simplest explanation, and one that captures the idea, is a song that Maple Thomas sang, "Free to be You and Me. Free to be, if you were a girl—doctor, lawyer, Indian Chief. Anything you want to be. And if you're a boy, and you like teaching, you like nursing, you would like to have a doll, that's OK too. That notion that we should each be free to develop our own talents, whatever they may be and not be held back by artificial barriers—manmade barriers certainly not heaven sent.*

> *Ruth Bader Ginsburg*

Table 3.1: DE&I in relation to KCG model

DE&I in relation to KCG Model	
Diversity, Equity, and Inclusion	KCG Model
Humankind is one species. Our shared humanity is represented by male and female kind adorned by a variety of skin hues or tones. Human Diversity is any difference between individuals and groups; it may include race, gender, nationality, religion, sexual orientation, ethnicity, socio-economic status, physical and mental abilities or disabilities, ideas, thoughts, perspectives, values, etc.	Knowledge prepares the groundwork for creative solutions to emerge from data-driven awareness and/or data-mined Knowledge-informed information. Humankind shares one planet—Earth—and all its natural resources but unnaturally divided by human-made norms. These divisive norms make it impossible for far too many within the current human generation to meet its own needs while expected to ensure future generations have the resources to meet their needs. Organizations can accentuate our shared humanity in their equity and inclusion practices through commitments to socially responsible decision-making processes and activities. Socially responsible commitments are informed actions that create a healthy balance in organizational priorities around people, profits and planet and contribute to sustainable development.

Equity is treating everyone fairly based on their individual or group needs—equity rights. The outcomes of equity rights are the elimination of barriers that harbor discriminatory norms such as denial of opportunity, lack of access, unfair treatments and all forms of societal disparities that advantages one racial or gender group over another.	Creativity converts informed knowledge into just and fair socially responsible actions or results leading to sustainable development outcomes. Humankind's divisive norms are best addressed through human creativity. Humans created these divisive norms, and only humans can eliminate them through creative solutions. Organizations can address societal inequities by assessing its own decision-making processes and activities throughout its eco-system and ensuring that they are fair and just practices. When these practices fall short of socially responsible and sustainable development norms, they should be corrected promptly, or a measurable plan developed to address them overtime.
Inclusion is the intentional act to not exclude people or treat them in an unfair or unequal manner because of their race, gender, sexual orientation, or other discriminatory factors. At the root of inclusion is fairness and equality for all within the spheres where they belong.	Governance establishes just and fair decision-making and operational practices, rules of engagement and paths to an inclusive organizational eco-system. Humankind's segregation and discriminatory practices are unnatural and human-made and are birthed or upheld by fear and hate practices, typically reinforced by learned values, behaviors, laws, and even organizational practices. Organizations can address segregation and discrimination within their workforce, workplace, and work-partners through actionable steps that create inclusive norms, best established through social responsibility and sustainable development norms.

When the KCG model is integrated into a DE&I framework, it creates a synergic bond for achieving organizational wholeness. Although we do not often associate wholeness with organizations as we do with people, it is still an aspirational goal for organizations to reach for the DE&I stars in balancing their profits, planet, and people objectives. Organizations that set audacious goals such as Coca Cola attempted with their 30% law firm diversity policy (whose implementation was flawed but intentions were good) can expect to do better than where they were when the goal was first set because the adage that shooting for the moon and landing among the stars is always a win-win proposition. Within the KCG Model,

- Diversity must be knowledge-informed because it showcases our comfort levels in *who* we are and celebration of *what* we share— our humanity. We cannot talk about diversity within the context of superiority of a racial or gender group over another and segregation as a necessary practice.

- Equity is creativity-driven because it establishes our <u>commitment</u> in *when* and *where* we express our individual unique identities or live through imposed identities in the areas of ownership, belonging and participation. The levels of committed ownership, belonging and participation are at the heart of fair equity distribution when and where we show up affecting our abilities to fully express our higher purpose. How we resolve inequities in our organizations and society is dependent on whether we believe in our shared humanity and earthly resources.
- Inclusion is governance-based because it reveals confidence in our shared humanity by *how* we relate to one another and by our celebration of *why* we belong to each other. Inclusion is measured by a pendulum with governance/leadership on one side and dominance/leadership on the other; its pivot reveals how we relate to one another, and the results are why we belong to each other. At the core of inclusion is doing unto others what you wish done to you.
- Wholeness represents our comfortableness, commitment and confidence in our shared humanity and shared responsibility to all of nature.

Together, knowledge, creativity and governance/dominance set the stage upon which we see, interact, and are influenced by DE&I.

Figure 3.2: Ajiake KCG model—an organizational wholeness continuum

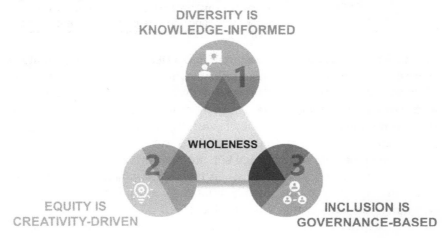

WHOLENESS

Wholeness has several definitions, but by defining "whole" we get the essence of its use in bringing our broken humanity to a place of some level of completeness. "Whole" is defined as all of something or the full amount. It is when all the parts of something are functioning well together that you have wholeness. A society, community, or country may celebrate its diversity, yet still exclude far too many of its members from participating in its economic engine. An organization can tout its inclusion strategies in well-crafted vision and mission statements, but the actual numbers and respect for varied opinions may betray inconsistencies. Wholeness is a determinant of how well a society, or an organizational DE&I environment exists and functions as a coherent whole. Wholeness represents our comfortableness (diversity), commitment (equity) and confidence (inclusion) in our shared humanity and our shared responsibility to one another.

Figure 3.3: The road to organizational wholeness

The Road to Organizational Wholeness:
Diversity, Equity & Inclusion in the Knowledge, Creativity & Governance (KCG) Model

04. WHOLENESS
Wholeness represents our comfortableness, commitment and confidence in our shared responsibility to all of nature

03. INCLUSION
Inclusion is governance-based and reveals confidence in our shared humanity by how we relate to one another and by our acceptance of why we belong to each other

02. EQUITY
Equity is creativity-driven and establishes our commitment in when and where we express our individual unique identities or live through imposed identities in the areas of ownership, belonging and participation

01. DIVERSITY
Diversity is knowledge-informed and showcases our comfortableness in who we are and acceptance of what we share in common—our humankind

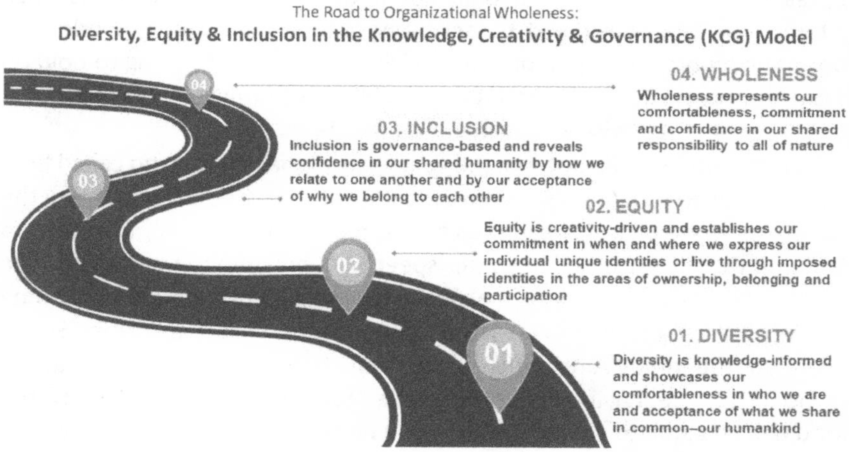

Lessons from President John F. Kennedy Moon Speech and Its Application to DE&I as a Moderator for Social Responsibility and Sustainable Development

Although the Moon Speech was not a DE&I speech, I use it here to showcase its application to organizational life where social responsibility and sustainable development norms are moderated by DE&I. Humankind going to the moon and DE&I as an organizational priority in decision-making processes and activities are novel, but not impossible, irreconcilable ideals. They both begin with acknowledged gaps between where we are currently and where we know we could be—the essence of translating knowledge to actionable steps and decisions.

On September 12, 1962, President John F. Kennedy gave his Moon Speech to convince Americans that going to the moon was not simply an option, but the right thing to do regardless of the financial and other costs. This speech provides a good example of making a case for change using the KCG model, the spirit of which is instrumental for leaders today. While the moon speech was aspirational, it also demonstrates what can be achieved where there is the political or organizational will to transform past systemic and structural decision-making and activities into a fairer and more just DE&I-centric approach.

The space age President Kennedy was calling Americans to embrace was going to cost each person additional taxes, with no foreseeable benefits at the time. The truth is that a racially reconciled nation and world will also cost something, at least to those who benefit from the imbalances that this reconciliation addresses. For some it would involve acknowledging the effects of the oppressive nature of systemic and structural racism to the oppressed and making a personal commitment not to propagate such systems. For others, it could be accepting a minority-majority world that does not support the notion of white privilege anymore. Fighting to hold on to a worldview that has shaken itself to pieces is perhaps instinctive but is neither prudent nor wise and worse off, unsustainable.

President Kennedy became the space-age global leader who called first, on Americans to embrace the moment and lead the world in conquering the mystery of space by sending a man to the moon and returning him safe to planet Earth. The President used this speech to galvanize the nation and the world to work together to conquer space for the good of humanity at a time of heightened tension between the United States and the former Soviet Union. At the time, Americans were conflicted about the potential for weapons in space, having experienced the Cuban missile crisis in which the world almost came to an end because of a nuclear war that no nation would have survived. When the Soviet Union snuck nuclear weapons into Cuba, allowing it to strike the United States more quickly, a crisis was triggered; the only option was for either the Soviets to remove the missiles, or face an escalated response.

This is not unlike an organization trying to persuade its employees that DE&I is good for its profits, people and planet when they are sympathetic to racist beliefs and values. How then does an organization's leadership move beyond policies and procedures and into the hearts and souls of its employees, to convince them to reject hate and discriminatory practices?

One approach is to quantify in real dollars and cents the costs of lack of diversity and inclusion along with other inequalities in an organization's financial reporting. Included in this report should be the currently realized and potential benefits of a diverse and inclusive workforce. Here is how President Kennedy addressed the issue of selling the people on a task whose benefits were diverse and long-term. On the costs of leading the space age quest, President Kennedy reported to the nation:

> To be sure, all this costs us all a good deal of money. This year's space budget is three times what it was in January 1961, and it is greater than the space budget of the previous eight years combined. That budget now stands at $5,400 million a year--a staggering sum, though somewhat less than we pay for cigarettes and cigars every year. Space expenditures will soon rise some more, from 40 cents per person per week to more than 50 cents a week for every man, woman and child in the United States, for we have given this program a high national priority--even though I realize that this is in some measure an act of faith and vision, for we do not now know what benefits await us.

On the known benefits of leading the space age quest, President Kennedy also reported to the nation:

> We choose to go to the moon. We choose to go to the moon in this decade and do the other things, not because they are easy, but because they are hard, because that goal will serve to organize and measure the best of our energies and skills, because that challenge is one that we are willing to accept, one we are unwilling to postpone, and one which we intend to win, and the others, too. It is for these reasons that I regard the decision last year to shift our efforts in space from low to high gear as among the most important decisions that will be made during my incumbency in the office of the Presidency...Within these last 19 months, at least 45 satellites have circled the earth. Some 40 of them were "made in the United States of America" and they were far more sophisticated and supplied far more knowledge to the people of the world than those of the Soviet Union.

> The Mariner spacecraft now on its way to Venus is the most intricate instrument in the history of space science. The accuracy of that shot is comparable to firing a missile from Cape Canaveral and dropping it in this stadium between the the 40-yard lines. Transit satellites are helping our ships at sea to steer a safer course. [The] Tiros satellites have given us unprecedented warnings of hurricanes and storms, and will do the same for forest fires and icebergs. We have had our failures, but so have others, even if they do not admit them. And they may be less public.

When DE&I become part of an organization's transactional medium or currency for negotiating change, it empowers dialogues to be more purposeful and measurable. If a senior leader's promotion or bonus were tied to how well they have assisted the organization in closing inequity gaps, you can be sure that they would take the task seriously.

Knowledge-informed Diversity Precepts
KNOWLEDGE AND DIVERSITY

Knowledge swings on the pendulum of good and evil; without understanding where we are in the diversity spectrum, equity and inclusion will wither on the vine. While we enter the world naked with no innate knowledge about our human differences, these differences are taught and learned over time through a societally-imposed lens of good and evil. There is no such thing as innate racism or sexism or other -isms that divide us, limit access to resources to some, create barriers of entrance to others and limit our wholeness as a human race. As Nelson Mandela eloquently stated:

> "No one is born hating another person because of the color of his skin or his background or his religion. People must learn to hate, and if they can learn to hate, they can be taught to love, for love comes more naturally to the human heart than its opposite."
>
> Nelson Mandela

Organizations seeking to address DE&I challenges and opportunities must look within their organizational knowledge- or awareness-base to understand the "knowledge current" that runs through the thoughts and decision-making processes of all stakeholders—internal and external about our shared humanity. How a person views or relates to diversity is a mirror into how they see themselves as a member of humanity. These beliefs far outweigh anything the DE&I policies and procedures may say, partly because the human mind is highly self-interested. For example, an organization may perceive itself as diverse through the eyes of color or gender, but this knowledge may not be from a holistic perspective because its institutional "knowledge currents" and practices are too deeply ingrained and influenced by the experiences and learned behaviors of its individual employees and other stakeholders.

It is common today to visit a corporate website to read well-crafted DE&I policies and practices, only to find 80-90% of its leadership as white while 80-90% of the people presented in the pictures representing the low- and mid-level staff as colored folks and women. A deeper dive might also show dismal numbers in this low- and mid-level, despite the diversity in the photos. Why this disconnect on the part of all involved within an organization's eco-system—leadership, management, rank-and-file employees, external stakeholders? This disconnect is not just in the corporate world, but it is self-evident throughout society's institutions, including sports organizations and even nonprofits. It is safe to say that this is not a result of shortage of minority talents but a shortage of the political will of those holding the power to dismantle structural and systemic discriminatory practices entrenched by societal values. A systemic response is needed to these discriminatory values, behaviors and practices and all hands must be on deck to make the change sustainable over time: leadership, midlevel management, and employees.

This is the reason why we need diverse opinions and thoughts from all stakeholders in formulating our organizational knowledge and understanding of diversity, especially as it relates to the socio-cultural dynamics that frame the values and behaviors of key employees—their world view. Without these diverse inputs, we tend to formulate "unicorn" visions, missions and strategic objectives that reflect our learned values. They may benefit some but exclude others, and they set the stage for governance that reflects impractical DE&I strategies.

These issues can no longer be relegated to the human resources or development functions with no meaningful authority. Just as with the race to lead the space age for the good of humanity, the advent of globalization is calling out for bold and decisive leadership that sees DE&I as integral to creating an organizational culture that leads to wholeness. After all, life is a gift nature grants to all regardless of skin color, and this is what matters to the employees of today. Employees want to know that they matter to their organizations as human beings, sharing their talents with the expectation that they will be valued and compensated fairly.

AWARENESS OF THE AGE

The leadership of an organization should have a sense of where it is on the DE&I spectrum and where the rest of the world stands on the matter. Awareness is the first step on the knowledge continuum. As the space age was taking off, President Kennedy addressed the joint session of Congress on May 25, 1961, a little over a year before he delivered the Moon speech; in this speech he demonstrated a keen awareness of exactly where the country was:

> With the advice of the Vice President, who is Chairman of the National Space Council, we have examined where we are strong and where we are not, where we may succeed and where we may not. Now it is time to take longer strides--time for a great new American enterprise--time for this nation to take a clearly leading role in space achievement, which in many ways may hold the key to our future on earth.

In like manner, DE&I awareness is more than having written policies, procedures, or statements to regulate behavioral decorum. It requires a real assessment that accounts for the worldviews that dominate citizens or employees and all other stakeholders' consciousness. The assessment does not have to be a formal psychological exercise, but it should tap into the socio-cultural tendencies of its leadership, managers, and those on the frontline of decision-making.

Every generation in the workforce today has their own diversity and inclusion influencers, and they may not be the same. What all generations shares are a propensity for implicit as well as explicit biases. While the form may differ by person, their positive or negative manifestations are certainly real to those on the receiving side. Social media has added its own complications. For example, if a manager grew up in segregated America in the 50s and 60s, an organization should be aware that they may have been influenced by the civil rights violations that gave rise to the civil rights movement either as a supporter or non-supporter. How this citizen or employee transitioned over the years in their worldviews about civil rights matters should be part of the social dialogue because it is instructive and can help enrich the dialogue – if it is without judgmental acrimony. Even more so when it involves power and authority and the exercise of it for or against others less powerful or subordinate. On the other hand, a manager who grew up in the 90s and in the 21st century may not have experienced a segregated America, but they could still have acquired biased indifference along the way, which could be part of a meaningful racial, equity and inclusion dialogue in the workplace. Above all, social media influencers can have a direct influence on how an employee makes work-related decisions notwithstanding what is written in the organization's policy or procedures or its DE&I pursuits.

When we assume that individuals have dealt with their negative biases, especially those that pertain to race and gender, we often discover that we were gambling with fate and minimizing the potency of the fear and hate that lie within. Assuming racial and gender worldviews have changed with the times without painful but meaningful dialogue may be a contributing factor as to why organizations get into trouble with discrimination lawsuits.

For example, many police officers captured on film abusing citizens belong to departments that have explicit, well-crafted DE&I policies and practices; obviously these policies did not translate to real-life just and fair behaviors on the beat. Why? Because it is unnatural to expect persons who consume materials and messages from "hate enterprises" to become DE&I champions when they're on the clock, or practitioners without mitigating natural intervention. Newton was right in stating that for every force there must be an equal and opposite force for change to happen.

It is important to be realistic by accepting the fact that the best-crafted DE&I policies and procedures, and the most elegant speeches about the subject, cannot erase entrenched biases and stereotypes. These are strongholds not easily dismantled by pep talks. Once we accept this reality, societies and organizations will be well-served by allocating the right resources or energy to the right DE&I problems or challenges. It oftentimes begins with a truthful assessment of where we are in the DE&I conversation, where we hope to be and what it will take to get us there—the full social responsibility spectrum.

President Kennedy knew what the competition was doing or hoping to do in space and told Congress why America needed to make its own decision about this commitment, and why:

> Recognizing the head start obtained by the Soviets with their large rocket engines, which gives them many months of lead-time, and recognizing the likelihood that they will exploit this lead for some time to come in still more impressive successes, we nevertheless are required to make new efforts on our own. For while we cannot guarantee that we shall one day be first, we can guarantee that any failure to make this effort will make us last.

President Kennedy looked at the data and clearly explained where the nation was and where it could be by making the right decisions when it mattered. Like President Kennedy, leaders of organizations today must be able to make a clear and concise case for why DE&I matters are important bottom-line impacting issues. Leaders facing DE&I challenges and realities share similar challenge as President Kennedy dealing with the need to lead a sea change in space explorations. The difference is, despite the hugely aspirational nature and intangible immediate benefits of the space race, it was still a more compelling and more politically universal flag around which to rally for many than it is for DE&I today. Unless, of course, we allow our shared humankind to moderate. Getting in the front end of change demands is always the best and productive option. Acknowledging that our world has been meaningfully changed by technological innovations is not a weakness, because globalization is an irreversible new normal. This is true both for economic ties and the speed at which news travels around the planet and the voracious ways social media is consumed by so many—the good, the bad and the ugly. The public slaughter of George Floyd enraged the whole world and compelled millions of people around the world to join the Black Lives Matter movement for change, because our human sensitivities and sensibilities demanded a collective response. But the response to incidents like these have a shelf-life unless they are accompanied by systemic sea change measures.

ACKNOLEDGEMENT OF OUR SHARED HUMANITY

Our broken humanity is made more broken by learned racism and other forms of negative isms. This inhibits our shared humanity and forces us into pockets of existence within "safe" demographics. This global phenomenon was no doubt exacerbated by colonialism and slave trades that created significant inequalities in our societies, organizations, and governments. They were further cemented by global institutions established after World War II that did not consider majority of the world as stakeholders—just those from the West who were at the table of decision at that time. These learned -isms inform our decision making and the way we perceive and interact with the world around us—profits, people, planet. Organizational policies and procedures can't go faster or farther than the people expected to follow and implement them. When the leadership of an organization and its management team include broken people, the best policies and procedures in the world aren't going to magically get results.

Organizations unfortunately are expected to work almost in the dark with this preexisting knowledge-base, as employees and stakeholders are all mired in those -isms that they learned before coming into the organization. These behaviors, value systems and worldviews are often not systematically challenged or addressed when dealing with DE&I matters—making any form(s) of remedies difficult to apply and sought after results difficult to realize.

Crossing the distance between reality and aspiration is the real challenge. President Kennedy recognized this, and began his Moon speech by addressing how to bridge the gap between what we already know with where we know we should be—the essence of the human awareness and knowledge change continuum:

> We meet at a college noted for knowledge, in a city noted for progress, in a State noted for strength, and we stand in need of all three, for we meet in an hour of change and challenge, in a decade of hope and fear, in an age of both knowledge and ignorance. The greater our knowledge increases, the greater our ignorance unfolds. Despite the striking fact that most of the scientists that the world has ever known are alive and working today, despite the fact that this Nation's own scientific manpower is doubling every 12 years in a rate of growth more than three times that of our population as a whole, despite that, the vast stretches of the unknown and the unanswered and the unfinished still far outstrip our collective comprehension.

Diversity is knowledge-based or knowledge-informed and it showcases our comfortableness in who we are and our acceptance of what we share— our humanity. If a person has deep-rooted beliefs of racial or ethnic superiority, they may go through the emotions and processes of DE&I training or seminar, but as a stakeholder their commitment will be limited at best. Until this person becomes comfortable in his or her personhood within the human family, their ingrained worldview will usually be their default modus operandi. President Kennedy captured the essence of our integrative human knowledge continuum as follows:

> No man can fully grasp how far and how fast we have come, but condense, if you will, the 50,000 years of man's recorded history in a time span of but a half-century. Stated in these terms, we know very little about the first 40 years, except at the end of them advanced man had learned to use the skins of animals to cover them. Then about 10 years ago, under this standard, man emerged from his caves to construct other kinds of shelter. Only five years ago man learned to write and use a cart with wheels. Christianity began less than two years ago. The printing press came this year, and then less than two months ago, during this whole 50-year span of human history, the steam engine provided a new source of power.
>
> Newton explored the meaning of gravity. Last month electric lights and telephones and automobiles and airplanes became available. Only last week did we develop penicillin and television and nuclear power, and now if America's new spacecraft succeeds in reaching Venus, we will have literally reached the stars before midnight tonight. This is a breathtaking pace, and such a pace cannot help but create new ills as it dispels old, new ignorance, new problems, new dangers. Surely the opening vistas of space promise high costs and hardships, as well as high reward.

Each organization would have its own unique culture framed by the individual and collective experiences of its employees and all other stakeholders. Organizational leaders in crafting diversity and inclusion policies and procedures should be cognizant of the underlining socio-cultural and political current that runs through its human ecosystem. Familiarity with the founders, what was happening in society at the time of the founding, and the prevailing mindsets of the originating citizens or employees that still dominate the current mindset are some of the areas to consider.

This knowledge will inform the leadership about the effectiveness of its treatment of DE&I as social responsibility, so they can assess whether it has created as President Kennedy wisely asserted "… new ills as it dispels old, new ignorance, new problems, new dangers." Consider the fact that humanity has had gender problems from the beginning of time, and that despite our progress we are still dealing with gender insensitivity and inequalities in pay, respect, and appreciation of our differences. The late

United States Supreme Court Judge Ruth Bader Ginsburg summarized this truth succinctly in a 2015 Bloomberg Interview:

> I was a law school teacher, and that's how I regard my role here with my male colleagues who haven't had the experience of growing up female, and don't fully appreciate the arbitrary barriers that have been put in women's way.

The willingness of an organization to embrace diversity in its decision-making and accountability structures have direct impact to its social responsibility commitments and it begins with a clear acceptance of our shared humanity. This in turn affects its transparency and ethical behavior in how the organization evaluates its progress in taking stakeholders' interests into account and in its compliance with applicable law, consistent with international norms of behavior and in its integration of these principles into daily operations (ISO 26000 2010). Archbishop Desmond Tutu summed it up well: *"All of our humanity is dependent upon recognizing the humanity in others (Twitter 2015)."*

Depending on where the pendulum rests in its DE&I continuum, an organization acting on its social responsibility knowledge will be better equipped to incorporate constructive principles, ideals, and benefits in addressing diversity issues. When an organization is aware of its own history and understands what it needs to do to bridge the gap between knowledge and reality, only then can it craft effective DE&I policies, procedures and practices suitable for its unique circumstances. Otherwise, they're just guessing at best and engaging in performative DE&I window-dressing at worst.

Creativity-driven Opportunity/Reconciliation/Disruption Considerations

Our humanity is something we all share regardless of skin color, gender, or status. As mortals, we are born and die naked without the ability or capability to bring our own resources into the world or carry the ones we inherited or accumulated over a lifetime. From birth onward, we are all subject to sickness, aging, and eventual death. These are things we can't control. What we do have control over are the choices we make during our lives, especially when we reach an age of accountability.

To be sure, if humanity is fundamentally flawed by virtue of its mortality, it should be no surprise that our systems and structures would also be imperfect. This means that our economic, environmental, and social systems need restructuring from time to time because each has the potential for creating or perpetuating systemic problems, especially those that divide us. Many of these problems have, frankly, existed since the beginning of time. Our awareness of these problems is usually the first step—knowledge. How we solve them is the second step—using these means based on knowledge. The third step is how to make what we have created stand the test of time and for that we need rules of engagement or governance.

The world has faced global problems before, not unlike the ones faced by organizations today in dealing with DE&I. Equity issues and challenges in how our shared planet's resources are owned or used have always been with humanity. Repeatedly, in countless ways that have varied by country and time, individual human rights and freedom to exercise those rights have been constrained by human actions and impositions—perceived and real. This explains why we need creativity-driven equity considerations: to right the wrongs and free ourselves from ingrained biases about who belongs where, who owns what, and who can participate freely in our shared human endeavors.

CREATIVITY AND EQUITY

Creativity is the mother of equity, because without using the knowledge we have acquired and steer it towards a course of justice, equity cannot be born. When an organization understands the "real life currents" that run through its internal and external stakeholders' worldviews, this diversity awareness and knowledge gives it the key to creatively develop appropriate measures to address the inequalities.

To be sure, an organization's inequalities and inequities are rooted in societal systemic and structural social contracts put in place by those in a position of privilege at the time they were founded. For some, this can be a very long time ago, when those social contracts might have reflected some deeply inequitable assumptions.

Equity is creativity-driven and underscores our fairness commitment in when and where we express our individuality without imposing dehumanizing values on others. Every person has an inalienable right to life, liberty, and the pursuit of happiness. These manifest in a sense of belonging, ownership, and participation in decisions and practices that involve and/or impact them.

When all is said and done, equality for all in all things is not practical, but equity or fairness to all in all things is possible. Fairness is not a benevolent gift we give to others out of the goodness of our hearts, but the goodwill we extend to all because of our shared journey on planet earth. We are always our brothers' and sisters' keepers, because it is the loftiest trajectory we can pursue in honor of our shared humanity.

When people or employees believe that organizational systems are against them, they are not likely to use their creativity to the fullest in addressing issues that weigh the organization down. When public agencies use public policies to marginalize or disadvantage one group over another, such as locating freeways or sanitary facilities in poor and/or minority communities, then equity dialogues and demands are inevitable.

Contrary to what some people think, equity and equality are not terms solely owned by communists or socialists. Supporting human rights doesn't mean everyone must wear the same clothes, eat the same rationed food, and earn the same pay just for showing up at work. Equity influencers give us the framework to creatively develop solutions to diversity and inclusion issues by asking the tough questions as to how we got to where we are and what we must do to ensure we do not remain there. To bridge equity gaps, we need a three-part lens, whose components can work independently or in concert, to create fair, equitable, and sustainable systems. The three fairness lenses of equity are: opportunity, reconciliation, and disruption:

Figure 3.4: Ajiake 3-step equity lens model

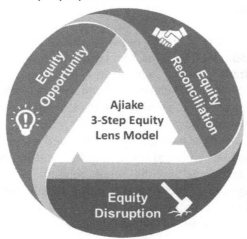

Equity opportunity gives us actionable steps for what must be done now to correct unjust or unfair practices. Equity reconciliation requires us to reconcile inconsistent, unjust, or unfair values, behaviors, and traditions by bringing these practices in line with fair and just ones that we profess to believe in. Equity disruption compels us to disrupt or stop the madness of perpetuating unjust and unfair practices because our shared humanity demands it.

The 3-Equity Lens Model Applied to DE&I

Applying these 3-Step Equity Lens model to DE&I as a moderator for social responsibility and sustainable development helps bring clarity to unjust policies and practices, and brings into focus what must be done to align these practices with those of a more just and equitable world:

Equity Opportunity (EO) focuses on opportunities to adjust or correct current inequitable or biased practices (racial, gender and others) with socially responsible fair and just ones.
Equity Reconciliation (ER) focuses on systemic biases (racial, gender and others) and equity norms (values, behaviors, traditions, and activities) that should be reconciled, improved upon, or replaced with socially responsible systemic fair and just ones.
Equity Disruption (ED) focuses on the unjust or unfair decision-making practices and discriminatory social contracts that must be stopped for socially responsible equity framework (racial, gender and others) to develop sustainable root.

1. Equity Opportunity

Every country in the world today has its own systemic and structural injustices woven into its societal fabric and consciousness. While some countries have seen significant improvement over time, others perpetuate the same injustices generation after generation. At issue quite often is the privileged folks who are unwilling to give up what they feel is their birthright, both in terms of tangible and intangible benefits. In some societies, the privileged group is hell-bent on not giving an inch, while expecting accolades for their public displays of concern for shared experiences and collective progress.

Gender inequities are some of the most divisive and destructive norms. When 50% or more of a country's population is marginalized because they are women, that means that 50% of a country's potential sustainable development or more is lost, both now and in the days to come. Understanding this opens the door for us to create equity opportunities within organizations that do not require seismic switch in our decision-making processes and activities, just the will to pursue fair and just practices.

Changing old and well-established orders are tough, because there are so many stakeholders who want to keep the status quo; they're often afraid of how change might impact them. President Kennedy knew that the United States was behind the Soviet Union when it came to manned flights and admitted to this inequity in their space programs. Importantly, the President did not make excuses or cover up the fact that America was behind the Soviet Union; he was honest about the situation, which enabled him to set realistic, if ambitious, goals for addressing the problem. Admitting that systemic and structural racism are woven into the American fabric opens the door to see the low hanging fruits of possible change and to seize on these opportunities. The equity opportunity in Kennedy's case was making sure that America was not left behind in the space race by playing second fiddle to the Soviet Union. Such a scenario could have led to geopolitical and economic imbalances akin to inequity practices wherein Americans might become subject to the Soviet Union's dictates. President Kennedy stated:

> To be sure, we are behind, and will be behind for some time in manned flight. But we do not intend to stay behind, and in this decade, we shall make up and move ahead. The growth of our science and education will be enriched by new knowledge of our universe and environment, by new techniques of learning and mapping and observation, by new tools and computers for industry, medicine, the home as well as the school. Technical institutions, such as Rice, will reap the harvest of these gains. And finally, the space effort itself, while still in its infancy, has already created a great number of new companies, and tens of thousands of new jobs.

Change, of course, is threatening. Integrating DE&I as currency for negotiating value-added decisions and performing organizational activities will no doubt have its own detractors who would prefer for the change to be gradual if at all.

On April 4, 1967, at a meeting of Clergy and Laity Concerned about the War in Vietnam, Dr. Martin Luther King gave a speech he titled, *"Beyond Vietnam: A Time to Break the Silence."* In this speech, Dr. King agreed with the theme of the meeting: *"A time comes when silence is betrayal."* This truth is also applicable for organizations that pursue supposed social responsibility and sustainable development while ignoring DE&I matters, limiting its power of transformation to superficial metrics. Here is an abbreviated version of Dr. King's speech:

> These are revolutionary times. All over the globe men are revolting against old systems of exploitation and oppression and out of the wombs of a frail world new systems of justice and equality are being born. The shirtless and barefoot people of the land are rising up as never before. "The people who sat in darkness have seen a great light." We in the West must support these revolutions. It is a sad fact that, because of comfort, complacency, a morbid fear of communism, and our proneness to adjust to injustice, the Western nations that initiated so much of the revolutionary spirit of the modern world have now become the arch anti-revolutionaries...A genuine revolution of values means in the final analysis that our loyalties must become ecumenical rather than sectional. Every nation must now develop an overriding loyalty to mankind as a whole in order to preserve the best in their individual societies...We are now faced with the fact that tomorrow is today. We are confronted with the fierce urgency of now. In this unfolding conundrum of life and history there is such a thing as being too late. Procrastination is still the thief of time.

For those who occupy positions of privilege to be truly free and create a meaningful and peaceful coexistence for their posterity, they must seize the moment and seek equity opportunities to right the wrongs of the past that may have privileged them, because while they might be benefiting in the short term, their long-term sustainability demands change. These call for taking actionable steps that seek to create Equity Opportunity strategies for funding, procurement, engagements, hiring, promotions, and in every sphere where there is systemic and structural unfairness.

2. Equity Reconciliation

There are times when systemic and structural injustices in society and organizations must be reconciled for fair and equitable resolution to occur, and organizational leaders should make the change happen. A systemic and structural unjust and unfair practice requires more than just platitudes to remedy. It also requires systemic and structural fair and just practices that account for areas of the injustice and mitigates or eliminates them. This approach screens out the gaslighting or conflating of the issues so that answers are not formed around questions that were not asked.

No condition is permanent in life, just like there should be no permanent enemies on social justice issues. Our shared humanity calls for liberty and the pursuit of happiness for all. Historically, demographic changes and power structures have transformed majority groups into the minority and made wealthy families poorer; change is inevitable. But when the poor are given opportunities to move up, in a system designed to address inequities wherever they're found, all of society benefits.

In those times when we face the perennial consequences of inequalities, we must be courageous to find creative means to realign the imbalance by reconciliations. To do this, we need data to show how deep and widen the gap might be between what we say about ourselves and the reality. In the case of the United States, the country was born with an original sin, slavery, with the concomitant sin of racism; together they shaped the consciousness of the nation. Against this backdrop are three documents—the Constitution, Declaration of Independence and Emancipation Proclamation—all clamoring for freedom, justice, and fairness for all its citizens. It is up to us to bridge the gap between the aspirations of these documents and the realities of the inequitable system that flourished alongside them, selectively wielding their words (or ignoring them) to justify ideals that run counter to their intent.

For America to continue its journey towards becoming a more perfect union, it needs to reconcile the glaring inconsistencies between its founding documents and its systemic and structural racism embedded in everyday realities of its minority groups. Therefore, Martin Luther King became the prophet to the nation challenging the consciousness of White Americans to come to the table of brotherhood and sisterhood for the nation to be whole in purpose, mission, and wellness.

In 1963 during the March on Washington for Jobs and Freedom, many well-meaning religious and political leaders advised the civil rights leaders to slow down and allow the nation to organically change and give Black people their inalienable rights for freedom, liberty, and the pursuit of happiness. Just like the fierce urgency in 2020 to integrate DE&I as currency for social responsibility, Dr. King addressed the issue of waiting for race relations to work itself out over time head on:

> This is no time to engage in the luxury of cooling off or to take the tranquilizing drug of gradualism. Now is the time to make real the promises of democracy. Now is the time to rise from the dark and desolate valley of segregation to the sunlit path of racial justice. Now is the time to lift our nation from the quick sands of racial injustice to the solid rock of brotherhood.

The "tranquilizing drug of gradualism" is usually a drug of choice for the privileged, not for those who are reeling from the impacts of systemic and structural injustices. For the underprivileged, waiting for the stars to be aligned in their favor is not a plan of action. For the underprivileged and marginalized, the adage coined because of the space age, "Houston, we've had a problem" remains true until the problem of racial and gender inequities is solved. Bringing some balance to the inequity is what they want, and therefore leaders should look for ways to make this reconciliation a reality. President Kennedy was able to make the case for space exploration by reconciling it with aspirational social responsibility goals and the economic sustainable pursuit of any city, state, or region:

> Space and related industries are generating new demands in investment and skilled personnel, and this city and this State, and this region, will share greatly in this growth. What was once the furthest outpost on the old frontier of the West will be the furthest outpost on the new frontier of science and space. Houston, your City of Houston, with its Manned Spacecraft Center, will become the heart of a large scientific and engineering community.

Organizations that acknowledge America's racial disharmony and their impacts can make a business case for why DE&I are social responsibility and sustainable development matters. The shifting American demographics towards a truly diverse population, one in which there will be no single racial majority, is a starting point for refocusing an organization's sustainable workforce plan and to remove barriers to diversity and inclusion.

3. Equity Disruption

There are times and situations when we face systemic and structural practices that are so reprehensible that they must be disrupted or abandoned, because as Dr. Martin Luther King Jr., reminded us, *"This is no time to engage in the luxury of cooling off or to take the tranquilizing drug of gradualism."* In these situations, continuing these structural injustices or allowing them to fester is tantamount to madness. Inequity matters like changing old values and behaviors do not simply work themselves out or disappear over time. If anything, they become entrenched with people who demand the continuation of their privileged position regardless of who else is negatively affected. For change to happen in these cases, we need to develop creativity-driven equity disruptors in response to these reprehensible behaviors, values, and systems because attempting unrealistic reforms is just as bad as ignoring them. It may even be worse, because the presence of a superficial and ineffective DE&I-oriented reform effort may prevent more meaningful change from taking place.

President Kennedy in his Moon speech also faced a nation reluctant to take a gamble on the space race. After all, the population had seen and experienced the horrors of World War 2, the proliferation of nuclear weapons, and the near-global disaster of the Cuban Missile Crisis.

Those who grew up in the late fifties and early sixties knew just how close the world came to fighting World 3 less than two decades after World War 2 ended. The only thing that averted all-out nuclear warfare was the Soviets' decision to back down and remove their nuclear missiles in Cuba. Had they not done so, it's quite possible that none of us would be here today.

The development and ownership control of nuclear weapons by five countries—U.S., USSR, Britain, France and later, Israel— created a check and balance or equity system in Europe and around the world. China, India, Pakistan, and South Africa have since become nuclear powered nations as well, providing balancing regional roles. However, at the time that space exploration was still new, it was presumed that whoever controlled it would have tremendous sway over life on earth. Convinced and determined that the only country that would use its technological leadership for the benefit of humanity was the United States, President Kennedy set out to convince the rest of the nation to forego its reluctance and instead join him in this space age proposition:

> So it is not surprising that some would have us stay where we are a little longer to rest, to wait. But this city of Houston, this State of Texas, this country of the United States was not built by those who waited and rested and wished to look behind them. This country was conquered by those who moved forward--and so will space. William Bradford, speaking in 1630 of the founding of the

Plymouth Bay Colony, said that all great and honorable actions are accompanied with great difficulties, and both must be enterprised and overcome with answerable courage. If this capsule history of our progress teaches us anything, it is that man, in his quest for knowledge and progress, is determined and cannot be deterred. The exploration of space will go ahead, whether we join in it or not, and it is one of the great adventures of all time, and no nation which expects to be the leader of other nations can expect to stay behind in the race for space.

President Kennedy wisely called the nation out of the doldrums of gradualism into the fierce urgency of leading the space age, and every generation of Americans since then has benefited from it. In like manner, today's organizational leaders must make DE&I a priority and a currency for systemic and organization-wide change. Corporate leaders need to convey a sense of urgency in disrupting divisive norms (values, behaviors, and traditions) that divide us and promote white supremacy or gender inequities, just like Kennedy did in galvanizing the nation for space missions. Kennedy succeeded in motivating American society to pursue a transformational achievement in an astonishingly short period of time because he was also willing to put the resources needed in place to achieve the goals.

During the next 5 years the National Aeronautics and Space Administration expects to double the number of scientists and engineers in this area, to increase its outlays for salaries and expenses to $60 million a year; to invest some $200 million in plant and laboratory facilities; and to direct or contract for new space efforts over $1 billion from this Center in this City.

In like manner, organizational leaders must also be open to the economic data that supports the value of having an inclusive workforce which promotes equity as its *modus operandi*. Hence, organizational leaders must be willing to put the necessary resources needed to achieve a diverse, equitable and inclusive workforce and workplace. If we can develop a successful moon mission in under a decade, surely, with the right leadership and ambitions, we can make meaningful transformational strides towards a more equitable and just society, beginning with our organizations and leaders.

Figure 3.5: Ajiake 3-Step Equity Lens summarized

Equity Reconciliation (ER) focuses on systemic biases (racial, gender and others) and equity norms (values, behaviors, traditions, and activities) that should be reconciled, improved upon, or replaced with socially responsible systemic fair and just ones.

Equity Disruption (ED) focuses on the unjust or unfair decision-making practices and discriminatory social contracts that must be stopped for socially responsible equity framework (racial, gender and others) to develop sustainable root.

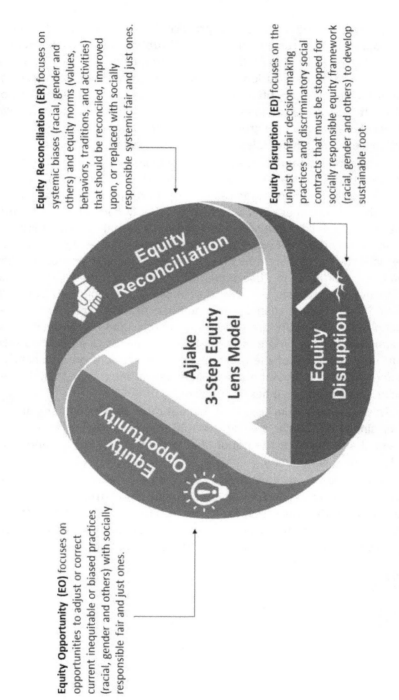

Equity Opportunity (EO) focuses on opportunities to adjust or correct current inequitable or biased practices (racial, gender and others) with socially responsible fair and just ones.

Governance-centered Inclusion Actionable Steps

Governance-centered inclusionary practice is the institutionalization of equity opportunities, reconciliations, and disruptions by including everyone within its ecosystem—creating an environment of belongingness. Governance-centered inclusion is the barometer that tells the story of where we are, highlighting the difference(s) between our stated policies and our realities. It reveals the confidence in our shared humanity by how we relate and includes all the people groups represented in our demographic sphere of influence in meaningful roles within our organizational ecosystem.

To be sure, we cannot always plan out life perfectly, but we can always meet and work with life wherever it finds us. This is true for organizations which have not grown organically using DE&I principles, values, and governance. Sometimes, organizations are simply compelled by business realities or stakeholder demands—internal and external—to examine and fix their inclusion problem. Frequently the response is to take highly visible but superficial steps – perhaps hire a few people belonging to groups that have been left out or appoint a board member or two from these groups. Then they pound their chests and sing the "mission accomplished" song. Yet, inclusion is much more than a simple numbers fix. While inclusive numbers of people from all groups are important, the roles and responsibilities they are assigned are even more important. Change needs to go beyond token inclusion. When most of the organization's leadership is predominantly of one demographic, it says far more about its values and culture than the DE&I policies and procedures it has on the books.

This explains why inclusion is a celebration of our shared humanity and all its similarities while valuing our differences, allowing them to be expressed and rejecting the notion that one or a few people represent a whole group or community.

Governance-centered inclusion sets forth actionable steps and should document our equity response to systemic and structural inequities, whatever form they may take. Therefore, it is from this knowledge that we create our equity path and work towards governance-centered inclusion framed by redemptive, restorative, and responsible principles:

Figure 3.5: Ajiake 3-step inclusion and belonging principles

Racial Inclusion Principle 1:

Redemption-driven (RD) principle should guide steps or opportune actions taken to create visible, practical, and measurable socially responsible inclusive (racial, gender and others) organizational eco-system.

There are, unfortunately, people today in organizations across the globe who believe that DE&I matters are overblown. For example, there are experts who argue that we should just allow racial profiling in securing employment to wear itself out with time, or to allow demographic changes to upend the majority/minority paradigm. The same goes for gender pay disparities and other inequalities. In the history of humankind, those that hold power do not willingly give it up without resistance. Inequities are sustained by those who currently benefit from the structural imbalance; they will want to keep the status quo until a demand for change is placed on it. The age of globalization has made DE&I an inevitable socially redemptive principle for crafting equity opportunity considerations in dealing with diversity and inclusion matters.

The human history of inclusion has not favored minority groups and women around the world. These groups always suffer the fallout from any inequity. The first inclusion principle therefore should guide us towards redeeming what was historically deprived these groups as a first step towards a holistic community. This principle accepts affirmative action measures as the first step in breaking the door open for real progress on DE&I to manifest, but affirmative action cannot be the only option in addressing systemic and institutional problems. It's the beginning of a solution, not the end.

In challenging his contemporaries to redeem their time by leading the explorations of space age, President Kennedy invoked the sacrifices of previous generations that provided the benefits that they were enjoying at that time. This linkage gave the President the moral authority to demand that society take the needed risks and seize the opportunities of the moment:

> Those who came before us made certain that this country rode the first waves of the industrial revolutions, the first waves of modern invention, and the first wave of nuclear power, and this generation does not intend to founder in the backwash of the coming age of space. We mean to be a part of it--we mean to lead it. For the eyes of the world now look into space, to the moon and to the planets beyond, and we have vowed that we shall not see it governed by a hostile flag of conquest, but by a banner of freedom and peace. We have vowed that we shall not see space filled with weapons of mass destruction, but with instruments of knowledge and understanding.

President Kennedy invoked the positive power of the image of those who paved the way so Americans could enjoy the benefits of their sacrifices. When it comes to systemic and structural inequities, the shared magnitude of their negative power over minority groups should be an even more compelling reason for change.

Before there was globalization, the world had already experienced the devastations of two world wars and the development of nuclear weapons. The Holocaust and the murder of millions of Jews because of hate, the civil rights movement in the United States, the Independence movements from around the world against colonialism, and all the other wars and movements (women's rights, environment, LGBTQ rights, etc) since then serve as reminders of where we have been as a human race.

These experiences not only shaped the world we live in today, but also call us to be the change needed to move our organization's DE&I commitments forward. The age of globalization compels us to redeem our broken humanity through our sense of social justice; this is not the first time such calls have rung out. On the eve of the Moon landing on July 16, 1969, a group of about 500 civil rights protesters led by civil rights icon Rev. Ralph Abernathy gathered at the gates of the Kennedy Space Center to protest the launch.

Rev. Abernathy and his group brought with them two mules and a wooden wagon as metaphors for the families who lacked affordable housing and food. Remarkably, NASA Administrator Thomas Paine came to the gates and engaged Rev. Abernathy in a dialogue to listen to understand the issues of their protest.

Rev. Abernathy reportedly said: "One-fifth of the population lacks adequate food, clothing, shelter and medical care," and suggested that the money for the space program should have been spent *"to feed the hungry, clothe the naked, tend the sick, and house the shelterless (Niiler 2021)."* Rev.

Abernathy asked NASA to "support the movement to combat the nation's poverty, hunger and other social problems," and that "NASA technical people work "to tackle the problem of hunger *(Niiler 2021)."*"

NASA Administrator Paine replied:

> "If we could solve the problems of poverty in the United States by not pushing the button to launch men to the moon tomorrow...then we would not push that button...[He further challenged Rev. Abernathy to] "... hitch his wagons to our rocket, using the space program as a spur to the nation to tackle problems boldly in other areas, and using NASA's space successes as a yardstick by which progress in other areas should be measured (Niiler 2021)."

Even as the United States with the new NASA Artemis Program is again planning to send humans to the moon—some fifty years later—unfortunately, most cities in American are still dealing with affordable housing and hunger issues. And cities around the world face the same problems. Pope Francis captured this sentiment well:

> These days there is a lot of poverty in the world, and that's a scandal when we have so many riches and resources to give to everyone. We all have to think about how we can become a little poorer.

Inequities in society, reflected in organizational life, present us with equity opportunities to right wrongs and create inclusive clusters of progress even when entire systems still beg for reform. Just because small changes may not be able to solve everything doesn't mean they're not worth doing. These quick equity opportunity fixes can be as simple as a teacher devoting more time to a struggling disadvantaged kid to a hiring manager instituting equity opportunity recruiting strategies to procurement managers using equity opportunity procurement to spread the wealth, or perhaps a public institution using funds to create an equity opportunity loan fund to assist groups disenfranchised from traditional lending institutions. The bottom line is that equity opportunity gives us the freedom and tools to do good immediately, wherever we are, as opposed to throwing our hands up at the magnitude of the problem.

RACIAL INCLUSION PRINCIPLE 2:
Restoration-focused principle should guide steps or on-going actions that identify entrenched inequitable inclusion barriers (racial, gender and others) and replaces them with socially responsible fair and just ones.

There are norms that are so destructive, entrenched, and pervasive that they require a systemic approach to restoring any form of human normalcy through social responsibility and sustainable development norms. In the age of globalization where the internet, cellphones, and social media have radically transformed human connectedness, this is the time for DE&I to be moderating our social responsibility and sustainable development pursuits, because now the stakeholders of interests and of expectations are all over the planet Earth.

"To whom much is given, much is required" is a true mantra for social responsibility. Organizations whose products and services have made them global titans have a social responsibility to make the world a better place by leading the way in DE&I matters. When President Kennedy gave the Moon speech, these benefits were but a wish and a prayer:

> Yet the vows of this Nation can only be fulfilled if we in this Nation are first, and, therefore, we intend to be first. In short, our leadership in science and in industry, our hopes for peace and security, our obligations to ourselves as well as others, all require us to make this effort, to solve these mysteries, to solve them for the good of all men, and to become the world's leading space-faring nation.

President Kennedy's articulation of the purpose to benefit the United States first has yielded tremendous fruits for American enterprises over the last fifty years. The seeds planted in this space race later led to IBM, Amazon, Apple, Google, Twitter, HP, WhatsApp, Microsoft, Facebook/Meta, Snapchat, INDEED, CISCO, Intel, Salesforce, Oracle, and other technology companies great and small, each of which has products and services that impact people in every corner of the globe. But in laying the foundation, President Kennedy took an inclusive approach by putting people's interests first before the goal to be the first to conquer space: *"Yet the vows of this Nation can only be fulfilled if we in this Nation are first, and, therefore, we intend to be first."*

We must likewise put our shared humankind at the forefront of our social responsibility and sustainable development constructs and aggressively work to eliminate the divisive norms we inherited from previous generations and those we formed or conformed to in our time. Placing the needs of people first (all people) is critical. Most organizations which ascribe to social responsibility see people as their greatest asset. As JPMorgan Chase Bank articulated:

> Diversity brings together people with unique perspectives, and inclusion creates opportunities for all individuals to contribute and work together to achieve success as a whole. We believe working in an inclusive environment motivates exceptional effort, or—put more simply—it makes us all better at what we do.

While this is a wholeness-birthing DE&I framework, the wholesome buy-in from the rank-and-file employees is where the rubber meets the road. The challenge is that each person that joins a company comes prepackaged with both internal and external filters that have more pull than the organization's inclusion mantra. Dr. Martin Luther King addressed this personal-division realms in his December 11, 1964, Nobel Lecture he titled the quest for peace and justice:

> Every man lives in two realms, the internal and the external. The internal is that realm of spiritual ends expressed in art, literature, morals, and religion. The external is that complex of devices, techniques, mechanisms, and instrumentalities by means of which we live. Our problem today is that we have allowed the internal to become lost in the external. We have allowed the means by which we live to outdistance the ends for which we live. So much of modern life can be summarized in that arresting dictum of the poet Thoreau: "Improved means to an unimproved end". This is the serious predicament, the deep and haunting problem confronting modern man. If we are to survive today, our moral and spiritual "lag" must be eliminated. Enlarged material powers spell enlarged peril if there is not proportionate growth of the soul. When the "without" of man's nature subjugates the "within", dark storm clouds begin to form in the world. This problem of spiritual and moral lag, which constitutes modern man's chief dilemma, expresses itself in three larger problems which grow out of man's ethical infantilism. Each of these problems, while appearing to be separate and isolated, is inextricably bound to the other. I refer to racial injustice, poverty, and war (The Nobel Prize 1964).

The cure for this is having consistent DE&I dialogues/conversations, training, performance metrics, internal and external advisory groups – all reinforcements that can be and should be achieved within a DE&I moderated social responsibility plan. To be sure, an organization cannot spend all its resources addressing issues that are society-deep and ignore its core businesses or services—the reason it exists. Nonetheless by integrating DE&I into its decision-making systems and activities, an organization can pursue an inclusive approach in recruiting and engaging as many people as possible into the development of creativity-driven equity reconciliation considerations that meaningfully address diversity and inclusion.

Racial Inclusion Principle 3:
Responsibility-centered principle should guide steps or actions taken to stop or disrupt divisive norms (the status quo values, behaviors, traditions, and activities) that obstruct socially responsible inclusive (racial, gender and others) practices.

Divisive norms that are in obvious opposition to our shared humanity must be stopped, but responsibly without creating unintended consequences. This principle guides actionable steps that must be neither excessively tolerant nor punitive, but instead centered on ending normalized unjust and unfair racial and gender inequitable decision-making practices. For example, decision-making practices that assume that certain racial or gender groups cannot do certain kinds of jobs must be stopped because they are not based on facts but on bias. To assume that a minority or woman cannot be a referee or coach in a professional football or soccer game is discriminatory. The racial or gender group one belongs to does not automatically make them innately good in a profession that requires skillsets to be developed. Similarly, Black attorneys in the case of Coca Cola's diversity policy should be able to work on Coca Cola's new businesses as much as White attorneys and leaving them out because of entrenched systemic racism should not be tolerated.

In the 21st century, we cannot continue to tolerate norms that discriminate or disadvantage minority groups just because they've been around for such a long time. This kind of thinking is retrogressive at best and entitlement-centered at worst. At the same time, we should be guided by a non-punitive approach that does not zealously punish a person for the wrongs of their racial group.

Then, there are situations when we must write the systemic and structural inequities out of existence through governance-centered inclusion decisions. Entrenched systemic discriminatory practices are hard to eliminate by executive order, but it is a necessary first step. Slavery, America's original sin, was written out of existence by President Lincoln's Emancipation Proclamation executive order. A century later, another executive order by President Lyndon Johnson introduced Affirmative Action to address the festering lack of progress on race relations. Yet today we're facing another massive racial reckoning, sparked by police brutality and enduring systemic and structural racism. The executive orders, valuable though they were, did not "solve" the problem.

Affirmative Action was intended to force integration of African Americans and women into the corporate world, where they had long been ostracized by segregation. It was intended as a bridge to the promised land of equal employment and equal opportunity under the law. Inside this promised land, the nation already should have been at a socially responsible state where equity was no longer a regulated expectation but a necessary normality. Over five decades after Affirmative Action, the nation that sent men and women into space and brought most of them home safely should have managed the transition into a socially responsible society where systemic and structural racism and gender inequities are customs of the past. Yet, we are still saddled with old hatreds and new names for the same tired ideologies. White supremacists and nationalists continue their insatiable demands for attention, directing the national racial discourse in a way of their choosing and away from the constructive dialogue that threatens them. As a rallying point for the prejudiced, Affirmative Action has become a nemesis instead of a pathway to America's Mission Accomplished Generation's socially responsible destiny.

Figure 3.7: Ajiake 3-step inclusion & belonging principles summarized

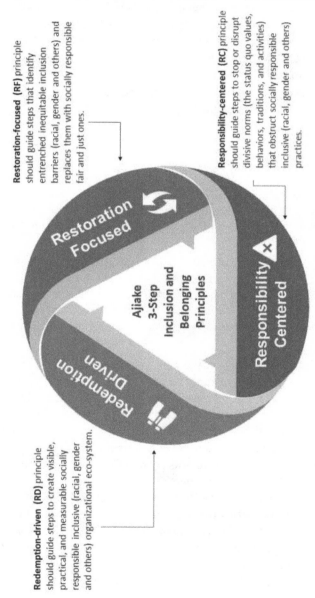

Restoration-focused (RF) principle should guide steps that identify entrenched inequitable inclusion barriers (racial, gender and others) and replaces them with socially responsible fair and just ones.

Responsibility-centered (RC) principle should guide steps to stop or disrupt divisive norms (the status quo values, behaviors, traditions, and activities) that obstruct socially responsible inclusive (racial, gender and others) practices.

Redemption-driven (RD) principle should guide steps to create visible, practical, and measurable socially responsible inclusive (racial, gender and others) organizational eco-system.

One simple but key benefit of early space exploration was the picture of planet Earth from space. When American astronaut Bill Anders took that famous picture of the world, it disrupted our worldview of our planet Earth as segregated geographic enclaves. This earthrise picture gave humanity its first breathtaking picture of the world we live in, a view that was not carved out into national boundaries as every map tends to be. That picture also showed in very graphic form how eerily isolated we are from all the elements of space and everything else in the cosmos. It further revealed our shared vulnerability as one globe—hanging on nothing, dancing to a rhythm we cannot control. The only control we have is ensuring we do not make our home uninhabitable by our actions.

When President Kennedy uttered the following words in his moon speech, he was not only being insightful, but also prophetic:

> We set sail on this new sea because there is new knowledge to be gained, and new rights to be won, and they must be won and used for the progress of all people. For space science, like nuclear science and all technology, has no conscience of its own. Whether it will become a force for good or ill depends on man, and only if the United States occupies a position of pre-eminence can we help decide whether this new ocean will be a sea of peace or a new terrifying theater of war.

> I do not say we should or will go unprotected against the hostile misuse of space any more than we go unprotected against the hostile use of land or sea, but I do say that space can be explored and mastered without feeding the fires of war, without repeating the mistakes that man has made in extending his writ around this globe of ours.

Today, because of what we know about our planet Earth from space exploration, we have more reason than ever to unite as one human race to fight global warming, climate change and collectively take other precautionary actions for our sustainable development and those of our posterity. Our social responsibility commitments are aimed at sustainable goals. Yet, no organization whose decisions and activities impacts diverse stakeholders can afford to pursue sustainable development without also addressing DE&I as an integral part of its social responsibility practices. We can achieve sustainable goals "without feeding the fires of..." racism and hate, "... without repeating the mistakes that man has made in extending his writ around this globe of ours" in sowing hate and divisions in the areas of our diversity. If we can focus on these earth-sustaining measures, we will be able to make significant progress on our race and gender relations and other discriminatory organizational practices that make us less diverse and inclusive.

Together, we can begin to create equity cultures that disrupt systems and structures that self-perpetuate within our organizations, societies, and nations. In establishing governance-centered inclusion actionable steps, organizations already have the nomenclature in place for promoting sustainable development. We use these nomenclatures to discuss climate change and global warming and environmental matters. By incorporating this terminology into the DE&I discourse, we help propel its adoption forward towards the sphere of wholeness.

Table 3.2: The 3-Step equity lens model linked to the 3-Step inclusion principles

3-Step Equity Lens Model	3-Step Inclusion Principles
Equity Opportunity (EO) focuses on opportunities to adjust or correct current inequitable or biased practices (racial, gender and others) with socially responsible fair and just ones.	**Redemption-driven (RD)** principle should guide steps or opportune actions taken to create visible, practical, and measurable socially responsible inclusive (racial, gender and others) organizational eco-system.
Equity Reconciliation (ER) focuses on systemic biases (racial, gender and others) and equity norms (values, behaviors, traditions, and activities) that should be reconciled, improved upon, or replaced with socially responsible systemic fair and just ones.	**Restoration-focused (RF)** principle should guide steps or on-going actions that identify entrenched inequitable inclusion barriers (racial, gender and others) and replace them with socially responsible fair and just ones.
Equity Disruption (ED) focuses on the unjust or unfair decision-making practices and discriminatory social contracts that must be stopped for a socially responsible equity framework (racial, gender and others) to develop sustainable root.	**Responsibility-centered (RC)** principle should guide steps or actions taken to stop or disrupt divisive norms (the status quo values, behaviors, traditions, and activities) that obstruct socially responsible inclusive (racial, gender and others) practices.

Chapter Four

THE SEVEN PRINCIPLES OF SOCIAL RESPONSIBILITY MODERATED BY DE&I

Organizations do not operate in a vacuum. They share a great deal with one another, essentially forming part of an ecosystem with other organizations. This is also true in terms of how an organization goes about its DE&I journey. By integrating best practices already vetted by over 500 experts from over 125 countries into its DE&I practices, an organization can confidently ensure that its social responsibility pursuits are on solid foundations.

Why do organizations need to be guided by social responsibility principles? One overarching reason is that an organization's decisions and activities showcases its values, behaviors, and practices that have impacts on its internal and external ecosystems. These ecosystems are wrapped around prosperity (profit), people and planet. One organization's decisions and activities can positively or adversely impact the socio-economic vitality of a region. Shared principles provide the integrated framework for addressing both economic and social issues without sacrificing the environment along the way.

Guided principles like the seven principles of social responsibility are necessary because they provide the framework for decision making and practices to be consistently applied as appropriate throughout the organization. DE&I—an emerging social science for ending our humankind's divisive norms—serves as an effective moderator for developing socially responsible organization-wide fair and just norms driven by actionable equity plans, deliberate inclusive practices, and relevant performance metrics. The results could be the emergence of vistas of prosperous organizations bringing belonging and wholeness to our broken humankind and our endangered planet.

To achieve these, an organization should be guided by principles that are universal humankind's values in decisions and activities. ISO 26000, though not a requirement for certification standards, can help articulate these principles for organizations. It was intended to assist organizations in clarifying –

ISO
… what social responsibility is, helps businesses and organizations translate principles into effective actions and shares best practices relating to social responsibility, globally. It is aimed at all types of organizations regardless of their activity, size or location.

ISO 26000:2010

ISO 26000 addresses the Principles of Social Responsibility and provides seven guidelines that, when moderated by a DE&I construct, provide a structured behavioral framework for an organization's rules of conduct and engagement with all its stakeholders—internal and external—in the areas of accountability, transparency, ethical behavior, respect for stakeholder interests, respect for the rule of law, respect for international norms of behavior, and respect for human rights:

ISO 7-Principles of Social Responsibility

PRINCIPLE 1: *ACCOUNTABILITY* MODERATED BY DE&I

Accountability within a socially responsible organization should be guided by shared values and standards that work for everyone in the organization, in equitable and measurable ways. Accountability, like the rests of the principles within an organization moderated by DE&I should also be guided by a Knowledge-informed diversity principle, framed by creativity-driven equity opportunity/ reconciliation/ disruptions lens, and codified in governance-centered inclusion actions, policies, and procedures.

ACCOUNTABILITY
Knowledge-informed diversity call to action

An organization should hold itself accountable for all its diversity, equity, and inclusion omissions and commitments and their profits-prosperity, people, and planet impacts within its internal and external ecosystems.

This principle implies that an organization should accept appropriate DE&I enquiries and the associated responsibility of responding to the enquiries within the context of its overall organization-wide accountability principles.

ISO *Accountability involves an obligation on management to be answerable to the controlling interests of the organization and on the organization to be answerable to legal authorities with regard to laws and regulations. Accountability for the overall impact of its decisions and activities on society and the environment also implies that the organization's answerability to those affected by its decisions and activities, as well as to society in general, varies according to the nature of the impact and the circumstances.*

Being accountable will have a positive impact on both the organization and society. The degree of accountability may vary, but should always correspond to the amount or extent of authority. Those organizations with ultimate authority are likely to take greater care for the quality of their decisions and oversight. Accountability also encompasses accepting responsibility where wrongdoing has occurred, taking the appropriate measures to remedy the wrongdoing and taking action to prevent it from being repeated.

ISO 26000:2010, pages 10-11.

ACCOUNTABILITY
Creativity-driven equity opportunity/reconciliation/disruption

Accountability for DE&I should include the acceptance of responsibility for any wrongdoing, lapses, or inequities in the organization's management, operations and in its products and services deliveries as well as in all areas where its decisions and activities have significant impacts on its stakeholders. The organization should look for equity opportunities to strengthen its accountability structures, reconcile any preferential accountability practices, and close any loopholes in its accountability procedures. Key equity issues to consider:

1. Does your organization have appropriate DE&I policies, decisions, and activities as part of its overall vision and mission statements? **(Speaks to Equity Opportunity)**

2. Has your organization conducted a recent assessment in the areas of DE&I and established an appropriate equity masterplan or equity mitigation plan? **(Speaks to Equity Reconciliation)**

3. Does your organization accept full responsibility for accounting, responding and/or reporting on its DE&I plan to its stakeholders on a regular basis? **(Speaks to Equity Disruption)**

Table 4.1: Accountability principle moderated by the 3-Step Equity Lens model:

1. DE&I ACCOUNTABILITY PRINCIPLE	
Equity Opportunity	Organizations should consider its management approach in addressing DE&I issues as an obligation and be responsive for answering to the controlling interests of the organization on DE&I matters as well as to those impacted. While management should be answerable to legal authorities on DE&I laws and regulations, it should also seek to go beyond these legal requirements where possible.
	Going beyond the legal requirements should be guided by equity opportunity lens in seeking to correct historical injustices and the barriers created around them in insulating organizations from being accountable to minority and vulnerable groups impacted by their decisions and practices.
Equity Reconciliation	Organizations should assess and reconcile its decision-making processes and practices to ensure that their overall impacts on society and the environment are consistent with its DE&I commitments. While the nature of the impacts and circumstances may vary from stakeholder to stakeholder, accountability to all stakeholders should be consistent in their fairness and forthrightness.
Equity Disruption	In situations where a socially responsible organization discovers practices that are adversarial to its DE&I commitments in being accountable to all stakeholders especially minority and vulnerable groups, it should take responsibility for its actions and take appropriate

| | steps to ensure that they are stopped and not repeated in any other creative form. |

ACCOUNTABILITY
Governance-centered inclusion actionable steps

Socially responsible organizations moderated by DE&I should have positive impacts on all stakeholders and the environment because they intentionally make themselves accountable to these stakeholders for the betterment of both the organization and society. The degree of accountability an organization exerts should correspond to the authority it has over each section within its ecosystem. This authority influences the overall actionable steps it develops or practices it stops to address DE&I matters. For example, In the second case study in Chapter one, Coca Cola exerted its authority over its internal legal department and achieved significant diversity and inclusion results. However, when it tried to exert the same accountability authority over its external law firm partners, it ran into trouble because they were not involved in developing the DE&I solutions even though the diversity policy had merit.

Figure 4.1: Governance-centered accountability questions

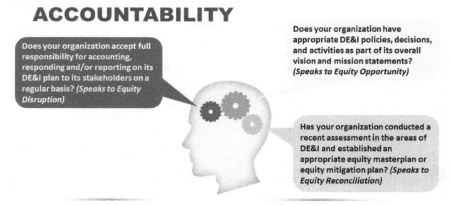

PRINCIPLE 2: *TRANSPARENCY* MODERATED BY DE&I

Transparency principle should be guided by shared values and standards that create a culture of trust and fairness in which organizational decisions and activities are made clear to both internal and external stakeholders.

TRANSPARENCY
Knowledge-informed diversity call to action

An organization should be transparent in its diversity, equity, and inclusion decisions and activities and their known impacts on its internal and external stakeholders and the environment at large.

This implies that an organization should be transparent in all its decisions and activities that impact its stakeholders, especially those belonging to the minority and vulnerable groups, traditionally overlooked and underserved. It also implies that the organization should be transparent in addressing, within reasonable timeframes, all inequities and lack of inclusion identified in its decisions and activities and not necessarily wait until it has conducted an assessment or developed a reporting mechanism—although both are good practices.

However, transparency does not mean that the organization is obliged to disclose proprietary information, including anything that is legally protected, or which has the potential to breach *"...legal, commercial, security or personal privacy obligations."*

ISO *The principle of transparency does not require that proprietary information be made public, nor does it involve providing information that is legally protected or that would breach legal, commercial, security or personal privacy obligations. An organization should disclose in a clear, accurate and complete manner, and to a reasonable and sufficient degree, the policies, decisions and activities for which it is responsible, including their known and likely impacts on society and the environment. This information should be readily available, directly accessible and understandable to those who have been, or may be, affected in significant ways by the organization. It should be timely and factual and be presented in a clear and objective manner so as to enable stakeholders to accurately assess the impact that the organization's decisions and activities have on their respective interests.*

ISO 26000:2010, Pages 10-11.

TRANSPARENCY
Creativity-driven equity opportunity/reconciliation/disruption

When creating, implementing, and/or promoting a DE&I moderated organization-wide transparency principled culture, it should be clear and intentional, without pretense, and appropriately pitched to the awareness levels of various stakeholders. DE&I moderated starter questions to ponder through Equity opportunity/reconciliation/disruption lens include:

1. Are your organization's DE&I commitments known, clearly written, readily available, directly accessible and understandable to those who have been, or may be affected in significant ways by them? **(Speaks to Equity Opportunity)**
2. Does your organization disclose in a clear, accurate and complete manner and to a reasonable and sufficient degree, its DE&I policies, decisions and activities for which it is responsible, including the known and likely impacts on individuals, the organization, society and the environment? **(Speaks to Equity Reconciliation)**
3. If your organization' s DE&I information is not timely, factual, or presented in a clear and objective manner to enable stakeholders to accurately assess the impact that the organization' s decision and activities have on their respective interests, are there plans to change these practices? **(Speaks to Equity Disruption)**

Table 4.2: Transparency principle moderated by the 3-Step Equity Lens model

2. DE&I TRANSPARENCY PRINCIPLE	
Equity Opportunity	A socially responsible organization should be transparent in its DE&I commitments and disclose them *"in a clear, accurate and complete manner, and to a reasonable and sufficient degree."* These DE&I commitments should be integrated into its policies, decisions and activities and where possible callout the impacts or likely impacts to minority and vulnerable groups and how to mitigate against their occurrence.
Equity Reconciliation	A socially responsible organization should commit to ongoing assessment of its decision-making processes and practices against a DE&I backdrop to ensure that *"readily available, directly accessible and understandable"* information is not withheld from *"those who have been, or may be, affected in significant ways"* such as minority and vulnerable groups. This transparency should be part of its DE&I commitment.
Equity Disruption	A socially responsible organization should not withhold from or present information that impact minority and vulnerable groups late or give them inaccurate information different from the ones provided to a majority group. All stakeholders should be identified and provided timely information enabling them to accurately assess the *"impact that*

> the organization's decisions and activities have on their respective interests."

TRANSPARENCY
Governance-centered inclusion actionable steps

In developing, improving, or implementing decision making tools, policy and procedures, socially responsible organizations should consider how information disclosed is received and understood by all stakeholders, including minority and vulnerable groups. Sometimes, stakeholders with shared cultural experiences are the best framers of information for their respective groups. Other times educational levels could be a barrier to understanding critical information that impact stakeholders; a socially responsible organization should be able to accommodate or mitigate for any communication barriers. For example, in planning to locate a waste treatment plant in a minority neighborhood where most of the population has only a high school education or less, providing them with complicated engineering plans about the project is not good-faith transparency. True transparency is sharing in an understandable way how the waste treatment plant could impact them economically, environmentally, and socially.

Figure 4.2: Governance-centered transparency questions

TRANSPARENCY

Are your organization's DE&I commitments known, clearly written, readily available, directly accessible and understandable to those who have been, or may be affected in significant ways by them? *(Speaks to Equity Opportunity)*

If your organization's DE&I information is not timely, factual, or presented in a clear and objective manner to enable stakeholders to accurately assess the impact that the organization's decision and activities have on their respective interests, are there plans to change these practices? *(Speaks to Equity Disruption)*

Does your organization disclose in a clear, accurate and complete manner and to a reasonable and sufficient degree, its DE&I policies, decisions and activities for which it is responsible, including the known and likely impacts on individuals, the organization, society and the environment? *(Speaks to Equity Reconciliation)*

ISO 26000 provides the following applicable guidance:

ISO   *An organization should be transparent regarding:*
- *the purpose, nature and location of its activities;*
- *the identity of any controlling interest in the activity of the organization;*
- *the manner in which its decisions are made, implemented and reviewed, including the definition of the roles, responsibilities,*

accountabilities, and authorities across the different functions in the organization;

o *standards and criteria against which the organization evaluates its own performance relating to social responsibility;*
o *its performance on relevant and significant issues of social responsibility;*
o *the sources, amounts and application of its funds;*
o *the known and likely impacts of its decisions and activities on its stakeholders, society, the economy and the environment; and*
o *its stakeholders and the criteria and procedures used to identify, select and engage them.*

ISO 26000:2010, Pages 11.

PRINCIPLE 3: ETHICAL BEHAVIOR MODERATED BY DE&I

Ethical behavior principle should be guided by shared values that work for everyone in the organization in equitable and measurable ways and when moderated by DE&I create consistent behavioral walk-the-talk ecosystem without regard for position, race or gender.

ETHICAL BEHAVIOR
Knowledge-informed diversity call to action

An organization should behave ethically in all diversity, equity, and inclusion matters and hold itself and its external partners to ethical behavior standards

This principle implies that an organization ought to be willing to face the realities of its DE&I deficits without sweeping them under the rug or using a positive spin to mislead people about the state of the organization on DE&I issues. Any discussion on ethical behavior standards should be processed through the lens of DE&I and include concern for people, planet, and profit with a commitment to address all stakeholders' interests. Not having an expected organizational behavior around DE&I matters leaves an organization's adherence to subjective interpretations which can detract from its efforts overall and is generally not a consistent approach. Ethical behavior, including anything that impacts DE&I matters, should be consistent across the board. At a minimum, an organization should evaluate or create its organizational DE&I ethical behavior principle and it should be:

1. jointly developed with both internal and external stakeholders, in order that all equity-related issues would be captured and addressed from the widest possible framework

2. integrated into the organization's governance and communication mechanisms to ensure everyone is figuratively "singing from the same songbook"

ISO *An organization's behavior should be based on the values of honesty, equity and integrity. These values imply a concern for people, animals and the environment and a commitment to address the impact of its activities and decisions on stakeholders' interests.*

ISO 26000:2010, page 11.

ETHICAL BEHAVIOR
Creativity-driven equity opportunity/reconciliation/disruption

When assessing an organization's ethical behavior relative to DE&I, considerations should be given to opportunities to ensure it is uniformly applicable, supports our shared humanity, and disrupts any double standards based on privileged status. Key equity issues to consider:
1. Is your organization's behavior around DE&I based on the ethics of honesty, equity and integrity? **(Speaks to Equity Opportunity)**
2. Does your organization proactively promote ethical conduct by defining and communicating its standards of ethical behavior expected from its governance structure, personnel, suppliers, and contractors? **(Speaks to Equity Reconciliation)**
3. Do these standards of expected ethical behavior include owners, managers, and particularly those that have "the opportunity to significantly influence the values, culture, integrity, strategy and operation of the organization and people acting on its behalf, while preserving local cultural identity?" **(Speaks to Equity Disruption)**

Table 4.3: Ethical behavior principle moderated by the 3-Step Equity Lens model

3. ETHICAL BEHAVIOR PRINCIPLE	
Equity Opportunity	An organization should examine its ethical behavior to ensure they are based on values that promote DE&I. This gives the organization the opportunity to adjust or make corrections in its values and behaviors that conflict with its stated DE&I commitments.
Equity Reconciliation	An organization should assess, identify, correct or establish a plan to correct values and behaviors that are inconsistent with its DE&I commitments to address the impacts of its activities and decisions on

	all stakeholder interests, including those that have known impacts on minority and vulnerable groups, animals and the environment.
Equity Disruption	An organization, upon identification of unethical behavior, should have a process in place to stop it and prevent it from recurring.

ETHICAL BEHAVIOR

Governance-centered inclusion actionable steps:

When an organization does not have minority and vulnerable groups represented in its ranks, developing a DE&I ethical behavior policy and procedures may be challenging but not impossible. In this type of situation, socially responsible organizations are well served when they bring in external voices that represent these groups to assist in crafting their ethical behavior policies and procedures as a step on their equity and inclusion journey. This adds values of honesty, equity and integrity to the organization's DE&I commitments.

Figure 4.3: Governance-centered ethical behavior questions

ETHICAL BEHAVIOR

Is your organization's behavior around DE&I based on the ethics of honesty, equity and integrity? *(Speaks to Equity Opportunity)*

Do these standards of expected ethical behavior include owners, managers, and particularly those that have "the opportunity to significantly influence the values, culture, integrity, strategy and operation of the organization and people acting on its behalf, while preserving local cultural identity?" *(Speaks to Equity Disruption)*

Does your organization proactively promote ethical conduct by defining and communicating its standards of ethical behavior expected from its governance structure, personnel, suppliers, and contractors? *(Speaks to Equity Reconciliation)*

ISO 26000 provided the following guidance:

An organization should actively promote ethical behavior by:

- *identifying and stating its core values and principles;*
- *developing and using governance structures that help to promote ethical behavior within the organization, in its decision making and in its interactions with others;*

- identifying, adopting and applying standards of ethical behavior appropriate to its purpose and activities and consistent with the principles outlined in this International Standard;
- encouraging and promoting the observance of its standards of ethical behavior;
- defining and communicating the standards of ethical behavior expected from its governance structure, personnel, suppliers, contractors and, when appropriate, owners and managers, and particularly from those that have the opportunity, while preserving local cultural identity, to significantly influence the values, culture, integrity, strategy and operation of the organization and people acting on its behalf;
- preventing or resolving conflicts of interest throughout the organization that could otherwise lead to unethical behavior;
- establishing and maintaining oversight mechanisms and controls to monitor, support and enforce ethical behavior;
- establishing and maintaining mechanisms to facilitate the reporting of unethical behavior without fear of reprisal;
- recognizing and addressing situations where local laws and regulations either do not exist or conflict with ethical behavior;
- adopting and applying internationally recognized standards of ethical behavior when conducting research with human subjects; and
- respecting the welfare of animals, when affecting their lives and existence, including by providing decent conditions for keeping, breeding, producing, transporting and using animals.

ISO 26000:2010, pages 11-12.

PRINCIPLE 4: RESPECT FOR STAKEHOLDER INTERESTS MODERATED BY DE&I

Respect for stakeholder interests when moderated by DE&I should be inclusive of all stakeholders, not just those the organization prefers. Minorities and vulnerable groups in organizational settings are often not seen, not heard, not valued and expected to accept such norms as historical truisms.

RESPECT FOR STAKEHOLDER INTERESTS
Knowledge-informed diversity call to action

An organization in dealing with diversity, equity, and inclusion matters should "respect, consider and respond to the interests of all stakeholders (ISO 26000 2010)" including minority and vulnerable groups.

This principle implies that DE&I is integral to the interests of all stakeholders who are impacted by the decisions and activities of the organization in the three spheres of social responsibility: economy, environment and social. Therefore, any knowledge or awareness discourse surrounding respect for stakeholder interest should be informed by facts, information, and skills gained from diverse experiences or attained from education or organizational assessments. This principle also leaves room for identifying stakeholders. When they do, they should be integrated and not dismissed for arbitrary reasons such as the passage of a specified period.

ISO *Although an organization's objectives may be limited to the interests of its owners, members, customers or constituents, other individuals or groups may also have rights, claims or specific interests that should be taken into account. Collectively, these individuals or groups comprise the organization's stakeholders.*

ISO 26000:2010, page 12.

RESPECT FOR STAKEHOLDER INTERESTS
Creativity-driven equity opportunity/reconciliation/disruption

In assessing an organization's systems on respecting stakeholders' interests, DE&I should help frame the discussion and help inform on the right tone for setting an overarching principle. In using DE&I as a lens, a socially responsible organization should look for opportunities to create an equitable and inclusive work-culture and workplace, to reconcile its decision-making processes and practices with any DE&I commitments guided by stakeholder involvement and in disruption of practices that perpetuate the inequalities of society. The organization should not neglect stakeholders who do not know their rights or how to advocate for their interests. Key issues to ponder include:

1. Has your organization identified all known DE&I stakeholders? **(Speaks to Equity Opportunity)**
2. Has your organization reconciled and aligned its DE&I expectations or stated commitments with other stakeholders' interests, including the broader expectations of its responsibility to sustainable development and interests in a fair and wholesome workplace for all? **(Speaks to Equity Reconciliation)**
3. In your stakeholder identification process, are individuals or groups who may have rights, claims or specific interests, but who are not owners, members, customers, or constituents included? **(Speaks to Equity Disruption)**

Table 4.4: Respect for stakeholder interests principle moderated by the 3-Step Equity Lens model

4. RESPECT FOR STAKEHOLDER INTERESTS PRINCIPLE	
Equity Opportunity	Respect for stakeholder interests begins by an organization first identifying and engaging all stakeholders impacted by its decisions and activities.
Equity Reconciliation	An organization should assess, identify, and engage all stakeholders, including those who may not be directly impacted by its decisions, products, services or practices. If the organization is faced with new stakeholders of which it was previously unaware, especially minority and vulnerable groups, it should have a process for engaging them immediately and incorporating them into its model.
Equity Disruption	An organization should stop seeing stakeholders only as *"owners, members, customers or constituents"* but must be more inclusive of those who *"have rights, claims or specific interests"* as well.

RESPECT FOR STAKEHOLDER INTERESTS
Governance-centered inclusion actionable steps

Stakeholder identification and engagement is a critical part of organizational social responsibility. Socially responsible organizations go the extra mile in assisting stakeholders who do not have the experience or culture that would allow them to effectively advocate for their interests. The adage "closed mouths don't get fed" should not apply here, because quite often minority and vulnerable groups have been silenced by systemic and structural racism, gender inequalities and other discriminatory practices. In many cases, they stopped advocating for themselves long ago because it got them nowhere, and even led to negative consequences. Yet, these minority and vulnerable groups often end up getting more adversely impacted by bad corporate decisions because their voices are not included in the decision and activities.

Figure 4.4: Governance-centered respect for stakeholder interests' questions

RESPECT FOR STAKEHOLDER INTERESTS

Has your organization identified all known DE&I stakeholders? *(Speaks to Equity Opportunity)*

In your stakeholder identification process, are individuals or groups who may have rights, claims or specific interests, but who are not owners, members, customers, or constituents included? *(Speaks to Equity Disruption)*

Has your organization reconciled and aligned its DE&I expectations or stated commitments with other stakeholders' interests, including the broader expectations of its responsibility to sustainable development and interests in a fair and wholesome workplace for all? *(Speaks to Equity Reconciliation)*

ISO 26000 provided the following guidance:

ISO

An organization should:
- ☐ *identify its stakeholders;*
- ☐ *recognize and have due regard for the interests as well as the legal rights of its stakeholders and respond to their expressed concerns;*
- ☐ *recognize that some stakeholders can significantly affect the activities of the organization;*
- ☐ *assess and take into account the relative ability of stakeholders to contact, engage with and influence the organization;*
- ☐ *take into account the relation of its stakeholders' interests to the broader expectations of society and to sustainable development, as well as the nature of the stakeholders' relationship with the organization; and*
- ☐ *consider the views of stakeholders whose interests are likely to be affected by a decision or activity even if they have no formal role in the governance of the organization or are unaware of these interests.*

ISO 26000:2010, page 12.

PRINCIPLE 4: RESPECT FOR THE RULE OF LAW MODERATED BY DE&I

An organization's principle to respect the rule of law should also be applicable to the spirit of the law especially in social and environmental areas where the law may be silent and yet the adverse impacts are disproportionately felt by marginalized and vulnerable groups.

RESPECT FOR THE RULE OF LAW
Knowledge-informed diversity call to action

"An organization should accept that respect for the rule of law is mandatory (ISO 26000 2010)" **and so too, should be its commitments to diversity, equity, and inclusion which may sometimes exceed what is required by law.**

This principle implies that DE&I policies, decisions and activities should be consistent with the rule of law, be made mandatory, and be adequately communicated to all stakeholders so that the policies are not subject to individual or organizational interpretations. This principle also recognizes that there are times and situations when existing laws do not go far enough to combat systemic and structural inequities. In these situations, the organization has a social responsibility to transcend these laws. In cases where they cannot change or influence the system to change, they should reconsider continued association with that eco-system (local, region or country).

> **ISO** *The rule of law refers to the supremacy of law and, in particular, to the idea that no individual or organization stands above the law and that government is also subject to the law. The rule of law contrasts with the arbitrary exercise of power. It is generally implicit in the rule of law that laws and regulations are written, publicly disclosed and fairly enforced according to established procedures. In the context of social responsibility, respect for the rule of law means that an organization complies with all applicable laws and regulations. This implies that it should take steps to be aware of applicable laws and regulations, to inform those within the organization of their obligation to observe and to implement those measures.*
>
> *ISO 26000:2010, page 12.*

RESPECT FOR THE RULE OF LAW
Creativity-driven equity opportunity/reconciliation/disruption

An organization's DE&I should be framed to conform with existing laws, but should go beyond the laws when they fall short of promoting socially responsible values. These transcendent organizational policies and procedures should address equity opportunities, reconciliation, and disruption mechanisms. Some key questions to consider:

1. Are your DE&I policies and commitments written, publicly disclosed, and fairly enforced in accordance with established procedures? **(Speaks to Equity Opportunity)**

2. Are your organization's DE&I commitments consistent with related laws and adhered to by all, regardless of position within the organization? **(Speaks to Equity Reconciliation)**
3. Are there processes within your organization to ensure that awareness of applicable laws and regulations or your corporate policies and procedures related to DE&I are known and up-to-date, and that this information is appropriately disseminated? **(Speaks to Equity Disruption)**

Table 4.5: Respect for the rule of law principle moderated by the 3-Step Equity Lens model

5.	RESPECT FOR THE RULE OF LAW PRINCIPLE
Equity Opportunity	An organization must not only comply with all applicable laws and regulations, it must also instruct everyone within its organization to do the same. This includes all laws and regulations as well as managerial obligations that address diversity, equity and inclusion and organization leaders should ensure that all employees and contractors observe and implement them.
Equity Reconciliation	An organization should assess all laws and regulations as well as its DE&I managerial obligations to ensure that its decision-making processes and practices are in concert with them. Where there are identified differences or gaps, an organization should ensure that it makes the correction or develop a plan that when implemented will bring it to compliance.
Equity Disruption	Respect for the rule of law implies that socially responsible organizations stop decision-making processes and practices that are illegal and that are adversarial to creating a diverse, equitable and inclusive workforce and workplace.

RESPECT FOR THE RULE OF LAW
Governance-centered inclusion actionable steps

In developing inclusive actionable steps, a socially responsible organization should be guided by DE&I and be clear on the difference between the supremacy of the law and the supremacy of our shared responsibility to humanity and the planet. The idea that no individual, organization, or government is above the law speaks to the supremacy of law which should be adhered to in constructing DE&I commitments. However, individuals, organizations and governments do have a responsibility to ensure that their respective actions do not deprive present or future humanity the opportunity and resources they need to be successful.

Figure 4.5: Governance-centered respect for the rule of law questions

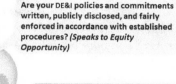

RESPECT FOR THE RULE OF LAW

Are there processes within your organization to ensure that awareness of applicable laws and regulations or your corporate policies and procedures related to DE&I are known and up-to-date, and that this information is appropriately disseminated? *(Speaks to Equity Disruption)*

Are your DE&I policies and commitments written, publicly disclosed, and fairly enforced in accordance with established procedures? *(Speaks to Equity Opportunity)*

Are your organization's DE&I commitments consistent with related laws and adhered to by all, regardless of position within the organization? *(Speaks to Equity Reconciliation)*

ISO 26000 provided the following guidance:

An organization should:

o *comply with legal requirements in all jurisdictions in which the organization operates, even if those laws and regulations are not adequately enforced;*

o *ensure that its relationships and activities comply with the applicable legal framework;*

o *keep itself informed of all legal obligations; and*

o *periodically review its compliance with applicable laws and regulations.*

ISO 26000:2010, page 12.

PRINICIPLE 6: RESPECT FOR INTERNATIONAL NORMS OF BEHAVIOR MODERATED BY DE&I

A DE&I framework should be guided by shared respect for international norms of behavior because any sustainable development pursuits touch on our shared humankind. The United States, regrettably, has a long history of rejecting international rules and standards "imposed by others" even when they make sense or are even congruent with American policies and/or values. However, while American government and society generally resists international frameworks, most of the global corporations today are based in its shores. This can create conflicts for these US-based corporations who must follow both US laws as well as laws in other countries where they do business. DE&I as a social responsibility currency can serve as that diplomatic bridge in creating decision-making activities that respect all the disparate legal frameworks within which the organizations operate.

RESPECT FOR INTERNATIONAL NORMS
Knowledge-informed diversity call to action

An organization that aspires to be socially responsible should address DE&I matters as part of that pursuit and "should respect international norms of behavior while adhering to the principle of respect for the rule of law (ISO 26000:2010)."

This principle implies that to avoid complicity, an organization should include DE&I matters as an integral part of its adherence to the principle of respect for the rule of law and respect for international norms of behavior. Complicity in legal terms can mean acts of omission with a significant impact on the commitment of an illegal act, while in non-legal terms, it implies participation in an illegal act by not exercising due diligence.

 Complicity has both legal and non-legal meanings.

In the legal context, complicity has been defined in some jurisdictions as being party to an act or omission having a substantial effect on the commission of an illegal act such as a crime, while having knowledge of, or intent to contribute to, that illegal act.

Complicity is associated with the concept of aiding and abetting an illegal act or omission.

In the non-legal context, complicity derives from broad societal expectations of behaviour. In this context, an organization may be considered complicit when it assists in the commission of wrongful acts of others that are inconsistent with, or disrespectful of, international norms of behaviour that the organization, through exercising due diligence, knew or should have known would lead to substantial negative impacts on society, the economy or the environment. An organization may also be considered complicit where it stays silent about or benefits from such wrongful acts.

ISO 26000:2010, page 13.

RESPECT FOR INTERNATIONAL NORMS
Creativity-driven equity opportunity/reconciliation

In reviewing its existing DE&I framework, an organization should also consider its respect for international norms of behavior as a guide, to make sure that it doesn't transgress against local legal standards. Some questions to consider on the opportunity, reconciliation and disruption influencers include:

1. Does your organization have a policy and procedure that guides its engagement or disengagement from situations where the law or its implementation—especially those dealing with DE&I—conflicts with international norms of behavior? **(Speaks to Equity Opportunity)**

2. Does your organization periodically examine its relationships with other organizations to ensure that it is not complicit by continuing association with organizations whose activities—especially those dealing with diversity, equity, and inclusion—are not consistent with international norms of behavior? **(Speaks to Equity Reconciliation)**

3. Does your organization have the "organizational will" and unfettered commitment to use its clout to proactively seek to influence relevant organizations and authorities whose actions—especially those dealing with DE&I—conflict with international norms of behavior? **(Speaks to Equity Disruption)**

Table 4.1: Respect for international norms of behavior principle moderated by the 3-Step Equity Lens model

6. RESPECT FOR INTERNATIONAL NORMS OF BEHAVIOR PRINCIPLE	
Equity Opportunity	An organization should, as feasible and appropriate, review the nature of its relationships and activities within jurisdictions where its DE&I commitments are in concert with international norms of behavior but in conflict with the implemented local or national jurisdictional law.
Equity Reconciliation	An organization should identify and engage in legitimate opportunities and channels where it can influence relevant organizations and authorities on its DE&I commitments that are consistent with international norms of behavior.
Equity Disruption	An organization should avoid being complicit on its DE&I commitments which are consistent with international norms of behavior by the activities of its partner organizations that are inconsistent with such norms.

RESPECT FOR INTERNATIONAL NORMS
Governance-centered inclusion actionable steps

Globalization has exposed the limits and obligations of organizational responsibility when it comes to international law. While globalization was driven by first-world economic interests, the newly interconnected situation has gone beyond these countries and touched just about every human being on earth either now or the very near future. All countries in the world have laws that have been outpaced or rendered obsolete by globalization. The United States Congress is struggling to keep up with the rapid deployment of new technologies that run circles around existing laws. The changes have had the unexpected effect of giving technology companies vast powers that transcends nation-states, creating relationships and abuses unlike anything previously experienced.

The United States, one of the most advanced countries in the world, is struggling to create laws fast enough to regulate or curtail the impacts of the decisions and activities of companies like Meta/Facebook, Instagram, Tiktok, Roblox, Discord, Snapchat, etc. The same is true of the European Union and other continental bodies—all trying to keep up with new international norms of behavior while enforcing existing laws. This situation is far worse in developing countries where their citizens have leapfrogged into the modern era courtesy of the internet and cell phones, leaving their laws desperately lagging.

While governments try to regulate and bring balance to the world digitally turned upside down, organizations have significant roles and responsibilities; they have an opportunity to use their influence to broker peace, advance diversity and inclusion and create a more equitable world. These roles and responsibilities are best handled through a social responsibility and sustainable framework moderated by DE&I. This gives socially responsible organizations a roadmap to help navigate through issues that may cause them to be complicit in adhering to international norms of behavior while respecting the rule of law in each jurisdiction where their products and services are in use. With these roadmaps, organizations would have already done the assessments that guide the actionable steps developed and the activities and practices to be stopped or discontinued in order not to be complicit.

Figure 4.6: Governance-centered respect for international norms of behavior questions

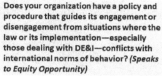

RESPECT FOR INTERNATIONAL NORMS OF BEHAVIOR

Does your organization have the "organizational will" and unfettered commitment to use its clout to proactively seek to influence relevant organizations and authorities whose actions—especially those dealing with DE&I—conflict with international norms of behavior? *(Speaks to Equity Disruption)*

Does your organization have a policy and procedure that guides its engagement or disengagement from situations where the law or its implementation—especially those dealing with DE&I—conflicts with international norms of behavior? *(Speaks to Equity Opportunity)*

Does your organization periodically examine its relationships with other organizations to ensure that it is not complicit by continuing association with organizations whose activities—especially those dealing with diversity, equity, and inclusion—are not consistent with international norms of behavior? *(Speaks to Equity Reconciliation)*

ISO 26000 provides the following guidance:

o   In situations where the law or its implementation does not provide for adequate environmental or social safeguards, an organization should strive to respect, as a minimum, international norms of behaviour.

o   In countries where the law or its implementation conflicts with international norms of behaviour, an organization should strive to respect such norms to the greatest extent possible.

o   In situations where the law or its implementation is in conflict with international norms of behaviour and where not following these norms would have significant consequences, an organization should, as feasible and appropriate, review the nature of its relationships and activities within that jurisdiction.

o   An organization should consider legitimate opportunities and channels to seek to influence relevant organizations and authorities to remedy any such conflict.

o   An organization should avoid being complicit in the activities of another organization that are not consistent with international norms of behaviour.

ISO 26000:2010, page 13.

PRINCIPLE 7: RESPECT FOR HUMAN RIGHTS MODERATED BY DE&I

A socially responsible organization should consider using DE&I commitments as a moderator for its human rights commitments. DE&I and respect for human rights are intrinsically tied together at the hip because an organization cannot respect human rights without touching on DE&I matters.

RESPECT FOR HUMAN RIGHTS
Knowledge-informed diversity call to action

An organization should respect human rights and recognize their inalienable affinity to diversity, equity, and inclusion, both in their importance and in their global applications.
This principle implies that DE&I is at the heart of any human rights recognition informed by our shared humanity. When a person's human rights are violated, it is an indication of the value – or lack thereof – placed on their humanity by the violator(s). This is true both for an organization's workforce and for those kept from the workforce because of discriminatory practices, which may manifest through corporate decision-making, hiring, and retention policies and procedures.

RESPECT FOR HUMAN RIGHTS
Creativity-driven equity opportunity/reconciliation/disruption

DE&I and Respect for Human Rights are affinity partners because they are concerned about upholding a vision of humanity wherein our endowed individual and communal rights are respected. Where these human rights are or could be violated, we should seek ways to create an equity opportunity, reconciliation, or disruption framework to effectively address the situation(s). Some key questions to consider:
1. Does your organization have a DE&I policy and procedure in place to avoid taking advantage in situations where human rights are not protected? **(Speaks to Equity Opportunity)**
2. Has your organization reviewed its decision-making processes and practices to ensure they adhere to the principle of respect for international norms of behavior in situations where human rights are not protected? **(Speaks to Equity Reconciliation)**
3. Where your organizational decision-making process or practice fails to provide for responsible protection of human rights, are there

demonstrable actions taken to correct it/them? **(Speaks to Equity Disruption)**

Table 4.7: Respect for human rights principle moderated by the 3-Step Equity Lens model

7. RESPECT FOR HUMAN RIGHTS PRINCIPLE	
Equity Opportunity	An organization should as a basic step include in its DE&I commitments that it would not take advantage of situations where human rights are not protected and instead respect these human rights by including them in its decision-making processes and practices.
Equity Reconciliation	An organization should assess its partner relationships, especially in those locations "where the law or its implementation does not provide for adequate protection of human rights." In this situation, the organization should make known its adherence to and respect for international norms of behavior as well as its DE&I commitments through its decision-making processes and practices that protect human rights.
Equity Disruption	In situations where an organization discovers that its own DE&I commitments fall short of respecting or protecting human rights, it should act quickly to rectify this in its policy and procedures. The organization should also take steps to ensure that its decision-making processes and practices respect human rights, even when policies of its partner organizations do not.

RESPECT FOR HUMAN RIGHTS
Governance-centered inclusion actionable steps

Human Rights are universal rights. Every human being deserves to be treated with dignity and to have their humanity respected. In developing actionable steps or reviewing existing ones guided by the principle of respect for human rights, socially responsible organizations should also consider DE&I as a moderator along with the 3-step inclusion principles as guide for the discussions and commitments.

Figure 4.7: Governance-centered respect for international norms of behavior questions

RESPECT FOR HUMAN RIGHTS

Where your organizational decision-making process or practice fails to provide for responsible protection of human rights, are there demonstrable actions taken to correct it/them? *(Speaks to Equity Disruption)*

Does your organization have a DE&I policy and procedure in place to avoid taking advantage in situations where human rights are not protected? *(Speaks to Equity Opportunity)*

Has your organization reviewed its decision-making processes and practices to ensure they adhere to the principle of respect for international norms of behavior in situations where human rights are not protected? *(Speaks to Equity Reconciliation)*

ISO 26000 provided the following guidance:

 An organization should:

o *respect and, where possible, promote the rights set out in the International Bill of Human Rights;*

o *respect the universality of these rights, that is, that they are indivisibly applicable in all countries, cultures and situations;*

o *in situations where human rights are not protected, take steps to respect human rights and avoid taking advantage of these situations; and*

o *in situations where the law or its implementation does not provide for adequate protection of human rights, adhere to the principle of respect for international norms of behaviour.*

ISO 26000:2010, pages 13-14.

Chapter Five

DE&I AS MODERATOR FOR ORGANIZATIONAL GOVERNANCE AND STAKEHOLDER RELATIONS

Organizational governance is the decision-making and implementation system by which objectives are pursued. It is through this system that an organization carries out its vision, mission, strategic goals, and objectives, through an applied sets of values and behaviors. It is also through organizational governance that DE&I can be established as a currency for negotiating systemic changes in values, behaviors, and practices.

Stakeholder relations are critical to effective governance. When they're open, transparent, and inclusive, they keep the wheels of organizational governance well-oiled; when they're not, they generate friction or conflict. When an organization recognizes and embraces its social responsibility and judiciously identifies and engages its stakeholders, the embracement of DE&I become part of its overall moderating currency. I am using "currency" within the context of exchanging or facilitating dialogue and negotiations around DE&I throughout an organization's eco-system. I am also deliberately using the term "embracement" here to signify the importance of DE&I as currency for social responsibility and stakeholder relationship in both identification and engagement. Together, organizational governance and stakeholder relations form the ecosystem for a sustainable organization driven by a vision of wholeness.

A sustainably-driven organization, by its very nature, seeks to find wholeness in ecosystems of people, planet, and profit. A wholeness diversity-driven constellation is the product of a conscious integration of diversity, equity, and inclusion in a continuum of ownership, belonging and participation. As the organization works towards perfecting its DE&I continuum, diversity's gravity pulls the other two into an integrated whole in celebration of our shared humanity, shared responsibilities and shared global resources—human and material alike.

Unadulterated equity and inclusion is anchored by belief in our shared humanity, which is the cornerstone of diversity. However, the belief in our shared humanity is a gift we must give to ourselves first before we can share it with others. The more we are comfortable with our individual or shared humanity, the more willing we are to see equity and inclusion as necessary paths to our individual and organizational journey towards wholeness.

Figure 5.1: Relationship between an organization, its stakeholders and society

Note: Societal expectations may differ from Stakeholders' interests. Adapted by Matthew Ajiake from ISO 26000

DE&I THROUGH THE EYES OF ORGANIZATION GOVERNANCE

Organizations—by their economic power and influence over policymakers (who set the rules and regulations that become law)—are an active force unto themselves and have the strength to tackle systemic and structural racism and inequalities with expediency, and often with more tangible social results than legislated mandates. These organizations can channel their unregulated power and influence into social responsibility commitments with the potential to impact generations in equity opportunity creation, equity reconciliation stabilization, and equity disruption termination.

ORGANIZATIONAL GOVERNANCE
Knowledge-informed diversity call to action

An organization's decision-making processes are enhanced when the embracement of diversity and inclusion is seen as a means of achieving its social responsibility goals. At issue are the powers organizations wield within their internal eco-systems as well as society at large. We have experienced these powers and influences from high-tech companies whose reach exceeds nation states. With offices in dozens of countries, an organizational infrastructure that connects layers of management from around the world in an instant, and vast financial resources, many high-tech companies have achieved a measure of operational independence and influence that transcends any particular country.

With such vast and far-reaching power and influence comes a corresponding social responsibility to include DE&I in their internal power structures. Put simply, organizational governance is driven by people. People make the rules, follow the rules, and enforce the rules. This makes a compelling case to incorporate diversity in the decision-making organizational structures. Racial and gender inequalities frankly threaten any sustainable and social responsibility goals and objectives. For example, "The power of parity" 2015 report from McKinsey Global Institute (MGI) stated that *"…no country has achieved gender equality in the workforce without first narrowing gender gaps in society (Devillard, Sancier-Sultan, Zelicourt, & Kossoff 2016)."* ISO 26000 provides the following insight into organizational systems:

ISO *Leadership is also critical to effective organizational governance. This is true not only for decision making but also for employee motivation to practice social responsibility and to integrate social responsibility into organizational culture. Organizational governance can comprise both formal governance mechanisms based on defined structures and processes and informal mechanisms that emerge in connection with the organization's culture and values, often influenced by the persons who are leading the organization. Organizational governance is a core function of every kind of organization as it is the framework for decision making within the organization. Governance systems vary, depending on the size and type of organization and the environmental, economic, political, cultural and social context in which it operates. These systems are directed by a person or group of persons* *(owners, members, constituents or others) having the authority and responsibility for pursuing the organization's objectives.*

ISO 26000:2010, pages 21-22.

Organizational governance tuned to the frequency of DE&I uses social responsibility nomenclatures as a normalizing currency for communicating core values, behaviors and practices that celebrate our shared humanity and protect the planet. An organization cannot be holistic in its sustainable development goals when it ignores DE&I as a means for achieving it. In the context of DE&I within a social responsibility construct, organizational governance is both a core subject for establishing just parameters for its operations and a means for carrying out its social responsibility values through its behavior. ISO 26000 provides the following precepts as guidance:

ISO *Effective governance should be based on incorporating the principles of social responsibility...into decision making and implementation. These principles are accountability, transparency, ethical behaviour, respect for stakeholder interests, respect for the rule of law, respect for international norms of behaviour and respect for human rights...In addition to these principles, an organization should consider the practices, the core subjects and the issues of social responsibility when it establishes and reviews its governance system.*

ISO 26000:2010, page 22.

Figure 5.2: Social responsibility: 7 core subjects—a holistic integrated approach

ISO Social Responsibility: 7 Core Subjects

Adapted by author from ISO 26000:2010.

ORGANIZATIONAL GOVERNANCE
Creativity-driven equity opportunity/reconciliation/disruption

Organizational decision processes and structures are never perfect; they are created and implemented by people, who are intrinsically imperfect. One key area where these imperfections are most apparent is in inequalities in economic, social and environmental spheres, which adversely impact minority and vulnerable groups. In developing, reviewing, or updating its DE&I master plan, an organization should consider using equity opportunity, reconciliation, and disruption as lenses to ascertain the effectiveness of its decision-making processes and structures when integrating diversity and inclusion into its social responsibility framework. ISO 26000 provides the following guide:

ISO *Every organization has decision-making processes and structures. In some cases, these are formal, sophisticated and even subject to laws and regulations; in other cases they are informal, rooted in its organizational culture and values. All organizations should put in place processes, systems, structures, or other mechanisms that make it possible to apply the principles and practices of social responsibility.*

ISO 26000:2010, page 22.

An organization's decision-making systems, processes and structures are the first and best lines of effectuating societal change and exerting influence over societal discriminatory practices and related challenges. This is because organizations can implement an example of what wholeness should be within their own ecosystems that also have direct linkage to societal change. Doing so makes advocating for systemic and structural changes in society and culture more effective and results-driven.

While historically, nation-states may have or continue to implement affirmative action laws to counterbalance past discriminatory practices, organizations have a far deeper and stronger power to change these unjust and unfair practices by choosing to operationalize values that uphold our shared humanity and shared planet. Organizations achieve an equitable and inclusive organizational culture within a diverse workforce and with its external work partners by clearly stating its DE&I aspirations and commitments in ways that influence its activities. The following represents some DE&I customized focus repurposed from ISO 26000 guidance:

- The organization should extend its DE&I aspirations and commitments into its mission statements by clear and concise references to its DE&I commitments within its social responsibility framework while establishing its DE&I actionable steps guided by the 3-Step Inclusion principles and the principles and issues of social responsibility.

- When utilizing DE&I as the currency or language for translating socially responsible values and principles into appropriate behavior, an organization should also consider the adoption of written codes of conduct or ethics that clearly state its commitments to diverse and inclusive workforce, workplace and work partnership with external organizations (ISO 26000 2010).

- Organizations should also demonstrate its unambivalent DE&I commitments within a social responsibility framework by integrating them into its key elements within its organization-wide strategy codified in its policies, processes, and systems and exemplified in its decision-making behavior (ISO 26000:2010).

In addressing equity issues, an organization should look through its governance structure, decision-making and activities systems and processes to ensure that they are not adverse or impede its stated and/or written DE&I commitments and practices. To be effective in establishing its DE&I Commitments, an organization should consider using the 3-Step Equity lens—equity opportunity, reconciliation and disruption—as its guideposts for assessing its social responsibility framework. It should organize itself around the seven ISO 26000 core subjects: (a) organizational governance, (b) human rights, (c) labor practices, (d) the environment, (e) fair operating practices, (f) consumer issues, and (g) community involvement and development. To determine which core subject is relevant to a DE&I matter, the following repurposed extrapolations from ISO 26000 could be used as reference:

- ☐ List all applicable activities and their linkages to DE&I
- ☐ Identify all known DE&I stakeholders with room to adjust for additional stakeholders when they become known
- ☐ Identify the internal activities of the organization with its DE&I implications as well as those of its external partners within its sphere of influence. Remember that an organization's external partners or stakeholders' decisions and activities may significantly reflect on its own decisions and activities
- ☐ Determine which core subjects and issues touch DE&I matters and how they manifest when the organization and other organizations within its sphere of influence and/or in its value chain interact and carryout the DE&I-related activities while abiding by all applicable laws
- ☐ Examine the many ways in which the organization's DE&I policy and commitments impact its sustainable development plans, decisions and activities, and its varied stakeholders

□ Examine the ways in which stakeholders and DE&I-moderated social responsibility issues impact the organization's plans, decisions, and activities, and

□ Identify all DE&I issues related to social responsibility in day-to-day activities, including those that arise periodically under specific situations.

In utilizing the 3-Equity Lens to develop or overhaul an organization's decision-making systems and activities, DE&I matters should be considered even when there are no existing laws addressing them directly. Remember that social responsibility is a means by which an organization does the right thing because doing so positively impacts our social contracts and extends our decisions and activities into the sphere of sustainable development.

ISO *Even for core subjects or issues covered by the law, responding to the spirit of the law may in some cases involve action beyond simple compliance. As an example, although some environmental laws and regulations limit emissions of air or water pollutants to specific amounts or levels, an organization should use best practice to further reduce its emissions of those pollutants or to change the processes it uses so as to completely eliminate such emissions. Other examples are a school that voluntarily decides to reuse rainwater for sanitary purposes, and a hospital that could decide not only to comply with laws regarding its labour practices, but also to launch a special programme for supporting the work-life balance of its personnel.*

ISO 26000:2010, page 71.

Utilizing DE&I as a moderator for organizational governance through the core subjects of social responsibility is a reasonable approach to promoting the practical use of the principles and practices of social responsibility. It's also a way of appropriately identifying and engaging all stakeholders. Where there are gaps, the organization should consider creative solutions and options. The following questions may assist in the dialogue:

1. Is your organization sensitive and committed to DE&I as a social responsibility currency for negotiating value-added decisions and performing routine business activities?

2. Does your organization have decision-making processes and structures which promote DE&I within a social responsibility construct and which effectively integrate these into its principles and practices?

3. Has your organization recognized and accepted its responsibility to the community in which it operates, as well as to all stakeholders

who are directly impacted by, and have direct interests in, its activities?

4. Has your organization developed mechanisms for identifying and engaging all appropriate stakeholders?

5. Does your organization have diversity, equity, and inclusion processes, systems and structures that make applying the principles and practices of social responsibility possible?

6. Does your organization follow through on its stated DE&I goals and priorities through periodic reviews

ORGANIZATIONAL GOVERNANCE
Governance-centered inclusion actionable steps

Socially responsible organizations have decision-making processes and structures that support the seven principles and seven subjects of social responsibility. When moderated by DE&I commitments, they create an eco-system where diversity, equity and inclusion thrive. It is within an organization's decision-making processes and structures that DE&I commitments are best showcased and evaluated periodically to ensure the organization walks its DE&I talk:

1. Translate DE&I priorities for action on core subjects and challenges into organizational objectives that are manageable strategies, processes and timelines

2. Ensure that DE&I objectives are specific, measurable, and verifiable, with input from relevant stakeholders

3. Establish detailed plans for achieving the stated DE&I objectives, including identifying all roles and responsibilities, timelines, budgets and corresponding impacts on other organization-wide activities.

Applying these principles and practices through routine activities enriches the dialogue in the entire organization. Utilizing the 3-Step Inclusion principles as a guide, an organization can use the following ISO 26000 guidance, repurposed here when utilizing DE&I as the moderator for organizational governance:

An organization's decision-making processes and structures moderated by DE&I should enable it to:

☐ *Develop DE&I strategies, objectives, and targets in concert with its overall social responsibility commitments*

☐ *Demonstrate leadership commitment and accountability to DE&I as an integral driver for social responsibility and sustainable development*

☐ *Create and nurture a DE&I environment and culture in which the principles of social responsibility are practiced*

- Create a sustaining system for rewarding DE&I and other social responsibility performance through economic and non-economic incentives
- Use DE&I as a lens for judging financial, natural and human resource efficiencies
- Promote a fair opportunity moderated by DE&I that allows underrepresented groups (women, back and brown racial and other ethnic groups) to occupy senior positions in the organization
- Use DE&I as moderator to balance the needs of the organization and its stakeholders to satisfy both immediate needs of current generations and those of future generations
- Establish two-way DE&I communication processes with stakeholders, identifying areas of agreements and disagreements and negotiated measures taken to resolve possible conflicts
- Encourage effective participation of all levels of employees in the organization's DE&I and other social responsibility activities
- Balance the level of authority, responsibility and capacity of people who make decisions that have DE&I implications on behalf of the organization
- Keep track of the implementation of DE&I decisions to ensure that these decisions are practiced in a socially responsible manner conducive to accountability for the results of the organization's decisions and activities (positive or negative), and
- Periodically review and evaluate the organization's governance processes as they relate to DE&I; adjust DE&I processes according to the outcome of the assessment and communicate changes throughout the organization, and, when applicable, to the external stakeholders.

Adapted & repurposed from ISO 26000:2010, pages 22-23.

DE&I THROUGH THE EYES OF STAKEHOLDER RELATIONS

When an organization recognizes and embraces its social responsibility and properly engages its stakeholders, the embracement of DE&I becomes part of its overall moderating currency. Together, they form the ecosystem for a wholeness-driven, sustainable organization.

According to the Merriam-Webster dictionary, the term "Embracement" signifies the readiness to "embrace a cause...to take in or include as a part, item, or element of a more inclusive whole...to be equal or equivalent to..." As a social responsibility currency, DE&I provides the knowledge we need to embrace our common humanity, expose inequities (and creatively seek answers for them), and challenge us to pursue intentional inclusion actions in celebration of our shared humanity.

Recognition of our shared humanity leads to a recognition of our social responsibility, the cornerstone of our human diversity. While identifying the issues unfurled by the impacts of an organization's decision-making and activities and determining how to address them in a way that leads to sustainable development, is the essence of social responsibility, at its core is how we value DE&I as a continuum leading to organizational wholeness. To fully be socially responsible, an organization must also holistically identify and engage its stakeholders, anchored by a properly inclusive worldview. This continuum and worldview are guided by the KCG model:

1. Knowledge-informed diversity call-to-action social responsibility
2. Creativity-driven equity stakeholder engagement
3. Governance-centered inclusion actionable steps within social responsibility and stakeholder engagement

STAKEHOLDER RELATIONS
Knowledge-informed diversity call to action

Knowledge-informed diversity and social responsibility extends to everything we know about social responsibility, by emphasizing our shared humanity as the key mitigating factor. No amount of pursuing social responsibility decisions and activities will lead to wholeness if our concept of our shared humanity segregates people into different human races and other forms of discriminatory classifications. Yet, understanding organizational social responsibility brings us all closer to some comfort level that diversity is Knowledge-informed and showcases who we are collectively, illustrating why celebrating what we have in common brings us individually and organizationally closer to wholeness.

In ISO 26000, we find three identified relationships which lead to social responsibility. These include: (1) between the organization and society, (2) between the organization and its stakeholders, and (3) between the stakeholders and society. Extending this thought to diversity, we see the relationship between a diverse community (society) and diverse stakeholders within the communities in which the organization is located and anywhere that its influence is felt:

1. **Between the organization and its diverse community**: an organization should be knowledgeable about its impacts on all communities in which its products and services are utilized. This knowledge cannot be limited to only those in which it has a physical presence or location, but should extend to those in which it has influence. Since this influence sometimes extends beyond local, regional and national boundaries—as is the case with multinational corporations—the expectations and responsible behavior on their impacts should be viewed from a global perspective as well.

2. **Between the organization and its diverse stakeholders**: the global nature of businesses and organizations today requires them to identify and be knowledgeable about those impacted by their decisions, activities, products and services—those who have a stake or interest. These impacts can be potential or actual but they create a stakeholder relationship that does not necessarily have to be obligatory in nature for the relationship to exist.

3. **Between the diverse stakeholders and diverse community**: globalization and the configurations of society and communities have become less physical boundary defined. Organizations on a social responsibility path should be knowledgeable about the difference between its relationship with those impacted by its decisions and activities (stakeholders) from the expectations of the communities or societies at large. When a contractor delivers a service to an organization, their interest in getting paid on time is different from the expectations of society concerning its social responsibility behavior in its decisions and activities.

Figure 5.3: DE&I as moderator for 3 stakeholder relationships

DE&I as Moderator for 3 Stakeholder Relationships

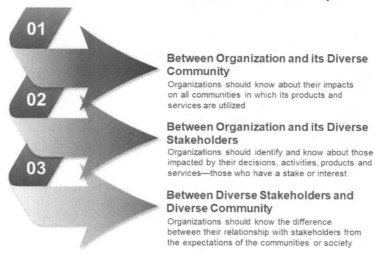

Between Organization and its Diverse Community
Organizations should know about their impacts on all communities in which its products and services are utilized

Between Organization and its Diverse Stakeholders
Organizations should identify and know about those impacted by their decisions, activities, products and services—those who have a stake or interest

Between Diverse Stakeholders and Diverse Community
Organizations should know the difference between their relationship with stakeholders from the expectations of the communities or society

Knowledge-informed diversity call to action social responsibility framework accounts for social, economic, and environmental relationships within the diversity, equity, and inclusion biosphere. These symbiotic relationships between DE&I and the social, economy and environmental spheres are not linear, but may take many forms based on interests and expectations. It takes a Knowledge-informed diversity lens to sort through the various interests that do get impacted by an organization's decisions and activities.

Recognize the core subjects and relevant issues of social responsibility as integral to any diversity plan

A Knowledge-informed sense of diversity and social responsibility requires recognition of the core subjects articulated in ISO 26000 as organizational governance, human rights, labor practices, the environment, fair operating practices, consumer issues, and community involvement and development. These core subjects also provide the systemic framework for addressing diversity-related issues, challenges, opportunities, and growth.

This Knowledge-informed process is informed by the following precept: What we do not quantify, we cannot measure; and what we cannot measure, we cannot take actionable steps to improve. The only way to reach our goals is to understand our current situation, and the distance between where we are now and where we want to be. Diversity issues form the bedrock of equity and inclusion issues and should be identified and assessed, and their significant impacts should be reported on as social responsibility so actionable steps can be developed to inform any required changes. These significant impacts should be linked to the stakeholders impacted such that any impacts may affect the organization's overall DE&I decisions and activities—all within a context of sustainable development.

Further, ISO 26000 recommended that while considering the core subjects and issues related to social responsibility, the organization also include its interactions with other organizations. This informs the notion that an organization's decisions and activities impacts stakeholders and even more so when diversity issues are at stake.

ISO *An organization seeking to recognize its social responsibility should consider both legally-binding and any other obligations that exist. Legally-binding obligations include applicable laws and regulations, as well as obligations concerning social, economic or environmental issues that may exist in enforceable contracts. An organization should consider the commitments that it has made regarding social responsibility. Such commitments could be in ethical codes of conduct or guidelines or in the membership obligations of associations to which it belongs.*

Recognizing social responsibility is a continuous process. The potential impacts of decisions and activities should be determined and taken into account during the planning stage of new activities. Ongoing activities should be reviewed as necessary so that the organization can be confident that its social responsibility is still being addressed and can determine whether additional issues need to be taken into account.

In some jurisdictions, DE&I are legally binding obligations included in applicable laws and regulations; in others, concern for DE&I is driven primarily by a concern for human rights or an organization's social responsibility. Regardless of where an organization finds itself on the question of diversity, the recognition that DE&I has significant positive impacts on its profit, people and planet's bottom line is the first step towards organizational wholeness.

Laws and regulations are very important, but the realization that the bottom line can be enhanced by embracing or paying attention to diversity is generally far more potent for private corporations. This requires continuous evaluative processes to identify the direct and potential impacts of the organization's decisions and activities. The knowledge derived from such continuous evaluative processes gives the organization the confidence that its DE&I performance is consistent with its social responsibility decisions and activities; when they are not, measures can be taken to address the gaps.

STAKEHOLDER IDENTIFICATION & ENGAGEMENT
Knowledge-informed diversity call to action

An organization's sphere of influence includes other organizations over which it wields influence and those with which it has ongoing relationships. While a socially responsible organization is not responsible for the diversity decisions and actions of every firm in this sphere, it is expected that in situations where it has such a relationship, that it will exercise its influence to encourage conformity to its norms. For example, many cities across the United States are using their legislative authority to influence the values they expect of other organizations which do business with them. This aligns with ISO 26000's recognition that a socially responsible organization addresses in a transparent and ethical manner all impacts directly associated with its decisions and activities within its internal and external ecosystems. An organization that values diversity and has reaped the benefits of it should be quick to aid others, because "to whom much is given, much is required." The stronger the relationship, the greater the opportunity to exercise influence.

It is true that an organization's control is technically limited to its own decisions and activities, but so too is its control over how much exposure it is willing to bear on behalf of those other organizations in its sphere of influence whose diversity values, ethical behavior and transparency may be opposed to its own. Therefore, an organization that has already settled its diversity issues is in a better place to inform and exercise its influence in promoting these values and ethical behavior across its value chain or supply chain. The bottom line is that in a Knowledge-informed diversity social responsibility organization, assessing its sphere of influence is par for the course. As we've seen, exercising due diligence in stakeholder engagements is a necessary path towards its own organizational wholeness.

STAKEHOLDER IDENTIFICATION & ENGAGEMENT
Creativity-driven equity opportunity/reconciliation/disruption

Creativity-driven equity stakeholder identification and engagement are crucial means for attaining and improving organizational social responsibility goals and objectives. Within the KCG model, equity is creativity-driven and establishes an organization's commitment to identify and engage its stakeholders wherever it finds them. This puts the burden on the organization to creatively identify and engage all stakeholders, enabling them to freely express their interests and exercise their rights in the areas of ownership, belonging, and participation within the organization's decisions and activities.

Stakeholder identification

Identifying an organization's stakeholders rests on who has a "stake" on the decisions and activities of the organization. These stakeholders can be individuals or organizations. Because they are affected by the organization's decisions and activities, a relationship is created. Both organizations and stakeholders may not know that a relationship exists between them, but it is still the organization's social responsibility to try to identify its diverse stakeholders. ISO 26000 takes a broad view of who these stakeholders include:

ISO   *Stakeholders are organizations or individuals that have one or more interests in any decision or activity of an organization. Because these interests can be affected by an organization, a relationship with the organization is created. This relationship need not be formal. The relationship created by this interest exists whether or not the parties are aware of it. An organization may not always be aware of all its stakeholders, although it should attempt to identify them. Similarly, many stakeholders may not be aware of the potential of an organization to affect their interests. In this context, interest refers to the actual or potential basis of a claim, that is, to demand something that is owed or to demand respect for a right. Such a claim need not involve financial demands or legal rights. Sometimes it can simply be the right to be heard. The relevance or significance of an interest is best determined by its relationship to sustainable development.*

Understanding how individuals or groups are or can be affected by an organization's decisions and activities will make it possible to identify the interests that establish a relationship with the organization. Therefore, the organization's determination of the impacts of its decisions and activities will facilitate identification of its most important stakeholders. Organizations may have many stakeholders. Moreover, different stakeholders have various and sometimes competing interests. For example, community residents' interests could include the positive impacts of an organization, such as employment, as well as the negative impacts of the same organization, such as pollution.

ISO 26000:2010, page 17.

Creativity-driven equity stakeholder identification begins with answers to the following sample questions from ISO 26000:

ISO *To identify stakeholders an organization should ask itself the following questions:*
- o *To whom does the organization have legal obligations?*
- o *Who might be positively or negatively affected by the organization's decisions or activities?*
- o *Who is likely to express concerns about the decisions and activities of the organization?*
- o *Who has been involved in the past when similar concerns needed to be addressed?*
- o *Who can help the organization address specific impacts?*
- o *Who can affect the organization's ability to meet its responsibilities?*
- o *Who would be disadvantaged if excluded from the engagement?*
- o *Who in the value chain is affected?*

ISO 26000:2010, pages 17-18.

Stakeholder engagement

The relationship between an organization's DE&I decisions and activities and its overall decisions and activities should be integrated. The two should not be treated as different, because they both have impacts on stakeholders and society at large. (Of course, while stakeholders are generally impacted because they have stakes or interests in the organization's decisions and activities, these may be different from that of society's expectations.)

The position of ISO 26000 is that stakeholders are those who have an "interest" in an organization's decisions and activities, while society has expectations of the organization, not necessarily an "interest". This differentiation allows the organization to engage stakeholders while also paying attention to society's concerns and expectations.

Stakeholder engagement is basically a dialogue between the organization and its stakeholder(s). This dialogue provides a framework for the organization to gain knowledge about the impacts of its decisions and activities on the stakeholders and on the communities/societies that they represent. Stakeholder engagement is at the heart of DE&I because it sets the stage for an organization to receive informed feedback on how to address its social responsibility:

ISO *Stakeholder engagement can take many forms. It can be initiated by an organization or it can begin as a response by an organization to one or more stakeholders. It can take place in either informal or formal meetings and can follow a wide variety of formats such as individual meetings, conferences, workshops, public hearings, round-table discussions, advisory committees, regular and structured information and consultation procedures, collective bargaining and web-based forums. Stakeholder engagement should be interactive and is intended to provide opportunities for stakeholders' views to be heard. Its essential feature is that it involves two-way communication.*

ISO 26000:2010, Page 18.

Extending this precept further under a KCG model, an organization should consider integrating the DE&I principles and the core subjects of social responsibility as guides when engaging stakeholders, to ensure positive impacts in all areas of its economic, environmental, and social "life" or ecosystem. In the KCG model, an organization's DE&I commitments are integrated into its overall vision and mission statements and are visibly represented in its strategic and operational goals and objectives and then implemented and reinforced through its daily activities. In this scenario, the DE&I currency is used across the entire organization's operations regardless of whether decisions and work activities are made or organized by function, matrix, or a combination of both. As currency for transactions and engagement, the DE&I principles and core subjects provide a means for actualizing the organization's vision and mission statements.

This places DE&I as a strategic datapoint or guide that informs the organization's decisions and activities and provides the assessment paths for measuring the impacts to stakeholder interests and community/society expectations as well as at the point of inception where stakeholder interests and community/society expectations intertwine.

Figure 5.4: Stakeholder identification and engagement through the lens of DE&I

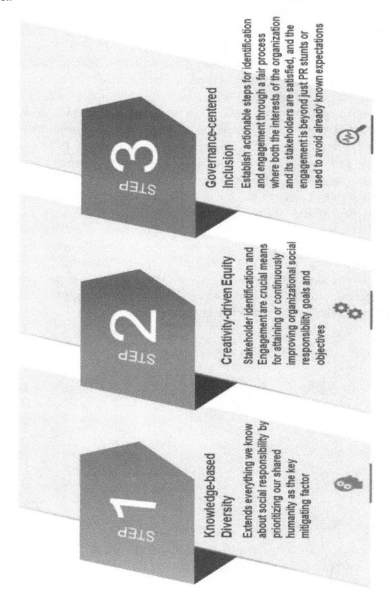

When an organization addresses DE&I issues outside of its everyday decisions and activities, the procedure is sometimes a disjointed afterthought, essentially reactionary or *ad hoc* in nature and in implementation. For example, an organization may look at a data point confirming that its employee ranks or suppliers or management demographics are not representative of the expectations of the communities or society from which all their "interested" stakeholders come. To solve this problem without resorting to a DE&I framework, some organizations would just use an ad hoc approach.

This might involve getting a few people together to come up with some nice diversity and inclusion statements, goals and objectives. But outside any inclusive framework, the exercise is pointless, because the hiring managers or the procurement staff may continue to make decisions every day that bear no resemblance to the organization's ad hoc commitments to DE&I. Further, as such efforts take place independent of any defined metrics or broader context, there are often no systemic ways to quantify the DE&I goals and objectives and no way for the organization to report on them in a useful way that encourages actual improvement.

When DE&I becomes natural in an organization's ecosystem, it guides everyday organizational decision and activities and creates an atmosphere for capturing data on how well an organization is doing in walking the talk of DE&I. A negative DE&I performance is not the end of the world but could instead be the beginning of a glorious future where all stakeholders are more engaged in solving the problems and community/society expectations are met over committed timeframes. As in the old Chinese adage, the journey of a thousand miles begins with knowing to take the first step.

Chapter Six

DE&I AS MODERATOR FOR HUMAN RIGHTS

E&I is front and center in any consideration of human rights because it encompasses the very concepts of social justice and fairness. Human rights are those inalienable, indivisible, universal, and interdependent rights that speak to the heart of our shared humanity. In general, the protection of individuals and groups against human rights abuses rests with the State, which has the responsibility of respecting and fulfilling human rights within its jurisdiction. ISO 26000 provides two broad categories of human rights to consider: (1) civil and political rights which pertain to freedom of expression and to life, liberty and equality before the law, and (2) economic, social and cultural rights which pertain to the right to food, employment, health, social security, and education. While the State plays key roles in upholding human rights within its jurisdictions through its laws, the International Bill of Human Rights and other core human rights covenants established over the years by the United Nations and other international groups also help set standards for these rights within the international community.

It is also generally accepted that preserving and protecting human rights goes beyond the relationship between the state and an individual or group. In these situations, non-state organizations have a social responsibility to uphold and respect human rights as well. In the sphere of social responsibility within the human rights context, ISO 26000 affirmed that organizations do *"benefit from a social and international order in which the rights and freedoms [of individuals and groups] can be fully realized."* (emphasis added). Understanding and accepting our shared humanity makes it easy to view DE&I as the social responsibility currency for bringing an organization closer to wholeness through its dialogues on values and behaviors which it incorporates into its decisions and activities. ISO 26000 provides the following guidance:

> **ISO** *The baseline responsibility of non-state organizations is to respect human rights. However, an organization may face stakeholder expectations that it go beyond respect, or it may want to contribute to the fulfilment of human rights. The concept of sphere of influence helps an organization to comprehend the extent of its opportunities to support human rights among different rights holders. Thus it may help an organization to analyse its ability to influence or encourage other parties, the human rights issues on which it can have the greatest impact and the rights holders that would be concerned.*
>
> *ISO 26000:2010, Page 24.*

HUMAN RIGHTS
Knowledge-informed diversity call to action

Human rights principles in ISO 26000 and DE&I principles are one and the same; they are universal, indivisible, inherent, interdependent and inalienable. As repurposed from ISO 26000 guidance, these DE&I principles are:

1. Universal, because they apply to every human being regardless of status;
2. Indivisible, because no human right may be selectively ignored;
3. Inherent, as they belong to every human being by virtue of our shared humanity;
4. Interdependent, because the realization of one right lead or contribute to the realization of other rights; and
5. Inalienable, because a person cannot give them up or be deprived of them by either institutions or governments (ISO 26000 2010).

HUMAN RIGHTS
Creativity-driven equity opportunity/reconciliation/disruption

Respecting human rights is the hallmark of an organization's commitment to DE&I. Unfortunately, it's not a common hallmark. Our shared humanity has been broken for a long time. All the divisive barriers that have kept us from individual and organizational wholeness are deeply ingrained in our psyche and reinforced by our everyday experience. Racism, tribalism, sexism, and gender inequalities, to name a few, did not simply happen overnight. They are well-entrenched social disorders with roots deep in our past that continue to plague our human realities and existence. Most people do not leave these values at home when they step into an organization's sphere.

For example, a person who belongs to a separatist group and attends their rallies on the weekend cannot be expected to come to work Monday through Friday and suddenly act as an advocate for human rights values and equity reconciliation. While it would be wrong to assume that everyone who goes to these rallies believes in the hate that they spew out, it is important to still respect the individual's rights and freedoms – without sacrificing the need for the organization to protect and preserve its rights to promote its diversity values, in pursuit of equity, and inclusion demands. In this front, ISO 26000 provides a sensible balance:

> **ISO** *States have a duty to protect individuals and groups against abuse of human rights, as well as to respect and fulfill human rights within their jurisdiction. States are increasingly taking steps to encourage organizations based in their jurisdiction to respect human rights where they operate outside that jurisdiction. It is widely recognized that organizations and individuals have the potential to and do affect human rights, directly and indirectly. Organizations have a responsibility to respect all human rights, regardless of whether the state is unable or unwilling to fulfil its duty to protect. To respect human rights means to not infringe the rights of others. This responsibility entails taking positive steps to ensure that the organization avoids passively accepting or actively participating in the infringement of rights. To discharge the responsibility to respect human rights requires due diligence. Where the state fails in its duty to protect, an organization may have to take additional measures to ensure that it respects human rights in all of its operations.*

> *ISO 26000:2010, page 24.*

Unless an organization deals with explicit and implicit bias head-on, its human rights equity-driven DE&I social responsibility framework would generally not lead to organizational wholeness. Why? The simple answer is that there may be too many DE&I issues passively or actively swept under the table because they are uncomfortable to discuss and address openly. Yet, there is freedom in addressing our deepest fears about our divided humanity within the figurative organizational home. An organization should consider its role in helping bridge the "divided-we-stand" mantra we so often find in society, a mantra that also shows up to work and interferes with our organizational life. We have all experienced toxic social or cultural environments in society; such environments can manifest anywhere – at work, school, or even religious establishments.

One cure for these societal ills is to incorporate the seven principles and practices and the seven core subjects of social responsibility into equity action plans, trainings, and performance metrics that are evaluated and monitored over time. It is also helpful to create internal equity groups or champions and an external stakeholder advisory group. These groups provide the go-to support system for sustainable practices to take hold and become organizational norms. Applying the ISO 26000 guidelines to integrate socially responsible behavior into an organization can be enhanced by utilizing DE&I as a currency for designing, updating or integrating social responsibility framework into an organization's entire eco-system. It does not help when one function within the organization is fully committed to DE&I in its decision-making processes and practices while another function totally ignores or pays lip service to the notion of creating a diverse, equitable and inclusive workplace. And any DE&I lip service from the ranks of an organization's leadership makes any concerted cultural change efforts much more difficult and near impossible to sustain minimal gains. ISO 26000 provides the following guidance:

ISO *An organization's opportunities to support human rights will often be greatest among its own operations and employees. Additionally, an organization will have opportunities to work with its suppliers, peers or other organizations and the broader society. In some cases, organizations may wish to increase their influence through collaboration with other organizations and individuals. Assessment of the opportunities for action and for greater influence will depend on the particular circumstances, some specific to the organization and some specific to the context in which it is operating. However, organizations should always consider the potential for negative or unintended consequences when seeking to influence other organizations. Organizations should consider facilitating human rights education to promote awareness of human rights among rights holders and those with the potential to have an impact on them.*

ISO 26000:2010, pages 24-25.

In pursuing a creativity-driven human rights equity opportunity, reconciliation and disruption path, an organization may consider the following eight human rights-related questions and the accompanying governance-centered inclusion actions. In addressing these actionable steps, an organization should consider the following three questions:

1. Are there equity opportunities for immediate actionable steps that address human rights issues?

2. Are there human rights issues that highlight the inconsistencies between the organization's policy and procedures and its practices that should be reconciled through the lens of fair and inclusive practices?

3. Are there human rights violations that must be disrupted or stopped because they are either against the law or violate our social justice sensibilities?

In reviewing or evaluating an organization's human rights social responsibility, ISO 26000 provides the following seven activities as guides:

 Human Rights

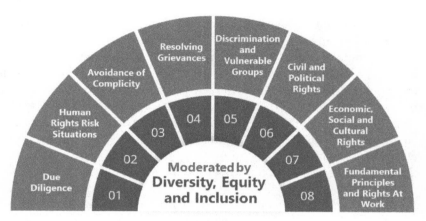

Human Rights Issue 1: DUE DILLIGENCE

Does your organization have a **DUE DILIGENCE** process that integrates DE&I matters as part of its human rights commitments to social responsibility?

DUE DILIGENCE
Knowledge-informed diversity call to action

Due diligence within the social responsibility paradigm encompasses the entire eco-system of an organization and includes its DE&I decision-making processes, activities and relationships—both internal and external. Remember that DE&I are human rights issues and due diligence is a proactive process in identifying risks and creating ways to avoid or mitigate them. Within a human rights framework, due diligence looks at comprehensive measures aimed at minimizing the risk of human rights violations in an organization's activities and relationships. When applying the ISO 26000 guidelines to socially responsible behavior, an organization should consider its own DE&I practices and those of other organizations within territories where its business activities occur or have an impact, to ensure that they are consistent with its human rights commitments. Where human rights abuses or lack of diversity, equity and inclusion exist, the organization should make its position known, either directly or indirectly, by developing, applying or restating its own DE&I Commitments and celebrating its successes wherever it has the influence to help shape the conversation and mitigate any challenges or problems (ISO 26000 2010).

DUE DILIGENCE
Creativity-driven equity opportunity/reconciliation/disruption

Extending this into DE&I matters, at issue is establishing a due diligence process where an organization's DE&I Commitments are reviewed within the national context in which the organization operates or where its activities or products or services are used (e.g. information delivery organizations like Facebook, Salesforce, and SAP). The goal is to assess the organization's actual or potential DE&I impacts for its activities—positive or negative consequences—and those of organizations whose activities are significantly linked to it (ISO 26000 2010). This was what the Coca Cola Legal Department attempted to practice with the diversity policy it tried to implement, as discussed earlier. ISO 26000 provides the following guidance:

> **ISO** *In identifying potential areas for action, an organization should strive to better understand challenges and dilemmas from the perspective of the individuals and groups potentially harmed. In addition to this self-evaluation, an organization may find that in some cases it is both possible and appropriate to seek to influence the behaviour of other entities towards enhancing their performance on social responsibility, particularly those with which it has close ties or where the organization considers the issues to be particularly compelling or relevant to its situation. As an organization gains experience in the area of enhancing performance on social responsibility, it may grow in its capacity and willingness to intervene with other entities to advocate this objective.*

> *ISO 26000:2010, pages 70-71.*

In addressing due diligence with DE&I as moderator, an organization should consider the application of the following 3-Step Equity lens model as means towards establishing socially responsible norms:

1. **Equity Opportunity**: Identify and immediately correct existing organizational decision-making processes and activities that are known to be biased and adversely impact minorities, indigenous tribes, women, and other discriminated groups. Where possible, also identify and state the organization's DE&I social responsibility position clearly to all its external partners, especially those whose

decision-making processes and activities are known to be biased in some way

2. **Equity Reconciliation**: Create, implement, or enhance tracking mechanisms for periodically evaluating decision-making processes and practices (including policy and procedure manuals) to ensure they are consistent with the organization's stated DE&I goals or commitments. Where these policy and procedures are inconsistent with the organization's stated DE&I goals and commitments, there should be corrective steps established to reconcile, improve, or replace them with socially responsible norms that are fair and just.

3. **Equity Disruption**: When decision-making processes and activities or norms are identified that outright discriminate or promote norms that discriminate against people of color, women and other disadvantaged groups, the organization should take immediate actions to stop such practices and activities or present a plan of action to end them. When these discriminatory norms are well known to exist within external partner organizations, the organization should consider whether to continue in these relationships.

DUE DILIGENCE
Governance-centered inclusion actionable steps

Governance-centered inclusion measures are how an organization commits to DE&I as a moderator for its social responsibility decision-making processes and activities. These actionable steps assist the organization in making its people and processes whole when it moves the organization forward in its social responsibility commitments. As an organization considers its DE&I due diligence roles and responsibility within its social responsibility framework, it should also consider its size and circumstances to ensure that it is acting wisely and appropriately. In designing, evaluating, or integrating DE&I due diligence within an organization's decision-making processes and practices, the following governance-centered inclusion components based on the organization's size and circumstances should be considered and framed by the 3-Step Inclusion Principles:

☐ Organizational policies related to human rights moderated by DE&I Commitments that give both those within the organization and those closely associated with it useful directions or guidance

☐ Means of assessing how DE&I Commitments are impacted by existing and proposed activities

☐ Means of integrating DE&I Commitments into human rights policies throughout the organization

- ☐ Means of tracking performance periodically and over time to measure DE&I Commitments' assimilation into the organization's decision-making processes and practices and where necessary, make course corrections in approach and priorities
- ☐ Appropriate actions to address the negative DE&I impacts of its decisions and activities.

Adapted & repurposed from ISO 26000:2010, pages 25 & 70.

Human Rights Issue 2: HUMAN RIGHTS RISK SITUATIONS

In **Human Rights Risk Situations**, does your organization have DE&I policy and procedure in place so as not to exacerbate or contribute to human rights abuses of minority and vulnerable groups?

HUMAN RIGHTS RISK SITUATIONS
Knowledge-informed diversity call to action

Systemic and structural racism, gender inequality, and discriminatory practices based on entrenched value systems that marginalize people groups provide fertile ground for human rights violations to manifest. Organizations need to recognize that they have a role to play in curtailing societal norms that discriminate and marginalize populations and thereby expose them to human rights abuses. Within the context of DE&I as moderator for an organization's social responsibility, there are DE&I-related risk situations and environments in which an organization faces pressure relating to the potential for or existing risk of human rights abuses. In these DE&I-related human rights risk situations, the organization should be balanced and fair in addressing unfair and inequitable DE&I matters, including negative impacts associated with its decision-making practices on minority and vulnerable groups and on the environment.

ISO *[A]n organization should consider the potential consequences of its actions so that the desired objective of respecting human rights is actually achieved. In particular, it is important not to compound or create other abuses. A situation's complexity should not be used as an excuse for inaction.*

ISO 26000:2010, page 26.

HUMAN RIGHTS RISK SITUATIONS
Creativity-driven equity opportunity/reconciliation/disruption

The exclusion of minority and vulnerable groups from decisions and activities which impact their economic, environment and social interests is one way in which organizations have perpetuated or contributed to human rights abuses in the past. When a society has a history of systemic racism and gender inequalities, it is primed for situations where minority and vulnerable groups are at risk of human rights abuses, whether these abuses are intentional or not. Organizations are in a better position to right these societal wrongs when they use DE&I as a moderator for establishing fair and equitable organization-wide social responsibility norms; utilizing the 3-Step Equity Lens model can assist in the process.

If an organization is unsure of what at-risk situations look like in real life circumstances within its own eco-system or within the society in which it operates, the following general guidance from ISO 26000 may be of assistance:

ISO There are certain circumstances and environments where organizations are more likely to face challenges and dilemmas relating to human rights and in which the risk of human rights abuse may be exacerbated. These include:

☐ conflict or extreme political instability, failure of the democratic or judicial system, absence of political or civil rights;

☐ poverty, drought, extreme health challenges or natural disasters;

☐ involvement in extractive or other activities that might significantly affect natural resources such as water, forests or the atmosphere or disrupt communities;

☐ proximity of operations to communities of indigenous peoples;

☐ activities that can affect or involve children;

☐ a culture of corruption;

☐ complex value chains that involve work performed on an informal basis without legal protection; and

☐ a need for extensive measures to ensure security of premises or other assets.

ISO 26000:2010, pages 25-26.

Systemic and structural divisive norms—racial, gender, sectarian, tribal, etc.,—all relate to the devaluing of our shared humankind both individually and collectively. The situations above could force an organization to make decisions or take a stand on its position on issues that may originate from societal broken norms and practices. The overarching goal in these situations is to always come out on the side of respect for human rights whether contributing to, promoting, or defending it. Human rights risk situations can be mitigated through a fair and honest introspection and actionable steps taken that incorporate DE&I as part of the organization's priorities. The 3-Step Equity lens model can assist socially responsible organizations determine the extent of the impact of the systemic DE&I-related risk situation on minority and vulnerable groups' human rights and to the organization's commitments to social responsibility norms that lead to sustainable development.

HUMAN RIGHTS RISK SITUATIONS
Governance-centered inclusion actionable steps

To address any of the situations listed above, an organization should develop an overarching DE&I policy that clearly states its position against any human rights abuses, whatever their provenance. This allows the organization's representatives to speak with a united voice as DE&I-related human rights risk situation arises, which puts less pressure on individual managers or executives to make their own judgment calls because the policy and supporting procedures have been thought through and responses clearly stated. In creating this "question asked and answered" policy and/or procedure, the organization should consider which of the 3-Step Inclusion Principles to use as guide (redemption-driven, restoration-focused, or responsibility-centered).

ISO Organizations should take particular care when dealing with situations characterized above. These situations may require an enhanced process of due diligence to ensure respect for human rights. This could for example be done through an independent human rights impact assessment. When operating in environments in which one or more of these circumstances apply, organizations are likely to be faced with difficult and complex judgements as to how to conduct themselves. While there may be no simple formula or solution, an organization should base its decisions on the primary responsibility to respect human rights, while also contributing to promoting and defending the overall fulfilment of human rights. In responding, an organization should consider the potential consequences of its actions so that the desired objective of respecting human rights is actually achieved. In particular, it is important not to compound or create other abuses. A situation's complexity should not be used as an excuse for inaction.

ISO 26000:2010, page 26.

Human Rights Issue 3: AVOIDANCE OF COMPLICITY

In your decision-making processes and activities, does your organization avoid complicity on DE&I matters, whether they are direct, beneficial, or silent?

The KCG framework provides a reasoned process for an organization to review its decision-making and activities to ensure it is not passively or actively complicit with abuses or inequities perpetrated by any of its partners. If an organization does find itself in a position such as this, it can use the creatively-driven equity solutions as part of its DE&I commitments which it incorporates into its policy and procedures.

AVOIDANCE OF COMPLICITY
Knowledge-informed diversity call to action

One of the reasons systemic and structural racism and gender inequality persists in society and organizations is directly related to the fact that far too many good people tend to do nothing about it. They may not agree with these inequities, but they don't engage in finding solutions or voice righteous indignation against unjust and unfair organizational and societal practices either. DE&I issues with persistently adverse impacts on minority groups are often enabled by such complicity. In a shared planet where norms divide our humankind, complicity stems from uncomfortableness in addressing or engaging in constructive dialogues about topics such as race, tribal or caste systems, unearned privileged status, etc. But without these difficult conversations, the inequity and exclusion cleavages persist. ISO 26000 makes the linkage succinctly: *"Complicity is associated with the concept of aiding and abetting an illegal act or omission."*

DE&I issues generally tend to be human rights issues, and they disproportionately disadvantage groups not because of their character but because of their race, gender, and other established societal discriminatory norms. When organizations carry out activities in countries and societies where norms divide our shared humanity, privileging one group over another based on unfair and unjust social contracts, it may be easier for them to pretend that they don't see or know about the problem—corporate complicity. Yet, organizations today, more than governments have both the power and the means to cause these dividing norms to stop through social responsibility practices. This explains why organizational leaders need Knowledge-informed information about when their actions – or lack thereof – on DE&I matters may put them in a complicit position.

ISO 26000 recommends that organizations review their own internal systems, processes, and security structures to ensure that they respect human rights, which, within the DE&I framework, includes security protection for both the victims and the whistleblowers of unjust and unfair practices. In this vein, it is important for all personnel to be trained on what norms or practices relating to DE&I make the organization and its leaders complicit. This training should extend to not just employees (fulltime and temporary), but to external partners (independent contractors and other partnering arrangements).

There should also be a clear escalating ladder process for addressing DE&I issues, with clear lines of authority of who is responsible for what decisions and, when necessary, engage external experts for assistance. For leaders who are unsure of what constitutes individual and organizational complicity, ISO 26000 provided this reasoned guidance on the differences:

ISO In the legal context, complicity has been defined in some jurisdictions as an act or omission having a substantial effect on the commission of an illegal act such as a crime, while having knowledge of, or intent to contribute to, that illegal act. Complicity is associated with the concept of aiding and abetting an illegal act or omission. In the non-legal context, complicity derives from broad societal expectations of behaviour. In this context, an organization may be considered complicit when it assists in the commission of wrongful acts of others that are inconsistent with, or disrespectful of, international norms of behaviour that the organization, through exercising due diligence, knew or should have known would lead to substantial negative impacts on society, the economy or the environment. An organization may also be considered complicit where it stays silent about or benefits from such wrongful acts.

ISO 26000:2010, page 26.

AVOIDANCE OF COMPLICITY
Creativity-driven equity opportunity/reconciliation/disruption

DE&I matters continue to be key areas around the world where potential complicity in human rights abuses manifest because of the decisions and practices of organizations. This complicity is sometimes even more onerous in societies where there are existing laws prohibiting such practices. Affirmative Action and Equal Employment Opportunities laws have been on the books for years in the United States. However, the workforce of most organizations doesn't represent the diversity of the communities in which they operate or the stakeholders that their product or services reach. India has had positive Affirmative Action laws since it gained its independence and incorporated them into its Constitution, yet the longstanding caste system, which has been in place for centuries, still dominates many of its social contracts, affecting how and why organizational decision-making processes and activities are structured.

How do organizations first comply with existing DE&I related laws and then go beyond them into behaving in a socially responsible manner? The best way to begin is by examining divisive norms, fueled by complicity, which are inconsistent with our shared values and expectations of socially responsible behavior. For example, every little boy knows the value and significant role his mother plays and continues to play in his life. Yet when he becomes a man and takes on a position of influence and power, women—a group to which his mother belongs—are viewed as second- or third-class citizens and he willingly accepts this norm or even champions it. This is a society-bred complicit behavior that is prevalent as a shared norm around the world.

It continues through our awareness of how divisive norms violate human rights, endangering or limiting individual or communal rights to life, liberty, and the pursuit of happiness. There was indeed a time when women stayed home and took care of the children while the men went off to work outside the home. A shared norm developed where men tended to make more money than women if they had to work because it was assumed her income was a second income for her family. Nonetheless, there were women who had to work because they were the only bread winners supporting their families—a reality that was not factored into the shared social contract. This contract persists today; the days of stricter gender roles in the family are gone, but most women continue to earn less than men in the workplace for the same work and most men in position to change this unfair and unjust norms look the other way—complicit in this shared divisive norm.

In examining how to create solutions to DE&I-related complicity issues, organizations should consider three distinct facets that ISO 26000 ably defined in its social responsibility construct which are repurposed here for a DE&I framework – direct, beneficial, and silent complicity:

- Direct complicity related to DE&I matters is when an organization knowingly assists another organization in violating human rights such as the systematic discrimination in employment against certain groups, the underpaying of women compared to their male counterparts for the same work performed, the clear devaluing of opinions of minority groups just because...

- Beneficial complicity related to DE&I matters is when an organization directly benefits from products it needs for its profitable business model produced from human rights violations such as when in its complex value chains, workers belonging to indigenous groups have their human rights violated by its suppliers without impunity.

- Silent complicity related to DE&I matters is when an organization fails to take action to correct unjust and unfair practices or raise concerns about these violations with the appropriate authorities such as when minority neighborhoods are forced to drink lead contaminated water while the majority or affluent neighborhoods have clean uncontaminated water.

Using the 3-Step Equity lens as guide, an organization can conduct its own assessment of areas within its decision-making processes and practices where it might be complicit (equity opportunity), examine its own practices for inconsistencies in its stated DE&I commitments (equity reconciliation), and decide on what practices to stop or discontinue because they cause harm or disadvantage other groups (equity disruption).

AVOIDANCE OF COMPLICITY
Governance-centered inclusion actionable steps

Governance-centered inclusion actionable steps are ways in which an organization addresses and institutionalizes the inequity and exclusionary practices it uncovers in its current decision-making processes and activities. Both the process of discovery, development, and implementation of actionable steps should be guided by the 3-Step Inclusion principles. Ideally, they should be redemption-driven, restoration-focused or responsibility-centered. ISO 26000 provided some reasoned guidance on how organizations can integrate as part of its due diligence steps that foster societal and legal social responsibility benchmarks, which I have repurposed here for DE&I.

An organization should:
- ☐ *not provide goods or services to organizations that uses them to carry out discriminatory or segregation norms (a form of human rights abuse);*
- ☐ *not enter into partnership (formal or informal) or contractual relationship with a partner that commits human rights abuses (consistent with DE&I-related abuses or complicity avoidance) in the execution of the contracted work or within the context of the partnership;*
- ☐ *inform itself about DE&I matters in relation to the social and environmental conditions in which purchased goods and services are produced or distributed;*
- ☐ *ensure it is not complicit in any displacement of people from their land through known discriminatory practices (like redlining, imminent domain, redistricting, or others) especially when they are inconsistent or do not conform to national law and international norms, and provide*

adequate compensation to the victims of such acts when it participated in them even when or where such practice was an accepted societal norm or legally justified;

☐ *consider making its position on DE&I matters publicly known through statements, or taking other action indicating that it does not condone human rights abuse, such as norms or acts of discrimination or marginalization occurring in social contracts or environmental degradation in the country concerned; and*

☐ *avoid relationships with organizations engaged in tribal, racial, or gender supremacy anti-social activities.*

Adapted & repurposed from ISO 26000:2010, page 27.

Human Rights Issue 4: RESOLVING GRIEVANCES

Does your organization have processes in place for **RESOLVING** DE&I-Related **GRIEVANCES**?

RESOLVING GRIEVANCES
Knowledge-informed diversity call to action

Humankind exists on one shared planet, but we are far from united. We have been divided by numerous harmful norms, established in most cases not by reason but by fear, survival customs, unexamined value systems, and unjust social contracts. This exposes every human relationship to conflicts and grievances. For organizations, the existence of grievances are not the problems; they are a dime a dozen. The problem lies in how grievances are resolved (or not resolved). Socially responsible organizations should view DE&I-related grievances in a broader context of human rights violations. One key to ensuring fairness is to have a mechanism in place to support those who believe their human rights have been abused, compromised, or ignored.

RESOLVING GRIEVANCES
Creativity-driven equity opportunity/reconciliation/disruption

Any comprehensive creativity-driven grievance resolution mechanism should be tiered by dealing with each grievance with a response of appropriate magnitude. For example, in our earlier discussion about JPMorgan Chase, it would be unfair to judge the senior management's DE&I commitments by the actions of a racist manager in a local branch. But when that one manager represents dozens and even thousands of employees, then the question becomes whether senior management knew about its DE&I-related grievance mechanism not working for the aggrieved and what steps they took to address them. The fact that it took a media report for the DE&I-related abuse by one of its managers to cause senior management to be either aware of the problem or respond publicly about it suggests that its DE&I commitments were not deeply entrenched in its operations.

One thing that's clearly missing from the Chase situation was a clear and effective pathway for dealing with problems. The African American customers who were discriminated against by the bank manager did not have an effective known mechanism for having their grievances heard other than going to the media. While it's helpful that the media was able to intervene, these customers shouldn't have had to go to the media to find a resolution. As ISO 26000 ably expressed, *"to discharge its responsibility to respect human rights, an organization should establish a mechanism for those who believe their human rights have been abused to bring this to the attention of the organization and seek redress."*

Every day, this lack of grievance or effective grievance mechanism or corrupted mechanisms continue to be the experience of minorities, despite well-intentioned and meticulously crafted DE&I commitments by institutions in America and across the world. In crafting effective DE&I grievance mechanism, organizations should consider utilizing the 3-Step Equity Lens model by:

- seeking equity opportunities to correct or adjust current grievance mechanism that are inaccessible, unjust, or unfair (equity opportunity)
- assessing its DE&I commitments against its organizational systems and practices on a continual basis to ensure there are no discrepancies between its stated policy and procedures with actual grievance resolution practices across its eco-system (equity reconciliation)
- ensuring that its DE&I-related abuse response does not encourage continued practices that sustain unjust or unfair behavior with weak deterrents or actions that block or prevent access to available legal channels (equity disruption).

RESOLVING GRIEVANCES
Governance-centered inclusion actionable steps

Governance-centered inclusion for resolving DE&I-related grievances should be a means by which an organization provides additional structure through actionable steps. This approach should not circumvent or undermine legal channels, but rather address DE&I-related grievances early, before they escalate beyond an organization's authority and become legal matters. The DE&I-related grievance resolution ladder and actionable steps benefit from the use of the 3-Step Inclusion Principles because the resulting grievance mechanism is redemption-driven, restoration-focused, and responsibility-centered. ISO 26000 provides further guidance:

ISO *An organization should establish, or otherwise ensure the availability of, remedy mechanisms for its own use and that of its stakeholders. For these mechanisms to be effective they should be:*

☐ *legitimate This includes clear, transparent and sufficiently independent governance structures to ensure that no party to a particular grievance process can interfere with the fair management of that process;*

☐ *accessible Their existence should be publicized and adequate assistance provided for aggrieved parties who may face barriers to access, such as language, illiteracy, lack of awareness or finance, distance, disability or fear of reprisal;*

☐ *predictable There should be clear and known procedures, a clear time frame for each stage and clarity as to the types of process and outcome they can and cannot offer, and a means of monitoring the implementation of any outcome;*

☐ *equitable Aggrieved parties should have access to sources of information, advice and expertise necessary to engage in a fair grievance process;*

☐ *rights-compatible The outcomes and remedies should accord with internationally recognized human rights standards;*

☐ *clear and transparent Although confidentiality might sometimes be appropriate, the process and outcome should be sufficiently open to public scrutiny and should give due weight to the public interest; and*

☐ *based on dialogue and mediation The process should look for mutually agreed solutions to grievances through engagement between the parties. Where adjudication is desired, parties should retain the right to seek this through separate, independent mechanisms.*

ISO 26000:2010, page 27.

Human Rights Issue 5: DISCRIMINATION AND VULNERABLE GROUPS

Have your organization's decision-making processes and activities been vetted to ensure that individuals belonging to **MINORITY** and **VULNERABLE GROUPS** are not **DISCRIMINATED AGAINST**?

Discrimination practices are common, longstanding divisive norms that marginalize our shared humankind. Every human being alive has experienced one form of discrimination or another—white, black, male, female, thin, fat, clean, dirty, fine, ugly – the list goes on. But there are groups that have suffered disproportionately from discriminatory practices targeting the group with which they identify. These groups include minorities within larger communities, women and girls, indigenous people, people with disabilities, children, migrants, and any other people discriminated against because of race, caste, religion, or other vulnerable distinctions. Organizations have a unique role to play in dismantling societal discrimination norms, but it must first begin with the commitment and sustained engagement of senior leadership. While policies and procedures are necessary, they are not the go-to authority when it comes to discriminatory practices. Instead, decision-makers use automatic, social and mental models thinking—consciously or unconsciously—in some cases overriding the good intentions spelt out in policies and procedures.

DISCRIMINATION AND VULNERABLE GROUPS
Knowledge-informed diversity call to action

Understanding discrimination and how it manifests is critical for organizations that pursue a social responsibility agenda moderated by DE&I. When groups are marginalized, they not only suffer from acts associated with the marginalization, but all of society – including larger organizations – also suffers because when anyone is dehumanized or devalued, it affects us all. For example, when corporations take advantage of indigenous people groups by mining their resources and destroying their environment, forcing the people and future generations to burn down rainforests just to survive, both current and future humanity pay the price and are diminished.

Further, divisive norms that discriminate against minority and vulnerable population groups and women are generally entrenched, and do not simply end by themselves. If anything, these discriminatory practices tend to be both perennial and perpetual in entrenching the disadvantages they create. This is even more reason that organizational leaders must be intentional in their DE&I commitments, ensuring that they produce an equitable and inclusive culture regardless of societal dysfunctions created by these divisive norms. While these discriminatory norms may have been birthed in society, they do not belong in organizations today because they are not forward-facing and undermine social responsibility and sustainable development pursuits. The relevant question for organizations becomes what constitutes discrimination. ISO 26000 provides the following useful guidance:

ISO *Discrimination involves any distinction, exclusion or preference that has the effect of nullifying equality of treatment or opportunity, where that consideration is based on prejudice rather than a legitimate ground.*

Illegitimate grounds for discrimination include but are not limited to: race, colour, gender, age, language, property, nationality or national origin, religion, ethnic or social origin, caste, economic grounds, disability, pregnancy, belonging to an indigenous people, trade union affiliation, political affiliation or political or other opinion. Emerging prohibited grounds also include marital or family status, personal relationships and health status such as HIV/AIDS status. The prohibition of discrimination is one of the most fundamental principles of international human rights law... Discrimination can also be indirect. This occurs when an apparently neutral provision, criterion or practice would put persons with a particular attribute at a disadvantage compared with other persons, unless that provision, criterion or practice is objectively justified by a legitimate aim and the means of achieving that aim are appropriate and necessary.

ISO 26000:2010, page 28.

DISCRIMINATION AND VULNERABLE GROUPS
Creativity-driven equity opportunity/reconciliation/disruption

Organizations can benefit tremendously by utilizing DE&I as a moderator for establishing a discrimination-free environment. It all begins with committed leadership on DE&I matters that sets the expectations of a discrimination-free workplace and commits the leadership and resources to achieve it. This continues by applying the 3-Step Equity Lens in reviewing or assessing where the organization is on discriminatory practices and where it hopes to be to become a socially responsible organization that maximizes the multi-faceted human resources available within its societal eco-system.

DE&I should not be a reactionary response to political or social unrest but an organizational calling card for its commitment to make this world a better place through its decision-making practices. A multifaceted workforce that enables the participation and inclusion of minority groups, women and other disenfranchised groups should be viewed as a sound value-added business proposition, not just a gesture of benevolence. A benevolent DE&I approach may be rooted in good intentions, but it is not necessarily driven by sound business practices and hence is often difficult to sustain. For example, hiring one person from a marginalized group in a workforce of hundreds is a token benevolence—management's kind gesture to DE&I.

Using the 3-Step Equity Lens model enables an organization to take a holistic, systemic, and intentional approach to creating a discrimination-free workforce, workplace, and work-partnerships when DE&I serves as a moderator. This approach gives the organization a tripartite strategy that integrates the triple bottom line of profit (prosperity), people and planet as a sound business model:

- **Equity Opportunity:** By focusing on the opportunities to adjust or correct current discriminatory or potentially discriminatory decision-making processes and practices, an organization can strengthen its social responsibility commitments through DE&I. ISO 26000 provides the following guidance:

ISO *An organization should take care to ensure that it does not discriminate against employees, partners, customers, stakeholders, members and anyone else with whom it has any contact or on whom it can have an impact...An organization can take a positive and constructive view of diversity among the people with whom it interacts. It could consider not only the human rights aspects but also the gains for its own operation in terms of the value added by the full development of multi-faceted human resources and relations.*

ISO 26000:2010, pages 28-29.

- **Equity Reconciliation:** By assessing its everyday decision-making processes and practices against systemic or potentially discriminatory practices as memorialized in its policy and procedures, an organization can discover areas where there are gaps or inconsistencies and use this information to improve upon them or replace them with more socially responsible ones. ISO 26000 provides the following guidance:

ISO *An organization should examine its own operations and the operations of other parties within its sphere of influence to determine whether direct or indirect discrimination is present. It should also ensure that it is not contributing to discriminatory practices through the relationships connected to its activities. If this is the case an organization should encourage and assist other parties in their responsibility to prevent discrimination. If this is not successful it should reconsider its relations with such organizations. It may, for example, undertake an analysis of typical ways in which it interacts with women, as compared with men, and consider whether policies and decisions in this regard are objective or reflect stereotyped preconceptions. It may wish to seek advice from local or international organizations with expertise in human rights. An organization may be guided by the findings and recommendations of international or national monitoring or investigative procedures.*

ISO 26000:2010, page 28.

- **Equity Disruption**: An organization can break the circle of societal discrimination norms by intentionally utilizing its own decision-making processes and activities to dismantle them within its own eco-system. It might be as simple as committing to engaging in conversations and taking actions that respectfully seek to understand and address perennial discriminations that have limited the abilities of minority and vulnerable groups because of entrenched systemic norms or social contracts. ISO 26000 provides the following guidance:

ISO *An organization should consider facilitating the raising of awareness of their rights among members of vulnerable groups...An organization should also contribute to redressing discrimination or the legacy of past discrimination, wherever practicable. For example, it should strive to employ or do business with organizations operated by people from groups historically discriminated against; where feasible, it should support efforts to increase access to education, infrastructure or social services for groups denied full access.*

ISO 26000:2010, page 28.

DISCRIMINATION AND VULNERABLE GROUPS
Governance-centered inclusion actionable steps

Governance-centered inclusion actionable steps allow an organization to document its DE&I commitments and illustrate how it intends to create a discrimination-free workforce, workplace and work-partnerships. In creating these actionable steps, organizations should consider the groups that have suffered entrenched disadvantages within their own societal eco-systems and areas where their product or services are used or have influence. ISO 26000 provides the following guidance:

ISO *The following examples of vulnerable groups are described together with specific related actions and expectations:*

☐ ***Women and girls*** *comprise half of the world population, but they are frequently denied access to resources and opportunities on equal terms with men and boys. Women have the right to enjoy all human rights without discrimination, including in education, employment and economic and social activities as well as the right to decide on marriage and family matters and the right to make decisions over their own reproductive health. An organization's policies and activities should have due regard for women's rights and promote the equal* treatment of women and men in the economic, social and political spheres.

- **People with disabilities** are often vulnerable, in part because of misperceptions about their skills and abilities. An organization should contribute to ensuring that men and women with disabilities are accorded dignity, autonomy and full participation in society. The principle of non-discrimination should be respected, and organizations should consider making reasonable provisions for access to facilities.
- **Children** are particularly vulnerable, in part because of their dependent status. In taking action that can affect children, primary consideration should be given to the best interests of the child. The principles of the Convention on the Rights of the Child, which include non-discrimination, a child's right to life, survival, development and free expression, should always be respected and taken into account. Organizations should have policies to prevent their employees engaging in sexual and other forms of exploitation of children.

- **Indigenous peoples** can be considered a vulnerable group because they have experienced systemic discrimination that has included colonization, dispossession from their lands, separate status from other citizens, and violations of their human rights. Indigenous peoples enjoy collective rights, and individuals belonging to indigenous peoples share universal human rights, in particular the right to equal treatment and opportunity. The collective rights include: self-determination (which means the right to determine their identity, their political status and the way they want to develop); access to and management of traditional land, water and resources; maintaining and enjoying their customs, culture, language and traditional knowledge free from discrimination; and managing their cultural and intellectual property. An organization should recognize and respect the rights of indigenous peoples when carrying out its decisions and activities. An organization should recognize and respect the principle of non-discrimination and the rights of individuals belonging to an indigenous people when carrying out decisions and activities.

- **Migrants, migrant workers and their families** may also be vulnerable owing to their foreign or regional origin, particularly if they are irregular or undocumented migrants. An organization should respect their rights and contribute to promoting a climate of respect for the human rights of migrants, migrant workers and their families.
- **People discriminated against on the basis of descent**, including caste. Hundreds of millions of people are discriminated against because of their hereditary status or descent. This form of discrimination is based on a history of rights abuse justified by the wrongful notion that some people are considered unclean or less worthy because of the group into which they are born. An organization

should avoid such practices and, where feasible, seek to contribute to eliminating these prejudices.

☐ **People discriminated against on the basis of race**. *People are discriminated against because of their race, cultural identity and ethnic origin. There is a history of rights abuse justified by the wrongful notion that some people are inferior because of their skin colour or culture. Racism is often present in regions with a history of slavery or oppression of one racial group by another.*

☐ *Other vulnerable groups include, for example, the elderly, the displaced, the poor, illiterate people, people living with HIV/AIDS and minority and religious groups.*

ISO 26000:2010, page 29.

Human Rights Issue 6: CIVIL AND POLITICAL RIGHTS

Does your organization acknowledge and respect the **CIVIL AND POLITICAL RIGHTS** of its employees and partners, including those from groups that have suffered persistent denial of their inalienable human rights?

Civil and political rights abuse are the first layers of human rights abuses because they allow perpetrators to devalue people and use this as justification to cause them harm or deny them rights accorded others. An organization should use DE&I as a moderator for reviewing or modifying its policy and procedures to ensure it is not complicit in acts that deny individuals their civil and political rights and dignity because of the racial or gender group to which they belong or identify.

CIVIL AND POLITICAL RIGHTS
Knowledge-informed diversity call to action

In 2020, a Minneapolis Minnesota Police Officer placed his knee on George Floyd's neck and snuffed the life out of his lungs. It was a real-life representation of the life experiences of black and brown people groups in America. The difference is that Mr. Floyd died, and in a very public venue, while the weight of prejudice and discriminatory practices slowly snuffs the life out of black and brown people every day by individual and shared lived experiences. As black people in America, we know that we are in a game of life where the odds are stacked against our success every day because of the systemic and perennial racism that devalues our humanity. It's like starting off by playing a game of soccer, and as soon as your team gets a penalty to even the score, the game is automatically switched to baseball, in a different field with the other team already fully suited up and equipped—uniform, cleats, bats, and mitts—while your team is still in its soccer gear. In other words, as soon as you start to even the playing field, the other team changes the rules to preserve their advantage. This is a simple rendition of what happens when people are denied their civil and political rights.

Organizations are expected by some to be agnostic on civil and political rights issues, while others expect them to be vocal advocates and champions. Organizations who are committed to social responsibility and want to see a workplace where DE&I dialogues are allowed to flow freely without condoning divisive norms can utilize DE&I as its moderator for establishing new norms that are stakeholder-driven. These new norms should be respectful of each person and their contributions or potential to the organization's bottom line must be valued and encouraged. ISO 26000 provides the following guidance on civil and political rights:

ISO *Civil and political rights include absolute rights such as the right to life, the right to a life with dignity, the right to freedom from torture, the right to security of person, the right to own property, liberty and integrity of the person, and the right to due process of law and a fair hearing when facing criminal charges. They further include freedom of opinion and expression, freedom of peaceful assembly and association, freedom to adopt and practise a religion, freedom to hold beliefs, freedom from arbitrary interference with privacy, family, home or correspondence, freedom from attacks on honour or reputation, the right of access to public services and the right to take part in elections.*

ISO 26000:2010, page 30.

CIVIL AND POLITICAL RIGHTS
Creativity-driven equity opportunity/reconciliation/disruption

Organizations should consider using the 3-Step Equity Lens as a guide in seeking to understand how minorities and women are marginalized and ignored and what to do about it. If civil and political rights are being abused or denied within their ecosystem, they need to know it. Engaging minorities and those who have been disadvantaged and marginalized historically in a dialogue can assist organizations to find equity opportunities, reconcile their stated DE&I values with their real-life experiences, and stop decisions and activities that deny people of their civil and political rights.

CIVIL AND POLITICAL RIGHTS
Governance-centered inclusion actionable steps

Governance-centered inclusion actionable steps on civil and political rights developed using the 3-Step Inclusion Principles can assist an organization in living up to its DE&I commitments by creating an environment where DE&I issues and challenges are discussed in a more collegial and respectful atmosphere, and solutions are collectively developed. ISO 26000 provides the following guidance for enabling this atmosphere:

> An organization should respect all individual civil and political rights. Examples include, but are not limited to, the following:
>
> ☐ **life of individuals**. Minorities and women have historically been devalued and therefore the value of their lives made to be less valuable than members of the majority racial group. An organization can reverse this practice by elevating the voice and participation of black and brown people in its entire eco-system. When, for example, an American is held hostage overseas, the media coverage and general societal response is not what racial group the person belongs, but the country. Organizations can have the same response when any member of its workforce has their civil and political rights abused, it should create a shared righteous indignation;
>
> ☐ **freedom of opinion and expression**. An organization should not aim to suppress anyone's views or opinions, even when the person expresses criticism of the organization internally or externally except when such expressed opinions compromises its DE&I policy. When employees or partners are not able to separate their hate opinions from the exercise of their organizational responsibilities, an organization should consider whether it should continue the relationship. This is even more important when minorities and women already come into most organizations outnumbered and in lower positions where their contributions are marginalized and their expressed opinion scrutinized and labeled. Organizational leaders should intentionally solicit the opinion of these disadvantaged groups and highlight their contributions to the organization's bottom line of profit, people and planet as visible modeling for its DE&I expectations;
>
> ☐ **freedom of peaceful assembly and of association.** Sometimes, organizations frown on peaceful assembly or associations or pretend they don't know that their employees participate in hate groups that advocate divisive norms. While organizations may choose to remain neutral on what groups their employees and partners belong to in their own personal time, it should not remain neutral when hate and separatist ideals are brought into its eco-system. Tolerance of peaceful assembly that promotes hate and segregation undermines our shared humanity and organizations should make its position known and express why racial hatred and segregation conflicts with its DE&I commitments. When its internal and external stakeholders are known to belong to separatists and hate groups, organizations should ensure that while performing their functions for which they receive compensation, all stakeholders follow its DE&I commitments. In this

situation, organizations should consider additional trainings, promote dialogues that strengthens its position, etc.;

☐ **freedom to seek, receive and impart information and ideas through any means, regardless of national borders.** *In the age of social media, this can become a double-edged sword, but organizations should ensure that its platform is not used to promote hate or segregation or the devaluing of other people groups or acts that makes it complicit on human rights abuses;*

☐ **the right to own property, alone or in association with others, and freedom from being arbitrarily deprived of property.** *Property ownership is one area where black and brown racial people groups have suffered significantly from racist policies. From redlining of black and brown communities to racially restrictive covenants in deeds that prohibit white property owners from selling their homes to black and brown people to lending institutions that deliberately deny them home loans, there are many ways that racism and its systemic practices continue in society. Organizations can redress these systemic and perennial racist practices through socially responsible actionable steps that blocks their manifestations or mirroring in its decision-making processes or activities; and*

☐ **access to due process and the right to a fair hearing before any internal disciplinary measure is taken.** *Organizations should ensure that minorities and groups that have suffered disproportional denial of their civic and politic rights be part of designing or updating any decision due process. This would reduce the unfair and unjust practices that are holdover from when black and brown people had no rights, and*

☐ **Any disciplinary measure should be proportionate and not involve physical punishment or inhuman or degrading treatment.**

Adapted & repurposed from ISO 26000:2010, page 30.

Human Rights Issue 7: ECONOMIC, SOCIAL AND CULTURAL RIGHTS

How does your organization incorporate DE&I as part of its **ECONOMIC, SOCIAL AND CULTURAL RIGHTS Agenda**?

Many of the world's divisive norms are anchored by one racial or tribal group's interest in controlling the economic, social and cultural rights of other groups in order to secure and preserve its own privileges. These divisive norms generally find their way into organizational eco-systems, where unfair social contracts are reflected in corporate policies and continue unabated.

ECONOMIC, SOCIAL AND CULTURAL RIGHTS
Knowledge-informed diversity call to action

Economic, social and cultural rights are the bedrock of sustainable development, which is defined as "… development that meets the needs of the present without compromising the ability of future generations to meet their own needs (WCED 1987)." Two key concepts accompanied the crafting of this definition:

1. the concept of 'needs', in particular the essential needs of the world's poor, to which overriding priority should be given; and
2. the idea of limitations imposed by the state of technology and social organization on the environment's ability to meet present and future needs (WCED 1987).

Since the industrial revolution began, the world has witnessed the ever-escalating rich versus poor divide; today it has reached an alarming scale that was unfathomable before. Despite all the wealth developed from our shared resources, the plight of the poor has grown even more extreme. When we add the impacts of global warming and climate change to the mix, it is even more clear that our economic development continues to be at the expense of our shared planet and the majority poor living in this generation and those in future generations. Consider that no billionaire earned their wealth without drawing upon the natural resources in our shared planet. Even knowledge-driven businesses still rely on stakeholders whose devices that connect them to the knowledge are made from natural resources uniting the triple bottom line of profit, people and planet in an inescapable dance. Economic, social and cultural rights are DE&I-related and addressing them begins first by understanding the cleavages. ISO 26000 provides the following guidance on economic, social and cultural rights:

ISO *Every person, as a member of society, has economic, social and cultural rights necessary for his or her dignity and personal development. These include the right to: education; work in just and favourable conditions; freedom of association; an adequate standard of health; a standard of living adequate for the physical and mental health and well-being of himself or herself and his or her family; food, clothing, housing, medical care and necessary social protection, such as security in the event of unemployment, sickness, disability, death of spouse, old age or other lack of livelihood in circumstances beyond his or her control; the practice of a religion and culture; and genuine opportunities to participate without* *discrimination in decision making that supports positive practices and discourages negative practices in relation to these rights.*

ISO 26000:2010, page 30.

ECONOMIC, SOCIAL AND CULTURAL RIGHTS
Creativity-driven equity opportunity/reconciliation/disruption

Using the 3-Step Equity Lens model, an organization can strategically develop and institute structures that enable it to respect and consider the economic, social and cultural rights of its stakeholders within the framework of its DE&I initiatives:

- **Equity Opportunity:** ISO 26000 provides the following guidance:

ISO *To respect these rights, an organization has a responsibility to exercise due diligence to ensure that it does not engage in activities that infringe, obstruct or impede the enjoyment of such rights.*

ISO 26000:2010, page 30.

- **Equity Reconciliation:** ISO 26000 provides the following guidance:

ISO *An organization should assess the possible impacts of its decisions, activities, products and services, as well as new projects, on these rights, including the rights of the local population.*

ISO 26000:2010, pages 10-11.

- **Equity Disruption**: ISO 26000 provides the following guidance:

ISO *[An organization] should neither directly nor indirectly limit or deny access to an essential product or resource, such as water. For example, production processes should not compromise the supply of scarce drinking water resources. Organizations should, where appropriate, consider adopting or maintaining specific policies to ensure the efficient distribution of essential goods and services where this distribution is endangered.*

ISO 26000:2010, pages 30-31.

ECONOMIC, SOCIAL AND CULTURAL RIGHTS
Governance-centered inclusion actionable steps

Governance-centered inclusion platform provides an organization the creative broad-mindedness to think outside the box and become part of the solution in preserving, protecting and advocating for the economic, social and cultural rights of its internal and external stakeholders as well as those outside these relationships. While recognizing that governments and other organizations are responsible for providing for these rights within societies, an organization can also contribute to their fulfillment. ISO 26000 provides the following examples on how organizations can become involved by:

ISO

☐ facilitating access to, and where possible providing support and facilities for, education and lifelong learning for community members;

☐ joining efforts with other organizations and governmental institutions supporting respect for and realization of economic, social and cultural rights;

☐ exploring ways related to their core activities to contribute to the fulfilment of these rights; and

☐ adapting goods or services to the purchasing ability of poor people.

ISO 26000:2010, page 31.

Human Rights Issue 8: FUNDAMENTAL PRINCIPLES AND RIGHTS AT WORK

How does your organization guarantee the **FUNDAMENTAL PRINCIPLES AND RIGHTS AT WORK** as part of its DE&I commitments?

FUNDAMENTAL PRINCIPLES AND RIGHTS AT WORK
Knowledge-informed diversity call to action

Fundamental principles and rights at work focus on labor matters and they are globally accepted as basic human rights issues. The International Labour Organization (ILO) recognizes the fundamental rights at work (ILO 1998) as the freedom of association and effective recognition of collective bargaining rights and the elimination of all forced labor, including child labor, and discrimination in employment and occupation. While fundamental principles and rights at work are now part of the legislative environment in most countries, these rights also need to be integrated as part of an overall organizational social responsibility framework.

FUNDAMENTAL PRINCIPLES AND RIGHTS AT WORK
Creativity-driven equity opportunity/reconciliation/disruption

There are corporations with socially responsible reputations who nonetheless fight fiercely against unionization efforts, often with great sophistication, resources, and unabashed success. In some cases, at issue is the very validity of collective bargaining as a tool for improving worker rights. These companies recognize the value of appearing socially responsible but are unwilling to make some of the deep organizational and cultural changes necessary to walk the DE&I talk. In reviewing, assessing or updating its current policies and procedures relating to labor laws against a DE&I background, an organization should use the framework on fundamental rights at work established by the International Labour Organization (ILO) as guide and this includes:

1. Eliminating discrimination in employment and occupation
2. Eliminating all compulsory and forced labor
3. Recognizing the right to collective bargaining and of association
4. Honoring the effective abolition of child labor (ILO 1998).

FUNDAMENTAL PRINCIPLES AND RIGHTS AT WORK
Governance-centered inclusion actionable steps:

Fundamental principles and rights at work are generally legislated by jurisdictions outside the purview of individual organizations. However, socially responsible organizations moderated by DE&I should still consider how its internal commitments adhere to the spirit and the law of these rights at work. ISO 26000 provides the following guidance:

☐ *freedom of association and collective bargaining*   *Workers   and employers, without distinction whatsoever, have the right to establish and, subject only to the rules of the organization concerned, to join organizations of their own choosing without previous authorization. Representative organizations formed or joined by workers should be recognized for purposes of collective bargaining. Terms and conditions of employment may be fixed by voluntary collective negotiation where workers so choose. Workers' representatives   should be given appropriate facilities that will enable them to do their work effectively and allow them to perform their role without interference. Collective agreements should include provisions for the settlement of disputes.*

Workers' representatives should be provided with information required for meaningful negotiations.

☐ **forced labour**   *An organization should not engage in or benefit from any use of forced or compulsory labour. No work or service should be exacted from any person under the threat of any penalty or when the work is not conducted voluntarily. An organization should not engage or benefit from prison labour, unless the prisoners have been convicted in a court of law and their labour is under the supervision and control of a public authority. Further, prison labour should not be used by private organizations unless performed on a voluntary basis, as evidenced by, among other things, fair and decent conditions of employment.*

☐ **equal opportunities and non-discrimination**   *An organization should confirm that its employment policies are free from discrimination based on race, colour, gender, religion, national extraction, social origin, political opinion, age, or disability. Emerging prohibited grounds also include marital or family status, personal relationships, and health status such as HIV/AIDS status. These are in line with the general principle that hiring policies and practices, earnings, employment conditions, access to training and promotion, and termination of employment should be based only on the requirements of the job. Organizations should also take steps to prevent harassment in the workplace by:*

  o   *regularly assessing the impact of its policies and activities on promotion of equal opportunities and non-discrimination;*
  o   *taking positive actions to provide for the protection and advancement of vulnerable groups; this might include establishing workplaces for persons with disabilities to help them earn a living under suitable conditions, and establishing or participating in programmes that address issues such as promotion of employment for youth and older workers, equal employment opportunities for women and more balanced representation of women in senior positions.*

☐ **child labour**   *The minimum age for employment is determined through international instruments. Organizations should not engage in or benefit from any use of child labour. If an organization has child labour in its operations or within its sphere of influence, it should, as far as possible, ensure not only that the children are removed from work, but also that they are provided with appropriate alternatives, in particular, education. Light work that does not harm a child or interfere with school attendance or with other activities necessary to a child's full development (such as recreational activities) is not considered child labour.*

ISO 26000:2010, pages 31-32.

Chapter Seven

DE&I AS MODERATOR FOR LABOR

The labor practices of an organization are more far-reaching than most organizations recognize or may be willing to accept. Organizations create jobs, and jobs give workers a means for meeting their economic and social needs, as well as providing them with dignity and significance. Without jobs, a community faces social problems. With productive, meaningful, and fairly compensated jobs, it is transformed in many ways: human development, community enhancement and shared prosperity. Socially responsible labor practices today are challenged because the supply chain doors have extended beyond the front doors of most organizations. The global value chain presents organizations with ancient but persisting practices such as child labor, debt-bondage, bonded labor—all with private actors playing roles traditionally assumed by human resources functions. What does an organization do when it discovers that within its ecosystem, products and services are been developed, produced, and distributed by the hands of workers whose human rights and dignity are denied or abused by such practices?

While the sum-total of any organization is its people, the idea extends beyond this internal stakeholder group of employees and includes all stakeholders who perform work on its behalf, such as subcontractors or independent contractors. Labor practices also define how, why and with whom work is performed, and how compensation is determined. Labor practices are therefore an essential part of social responsibility and impact communal stability (ILO 2008). ISO 26000 provides this broad categorization of labor practices:

ISO *Labour practices include the recruitment and promotion of workers; disciplinary and grievance procedures; the transfer and relocation of workers; termination of employment; training and skills development; health, safety and industrial hygiene; and any policy or practice affecting conditions of work, in particular working time and remuneration. Labour practices also include the recognition of worker organizations and representation and participation of both worker and employer organizations in collective bargaining, social dialogue and tripartite consultation...to address social issues related to employment.*

ISO 26000:2010, page 33.

The International Labour Organization (ILO), a United Nations agency, has provided guidance on labor matters since the 1940s. It is the premier global labor standards organization, focusing on three areas: governments, employers and workers. ILO defines productive work as one *"performed in conditions of freedom, equity, security and human dignity (ISO 26000 2010)."* In its 1944 Declaration of Philadelphia, ILO adopted a universal principle that labor is not a commodity and *"workers should not be treated as a factor of production and subjected to the same market forces that apply to commodities (ISO 26000 2010)."*

Through its International Covenant on Economic, social and cultural Rights and the Universal Declaration of Human Rights, ILO's principles are geared towards protecting workers' rights to earn a living in a manner of their choosing with fair working conditions. Labor laws, of course, vary from one country to another; it's the responsibility of each government to be consistent with the ILO standards in creating and enforcing its labor-related legislation, as well as ensuring that access to justice is readily available to both workers and organizations *(ISO 26000 2010)*. ISO 26000 provides the following guidance:

ISO *Where governments have failed to legislate, an organization should abide by the principles underlying these international instruments. Where the law is adequate, an organization should abide by the law, even if government enforcement is inadequate. It is important to distinguish between the government's role as the organ of state and its role as an employer. Government bodies or state-owned organizations have the same responsibilities for their labour practices as other organizations.*

ISO 26000:2010, page 34.

Why should organizations driven by a focus on profits abide by these principles if they don't increase their shareholders' values? The truth is that social responsibility and sustainable development are no longer optional in a world with enlightened stakeholders. There are, in fact, far more profits to be gained when an organization uses DE&I to moderate its activities and includes both environmental and social costs in its bottom line. Today's younger generations are not interested in organizations whose DE&I commitments are not life-giving, equitable and inclusive. In a competitive labor marketplace, the long-term survivability of an organization depends on its ability to attract the right workforce; to do so, they must have working conditions that are consistent with these international standards.

ISO 26000 recognizes that the labor policies and practices of an organization need to transcend its own boundaries and extend to work performed by others on its behalf, such as those performed by contractors, subcontractors, and other public and non-governmental sectors. In doing so organizations need to meet societal expectations that they will engage in labor practices that integrate DE&I as core business values.

LABOR PRACTICES
Knowledge-informed diversity call to action

A socially responsible organization should ensure that its policies and practices *and those of its partners and contractors* are compliant with international norms, and that practices are based on the principle of diversity embracement. For this to happen on a consistent basis, the organization needs to be guided by a knowledge-informed labor practices diversity call-to-action that is inherently tied to a fundamental principle of labor. Humankind's dignity has historically been tied to the jobs we do, going back to when our ancestors were hunter-gatherers. Jobs are at the center of a society's economic, environmental, and social engine, the vehicle used to transport divisive norms that favors one group over another across the generations. Consequently, to close the gap created by these divisive norms, we need DE&I as the driver for new redemptive, restorative, and responsible principles that create fair and just labor practices.

Labor practices are fundamental values that enable each generation to realize their fullest potentials in life, liberty and the pursuit of happiness while ensuring that future generations do the same. Labor practices are so important to society that four of the Ten Principles of the UN Global Compact are dedicated to labor:

Table 7.1: The ten principles of the UN Global Compact: labour

Principle 3:	Businesses should uphold the freedom of association and the effective recognition of the right to collective bargaining;
Principle 4:	The elimination of all forms of forced and compulsory labour;
Principle 5:	The effective abolition of child labour; and
Principle 6:	The elimination of discrimination in respect of employment and occupation.

- Principle 3 speaks to respect of the rights of employers and all workers to be able to promote and defend their occupational interests through group associations that includes activities such as the freedom to form groups, administer and elect its representatives without fear of impunity. This is one area where minority and vulnerable groups have historically been prevented from realizing any collective association because they are quick to be branded as revolutionary, communist or anti-establishment. The fear of not allowing minority and vulnerable groups to associate to pursue common interests is a relic from past unjust and unfair practices that an organization either has not addressed or poses a reckoning of some sort that the leadership is not willing or comfortable addressing. It is also a new frontier, enabling all stakeholders to build the strength of wholeness where strength in numbers make good advocacy and partnership for organizational leadership.

- Principle 4 speaks to respect for individuals to freely engage in work that is freely given, with the rights of both parties to terminate relations based on agreed-upon terms. Forced labor has disproportionately affected minority and vulnerable groups. While most socially responsible organizations today may not be involved in forced labor practices, because of the globalization of the supply chain ecosystem, it is still the responsibility of each organization to know the life-cycle structure of the labor used to produce its products or services. If for no other reason, this knowledge is important because it shields the socially responsible organization from being complicit.

- Principle 5 speaks to the exploitation of children when they are conscripted as slaves, used for illicit activities (such as trafficking of drugs or armed as soldiers) or exposed to work at a developmental age. The UN ILO Convention 182 established three types of work and the minimum age for admission to work or employment:
  - light work (developed countries 13 years and developing countries 12 years),
  - regular work (developed countries 15 years and developing countries 14 years), and

- o hazardous work (developed countries 13 years and developing countries 12 years).

Underage-to-work children of minority and vulnerable groups have traditionally been involved in the same divisive norms that marginalized their parents. They are impacted in areas such as their health, safety, and morals. Socially responsible organizations need to understand the full lifecycle of their products and services' ecosystem to account for all child labor abuses—where known—within their operations and value chains. This is consistent with the goal of seeking to not be complicit and conducting due diligence to ensure that all its stakeholders are following its DE&I principles and practices around shared holistic abolition of child labor.

- Principle 6 speaks to fair and just employment practices where a person is hired on the basis of ability to do the job; they cannot be denied employment due to divisive norms such as race, gender, age, sect, etc. Minority and vulnerable groups have long suffered these discriminatory employment practices that wounds their self-worth. It also goes beyond employment to how a person is treated once hired. Whether directly or indirectly, the employment ecosystem is full of areas where discriminations can fester even in salient practices or rules that are exclusionary but appear neutral or even inclusivity-inviting. Like other discriminatory rules and practices, employment systemic racial and gender inequities are strongholds—forces that do not concede to change on their own unless an equal and opposite force moderated by DE&I is unleashed to counter them.

LABOR PRACTICES
Creativity-driven equity opportunity/reconciliation/disruption

DE&I rules of engagements are generally embedded in labor practices even when they may not be specifically named or identified. ISO 26000 affirms that while labor laws will vary from country to country, it is generally agreed that the government is responsible for ensuring fair and equitable treatment of workers through:

1. Adoption of legislation which are consistent with the Universal Declaration of Human Rights and related ILO labour standards,
2. Enforcement of those laws, and
3. Assurance that both the organization and workers have needed access to justice (ISO 26000 2010).

But even when the State or government fails to address DE&I in its labor laws and practices, the organization still has a responsibility to do so within a broader context of social responsibility. Everyone has the right to earn a living by freely choosing work and the right to fair and equitable treatment at work. When States fail to enforce these principles, these rights can be compromised and abused, especially for minority and vulnerable people groups. This is even more true when the contracting party has the controlling power, which is usually the case. It is the reason why historically labor laws have been enacted to protect the interests of employees and others contracted for labor.

Creativity-driven labor practices equity considerations begin by upholding the International Labor Convention's 1944 Declaration establishing the fundamental principle that "labour" is not a commodity, and that workers should not be treated as a simple factor of production or equated to robots—even when they are programmed to have artificial intelligence. These considerations continue when an organization upholds all the other labor laws applicable locally. Labor practices would not need to be codified in law if employees and workers had historically been treated fairly. The truth is that even when these laws are on the books, it is stills a critical source of equity imbalance and equal rights violations, as indicated by the preponderance of labor-practice-related lawsuits. This explains why DE&I need to be a moderating voice in assessing an organization's labor practices as it bridges the gap between the law and its social responsibility. Overall, any labor law and organizational social responsibility assessment should include equity opportunity, reconciliation, and disruption as integrative lenses

 Labour Practices

LABOUR PRACTICES ISSUE 1: DE&I AS MODERATOR FOR EMPLOYMENT AND EMPLOYMENT RELATIONSHIP

Job creation and the power to employ people to work is a powerful tool for shaping both organizational and societal norms for good or evil. Human development cannot be fully realized without employment and the realization of life, liberty and the pursuit of happiness hinges on the quality and consistency of work for individuals, their respective communities, and the world. A life well-lived is anchored by employment which relies on decent work that is secure and fulfilling in both time and remuneration.

EMPLOYMENT AND EMPLOYMENT RELATIONSHIPS
Knowledge-informed diversity call to action

When labor is treated as a commodity without consideration for our shared humankind, a warped view of the employment market develops. Warped employment relationships are foundations of unjust and unfair decisions and practices that are often difficult to uproot because they become social contracts, mental models and mountains of privileges—hills sacred enough for some to gladly die upon. Yet, the impacts to minority and vulnerable groups can stymie economic growth for generations. During the founding years of the United States of America, slaves were used as free labor to build the infrastructures of the country. Particularly in the South, slave labor helped create the fourth largest economy in the world at that time.

Slaves became experts in all known trades of the day, including farming, road and rail construction, equipment repairs, etc. Infrequently mentioned is what happened to the children of slaves during and immediately after slavery—especially those who were less than 13 years old. These children of slavery were sometimes intentionally born to supply free labor and promote the sustainability of the owners' slavery enterprise. Men and women were forced to mate to produce children for the master to benefit. These children were born into slavery. At an early age, these slave children began to work in whatever profession their parents were employed in, and through that experience gained valuable work-related skillsets.

Based on today's UN Global Compact's 5th Principle, a 13-year-old slave child was work-eligible for light work in 1865 but may have started work much earlier. By the late 19th and early 20th centuries—the era of the industrial revolution—this same 13-year-old former slave in 1865 would be 48 years old by 1900—a time when Jim Crow laws of "separate but equal" had become an American employment and employment relationship stronghold. Consider that denying African Americans the right to sustainable employment based on race denied them the right to economic stabilization and their human dignity. This same 13-year-old in 1865, even though they had years of work experience, was deemed unemployable most of their adult life. Here is what we know today about the adverse long-term impact of child labor:

> Child labour is damaging to a child's physical, social, mental, psychological and spiritual development because it is work performed at too early an age. Child labour deprives children of their childhood and their dignity. They are deprived of an education and may be separated from their families. Children who do not complete their primary education are likely to remain illiterate and never acquire the skills needed to get a job and contribute to the development of a modern economy. Consequently, child labour results in under-skilled, unqualified workers and jeopardizes future improvements of skills in the workforce. Children have the same human rights as adults. But by virtue of their age and the fact that they are still growing and gaining knowledge and experience, they have some distinct rights as children. These rights include protection from economic exploitation and work that may be dangerous to their health, safety or morals and that may hinder their development or impede their access to education (UN Global Compact Principle 5).

For the 13-year-old in our focus and his or her generation, the various federal programs curated to assist their parents did not benefit their employment situation, just as it did not benefit their parents or their own children. There were no intentional programs to address the socio-cultural or socio-economic damage done to them, nor was their psychological wellbeing even considered as a matter of national importance. By 1870, just five years after the end of slavery, Jim Crow laws swept through the south in a sweltering fear-and-hate wave presented as "separate but equal" rights, upheld by the US Supreme Court in 1896 in the Plessy vs. Ferguson case. It was declared unconstitutional in 1954—almost 90 years later.

While slavery was abolished over 150 years ago, the unjust and unfair inequitable legacy of this system persists. This is instructive for socially responsible organizations with global footprint that must holistically be aware of its employment and employment relationship across an entire geographical ecosystem, including in places where child labor is still practiced. Today, the labor values of African Americans are still seen and compensated less than their white counterparts. Universally, minority and vulnerable groups—groups that are marginalized by caste systems or divisive norms—remain undervalued and undercompensated for their work and underrepresented in the workforce.

This is a failure at both the level of the government and of the individual companies that propagate and perpetuate these inequities. Although governments are responsible for regulating work, organizations have tremendous responsibility in ensuring that those they engage as workers directly or through intermediary arrangements are classified correctly and compensated fairly and do not include underage child labor. ISO 26000 provided the following guidance:

ISO *Not all work is performed within an employment relationship. Work and services are also performed by men and women who are self-employed; in these situations the parties are considered independent of each other and have a more equal and commercial relationship. The distinction between employment and commercial relationships is not always clear and is sometimes wrongly labelled, with the consequence that workers do not always receive the protections and rights that they are entitled to receive. It is important for both society and the individual performing work that the appropriate legal and institutional framework be recognized and applied. Whether work is performed under an employment contract or a commercial contract, all parties to a contract are entitled to understand their rights and responsibilities and to have appropriate recourse in the event that the terms of the contract are not respected.*

ISO 26000:2010, page 35.

EMPLOYMENT AND EMPLOYMENT RELATIONSHIPS
Creativity-driven equity opportunity/reconciliation/disruption:

Labor laws are necessary because the power structure is often unbalanced in employer-employee relationships, child labor relationships, etc. Each country today has the responsibility to regulate employer-employee relationships within internationally accepted standards as set forth by ILO and to ensure just and fair work relationships, workplaces and work conditions. Within this context, labor means work performed for compensation in contrast to work performed by volunteers. However, when volunteers are engaged, ISO 26000 recommends that organizations still address their duty of care and liabilities through the adoption of applicable policies and measures consistent with those for its regular employees. Socially responsible organizations look for opportunities to build equal access ecosystems where tolerance, occupational development and respect for cultural traditions are normalized in their employment and employment relationships. The UN Global Compact Principle 6 offers the following guidance:

- ☐ Institute company policies and procedures which make qualifications, skill and experience the basis for the recruitment, placement, training and advancement of staff at all levels
- ☐ Assign responsibility for equal employment issues at a high level, issue clear company-wide policies and procedures to guide equal employment practices, and link advancement to desired performance in this area
- ☐ Work on a case by case basis to evaluate whether a distinction is an inherent requirement of a job, and avoid application of job requirements that would systematically disadvantage certain groups
- ☐ Keep up-to-date records on recruitment, training and promotion that provide a transparent view of opportunities for employees and their progression within the organization
- ☐ Conduct unconscious bias training
- ☐ Where discrimination is identified, develop grievance procedures to address complaints, handle appeals and provide recourse for employees
- ☐ Be aware of formal structures and informal cultural issues that can prevent employees from raising concerns and grievances
- ☐ Provide staff training on non-discrimination policies and practices, including disability awareness. Reasonably adjust the physical environment to ensure health and safety for employees, customers and other visitors with disabilities.
- ☐ Establish programs to promote access to skills development training and to particular occupations.

UN Global Climate Principle 6).

In reviewing its employment and employment relationships, an organization should consider the 3-Step Equity Lens framework as guide to ensuring fair and just practices.

EQUITY OPPORTUNITY IN EMPLOYMENT AND EMPLOYMENT RELATIONSHIPS:

A socially responsible organization should look for opportunities to adjust or correct current inequitable or biased employment and employment relationships (racial, gender and others) with socially responsible fair and just ones. For example, they should ensure that work performed by employees or contractors from historically disadvantaged groups—like other majority groups—are classified correctly and compensated fairly, and listened to because they are also stakeholders of interest.

EQUITY RECONCILIATION IN EMPLOYMENT AND EMPLOYMENT RELATIONSHIPS:

Socially responsible organizations normalize continual assessments of their internal policies, systems and practices around employment and employment relationships to ensure that they are consistent with stated DE&I commitments and international human rights fundamental principles and rights at work. For example, if an organization discovers the use of child labor by one of its suppliers, it should state its objections clearly and develop responsible actions to require the supplier to stop such practices if they wish to continue the relationship. Another example, an organization should not only hire coaches from a majority group or from a group that got an early advantage in performing that role and not find such practice in conflict with any socially responsible DE&I construct. No one is born with a whistle in their mouth with programming to be a coach. They are learned skillsets just as racism and other forms of divisive norms:

willing to assume the responsibilities of an employer and to provide decent working conditions. An organization should use only those labour intermediaries who are legally recognized and where other arrangements for the performance of work confer legal rights on those performing the work...Home workers should not be treated worse than other wage earners;

☐ *not benefit from unfair, exploitative or abusive labour practices of its partners, suppliers or subcontractors, including home workers. An organization should make reasonable efforts to encourage organizations in its sphere of influence to follow responsible labour practices, recognizing that a high level of influence is likely to correspond to a high level of responsibility to exercise that influence. Depending upon the situation and influence, reasonable efforts could include: establishing contractual obligations on suppliers and subcontractors; making unannounced visits and inspections; and exercising due diligence in supervising contractors and intermediaries. Where suppliers and subcontractors are expected to comply with a code of labour practice, the code should be consistent with the Universal Declaration of Human Rights and the principles underlying applicable ILO labour standards; and*

☐ *where operating internationally, endeavour to increase the employment, occupational development, promotion and advancement of nationals of the host country. This includes sourcing and distributing through local enterprises where practicable.*

ISO 26000:2010, pages 35-36.

EQUITY DISRUPTION IN EMPLOYMENT AND EMPLOYMENT RELATIONSHIPS:

Socially responsible organizations seek to disrupt societal norms that abuse employee or subcontractor rights because of perennial or current prejudicial or harmful practices. For example, an organization should not hire people belonging to a minority group as perpetual temporary employees for work that requires full-time employees or keep women from jobs solely because of societal gender norms. If a man can be a referee for an American football or soccer game, so can a woman for the same game, even if all the players are men; after all, nobody raises an eyebrow when men referee women's sports events. Further, minorities and vulnerable groups should not be the first ones fired when an organization is forced to reduce staffing because it continues the historical discriminatory practices and betrays its DE&I commitments and messaging.

 An organization should:

- not seek to avoid the obligation that the law places on the employer by disguising relationships that would otherwise be recognized as an employment relationship under the law;
- eliminate any arbitrary or discriminatory dismissal practices;
- protect personal data and privacy of workers.

ISO 26000:2010, pages 35-36.

EMPLOYMENT AND EMPLOYMENT RELATIONSHIPS
Governance-centered inclusion actionable steps

All employment and employment relationships should be guided by the 3-Step Inclusion principles when creating, modifying, or enhancing related to policies and practices. These relationship changes or adjustments—to be socially responsible—must be redemption-driven, restoration-focused, and responsibility-centered.

How an organization addresses its DE&I continuum speaks to its established obligations and rights by ensuring that it legally recognizes workers either as employees or self-employed. This is even more important when minority and vulnerable groups are involved, as employers wield tremendous influence over their employees and contractors. Hence it becomes necessary for the organization's leadership to hold itself responsible for ensuring that all work is compensated appropriately and that workers are treated fairly as employees or contractors regardless of their gender, racial profile, or other diversity traits. Further, the leadership should be confident in its decision-making systems and activities that as an organization it does not arbitrarily discriminate based on artificial differentiators.

Governance-centered inclusion actionable steps in
EMPLOYMENT AND EMPLOYMENT RELATIONSHIPS

1. In reviewing your organization's policies and procedures around employment and employment relationships, how do they align with your DE&I policy, commitments, and corporate proclamations on the matter?
2. If there are gaps, what are the actionable steps and timelines you have identified to narrow or eliminate them based on the 3-Step Equity Lens model?
3. Were all relevant stakeholders identified and engaged in the review, modification or development of your policies and procedures around your DE&I moderated employment and employment relationships practices?

LABOUR PRACTICES ISSUE 2: DE&I AS MODERATOR FOR CONDITIONS OF WORK AND SOCIAL PROTECTION

Work conditions and social protection are DE&I issues and are critical to the preservation of human dignity and the establishment of a sense of social justice and fairness. These are generally established by national, regional, or other legally binding agreements between those who assign the work and those who perform it. Conditions of work and social protection are very much DE&I issues because they are social responsibility matters.

CONDITIONS OF WORK AND SOCIAL PROTECTION
Knowledge-informed diversity call to action

Organizations today are confronted with more challenges around conditions of work and social protection issues. These issues include a living minimum wage, gender pay equality, forced labor, and others. While minimum wage is generally legislated, actual living wages can be both legislated and corporate decisions. The minimum wage debate has fierce proponents on each side. Massively wealthy organizations like Walmart, Amazon, and other tech companies employ large numbers of people at or near the minimum wage. These companies often assert that the generous benefits they provide exceed the minimum wage requirements. Others in the service industry see minimum wage as an impediment to their profits, especially in areas with very low cost of living; a minimum wage designed to provide a living wage for those in a high-cost area might seem excessive to those elsewhere. Then there are those who note that because minimum wage legislations are slow in responding to inflation and other cost of living factors, workers are often forced to work two or more jobs just to rise above the poverty level. The bottom line is that a socially responsible organization ensures that its workers are adequately compensated with living wages that give them dignity and work-life balance consistent within the local, regional or national context where they live and work. ISO 26000 describes matters related to conditions of work and social protection as follows:

ISO *Conditions of work include wages and other forms of compensation, working time, rest periods, holidays, disciplinary and dismissal practices, maternity protection and welfare matters such as safe drinking water, sanitation, canteens and access to medical services. Many of the conditions of work are set by national laws and regulations or by legally binding agreements between those for whom work is performed and those who perform work. The employer determines many of the conditions of work...Fair and appropriate consideration should be given to the quality of conditions of work...Social protection refers to all legal guarantees and* *organizational policies and practices to mitigate the reduction or loss of income in case of employment injury, illness, maternity, parenthood, old age, unemployment, disability or financial hardship and to provide medical care and family benefit. Social protection plays an important role in preserving human dignity and establishing a sense of fairness and social justice. Generally, the primary responsibility for social protection lies with the state.*

ISO 26000:2010, page 36.

Organizations should ensure that conditions of work are not discriminatory, and that social protection is afforded those who have traditionally been marginalized by social norms. This is one area where socially responsible organizations are illuminated by their actions, which should consider the quality of life of their employees, subcontractors, and their families. Then there is the issue of forced labor, which is also part of workplace conditions where the rights of individuals are abused even if they are compensated. This is especially true in places where forced labor is still the norm even if official position is that it has been eradicated.

Forced labor is covered in the UN Global Compact Principle 4. Forced labor is work or service that is performed by a person who is under some form of threat to perform the work where such performance is not voluntary and from which the person cannot freely walk away. Forced labor can be perpetuated by state or private actors. State-imposed forced labor can be driven by ideological or political reasons, and they can include forced public works such as prisoners being hired out (without public authority supervision) to companies or individuals. Private actors in forced labor generally use a form of coercion or slavery or use it to settle debts such as debt-bondage or bonded labor (an ancient practice for debt repayments which can even include children and relatives of the debtor)—(UN Global Compact n.d.). Organizations that produce or offer products or services where the supply chain is varied and located in different parts of the world should be aware of the prevalence of forced labor. For global organizations, the leadership should at the very least understand forced labor and how to ensure that it does not exists in its ecosystem:

What Companies can do [about forced Labor]:
☐ Have a clear policy not to use, be complicit in, or benefit from forced labour;
☐ Where adherence to forced labour provisions of national laws and regulations is insufficient, take account of international standards;

- Ensure that all company officials have a full understanding of what forced labour is;
- Make available employment contracts to all employees stating the terms and conditions of service, the voluntary nature of employment, the freedom to leave (including the appropriate procedures) and any penalties that may be associated with a departure or cessation of work;
- Do not confiscate workers' identity documents;
- Prohibit business partners from charging recruitment fees to workers;
- Write employment contracts in languages easily understood by workers, indicating the scope of and procedures for leaving the job;
- Be aware of countries, regions, industries, sectors, or economic activities where forced labour is more likely to be a practice;
- In planning and conducting business operations, ensure that workers in debt bondage or in other forms of forced labour are not engaged and, where found, provide for the removal of such workers from the workplace with adequate services and provision of viable alternatives;
- Institute policies and procedures to prohibit the requirement that workers lodge financial deposits with the company;
- If hiring prisoners for work in or outside prisons, ensure that their terms and conditions of work are similar to those of a free employment relationship in the sector involved, and that they have given their consent to work for a private employer;·
- Ensure that large-scale development operations do not rely on forced labour in any phase; and
- Carefully monitor supply chains and subcontracting arrangements.

UN Global Climate Principle 4.

CONDITIONS OF WORK AND SOCIAL PROTECTION
Creativity-driven equity opportunity/reconciliation/disruption

DE&I enables an organization to take the long-view beyond mere profits for shareholders. When DE&I becomes the moderator, it provides the platform for an organization to examine its conditions of work and the social protections in its workplace to ensure they include fair and just socio-economic and environmental interests of minority and vulnerable groups. Together, DE&I has the potential to transform both the organization and society, resulting in far richer shared prosperity in terms of profits, people and planet. Applying the 3-Step Equity Lens model to conditions of work and social protection gives an organization a key value-added and performance-enhancing social responsibility framework.

EQUITY OPPORTUNITY IN CONDITIONS OF WORK AND SOCIAL PROTECTION

Equity Opportunities give an organization the flexibility to act on fair, equitable and humanity-validating opportunities that improve or fairly adjust conditions of work and social protections. For example, allowing workers to observe national or religious customs or giving pregnant women flexible work schedules that do not impede work are adjustments that would be easy to make. Paying living wages to workers is another example, and this does not necessarily mean just compliance with minimum wage laws but going beyond it. ISO 26000 provides the following guidance:

ISO   *An organization should:*
- *respect higher levels of provision established through other applicable legally binding instruments such as collective agreements;*
- *observe at least those minimum provisions defined in international labour standards as established by the ILO, especially where national legislation has not yet been adopted;*
- *provide decent conditions of work with regard to wages, hours of work, weekly rest, holidays, health and safety, maternity protection and ability to combine work with family responsibilities;*
- *wherever possible, allow observance of national or religious traditions and customs;*
- *provide conditions of work for all workers that permit, to the greatest extent possible, work-life balance and are comparable with those offered by similar employers in the locality concerned;*
- *provide equal pay for work of equal value;*
- *pay wages directly to the workers concerned, subject only to any restriction or deduction permitted by laws, regulations or collective agreements...*

ISO 26000:2010, pages 36-37.

EQUITY RECONCILIATION IN CONDITIONS OF WORK AND SOCIAL PROTECTION

Equity reconciliations allow the organization to conduct periodic assessments of its policies and procedures, internal systems, and decision-making practices to ensure that they are consistent with international and national labor laws and with its DE&I commitments. For example, should an organization discover that its policies are not in concert with international or national or local labor standards or its DE&I commitments, it should rectify the situation to conform to these standards. ISO 26000 provides the following guidance:

 An organization should:

- ☐ *ensure that the conditions of work comply with national laws and regulations and are consistent with applicable international labour standards;*
- ☐ *provide wages and other forms of remuneration in accordance with national laws, regulations or collective agreements. An organization should pay wages at least adequate for the needs of workers and their families. In doing so, it should take into account the general level of wages in the country, the cost of living, social security benefits and the relative living standards of other social groups. It should also consider economic factors, including requirements of economic development, levels of productivity and the desirability of attaining and maintaining a high level of employment. In determining wages and working conditions that reflect these considerations, an organization should bargain collectively with its workers or their representatives, in particular trade unions, where they so wish, in accordance with national systems for collective bargaining;*
- ☐ *comply with any obligation concerning the provision of social protection for workers in the country of operation...*

ISO 26000:2010, pages 36-37.

EQUITY DISRUPTION IN CONDITIONS OF WORK AND SOCIAL PROTECTION

Equity disruptions are ways in which an organization stops practices that make conditions of work inhumane or endangers workers' safety or thwarts international or national human rights laws. For example, an organization's leadership should consistently carry out its collective bargaining agreements based on principles of work and social protection and not unilaterally switch course when they no longer meet its business objectives without submitting such change to renegotiations. ISO 26000 provides the following guidance:

 An organization should:

- ☐ *respect the right of workers to adhere to normal or agreed working hours established in laws, regulations or collective agreements. It*

should also provide workers with weekly rest and paid annual leave;

☐ *respect the family responsibilities of workers by providing reasonable working hours, parental leave and, when possible, childcare and other facilities that can help workers achieve a proper work-life balance; and*

☐ *compensate workers for overtime in accordance with laws, regulations or collective agreements. When requesting workers to work overtime, an organization should take into account the interests, safety and well-being of the workers concerned and any hazard inherent in the work. An organization should comply with laws and regulations prohibiting mandatory and non-compensated overtime, and always respect the basic human rights of workers concerning forced labour.*

ISO 26000:2010, pages 36-37.

CONDITIONS OF WORK AND SOCIAL PROTECTION
Governance-centered inclusion actionable steps

Governance-centered inclusion actionable steps give organizations a platform to focus their decisions on conditions of work and social protection commitments. When these actionable steps are moderated by DE&I, they should be guided by the 3-Step Inclusion principles to ensure that they are redemption-driven, restoration-focused, and responsibility-centered in their social responsibility focus.

Governance-centered inclusion actionable steps in CONDITIONS OF WORK AND SOCIAL PROTECTION

1. In reviewing your organization's policies and procedures around conditions of work and social protection, how do they align with your DE&I policy, commitments, and corporate proclamations on the matter?

2. If there are gaps, what are the actionable steps and timelines you have identified to narrow or eliminate them based on the 3-Step Equity Lens model?

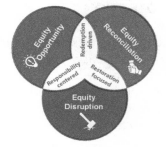

3. Were all relevant stakeholders identified and engaged in the review, modification or development of your policies and procedures around your DE&I moderated conditions of work and social protection practices?

LABOUR PRACTICES ISSUE 3: DE&I AS MODERATOR FOR SOCIAL DIALOGUE

Social dialogues within any organization are varied, as are the stakeholders' communications styles and interests. DE&I as the moderator offers organizations a good platform for categorizing and effectuating productive and positive norms, changing mechanisms built with inequitable and non-inclusive social contracts. With the advent of a plethora of global organizations—connected by technological tools—social dialogue has become a global phenomenon expanding the boundaries of employer-worker conversations. Increased communication allows for the sharing of preferences beyond local, regional or even national priorities and prerogatives. But increased communication tools do not necessarily mean effective social dialogue.

SOCIAL DIALOGUE
Knowledge-informed diversity call to action

Traditionally, social dialogues in organizations are generally thought to focus on exchanges of information, consultations, or bargaining negotiations between employer and workers and sometimes involving the government on economic or social issues that were of interests to them. These social dialogues sometimes take place between employer and workers in work-related agreements and disputes; other times they take place between the employer and the government on social policy matters. ISO 26000 provided the following overarching guidance:

> *Effective social dialogue provides a mechanism for developing policy and finding solutions that take into account the priorities and needs of both employers and workers, and thus results in outcomes that are meaningful and long lasting for both the organization and society. Social dialogue can contribute to establishing participation and democratic principles in the workplace, to better understanding between the organization and those who perform its work and to healthy labour-management relations, thus minimizing resort to costly industrial disputes. Social dialogue is a powerful means for managing change. It can be used to design skills development programmes contributing to human development and enhancing productivity, or to minimize the adverse social impacts of change in the operations of organizations. Social dialogue could also include transparency on social conditions of subcontractors.*
>
> *ISO 26000:2010, page 37.*

Since employers and workers generally have both mutual and competing interests, social dialogue becomes a necessary framework for addressing both. There are various social dialogues occurring within an organization's eco-system, at different levels and at different times. Workers may be frustrated because they do not believe their voices are heard in the employer's decisions concerning their welfare and well-being. Progressive employers look for new ways to share their profits with workers without going through bargaining processes that could become easily contentious when competing interests cannot be aligned. Others rely on perks that address traditional workers' concerns: staffing, scheduling, seniority pay, safety, and meeting carbon neutral and racial equity goals. It is in these benevolent practices that the divide becomes clear, and employers may take advantage in the social dialogues but not necessary the realm of social media.

For older workers that do not belong to the Gen Z and Millennial groups, all the concerns mentioned above are their bread-and-butter reasons for unionizing. For the Gen Z and millennials, it's more important that the organizations they work for engage in protecting and preserving the planet from global warming and climate change. When these issues are presented in opposition to unionizing drives, a progressive organization might easily divide the workers, making it impossible for them to unite despite their shared interests.

Social media has created a new level of knowledge within the workplace; employers and workers now have different, more informed social dialogues than previous generations, confirming the adage that knowledge is power. Although work structures have changed substantially since the impact of COVID-19, the need for workers' voices being heard in the organizational eco-system cannot and should not be silenced. Organized labor and those in the traditional workers representation space may still be using the traditional networking approach to engage their constituents on the same platform of issues—wages, benefits, retirement, disciplinary concerns, etc. However younger workers who grew up with social media—Gen Z and Millennials—have different employment concerns and different ways in which they want to negotiate with their employers. These divided paradigms create opportunities to unite around the organization's DE&I commitments without sacrificing one group's preference over the other when it comes to representations.

Figure 7.1: America's generations defined from 1928 to 1996-onward

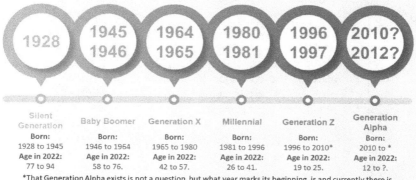

Silent Generation	Baby Boomer	Generation X	Millennial	Generation Z	Generation Alpha
Born: 1928 to 1945	**Born:** 1946 to 1964	**Born:** 1965 to 1980	**Born:** 1981 to 1996	**Born:** 1996 to 2010*	**Born:** 2010 to *
Age in 2022: 77 to 94	**Age in 2022:** 58 to 76.	**Age in 2022:** 42 to 57.	**Age in 2022:** 26 to 41.	**Age in 2022:** 19 to 25.	**Age in 2022:** 12 to ?.

*That Generation Alpha exists is not a question, but what year marks its beginning, is and currently there is no established consensus on when it began: 2010 or 2012, that is the question.

When using DE&I as moderator, employers and workers should decide together the various levels of these dialogues, what each level is authorized to negotiate and for what representative group(s). The age of social media has changed everything when it comes to how, why and by what means negotiations occur, are resourced, and documented. New agreements will need to be fostered as to when organizational issues become public domain issues.

Although social dialogue takes many forms within organizations such as bargaining units, employee councils, unions, consultative groups, etc., the roles are constantly changing. Today, both employers and workers' representatives use social media to support or undercut each other's messaging. When workers are considered stakeholders, they can assist in creating a work environment that is the core of socially responsible organizational pursuits. For larger organizations, bargaining units are sometimes necessary partnerships between employers and workers—allowing for mutually beneficial outcomes. The UN Global Compact Principle 3 provided the following guidance:

 What Companies [can do]:

In the workplace
- Respect the right of all workers to form and join a trade union of their choice without fear of intimidation or reprisal, in accordance with national law;
- Put in place non-discriminatory policies and procedures with respect to trade union organization, union membership and activity in such areas as applications for employment and decisions on advancement, dismissal or transfer;

- o Provide workers' representatives with appropriate facilities to assist in the development of effective collective agreement; and·
- o Do not interfere with the activities of worker representatives while they carry out their functions in ways that are not disruptive to regular company operations. Practices such as allowing the collection of union dues on company premises, posting of trade union notices, distribution of union documents, and provision of office space, have proven to help build good relations between management and workers, provided that they are not used as a way for the company to exercise indirect control.

At the bargaining table
- o Recognize representative organizations for the purpose of collective bargaining;
- o Use collective bargaining as a constructive forum for addressing working conditions and terms of employment and relations between employers and workers, or their respective organizations;
- o Address any problem-solving or other needs of interest to workers and management, including restructuring and training, redundancy procedures, safety and health issues, grievance and dispute settlement procedures, disciplinary rules, and family and community welfare;
- o Provide information needed for meaningful bargaining; and
- o Balance dealings with the most representative trade union to ensure the viability of smaller organizations to continue to represent their members.

UN Global Climate Principle 3.

SOCIAL DIALOGUE
Creativity-driven equity
opportunity/reconciliation/disruption:

Not all organizations are ideally suited to allow for bargaining units within their ecosystems. But all socially responsible organizations consider their employees and work-partners as stakeholders. By virtue of being stakeholders, employee concerns should be part of any organizational social dialogue. Further, it is not the responsibility of the employer or the government to dictate who represents workers' interests. Increasingly, the line between who the employer chooses to consult or negotiate with on behalf of the workers is becoming blurred because of the advent of global corporations and social media.

For many global organizations, unions are perceived as relics from the past and they push back on unionizing because they insist their workers' lucrative perks make them unnecessary. Older workers who generally favor unionizing are frustrated because they do not have a united stand as younger workers (Gen Zs and Millennials) have no reference point as to the unions' relevance. Yet, workers' voices must be part of the everyday social dialogue and their interests, however varied and decentralized, cannot be ignored or simply addressed through unilaterally presented benefits, however benevolent they may be.

For organizations struggling with creating an equitable and inclusive workforce, workplace and work-partners, DE&I can become a valuable moderator. Using the 3-Step Equity Lens model, an organization should examine its practices to create both organization-wide and societal changes on social dialogues about social contracts that are divisive and must be corrected to achieve sustainable development. ISO 26000 provided the following counsel:

> **ISO** *Trade unions and employers' organizations, as the chosen representatives of the respective parties, have a particularly important role to play in social dialogue...Social dialogue is based on the recognition that employers and workers have both competing and mutual interests, and in many countries plays a significant role in industrial relations, policy formulation and governance...Social dialogue can take many forms and can occur at various levels. Workers may wish to form groups with a broader occupational, inter-occupational or geographical coverage. Employers and workers are in the best position to decide jointly the most appropriate level. One way to do this is by adopting framework agreements supplemented by local organization-level agreements in accordance with national law or practice...At times, social dialogue may address contentious matters, in which case the parties can establish a dispute resolution process. Social dialogue can also concern grievances for which a complaints mechanism is important, particularly in countries where the fundamental principles and rights at work are not adequately protected. Such a grievance mechanism may also apply to a subcontracted workforce...International social dialogue is a growing trend, and includes regional and global dialogue and agreements between organizations operating internationally and international trade union organizations.*

> *ISO 26000:2010, pages 37-38.*

EQUITY OPPORTUNITY IN DE&I SOCIAL DIALOGUES

Both employers and workers would gain when social dialogues are also viewed as part of a holistic DE&I construct. Such focus presents the opportunities to use DE&I as moderator to find fair and just equitable solutions to disputes over employer-workers activities, roles, and responsibilities. Further, although disputes can be paralyzing when it comes to social dialogue in the workplace, DE&I-related ones like race or gender can be even more so. Using equity opportunity as a focus, both employers and workers can create a safe and collegial atmosphere to adjust or correct current inequitable or non-inclusive practices (racial, gender and shared profits/wealth, etc.) with socially responsible fair and just ones. It begins by establishing trust through adjustments or corrections to practices that are obviously biased towards any social dialogue.

ISO   *An organization should:*

☐ *recognize the importance for organizations of social dialogue institutions, including at the international level, and applicable collective bargaining structures;*

☐ *respect at all times the right of workers to form or join their own organizations to advance their interests or to bargain collectively;*

☐ *not obstruct workers who seek to form or join their own organizations and to bargain collectively, for instance by dismissing or discriminating against them, through reprisals or by making any direct or indirect threat so as to create an atmosphere of intimidation or fear...*

ISO 26000:2010, page 38.

Social dialogue provides a great platform for organizations to transform their practices into socially responsible ones. While social dialogues can take many forms, it is important to realize that when it comes to addressing inequalities in the workplace and in the communities impacted by an organization's decisions, identifying and engaging all impacted stakeholders is not only crucial, but necessary. That organizations have power and authority over workers is not debatable; how this power is exercised is where socially responsible norms come into play. Organizations that pursue social dialogues as a social responsibility moderated by DE&I should be aware of some organizational practices that might be unjust and unfair towards workers who support, entertain or participate in discussions about unionization or other representation. The following represent some of the ways in which these unjust practices manifest in social dialogues:

1. Launch an internal surveillance program to monitor workers' dialogue around collective representation activities or give the impression that such surveillance is ongoing to cause fear within the rank and file or produce distortion in the social dialogue echo chambers.

2. Threaten to deny promised benefits or wage increases, annual bonusses, promotions or other benefits already provided or in the pipeline to be provided.
3. Demonstrate disappointment when workers broach the subject of seeking potential collective representation and undermine the process by promising new benefits to deter them from pursuing it.
4. Threaten loss of job or conversion of current jobs to subcontracts when workers insist on unionizing or forming other associations to advocate for their collective interests.
5. Threaten to offset any gains achieved from unionized negotiations from existing benefits, thus making any collective bargaining wins an exercise in futility.
6. Engage in the solicitation of grievances and complaints and then use the data to target new benefits that derail any social dialogue around collective bargaining.
7. Prohibit or discourage the discussions amongst workers of disciplinary actions taken against anyone for entertaining or wanting to belong to a collective bargaining unit or record negative comments on workers' personnel files for participating on any collective bargaining or representation activities.
8. Imply or suggest that support for collective bargaining or any form of representation is tantamount to insubordination or a form of employer-intimidating or bullying (Streitfeld 2021).

Although the above are some practices that organizations may be engaged in "innocently," they are often performed quite deliberately, and injure workers' engagement as stakeholders of interest. They also create almost a police-state-like atmosphere. These practices will likely impede the free flow of social dialogues about social contracts, in a way that perpetuates divisive norms and makes a mockery of social responsibility pursuits. Groups that have been traditionally outside of the accepted norms continue to feel the pinch of these inequitable and non-inclusive organizational practices and bear the wounds to show for them. Organizations would benefit by using the 3-Step Equity Lens to assist in framing the dialogue around equity and inclusion matters.

EQUITY RECONCILIATION IN DE&I SOCIAL DIALOGUES

There are contentious DE&I-related social dialogues which have been uncomfortable to address openly for a long time, as well as emerging dialogues because of the new global focus on the subject. In these situations, both the employer and the workers should seek to regularly assess and reconcile the organization's DE&I commitments with its actual policies, decision-making processes, and practices. Where there are gaps, the focus should be improving upon existing agreements and commitments or replacing them with socially responsible alternatives that are fair and just. When social dialogues are moderated by DE&I, they become a continuum of actionable conversations – not just training events or organizational wide powwows (though these too have their rightful places). Social dialogues in informal settings by people that would not be caught dead discussing the inconsistencies in policies and practices on DE&I matters are a good segue to normalizing the difficult social norms that have divided us. These impromptu moments can bring our shared humanity to play and enable us to bridge gaps with actionable steps.

 An organization should:

☐ *where changes in operations would have major employment impacts, provide reasonable notice to the appropriate government authorities and representatives of the workers so that the implications may be examined jointly to mitigate any adverse impact to the greatest possible extent;*

☐ *as far as possible, and to an extent that is reasonable and non-disruptive, provide duly designated worker representatives with access to authorized decision makers, to workplaces, to the workers they represent, to facilities necessary to perform their role and to information that will allow them to have a true and fair picture of the organization's finances and activities...*

ISO 26000:2010, page 38.

EQUITY DISRUPTION IN SOCIAL DIALOGUES

Both employer and workers should recognize the need for representation from each of their perspectives in addressing DE&I matters. An organization would do well to engage all stakeholders in addressing its DE&I matters and not approach it from strictly top-down or press conference statements. In situations where adequate social dialogue protections do not exist through local, regional or national laws, organizations should not muzzle their employees from expressing themselves but rather create a valid complaints mechanism for addressing DE&I matters. ISO 26000 recommends that organizations also consider participating in social dialogues when appropriate *"... in employers' organizations as a means of creating opportunities for social dialogue and extending their expression of social responsibility through such channels."* The need for organizations to speak out to disrupt divisive social contracts through social dialogues is greater now than at any other time because of the power and influence of organizations today and of social media. Our shared humanity and planet demand that organizations collectively identify and engage to resolve structural and perennial divisive norms that previous generations failed to address and instead punted them forward.

 An organization should:

☐ *refrain from encouraging governments to restrict the exercise of the internationally recognized rights of freedom of association and collective bargaining. For example, organizations should avoid locating a subsidiary or sourcing from companies located in specialized industrial zones where freedom of association is restricted or prohibited, even if national regulation recognizes that right, and they should refrain from participating in incentive schemes based on such restrictions.*

ISO 26000:2010, page 38.

SOCIAL DIALOGUE
Governance-centered inclusion actionable steps

in formulating and facilitating its overall social dialogue on social responsibility, an organization should also consider DE&I as a currency for negotiating value-added decisions. Where appropriate, the organization should also consider involvement in relevant external organizations as a way to continue the DE&I social dialogue, where it can exercise its influence in dealing with inequalities as an expression of its social responsibility. Are the people working on creating and implementing DE&I policies and programs representative of the groups that have historically been marginalized and disenfranchised? Do they have an independent voice in all related social dialogues – including the freedom to negotiate, exchange information and other consultation practices without fear of reprisals? While they do not have to be members of the disenfranchised racial group, they still should be able to demonstrate their interest in practices that are diverse, equitable and inclusive. For instance, Benjamin Butler was the Chair of the House Judicial Committee who introduced the Civil Rights bill of 1875. In introducing the bill, Chair Butler shared his own experience watching African Americans fight and die in defense of a racially equitable America during the Civil War. Then he shared his own personal resolve to defend the civil rights of African Americans: *"May my right hand forget its cunning and my tongue cleave to the roof of my mouth if I ever fail to defend the rights of these men who have given their blood for me and my country. . . . God helping me, I will keep that oath (History, Art & Archives 2021)."*

The African-American legislators who served in the 43rd Congress with Chair Butler had no doubt that they could trust him. Of course, the Democrats attacked Butler to no end and his resolve eventually cost him reelection. In the transcendent scheme of life, Chair Butler went to meet his Maker knowing he stood for righteousness by defending the civil rights of the defenseless—a godlike attribute indeed!

Social dialogue on DE&I issues, while related to the broader issues an organization deals with as part of its eco-system, still requires a more systemic approach because divisive norms continue to be sustained by racism, gender inequalities, caste and tribal behaviors, and other forms of xenophobia. In approaching the creation, modification or updating of existing social dialogue practices, an organization should consider integrating the 3-Step Inclusion principles to provide the correct framework. Employers and workers engaged in DE&I-moderated social dialogue should agree to be guided by redemption-driven, restoration-focused, responsibility-centered principles as they discuss value-added decision-making processes and the performance of routine activities. This framework gives the organization's representatives the tools to find creative means to resolving inequities and inclusion challenges that have paralyzed societies for so long.

Governance-centered inclusion actionable steps in SOCIAL DIALOGUE
1. In reviewing your organization's policies and procedures around social dialogue, how do they align with your DE&I policy, commitments, and corporate proclamations on the matter?   2. If there are gaps, what are the actionable steps and timelines you have identified to narrow or eliminate them based on the 3-Step Equity Lens model?   3. Were all relevant stakeholders identified and engaged in the review, modification or development of your policies and procedures around your DE&I moderated social dialogue practices? 

LABOUR PRACTICES ISSUE 4: DE&I AS MODERATOR FOR HEALTH AND SAFETY AT WORK

Health and safety practices at work address how employers and workers think about them within a continuum of policies and procedures that frame organizational decisions and activities performed in a safe work environment across the organization's eco-system and beyond. Organizational life is often strongly manifested through an organization's health and safety culture. A health and safety culture cannot be developed or improved without senior leadership engagement and support. But it can also not be a culture that is handed down from a top-down approach, in which management makes all the decisions about health and safety and the workers have no say on the matter.

HEALTH AND SAFETY AT WORK
Knowledge-informed diversity call to action

The health and safety environment at work affects how employers and workers think about related policies and how they are developed or modified over time, especially as conditions of work change. Although traditionally, the workplace was assumed to be the one designated and maintained by the organization, COVID 19 and the Shelter-in-Place directives changed it all. Since COVID, a hybrid model has become part of the equation and now organizations are challenged to find new ways to support workers' behavior tied to health and safety at work—wherever that work is performed. Within the workplace, socially responsible organizations have generally addressed health and safety issues as economic bottom-line ones because they have been known to reduce overall costs, improve worker satisfaction, and make work performance easier.

But what happens when workers perform work in their homes? Is the organization also responsible for their physical, mental, and social well-being while working remotely? For example, wrist injuries and back pains have been correlated with sitting positions in the workplace and organizations generally have policies and procedures to address how to prevent them. Can these be extended to the home office? These are some of the simpler questions organizations are challenged with today. The complexity increases depending on the kind of work performed through the hybrid model.

Many global corporations today contend that today's workplaces are the safest they have ever been thanks to regulatory oversight from governmental agencies. Some go further to cite their perks and lavish benefits provided to workers today, some of which were unheard of in previous generations. Still at issue is whether workers believe that their health and safety concerns are being heard and taken seriously. Whether through unions or workers representative groups, health and safety issues must be addressed collaboratively.

ISO 26000 suggested using joint labor-management health and safety committees as an approach. In this approach, workers are involved in gathering information, reporting, recording, and investigating accidents, inspecting and responding to problems raised by management and workers, and developing and disseminating safety manuals and training programs:

ISO *Worker representatives on these committees should not be appointed by management but elected by the workers themselves. Membership in these committees should be equally divided among management and worker representatives and should include both men and women, whenever possible. The committees should be of sufficient size for all shifts, sections and locations of the organization to be represented. They should not be considered a substitute for works councils or workers' organizations..*

ISO 26000:2010, page 40.

Another aspect of health and safety at work that is even more important is the impact on minorities and disadvantaged groups. A racial group that has been historically marginalized by society often experiences the same marginalization or devaluation of their humanity in the workforce and workplace in the areas of health and safety unless there is an intentional DE&I commitment that overrides the stigmatization. It explains why minorities are often overrepresented in high-risk jobs and underrepresented in the management and supervisory ranks. One glaring problem with minorities caught in a no-voice, no-power tussle within an organizational ecosystem is that they are not taken seriously even when they report working conditions that cause them harm. Other times these minorities or society-driven disenfranchised groups are afraid to report their work-related health and safety concerns because of fear of losing their jobs or other punitive actions. ISO 26000 provides some guidance in this area:

ISO *Health and safety at work concerns the promotion and maintenance of the highest degree of physical, mental and social well-being of workers and prevention of harm to health caused by working conditions. It also relates to the protection of workers from risks to health and the adaptation of the occupational environment to the physiological and psychological needs of workers. The financial and social burden on society of work-related illness, injuries and death is heavy. Accidental and chronic pollution and other workplace hazards that are harmful for workers may also have impacts on communities and the environment. Health and safety concerns arise over dangerous equipment, processes, practices and substances (chemical, physical and biological).*

ISO 26000:2010, page 38.

HEALTH AND SAFETY AT WORK
Creativity-driven equity opportunity/reconciliation/disruption

An organization's health and safety culture determine and broadcasts the values and expectations practiced throughout its eco-system. This is partly because workers spend a significant portion of their time at work—40 or more hours—and the place where health and safety at work violations traditionally occurred before their impacts rumble through communities. In large corporations, unions or bargaining units advocated for the interests of workers. Labor unions helped curtail some of the dangers that workers and communities were subjected to by policies and corporate decisions that impacted them at work and in their neighborhoods. Today, righting the wrongs – potential and actual – before they even take root through DE&I moderated decision-making practices (informed by the 3-Equity Lens Model) is a forward-facing approach that becomes practical when health and safety at work are addressed together by all stakeholders. In reviewing the organization's health and safety eco-system, attention should be paid to equity opportunities, reconciliations, and equity disruptions.

EQUITY OPPORTUNITY IN HEALTH AND SAFETY AT WORK

Health and safety at work matters have a direct correlation to the organization's overall health and safety costs, which also impacts the three bottom lines of profit, people, and planet. This makes health and safety at work an area of DE&I focus because of its social responsibility implications. It includes prevention before and protection after injury or death occurs, the impact on the workers, their immediate families and community at large. Stakeholders' interests generally are not a straight-line net sum game when it comes to health and safety at work. When a mother or father is injured on the job and cannot earn a paycheck, the impact is not only felt by them but by all who depend on that income for their sustenance and wellbeing, including, for example, their local grocery provider. This is even more reason to address health and safety at work as a DE&I matter and look for opportunities to quickly correct unjust and unfair practices:

ISO *An organization should:*
- ☐ *understand and apply principles of health and safety management, including the hierarchy of controls: elimination, substitution, engineering controls, administrative controls, work procedures and personal protective equipment;*
- ☐ *communicate the requirement that workers should follow all safe practices at all times and ensure that workers follow the proper procedures;*

- provide the safety equipment needed, including personal protective equipment, for the prevention of occupational injuries, diseases and accidents, as well as for dealing with emergencies;
- provide adequate training to all personnel on all relevant matters;
- respect the principle that workplace health and safety measures should not involve monetary expenditures by workers; and
- base its health, safety and environment systems on the participation of the workers concerned and recognize and respect the rights of workers to:

  - obtain timely, full and accurate information concerning health and safety risks and the best practices used to address these risks;
  - freely inquire into and be consulted on all aspects of their health and safety related to their work;
  - refuse work that is reasonably considered to pose an imminent or serious danger to their life or health or to the lives and health of others;
  - seek outside advice from workers' and employers' organizations and others who have expertise;
  - report health and safety matters to the appropriate authorities;
  - participate in health and safety decisions and activities, including investigation of incidents and accidents; and
  - be free of the threat of reprisals for doing any of these things

ISO 26000:2010, page 39.

EQUITY RECONCILIATION IN HEALTH AND SAFETY AT WORK

When organizations commit to become socially responsible, they should also commit to treat health and safety at work as part and parcel of its DE&I culture. On Culture of Health, Robert Wood Johnson Foundation (RWJF) provides a holistic framework that can guide the health and safety at work culture moderated by DE&I:

A Culture of Health is broadly defined as one in which good health and well-being flourish across geographic, demographic, and social sectors; fostering healthy equitable communities guides public and private decision making; and everyone has the opportunity to make choices that lead to healthy lifestyles. This requires that society be free of systems and structures that perpetuate racial inequities. The exact definition of a Culture of Health can look very different to different people. A national Culture of Health must embrace a wide variety of beliefs, customs, and values. Ultimately it will be as diverse and multifaceted as the population it serves (Robert Wood Johnson Foundation n.d.).

This is a broad enough definition to slip in the organization's health at work decision-making processes and practices moderated by its customs, values, and beliefs—the very definition of an organization's culture. On Safety Culture, California's State Compensation Insurance Fund offered this "Safe at Work California" definition, which serves as a good holistic framework that supports organizational beliefs, customs, and values moderated by DE&I. It defines Safety Culture as:

> *The attitudes, beliefs, perceptions, and values that a company shares in relation to workplace safety. The foundation for building and maintaining a positive safety culture is a collaborative effort. It involves the owner, top management, supervisors, and employees. Other safety culture features include employee engagement, accountability, and cross-functional communication throughout the business. A positive safety culture emphasizes that safety is a core element designed into every aspect of the organization. It also emphasizes that safety is everyone's job, and that it is a measurable goal worth achieving (Safe 2020).*

Socially responsible organizations should periodically assess their health and safety policies and procedures and practices to make sure they are consistent with their DE&I commitments. Reconciling practice with policy requires the engagement of all stakeholders. ISO provides the following guidance:

ISO *An organization should:*

☐ *develop, implement and maintain an occupational health and safety policy based on the principle that strong safety and health standards and organizational performance are mutually supportive and reinforcing;*

☐ *analyse and control the health and safety risks involved in its activities;*

☐ *address the specific ways in which occupational safety and health (OSH) risks differently affect women (such as those who are pregnant, have recently given birth or are breastfeeding) and men, or workers in particular circumstances such as people with disabilities, inexperienced or younger workers...*

ISO 26000:2010, page 39.

EQUITY DISRUPTION IN HEALTH AND SAFETY AT WORK

In the twenty-first century, organizations stand at the crossroads of leading the rest of society and nation-states out of the doldrums of the impacts of industrial revolutions and divisive social norms. For a long time, health and safety were sacrificed at the altar of profit for a few industrialists. Some of these industrialists (to their credit), once they gained fame and notoriety, turned some of their wealth to address societal health and safety issues, but from a place of after-the-fact benevolence. Social responsibility is much more than benevolent gestures; it fundamentally hangs on the respect for the rule of law and conformity with legally binding obligations.

The fact that the industrial revolution led to the abuse of our environment and the misuse of people is not in question because global warming, climate change and global inequities are reflective mirrors of the excesses of this period—one that laid the foundation for our knowledge evolution today. Yet, during that era, the industrialists complied with some if not all existing health and safety at work laws—laws that struggled to catchup with the times and with the impacts of corporate decisions on people and society. These laws then did not preserve and protect our shared natural resources from corporate abuse because we now face global warming and climate change repercussions further exacerbated by the super-rich and the despondent-poor divide. This is not to exempt the technology and the knowledge revolutions from their own contributions to health and safety at work bad decision-making processes and practices. The difference is that today, organizations are less likely to get away with what would have been treated with kids gloves in the past because of global awareness and the ease with which information can be disseminated. At the very least,

ISO   *An organization should:*
- [ ] *record and investigate all health and safety incidents and problems in order to minimize or eliminate them;*
- [ ] *provide equal health and safety protection for part-time and temporary workers, as well as subcontracted workers;*
- [ ] *strive to eliminate psychosocial hazards in the workplace, which contribute or lead to stress and illness...*

ISO 26000:2010, page 39.

HEALTH AND SAFETY AT WORK
Governance-centered inclusion actionable steps

Without a full buy-in into our diverse shared humanity, it may be easier for a decision maker to designate a high-risk work environment as a panacea for solving equity and inclusion disparities by hiring or engaging individuals and organizations from marginalized groups. After all, if these marginalized groups are not perceived as equal in humanity, individuals representing them could easily be treated as a more expendable "commodity". It is through governance-centered inclusionary principles that balanced action steps are developed that are socially responsible and that do not lead to statistical numbing. In addition to the NYT lessons for the future list presented above, governance-centered inclusion should resolve the equity issues raised in health and safety at work by addressing them in actionable steps that move the organization forward in its social responsibility commitments. ISO 26000 provides the following guidance:

Governance-centered inclusion actionable steps in HEALTH AND SAFETY AT WORK

1. In reviewing your organization's policies and procedures around health and safety at work, how do they align with your DE&I policy, commitments, and corporate proclamations on the matter?
2. If there are gaps, what are the actionable steps and timelines you have identified to narrow or eliminate them based on the 3-Step Equity Lens model?
3. Were all relevant stakeholders identified and engaged in the review, modification or development of your policies and procedures around your DE&I moderated health and safety at work practices?

CASE STUDY 3:
Union Carbide Disaster in India and its consequential Impacts

On December 3, 1984, at about 12:40 A.M., Bhopal entered the history books as the place for one of the largest industrial accidents of modern times. Dangerously high levels of liquid MIC leaked from the Union Carbide India Limited (UCIL) Pesticide Plant. One of the Plant's three storage tanks released plumes of toxic gas into the air that was more lethal than cyanide. At the time of the accident, the official account estimated that at least 2,000 people were killed and over 200,000 injured in Bhopal city alone.

Five years after the accident, on February 15, 1989, Union Carbide Corporation (UCC) the parent company of UCIL agreed to a $470 million settlement with the Indian government to compensate victims (Richter 1989). Twenty-five years after the disaster, on June 6, 2010, eight former Executives of the Indian plant were found guilty of negligence. Seven of the eight executives were sentenced to two years in prison and fined $2,100 or 100,000 rupees while the eighth was deceased at the time of the sentencing (Kumar 2010). Overall, it took decades for people to be held accountable for the accident.

Background
In 1970, UCIL established a pesticide plant in north Bhopal. UCIL was a subsidiary of an American company—Union Carbide Corporation (UCC)–

which owned 50.9 percent of the plant. Indian interests, including the government of India, owned 49.1 percent (Diamond 1985). At issue later in this partnership is whether majority ownership translates to full control. Bhopal is the capital of the state of Madhya Pradesh, India. The Bhopal Municipality which covered about 285 square kilometers was topographically divided by two dams: the north dam was home to the slums and the railway station where the poor people lived. The south was more affluent, with modern buildings and villas.

In late 1977, UCIL began manufacturing the pesticide locally. The process for manufacturing the pesticide first involved the shipment of methyl isocyanate (MIC) and alpha-naphthol in stainless steel drums—the raw material—from the Union Carbide MIC plant in the United States. Then a cocktail of other chemicals, including monomethylamine (MMA) and phosgene, were used to complete the production cycle. Three underground storage tanks were built using "safe" technology materials to prevent leakage; together they had the capacity to store up to 68,000 liters of liquid MIC (Diamond 1985).

In the early 1980s, the Bhopal plant began manufacturing its own MIC based on the basic equipment and the technology transfer of the know-how provided by the UCC. From all indications this was a transactional deal between the Indian governments (national, state, and local) and Union Carbide (and its subsidiaries in the United States and in India). There were no known outreach efforts to prepare, warn or inform the community and its local authorities of what could happen to them and their loved ones in case of gas accident. In fact, the New York Times reported at the time:

> Nearly all the workers interviewed were making their first public statements since the disaster. They gave their accounts in Hindi through an interpreter; some declined to be identified. Virtually all the workers said they knew methyl isocyanate was dangerous and some said they knew it could be fatal, but the dozen workers said they underestimated its toxicity. No one said he knew it could kill many people quickly. The Union Carbide Corporation technical manual for methyl isocyanate is pointed on the hazards of the chemical and states that it "may cause fatal pulmonary edema," which is an accumulation of fluid in the lungs. But although the manual was distributed to managers that handle methyl isocyanate at the Bhopal plant and was seen by some of the workers there, most of the factory's employees had not read or understood it, according to former technical officials at the factory (Diamond 1985).

The employees reported a lack of functional testing equipment to diagnose gas leakages. Instead, they relied on their sense of smell to detect any leakage. Maintenance audits were conducted but the recommendations were seldom performed, and when they did it was only with acrimony. Saving money was the foremost consideration in any decision-making – not the health and safety concerns of the workers or community. The parent company UCC would use this as their self-defense. According to the New York Times report by Stuart Diamond, *"The Union Carbide Corporation was required by Indian law to design, engineer, build and operate its Bhopal chemical plant with local labor, materials, machines and staff unless the company could prove to the Indian authorities that local resources were unavailable (Diamond 1985)."*

UCC agreed to establish the plant because it could produce the pesticides with Indian cheap labor in a developing country, reduce its cost of goods sold and expand its customer base across South Asia. Yet, both the Indian government and UCC knew that the local host community lacked the trained workforce and adequate technology to maintain such delicate chemical infrastructure. From all indications, the Indian government did not put in place stringent regulations to monitor the activities at the plant and UCC had little incentive to reduce any people or environmental risks after the production operations began (Cassels 1993). After the accident, UCC laid the blame on "sabotage" by a disgruntled employee, while the Indian government blamed UCC for the design and operational failures at the Plant.

A cascading collage of unaddressed problems that led to the Bhopal Gas disaster

The UCIL plant had its share of coverage in the media prior to the accident, compounded during and afterwards. The following represents telling stories of a disaster that was avoidable:

- In 1976, there were complaints from the local trade unions about frequent pollution at the plant
- In 1980, there was a report of a worker getting splashed with phosgene in the cause of carrying out his job function
- On or about January 1982, 24 workers were exposed and admitted to the hospital because of a phosgene leakage. Post incident investigation documented those workers were not expected to wear protective masks even if they were required by regulations. Then there was the looming question whether the masks were supplied in the first place to the workers.
- On or about August 1982, a chemical engineer was overexposed to dangerous levels of liquid MIC and suffered severe burns over 30 percent of his body.
- On or about October 1982, the MIC supervisor suffered severe chemical burns while two of his workers were dangerously exposed to the gases.
- From 1983 through much of 1984, MIC, phosgene, carbon tetrachloride and monomethylamine leaked frequently individually or in combinations.
- By early December 1984, several of the valves and lines were in poor working conditions while the plant's safety systems were for the most part non-functional.
- Between late night of December 2 and the wee hours of the 3, one cascading problem after another began to manifest detailing a chemical plant that had not been maintained properly and staff that knew little about what to do in the face

of a pending disaster. When the siren went off about 12:50 am on December 3, it was quickly shutoff so as not to alarm the community, a practice that began long before this eventful day.

- When the local police called the plant to find out what was going on, they were first assured that everything was under control, at a time when everything had already spun out of control. Workers attested to the fact that keeping the police in the dark about gas leaks was a long established informal managerial practice.
- The residents of Bhopal found out about the accident the hard way; many choked to death from the gases in the air, some in their sleep, others as they tried to flee the town or run to the hospital for help. By daylight, dead human bodies and animal carcasses lay everywhere.
- The local hospital was not warned to expect a surge of people needing medical attention or what sort of chemical mayhem they were expected to treat. By the time they learned it was MIC exposure, the hospital staff discovered they had no prior knowledge of the chemical, nor were they equipped to treat such human poisoning in such a large scale while trying to stay alive themselves.

Source: Diamond 1985

The Bhopal plant eventually put so much toxic gas into the atmosphere that it apocalyptically snuffed life out of humans, animals, and plants. The Bhopal chemical leak occurred without fanfare because the show began long before the leak occurred. Later analysis revealed an even more damning picture of the impact:

BHOPAL DEATH TOLL	
Official death toll reported December 3-6	Over 3,000
Unofficial initial death toll	7,000 to 8,000
Deaths to-date	Over 15,000
Number affected	About 600,000
Compensation	Union Carbide agreed to settlement of $470m in 1989

Source: Indian Supreme Court, Madhya Pradesh government, Indian Council of Medical Research. Retrieved from: *http://news.bbc.co.uk/1/hi/world/south_asia/8725140.stm*

APPLYING THE 3-STEP EQUITY LENS TO THE BHOPAL DISASTER

We can use the 3-Step Equity lens to peripherally discuss how such a disaster could have been avoided, knowing full well that there were other mitigating circumstances not reported about the decision-making processes and practices that created an environment in which such a disaster could occur. On February 3, 1985, the New York Times published a list of lessons learned from the Bhopal disaster that could inform socially responsible organizations on what to consider as they transfer their hazardous technologies to developing countries or deploy them in marginalized or disadvantaged people's neighborhoods. These lessons for the future were gathered from interviews with hundreds of specialists, residents, and officials of Bhopal. I have repurposed the list here by assigning them at the end of each discussion of the 3-Step Equity Lenses.

EQUITY OPPORTUNITY: Most experts agree that the standards followed by UCC in the United States for mitigating the risks and potential risks posed by utilizing their technology to produce liquid MIC was not the same as those employed by its subsidiary in India. It's typical for global corporations to employ different policies and procedures abroad – this is in fact very often why they choose to locate plants overseas, away from costly oversight. To avoid this, organizations must adhere to globally consistent standards.

In 1970, the United States Congress passed the Occupational Safety and Health Act of 1970 to provide health and safety at work legal guidance on acceptable working conditions. This led to the creation of Occupational Safety and Health Administration (OSHA) in 1971 to ensure healthy and safe working conditions for American workers and to enforce workplace standards and laws. Providing outreach, education and training assistance to organizations was also included in the mix as a preventative measure. By all accounts, OSHA regulations and enforcement powers have kept American workers safe, communities protected from avoidable industrial accidents and corporations honest about their safe and healthy working conditions. Where there have been reported violations or accidents, OSHA has enforced compliance with legal and financial penalties.

India has its own occupational and environmental safety laws and regulations. All indications point to the fact that they are not as strictly enforced as OSHA standards. The records make it apparent that UCCIL operations in India violated many health and safety working conditions norms; they failed to train, educate or implement any outreach good faith effort to inform its employees and its external stakeholders about the toxicity of MIC. All these failures were low-hanging fruits—opportunities missed to do the right things for a socially beneficial project. The inequities go even further. The plant economically benefited the nation, the company and its corporate investors, but only the Bhopal people suffered the consequences of the catastrophe.

Lessons from the NYT's interviews applicable to Equity Opportunity:
- ✓ Hazardous facilities often pose added risks in developing nations, where skilled labor and public understanding are often lacking. Special training is needed to compensate for these extra risks.
- ✓ Public education is critical in developing countries, where people often do not understand the hazards of toxic substances. Repeated drills and clear warning signals are needed (Diamond 1985).

EQUITY RECONCILIATION: The Bhopal disaster demonstrated the complicity of both the Indian government and the United States' UCC in the face of the moral conventions that they ignored (Cragg 2005). The Indian government agreed to the setup of the Pesticide Plant in support of the green revolution initiative launched by the local Bhopal government to become self-sufficient in crop productions in the late 1960s. This move enabled Indian agricultural production to increase bountifully. The economic benefits were substantial; quoting an agricultural economist of a major international company located in India, the New York Times wrote just days after the accident *"that pesticides had helped India cut its grain losses from 25 percent of the crop 10 or 15 years ago, to 15 percent today Boffey 1984)."*

However, even the employees who were the most at risk underestimated the dangers from methyl isocyanate gas leakage. The community was left in the dark or actively misled about the potential dangers they faced. After all, the plant provided much-needed jobs and was the main economic sustaining engine for the community. The disconnect here as evidenced by the closed plant after the disaster was that all the decision-making processes and practices and justifications that placed profit above people and planet concerns were penny-wise and pound-foolish.

The Bhopal pesticide plant disaster was a classic example of a statistical numbing phenomenon, in this case concerning health and safety at work— all avoidable with a social responsibility commitment moderated by DE&I. Socially responsible organizations respect the rule of law and comply with legally binding obligations and commit to going beyond when obligations arise from ethical and other values that are communally shared. Social responsibility moderated by DE&I can provide the mirror for organizations to review or evaluate the effectiveness of their policies and procedures around health and safety at work issues and prevent the dangers of statistical numbing.

Psychologically, the larger the numbers involved in disasters or catastrophic events about people, planet, and profit matters, the harder it is for people to remain emotionally engaged. Ten thousand people dying of COVID-19 nationally causes grave concerns but past the half million-mark, people's engagement tend to wane. An equipment failure that has potential to cause tremendous damage but causes only minor damage if at all, can cause managers and supervisors to downplay the urgency of any maintenance work requiring overtime – until a catastrophic event occurs. When local indigenous people groups burn down trees in the Amazon just to survive daily living, the resulting impacts contributes to global warming and climate change which also has uncontrollable effects in other affluent areas around the world through flooding and fires.

What happened that fateful day in Bhopal demonstrated how difficult and emotionally disengaging it becomes for people when far too many warning signs are ignored (with no immediate consequences), too many maintenance jobs delayed or neglected, and too many stakeholders disenfranchised (especially those who should have a seat at the table) while business as usual rules daily operations.

A healthy reconciliation of balancing the economic development needs of the locals with the education, protection, and development of workforce (the people) and protection of the environment in the long run is the best foundation for sustainable profit or prosperity.

Lessons from the NYT's interviews applicable to Equity Reconciliation:
- ✓ The more rural areas of the developing world should not be used to test complex new technology.
- ✓ A sense of urgency about all safety problems and attention to worst-case possibilities - routine in industrial countries but often not transferred to developing countries - should be part of worker training, especially in plants with a high turnover of personnel.
- ✓ The company headquarters should audit its plants in developing countries frequently, perhaps more often than it audits plants at home.
- ✓ Sophisticated backup safety systems, often installed in industrial nations, are needed to compensate for lapses in training and staff in developing nations, where they are needed more (Diamond 1985).

EQUITY DISRUPTION: When it was discovered that there were no testing instruments provided to the workers for detecting gas leakage, management should have intervened from the get-go. Smelling for gas after a leakage is not a best practice, but a recipe for disaster. This and many other maintenance problems identified after the accident were present before the accident but never taken seriously enough to be mitigated. It was a colossal leadership and management failure.

The Bhopal community stakeholders—people, hospital officials, police, NGOs—as stakeholders of interest and of influence appeared to have been left out in the entire process. Even the workers were uneducated about the toxicity of MIC (Diamond 1985). While the governmental powers and the company acknowledged the existence of these stakeholders, their input, and the courtesy due them to be informed about a looming potential danger were marginalized at best. It is doubtful that if there had been predictions of two thousand or more deaths in case of disaster that the Bhopal management would have remained complicit knowing that the community was alarmed by such a prospect. But whether it is one or thousands of deaths predicted, the decision-making processes and practices should always err on the side of caution or prevention and stop activities that pushes it forward to disastrous outcomes.

✓ Company executives should be technically - not just administratively - trained in businesses that use toxic materials; such training can compensate for a lack of technical know-how in the local plant staff.

✓ Many areas of the developing world are growing rapidly and without zoning laws. Suitable buffers should be placed around the factory to prevent the dangers of crowding.

✓ Cultural differences between foreign and host countries should be considered. If preventive maintenance is a new concept, it should be more thoroughly taught.

✓ Host governments should closely and continually inspect hazardous factories and their managements, enforcing strict and quick sanctions for safety lapses.

✓ In making agreements with multinational companies, the governments of developing countries should consider only those technologies that can be safely handled in the long run. It may be necessary to change laws that mandate turning factories over to local control completely (Diamond 1985).

LABOUR PRACTICES ISSUE 5: DE&I AS MODERATOR FOR HUMAN DEVELOPMENT AND TRAINING IN THE WORKPLACE

Human development and training have become the epicenter for divisive norms, establishing divisions of the "haves and have nots" with under-and above-ground streams dotting vistas of inequities representing irrecoverable lost human dreams and stymied potentials. The workplace presents the best opportunities for workers to think beyond their current limitations and see the possibilities of what they could aim for and become. This makes human development and training in the workplace a critical DE&I matter that requires full attention and deployment of all needed resources to address discriminatory practices.

Socially responsible organizations can assist workers within their ecosystem and society at large as well. Inequities in human development and training are responsible for poverty, lack of educational opportunities for all, equal justice for all under the law, food insecurities, climate change, etc. Therefore, when socially responsible organizations commit to the human development of their workers and where possible invest in the human development within the communities where they operate or have influence, they inexplicably contribute to ending divisive norms in many streams— streams that sometimes don't fit the rubric of performance metrics. Human development and training have become humankind's epicenter for divisive norms, establishing divisions of the "haves and have nots" reinforced by many under and above ground streams of inequities with generational roots springing to the surface in every continent.

HUMAN DEVELOPMENT AND TRAINING IN THE WORKPLACE
Knowledge-informed diversity call to action

Human development and training in the workplace must transcend the core subjects needed by the organization to perform its operational activities. It should include the rethinking of human development beyond just profit concerns. It should be driven by the good intentions of ending all dividing norms established by systemic and structural discriminatory practices which marginalize vulnerable groups and keeps them disadvantaged, while robbing society of their ultimate human potential and purpose. In this vein, ISO 26000 provides the following wisdom:

ISO *Human development includes the process of enlarging people's choices by expanding human capabilities and functioning, thus enabling women and men to lead long and healthy lives, to be knowledgeable and to have a decent standard of living. Human development also includes access to political, economic and social opportunities for being creative and productive and for enjoying self-respect and a sense of belonging to a community and contributing to society.*

ISO 26000:2010, page 50.

HUMAN DEVELOPMENT AND TRAINING IN THE WORKPLACE
Creativity-driven equity opportunity/reconciliation/disruption

Human development and training are equity-driven matters and should be used to narrow or eliminate inequities and exclusionary practices in the workplace. Providing professional development and training opportunities to individuals from minority and vulnerable groups begins the journey to parity and organizational wholeness. Utilizing DE&I as currency gives organizations the means to create value-added human development and training programs that uplift those who have historically faced discriminatory practices. ISO 26000 provides the following insight:

ISO *Organizations can use workplace policy and initiatives to further human development by addressing important social concerns, such as fighting discrimination, balancing family responsibilities, promoting health and well- being and improving the diversity of their workforces. They can also use workplace policy and initiatives to increase the capacity and employability of individuals. Employability refers to the experiences,* *competencies and qualifications that increase an individual's capacity to secure and retain decent work.*

ISO 26000:2010, page 50.

HUMAN DEVELOPMENT AND TRAINING IN THE WORKPLACE
Governance-centered inclusion actionable steps

Governance-centered inclusion should aim to resolve equity issues in workplace training by addressing them in actionable steps that move the organization forward in its commitments to social responsibility. ISO 26000 provides the following guidance:

An organization should:

- [ ] *provide all workers at all stages of their work experience with access to skills development, training and apprenticeships, and opportunities for career advancement, on an equal and non-discriminatory basis;*
- [ ] *ensure that, when necessary, workers being made redundant are helped to access assistance for new employment, training and counselling;*
- [ ] *establish joint labour-management programmes that promote health and well-being.*

ISO 26000:2010, page 50.

Governance-centered inclusion actionable steps in HUMAN DEVELOPMENT AND TRAINING IN THE WORKPLACE

1. In reviewing your organization's policies and procedures around human development and training in the workplace, how do they align with your DE&I policy, commitments, and corporate proclamations on the matter?
2. If there are gaps, what are the actionable steps and timelines you have identified to narrow or eliminate them based on the 3-Step Equity Lens model?
3. Were all relevant stakeholders identified and engaged in the review, modification or development of your policies and procedures around your DE&I moderated human development and training in the workplace practices?

CASE STUDY 4:

The American human development and training story

As the United States began to look beyond the Civil War, Congress realized it had a human development problem that required immediate action for the benefit of both poor white and black citizens. Two critical Acts were put in place which together were meant to bring wholeness to a nation that had gone to war with itself: (1) the Morrill Act of 1862 and (2) the Freedmen and Refugees Act of 1865 and 1866. Both Acts were good examples of utilizing human development and training as a panacea for discriminatory practices and waste of human potentials.

Consider the human development challenges faced by poor whites and poor blacks after the Civil War and where both demographics are today in their respective communal human developments—a direct consequence of training opportunities provided to one group at the expense of the other. In 1865, the African American population was the highest skilled workforce in the South. They had built the plantation capitalist system that made the South the fourth-largest economy in the world, while they remained poor and destitute. They built the railroads and maintained the supportive infrastructures of the day. Yet, when the land-based institutions were established by the Morrill Act of 1862, the institutions that emerged catered predominantly to poor whites who at that time were far behind the African American population in human development in the workplace—the plantations and the railroad construction and maintenance infrastructures.

The knowledge developed from the experiences of African Americans about farming in the South and in general equipment infrastructures and their maintenances were no doubt part of the foundational knowledge-base curriculum used to teach the emerging science referred to as agriculture and mechanics arts or A&M. What became the curriculum for teaching agriculture and mechanic arts in the institutions that dotted the American landscape were human development excellences for which African Americans had already developed the foundation over the course of two centuries. Yes, it was through lived experience, not knowledge taught in a classroom, but it was still the development and transmission of valuable knowledge and skills.

THE MORRILL ACT OF 1862

In 1862, U.S. Congress established the Morrill Act introduced by Vermont congressman Justin S. Morrill, which created government sponsored or aided Agricultural institutions:

> Under the provisions of the act, each state was granted 30,000 acres (12,140 hectares) of federal land for each member of

Congress representing that state. The lands were sold and the resulting funds were used to finance the establishment of one or more schools to teach "agriculture and the mechanic arts." Though the act specifically stated that other scientific and classical studies need not be excluded, its intent was clearly to meet a rapidly industrializing nation's need for scientifically trained technicians and agriculturalists. Military training was required to be included in the curriculum of all land-grant schools, and this provision led to the establishment of the Reserve Officers Training Corps, an educational program for future army, navy, and air force officers.

Some states established new schools with their land-grant funds; others turned the money over to existing state or private schools to be used for the establishment of schools of agriculture and mechanics (these came to be known as "A&M" colleges). Altogether, 69 land-grant schools were founded, offering programs in agriculture, engineering, veterinary medicine, and other technical subjects. Cornell University in New York (in part), Purdue University in Indiana, Massachusetts Institute of Technology, Ohio State University, the University of Illinois (Urbana), and the University of Wisconsin (Madison) are among the best-known land-grant schools (Britannica 2017).

Expectedly for the times, most of the 69 land grant schools, whether publicly or privately held, disproportionately favored White students. This began the rise of white generational prosperity at the expense of black prosperity and is one of the reasons why every generation of America since has faced racial reckoning. Consider that at the time these land grant institutions were taking root, many freed slaves already had established skillsets and expertise in agriculture and mechanic arts. The school-aged, freed slaves would have excelled in these land grant schools had they been allowed to attend. How do we know this? Largely because they grew up using the actual farming best practices of the day in the plantation farms as child laborers.

Instead, what became of America was generations of African Americans were deliberately denied the education that would have enabled them to own and grow generational wealth and positioned them and their posterity to arise as an American success story alongside their White co-citizens. This is one of the fundamental reasons why there is still unfinished business in the American capitalism adventure.

THE FREEDMEN AND REFUGEE ACT OF 1865

"From reconstruction to deconstruction" became the anthem that created a two-America story and a lost opportunity to utilize human development and training as a national healing tool. The sad part about the lost racial reconciliation realization was that all the stars were lined up for its full manifestation during Reconstruction. Congress understood that to give both the freed slaves and the bankrupt poor whites the best equitable framework to rebuild their lives, it needed legislation to actualize equality under the law through an equity promise. The freedmen's Bureau Act was established on March 3, 1865 for that purpose:

> On March 3, 1865, Congress passed "An Act to establish a Bureau for the Relief of Freedmen and Refugees" to provide food, shelter, clothing, medical services, and land to displaced Southerners, including newly freed African Americans. The Freedmen's Bureau was to operate "during the present war of rebellion, and for one year thereafter," and also established schools, supervised contracts between freedmen and employers, and managed confiscated or abandoned lands (US Senate n.d.).

The Freedmen and Refugee Act addressed the critical human development and training issues of the day—both then and now (because it remains an unfinished agenda): making the African American population and poor Whites whole from systemic racism and bad economic policies—respectively and collectively—to build a future for themselves and their American posterity. Two paramount human development and training issues at the time were (1) land distribution or reallocation—an effective economic sustainability policy or growth tool intended to give freed slaves ownership of their destinies and (2) the establishment of educational institutions and the opportunities they create for expanding the human potential and prosperity.

President Abraham Lincoln, before his assassination, was both an advocate and supporter of reconciling a divided nation through policies that gave both poor whites and blacks the opportunities to jointly build their American success stories. President Lincoln believed this was the equitable and inclusive framework to guide the nation forward.

Lincoln was rejected by the Southern Whites and got elected as President without their votes—in fact they made sure he was not even on their ballots. Yet, during the Civil War, President Lincoln gave a speech where he expressed his sympathy for them. Instead of seeing the Southern Whites as adversaries worthy of annihilation, he took a different tone. Confronted by a woman who could not understand why he took a conciliatory position on the south, President Lincoln wisely responded:

> We are not enemies, but friends. We must not be enemies. Though passion may have strained, it must not break our bonds of affection. The mystic chords of memory will swell when again touched, as surely they will be, by the better angels of our nature.

Compare this magnanimity of beliefs acted out in support of human development and training programs like the Morrill Act and the eventual Freedmen and Refugee Act to the dastardly way his successor President Andrew Johnson approached both. In February 1866, the Freedmen bill was sent to President Johnson, with all indication that he would sign it into law. He surprised Congress when he vetoed it. In doing so, President Johnson provided the generic template consistently used since then to undermine or oppose any governmental program that benefits African Americans: "it's *an infringement on state or individual rights, too expensive, and represents discrimination against white people."* Never mind that the Freedmen and Refugees Act included provisions for poor White people; the narrative had been set.

Since Congress had placed the Freedmen's Bureau Act in the War Department under the President or Executive Branch, President Johnson argued it would create a military or police state throughout the country. President Johnson insisted that such an Act had the potential of becoming permanent by virtue of human nature because the enforcers are likely to find reasons for why their roles were indispensable and more time needed for the enforcement to become the norm. Further, President Johnson argued that since the Government did not provide any assistance to White people as a class in the past, it should not aid Black people regardless of whether they had toiled for free for their white masters for generations. He argued:

> *[Government] has never founded schools for any class of our own people; not even for ophans of those who have fallen in the defence of the Union...It has never deemed itself authorized to expend the public money for the rent or purchase of homes for the thousands, not to say millions, of the white race who are honestly toiling from day to day for their subsistence (Johnson 1866)."*

The above sentiments no doubt permeated the spirit of how President Johnson's administration carried out its policies and politics in favor of White ruling elite even when poor White people were used as the cover. The very Act that President Johnson opposed had provisions for poor Whites just as it did for freed slaves. Had the Act only benefitted only poor Whites and excluded black people, would President Johnson had signed it? The Bill clearly was for the benefit of both poor Whites and freed slaves but what transpired in America after that benefitted mostly White people.

At the time of President Johnson's veto, the land grant institutions as a new American school enterprise were already 4 years old when he claimed that government should not build schools for freed slaves because it had not done so for White people. This sentiment—shared by Southern politicians— would lead to the creation of "black codes" which barred whites and blacks from teaching black people or allowing them any formal education. These institutions disproportionately benefited White people, fully paid by the state, federal, and philanthropic funding, giving them an undue advantage in the agricultural and other fields and disadvantaging the black people. Before this, blacks were poised for even greater self-sufficiency within the American capitalistic system; the changes deliberately excluded them.

These examples of how an organization can address human development and training as a social responsibility was exactly what the US Congress had intended with the enactment of the Morrill and Freedmen and Refugee Acts. President Lincoln exemplified these values because he respected our shared humanity and sought to heal its divided norms. Americans and the world at large can only wonder what America would have become today, had President Lincoln lived. It's likely that the South would have found a champion of human development for both poor Whites and blacks and perhaps today Lincoln would be hailed as the Uniter-in-Chief.

Instead, President Johnson became the first Divider-in-Chief in post-Civil War America. His policies and unabashed support for southern whites—rich and poor—against the human development interests of black Americans emboldened those who wanted a separate but equal America even to this day. President Johnson knew and understood how advanced in workplace skills the African American community had become and the power they wielded in the capitalist economy of the South. In short, they represented a threat. In vetoing the Freedmen's Bureau Bill of February 1866, President Johnson described what probably represented the threat most poor Whites felt about having freed slaves as labor competitors:

His condition is not so exposed as may at first be imagined. He is in a portion of the country where his labor cannot be spared. Competition for his services from planters, from those who are constructing or repairing railroads, and from capitalists in his vicinage, or from other States, will enable him to command almost his own terms (Johnson 1866).

Yes, it was true that freed slaves did have advantages, having worked on most of the infrastructural projects of the time and in the process having developed more advanced marketable and on-demand skillsets. But in the court of social justice, it was unjust to purposefully disadvantage them when they had no generational wealth or access to capital to independently actualize these knowledge assets. They needed the government to balance the scales and provide help—help that President Johnson believed should be offered only to poor White people.

The above observation of the advantage African Americans had over their poor White counterparts was made when Frederick Douglass and the Black leadership of that day met with Johnson to ask for federal assistance in enabling the freed slaves actualize their respective life, liberty and pursuit of happiness American dream.

President Johnson as an astute student of history contended, and rightly so, that the Civil War was orchestrated by the plantation owners who owned the best and most productive real estate for farming cotton in the South. During the period before and after the war, cotton was king and it made the South the 4th largest economy in the world and the bedrock of a plantation capitalism economy. King cotton produced more millionaires in the South than in any other region in the country at the time, and made the slaves the best skilled labor force upon whose backs the plantation economy rested and the poorest demographic.

President Johnson knew that if the freed slaves participated in the free market without the discriminatory practices in the South, they would fare better than the poor Whites anywhere in the country but especially in the South. In vetoing the Freedmen's Bureau Bill, President Johnson made this case eloquently:

> He also possess a perfect right to change his place of abode; and if, therefore, he does not find in one community or State a mode of life suited to his desires, or proper remuneration for his labor, he can move to another, where that labor is more esteemed and better rewarded. In truth, however, each State, induced by its own wants and interests, will do what is necessary and proper to retain within its borders all the labor that is needed for the development of resources. The laws that regulate supply and demand will maintain their force, and the wages of the laborer will be regulated thereby. There is no danger that the exceedingly great demand for labor will not operate in favor of the laborer (Johnson 1866).

President Johnson knew very well that Blacks could not leave the South without getting killed, maimed or having other heinous crimes committed against their families. Ironically, in a plantation capitalistic system, had the laws of supply and demand been allowed to play out for the freed slaves, African Americans would be one of the richest and self-sustaining demographics alongside their White brothers and sisters, throughout the United States today. This is the evil that systemic and structural racism robbed America from achieving in its racial equity reconciliation journey when it chose instead to marginalize and disadvantage its Black citizens.

In May 1865, President Johnson appointed Maj. Gen. Oliver Otis Howard as commissioner of the Freedmen's Bureau. The Act provided the infrastructural systems required to implement human development programs meant to prepare Americans to lead the nations despite the formidable opposition from the Presidency. The national archive summarized the role the Act played:

> Although the Bureau was not abolished until 1872, the bulk of its work was conducted from June 1865 to December 1868. While a major part of the Bureau's early activities included the supervision

of abandoned and confiscated property, its mission was to provide relief and help formerly enslaved people become self-sufficient. Bureau functions included issuing rations and clothing, operating hospitals and refugee camps, and supervising labor contracts between planters and freedpeople. The Bureau also managed apprenticeship disputes and complaints, assisted benevolent societies in the establishment of schools, helped in legalizing marriages entered into during slavery, and provided transportation to refugees and freedpeople who were attempting to reunite with their family or relocate to other parts of the country. As Congress extended the life of the Bureau, it added other duties, such as assisting Black soldiers and sailors in obtaining back pay, bounty payments, and pensions (United States Senate n.d.).

Implemented by the spirit and the law, the Freedmen and Refugee Act would have made America great, not weaken it. After two and a half centuries (1619 to 1868) of repressive slavery labor system that used African Americans as free labor, the seven years allotted for changing things was unrealistically short. Yet, the pressure from the White Southerners, with the support from the White House, limited its impact. The notion that institutional slavery and its adverse impacts on African Americans was cured within 36 months (1865 to 1868) is like treating a stillbirth baby as though he or she was still alive post birth. Reclaiming one's lost human dignity and denied rights required much deeper generational investments in time and resources to be made whole.

This is instructive for organizational leaders today committed to the pursuit of social responsibility ideals. It is not a surprise that corporate and organizational leaders have not historically engaged about America's racial inequities dysfunction. Organizations tend to leave such issues to the government to resolve through political means.

The foundation for this complicity can be traced back to President Johnson's thinking that any movement towards racial equity was a journey to white disadvantage. It is an unjust idea that when black and brown people gain, white people lose. In truth, the equity plight of the millions of poor white people that President Johnson was supposedly advocating for was actually covered by the Freedmen Bill he vetoed. Therefore, his insistence that whites would suffer was a red herring and a cover story for what President Johnson and many Southerners feared to be a looming real possibility: Negro self-sufficiency under constitutional laws, which some misleadingly called "Negro Supremacy!"

Although he became the Divider-in-Chief, President Johnson's appointment of General Howard provides a good example of what organizational leaders can accomplish even when their bosses do not walk the social responsibility talk. General Howard used his influence and talent to assist in the creation of an institution that exemplified what the spirit of land grant institutions were meant to represent.

Howard University, named after General Howard would become one of the first land grant institutions to intentionally benefit freed slaves and represents one of the very few historically black institutions. Interestingly, the few black land-grant institutions also admitted white students, taking a more inclusive approach than their exclusively white counterparts. Some of the other early black institutions included Morehouse (1867), Hampton (1868), and Spellman (1881), to name a few. About Howard University:

> Shortly after the end of the American Civil War, members of The First Congregational Society of Washington considered establishing a theological seminary for the education of black clergymen. Within a few weeks, the project expanded to include a provision for establishing a university. Within two years, the University consisted of the Colleges of Liberal Arts and Medicine. The new institution was named for General Oliver Otis Howard, a Civil War hero, who was both the founder of the University and, at the time, Commissioner of the Freedmen's Bureau. Howard later served as President of the University from 1869 to 1874 (Wikipedia Contributors 2022).

> The U.S. Congress chartered Howard on March 10, 1867, and much of its early funding came from endowment, private benefaction, and tuition. (In the 20th and 21st centuries an annual congressional appropriation, administered by the U.S. Department of Education, funds Howard University and Howard University Hospital). In its first five years of operation, Howard University educated over 150,000 freed slaves (Wikipedia Contributors 2022).

The rapid pace with which Howard University came to fruition from planning to execution demonstrates what can happen when Americans of all races come together to address systemic and structural racial and gender inequities. This is instructive for leaders today who sincerely want to use their corporate influence for making our divisive norms a thing of the past. Corporate leaders are perhaps the most reliable players to lead the country to reclaim its lost destiny, because our political leadership is too fragmented and too knee-deep in the racial inequity quagmire to make meaningful progress.

From the time the Southern politicians were allowed back into the Union after the civil war, the battle to squash the racial equity agenda has been the main agenda of white supremacists and white nationalists who gravitate to politics as their preferred means for sustaining white power and privilege. Corporate and other non-political organizational leaders wield an often-unused power and influence to force equitable legislations—from rights to vote to standing up against any form of systemic and structural racism and gender inequities.

The United States' rise from the colonial days (when slave labor built its institutional power and economic infrastructure) through the period of Reconstruction (when the country took halting and frequently sabotaged steps towards its first racial equity reconciliation) and now into the twenty-first century (when systemic and structural racism still marginalizes its black and brown racial groups), the white racial group has disproportionately benefited from the credit side of the national socio-economic and political ledger. Therefore, when a white person growing up in the twenty-first century, enjoying the privileges that white prejudice built, believe they owe nothing to black and brown people, they are missing the point. For a racial equity accounting ledger to be balanced, both its credit and debit sides must be accounted for regardless of what time, amount or by whom the entry was made.

How far more racially equitable would the entire country be today if freed slaves had been allowed beginning in 1865 the opportunity to leverage their skills and fully participate in the labor market and higher education systems? What would our cities, suburbs and rural areas be today? Would white and black people working and living together because they shared a common history of demanding equal participation in the socio-economic and political development of America during and after reconstruction? None of this can happen without intentional investments in human development and training as panacea for discriminatory and inequitable norms.

Had President Lincoln not been killed, would the wealth distribution of America have had a foundational social justice framework where poor whites and freed slaves worked together to demand just distribution of the new American wealth? Just as European immigrants looked back and assisted their former homelands, perhaps Africa would have benefitted too if Black freedmen and women had established their own inheritance and success stories in America. Where would Africa be today if during the end of colonization in the 1950-60s they'd had the knowledge transferred from their well-established and successful African American relatives?

All these dreams of a harmonized and racially equitable America are now in the hands of organizations and new generations of citizens who are tired of the polarization and the unjust and unfair hand dealt the African American demographic. This is the America's Mission Accomplished Generation, who no longer have the stomach to endure the legacies—both for those on the receiving and giving ends. Most Americans—white, black and every shade in between—are genuinely seeking an end to racial and gender inequities, especially since the George Floyd ritual sacrifice. Protesters from every walk of life showed up in support of our shared humankind and loudly rejected the barbaric killings by Officers on the payroll of citizens. One thing is for sure, a good number of Americans must share in the fight to end racial and gender inequities in one generation. Perhaps we can draw inspiration from three individuals who demonstrate the power of human development and training.

The Real MCoy: Ever heard the cliché the "Real McCoy"? While there is dispute from experts as to when the cliché was first used, Elijah McCoy's inventions made him the strongest candidate. "Real McCoy" has become synonymous with genuine originality, the real undiluted stuff. Elijah was born May 2, 1844 in Canada to George and Mildred—African American parents who fled Kentucky in the United States through the underground railroad. Elijah's birth in Canada gave him the untethered opportunity to get formal education in the (segregated) Upper Canada schools in Scotland, Canada.

In Scotland, Elijah McCoy earned his Mechanical Engineering degree. He rejoined his family, not in Canada but in Ypsilanti, Michigan, where his parents had moved the family and his father worked for a family farm as a skilled tobacconist—a human development skillset he probably gained in the plantation workforce. Unable to be gainfully employed as a Mechanical Engineer, Elijah McCoy settled for a fireman and oiler job at the Michigan Central Railroad—a lesson in not despising small beginnings—and established his own home-based workshop to work on his craft.

Back then the train engines needed constant lubrication to prevent overheating and Elijah's job was to lubricate them. The young inventor believed the process was antiquated so he invented a cup that held the lubricant and through a tube fed it automatically to the engines. Violà! Our human experience with engine lubrication and overheating got upgraded. Since then, the impact of this discovery can be seen in widely varied applications—from train systems to oil-drilling and mining equipment to a variety of construction tools. The patent described the device as providing *"...for the continuous flow of oil on the gears and other moving parts of a machine in order to keep it lubricated properly and continuous and thereby do away with the necessity of shutting down the machine periodically (Bellis 2021)."* This was a transformative discovery because it meant trains did not have to stop so frequently. While there were other inventions that attempted to do the same thing, McCoy's patented invention became the real thing every engineer that knew their stuff wanted—the real McCoy!

McCoy moved to Detroit, where he continued to work on his many inventions and served as a consultant to the railroad industry. The Midwest Regional U.S. Patent and Trademark Office is named after him. In his lifetime, McCoy patented over 50 inventions, became an African American success story, and made humankind's life on planet a better experience. From the hallowing bowels of the underground railroad escape that gave his parents a new lease on life as freed human beings in Canada, Elijah McCoy was born a descendant of African Africans to change the railroad experience for all

Americans and the rest of the world because of the untethered human development training he received and his dedication to his craft.

George Washington Carver: Carver's father died weeks before his birth on or about 1864. Weeks later he and his mother were captured by slave raiders, only for the baby to be exchanged for a horse; his mother was carried away and separated from him for the rest of their lives. Despite such a dire welcome into the world, Carver ended up on the farm of a German couple who took care of him for the first decade of his life in Missouri and Kansas. The German couple observed early on the fascination the young boy had for nature as he would roam the countryside and pick up plants and study them carefully in his own world—a foundation that foretold the humble and minimalist life he would live as an adult agricultural researcher.

This is another demonstration of the strength and power in our shared humankind when divisive norms are shattered, and individuals are afforded human development and training opportunities. The couple encouraged his training, giving him the courage to not give up on his dreams. He left the Carver farm at ten to attend a school miles away, working odd jobs to pay for his education, living in shanty accommodations and supporting himself by whatever means necessary. Years later, Carver attended Simpson College in Indianola, Iowa; he later transferred to what is Iowa State University today, known as Iowa Agricultural College at the time. There, Carver earned both his bachelors and master's degree in 1894 and 1897 respectively.

In 1897, Booker T. Washington offered him the position of director of agriculture at the famous Tuskegee Institute. This institute gave Carver a platform to single-handedly change the agricultural economy of the south and the entire world. The life goal Carver set for himself was to develop different uses for crops so that poor farmers could improve their economic vitality through sustainable farming. Carver knew that cotton farming damaged the soil and without alternative crops the plantations had no sustainable future. Carver established a laboratory from materials collected around the institute. He took a plant considered as hog food– the peanut— and discovered 325 different uses for it. He also discovered additional 118 product lines for the sweet potato _(Bellis 2021)._

These transformational discoveries incentivized traditional cotton farmers to switch to peanuts, sweet potato, and pecan farming as an alternative to cotton. Carver refused to seek patents for his discoveries because he believed his work was inspired by God, saying that _"God gave them to me...How can I sell them to some else?"_ Both white and black farmers celebrated Carver as a great researcher whose work made their livelihood a sustainable reality. Carver's life work transformed the subsistence living of a famous peanut farmer's family—Jimmy Carter—long before he made a living at it and eventually became the President of the United States. President Carter's family net worth gained from peanut farming can be traced back to the knowledge, creativities, and governance genius of Carver—a recognition and honor that other white farmers in the south gladly gave him because it changed their economy and gave them new options for prosperity.

Carver died a centenarian (or almost) in 1943 and then President Franklin D. Roosevelt wrote the following epithet to his life's work: *"All mankind are the beneficiaries of his discoveries in the field of agricultural chemistry. The things which he achieved in the face of early handicaps will for all time afford an inspiring example to youth everywhere."*

Finally, how each organization becomes a healer organization in the discriminatory practices of society largely rests on its commitments to human development and training with an equity lens. The 3-Step Equity Lens model provides the framework to assist organizations take this ride towards racial and gender equity first in the workplace and hopefully in society. We should also integrate holistic solutions that address salient life-limiting killers (like pollutants in Bhopal) that overexposes black and brown people in their formative years to excessive pollutants resulting in truncated life expectancy and limited time in the labor markets because of past unjust policies. Carver lived to be a centenarian perhaps because he was not overexposed to pollutants in his early life and because of his adult lifestyle choices.

Figure 7.2: America's biggest pollution disparities

Biggest Pollution Disparities
Nationwide, Black people are exposed to greater-than-average concentrations of a dangerous form of pollution known as PM 2.5. People of color face more exposure from almost every type of source, while white people are less exposed.

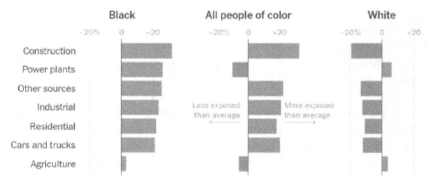

Other sources include pollution from commercial cooking, off-highway vehicles and equipment, and others. The cars and trucks category includes direct pollution as well as road dust.
Source: Tessum 2021.

America lost far too many real McCoys and Carvers, but there are even more real McCoys and Carvers just waiting to be developed, to the eventual benefit of humankind. All we must do is balance the scales and give all Americans (black and brown included) a fair and equitable opportunity to life, liberty and the pursuit of happiness.

Chapter Eight

DE&I AS MODERATOR FOR THE ENVIRONMENT

The Environment is the non-human tapestry upon which human decisions and activities live and manifest in living colors. Our shared planet was once a pristine, self-restoring ecosystem where the carbon emissions generated were offset by nature's cleansing biosphere. Since the days of industrial revolution, this balance has become a screeching and escalating nuisance to our shared planet and our privileged existence in it. In a big sense, our shared planet has become an extension of our divisive norms, and its preservation holds the keys to the very natural provisions that humankind needs to sustain itself both now and in the future. This makes the Environment a key DE&I matter, because it is at the core of our survival as a species, as well as being significant nexus to inequities in wealth, health, opportunity, and power structures.

THE ENVIRONMENT
Knowledge-informed Diversity Call to Action

Today, organizations rely on more natural resources than ever to produce products and deliver services through innovative solutions that have used just about every mineral known to humankind. Every day, organizations are becoming increasingly dependent on these products and services and these demands place a tremendous burden on our global ecosystem. This makes environmental stewardship a shared responsibility, and both individuals and organizations have roles to play in it.

No individual exists alone. We are all part of a shared planet inhabited by a transcendent humankind—where the actions of one generation positively or negatively impacts generations not yet born. In the same vein, all organizations contribute to the fidelity of the environment for all humankind in this and future generations whether through its activities, products or services or through its workers, workplaces, and work partners. John Donne, a 17th century English metaphysical poet captured the interrelatedness of this truth well:

"Devotions Upon Emergent Occasions and Seuerall Steps in my Sicknes - Meditation XVII, 1624"

No man is an island entire of itself,
Every man is a piece of the continent,
A part of the main.
If a clod be washed away by the sea,
Europe is the less,
As well as if a promontory were,
As well as any manor of thy friend's,
Or of thine own were.
Any man's death diminishes me,
Because I am involved in mankind.
And therefore never send to know for whom the bell tolls;
It tolls for thee.

In environmental issues, both the perpetrators and the victims are often intertwined as ably captured by the adage "no man is an island." Organizational leaders that make decisions and champion activities that tax our environment also face the consequences of climate change for example, regardless of the location of their actions or the place they call home. ISO provided a broader view:

ISO Society is facing many environmental challenges, including the depletion of natural resources, pollution, climate change, destruction of habitats, loss of species, the collapse of whole ecosystems and the degradation of urban and rural human settlements. As the world population grows and consumption increases, these changes are increasing threats to human security and the health and well being of society. There is a need to identify options to reduce and eliminate unsustainable volumes and patterns of production and consumption and to ensure that the resource consumption per person becomes sustainable. Environmental matters at the local, regional and global level are interconnected. Addressing them requires a comprehensive, systematic and collective approach.

Addressing environmental issues in a *"comprehensive, systematic and collective approach"* should include disparities that devour the hopes and dreams of minorities and vulnerable groups today. As is quite often the case, many of these groups are stymied in their ability to experience lives well-lived compared to their majority group contemporaries. Vulnerable groups around the world have been disproportionately impacted by environmental issues, making social responsibility and sustainable development essential vehicles for addressing these disparities moderated by DE&I. Both the UN Global Compact and ISO 26000 provide good guiding principles on the environment. The UN Global Compact has three principles specific to the environment:

Table 8.1 UN Global Compact: Environment

Principle 7:	Businesses should support a precautionary approach to environmental challenges;
Principle 8:	Undertake initiatives to promote greater environmental responsibility; and
Principle 9:	Encourage the development and diffusion of environmentally friendly technologies.

The following ISO 26000 principles provide an integrated organization-wide social responsibility and best applied inclusively when moderated by DE&I:

ISO An organization should respect and promote the following environmental principles:

- [ ] **environmental responsibility** In addition to complying with law and regulations, an organization should assume responsibility for the environmental impacts caused by its activities in rural or urban areas and the broader environment. In recognition of ecological limits, it should act to improve its own performance, as well as the performance of others within its sphere of influence;

- [ ] **precautionary approach** This is drawn from the Rio Declaration on Environment and Development...and subsequent declarations and agreements...which advance the concept that where there are threats of serious or irreversible damage to the environment or human health, lack of full scientific certainty should not be used as a reason for postponing cost-effective measures to prevent environmental degradation or damage to human health. When considering the cost-effectiveness of a measure, an organization should consider the long-term costs and benefits of that measure, not only the short-term costs to that organization;

☐ **environmental risk management**   An organization should implement programmes using a risk- based and sustainability perspective to assess, avoid, reduce and mitigate environmental risks and impacts from its activities. An organization should develop and implement awareness-raising activities and emergency response procedures to reduce and mitigate environmental, health and safety impacts caused by accidents and to communicate information about environmental incidents to appropriate authorities and local communities; and

☐ **polluter pays**   An organization should bear the cost of pollution caused by its activities according to either the extent of the environmental impact on society and the remedial action required, or the degree to which the pollution exceeds an acceptable level (see Principle 16 of the Rio Declaration [158]). An organization should endeavour to internalize the cost of pollution and quantify the economic and environmental benefits of preventing pollution in preference to mitigating its impacts based on the "polluter pays" principle. An organization may choose to co-operate with others to develop economic instruments such as contingency funds to cope with costs of major environmental incidents.

ISO 26000:2010, pages 41-42.

These principles should guide how socially responsible organizations deal with environmental matters and extend these to DE&I matters both as the right thing to do and as currency for negotiating value-added environment decisions and performing routine activities within its social responsibility framework. When all appropriate stakeholders are at the table of decision on environmental matters, their participation should enhance and not diminish the organization's social responsibility and sustainable development aspirations and actual performances.

Why the Environment solutions should be moderated by DE&I

Environmental Responsibility: Organizations that have an existing culture where values and behaviors have defined expectations are more likely to be socially responsible if these values and behaviors are diverse, equitable and inclusive. Even so, the fact that society has in general perpetuated humankind's divisive norms means that organizations are not exempt from these challenges within their ecosystems. Minorities and vulnerable groups tend to be rural and urban dwellers and have traditionally been absent at the table of decisions on environmental issues adversely impacting them.

Consider Cancer Alley, an 85-mile area between Baton Rouge and New Orleans where 150 petrochemical plants and refineries call home and are responsible for producing about 25% of all petrochemicals in the United States (Keehan 2018). The national average at risk of developing cancer is thirty individuals for every one million, but in Cancer Alley, that number is forty-six (Keehan 2018). Researchers have also found that African-American neighborhoods are over 16% more at risk than white neighborhoods (Keehan 2018). Even more, the poorer the census tract demographic, the higher the risk at over 12% compared to the higher income tract.

St. James Parish, which is located within the corridors of Cancer Alley, has a 48.8% African American population with 16.6% of its entire population living in poverty (Keehan 2018). When eleven of the plants located in St. James Parish were surveyed, the results showed that they employed between 4.9% and 19.4% African Americans (Keehan 2018). When in the very neighborhood where wealth is generated for one stakeholder group (the shareholders) and another stakeholder group is put at risk (minority and vulnerable groups) along with a damaged environment, social responsibility and sustainable development principles are also compromised.

If Cancer Alley can exist and continues to flourish in the United States— home of the Clean Air Act and formidable social justice activism – one can only wonder what it is like in other environmental sacrifice zones around the world where minority and vulnerable groups share similar fates. In Brazil, the Cubatao River is home to two million people living in an area known as the "Valley of Death" where 130 metallurgical and petrochemical industries are clustered, polluting both air and water. Sumgayit, Azerbaijan has earned the dubious moniker as "Baby cemetery" because of high infant mortality rates courtesy of decades of chemical manufacturing pollution by twenty-three local factories. Sumgayit remains home to over 275,000 people, victims of genetic mutation and elevated cancer rates that was no fault of theirs or luck from mother nature (Keehan 2018).

Bringing minorities and vulnerable groups to the table of decision or advocating for their interests should improve an organization's environmental management schemes and do not weaken it because they too are both stakeholders of interest and of influence. When environmental responsibility is championed by an organization's leaders and moderated by DE&I, it allows the rest of the organization to come along with solutions for an integrated and inclusive approach. The UN Global Compact Principle 8 provides the following guide:

Steps that the company could take to promote environmental responsibility would include the following:

- Define company vision, policies and strategies to include sustainable development — economic prosperity, environmental quality and social equity;
- Develop sustainability targets and indicators (economic, environmental, social);
- Establish a sustainable production and consumption programme with clear performance objectives to take the organisation beyond compliance in the long-term;
- Work with product designers and suppliers to improve environmental performance and extend responsibility throughout the value chain;
- Adopt voluntary charters, codes of conduct and practice internally as well as through sectoral and international initiatives to reach responsible environmental performance;
- Measure, track and communicate progress on incorporating sustainability principles into business practices, including reporting against global operating standards. Assess results and apply strategies for continued improvement; and
- Ensure transparency and unbiased dialogue with stakeholders.

UN Global Compact Principle 8

Environmental impacts can be far-reaching, but they are not often equitably distributed among all stakeholders. Quite often, minority and vulnerable groups are disproportionately impacted more economically and socially by these environment impacts from decisions and activities of organizations. If minorities and vulnerable groups are not at the table where decisions are made, their interests are not considered. This nexus of environmental and social responsibilities, ISO noted, requires a holistic education because *"environmental education is fundamental to promoting the development of sustainable societies and lifestyles."*

The UN in a Resolution adopted by the General Assembly on 25 September 2015, *"Transforming our world: the 2030 Agenda for Sustainable Development,"* captured the essence of a world where environmental and social responsibilities are both drivers for divisive norms and the very remedy needed to eradicate poverty and save the planet:

Today we are also taking a decision of great historic significance. We resolve to build a better future for all people, including the millions who have been denied the chance to lead decent, dignified and rewarding lives and to achieve their full human potential. We can be the first generation to succeed in ending poverty; just as we may be the last to have a chance of saving the planet. The world will be a better place in 2030 if we succeed in our objectives.

When more organizations utilize these environmental principles in their overall social responsibility framework, it ought to become easier over time to compare the results within the organization, its peer organizations, and beyond. These benchmark data will help inform and increase the knowledge-based environment diversity principles globally. This is where both the UN Global Compact and the GRI reporting standards become very useful tools.

On February 28, 2022, the UN's Intergovernmental Panel on Climate Change produced its Climate Change 2022 report, in which it sounded the loud alarm that the planet is being slowly cooked to extinction by uncontrolled humankind's activities. The report warned that over the next 18 years—by 2040—our world will experience even more dire impacts if we do nothing to mitigate the rise in greenhouse carbon emissions. The prospects for children alive today who will live to see the year 2100 is so dire, the report warned, that they would experience a planet where floods, droughts, wildfires, storms, and heat waves will become five times more frequent what they are today.

A consistent message in the report was the increasing vulnerabilities of minority and vulnerable groups around the world who lack the resources to plan for or recover from these climate-induced disasters and who live in regions and locations where the severity of these events is particularly damaging. Consider sea level rise as an example. The IPCC report surmised:

 Coastal cities and settlements play a key role in moving toward higher climate resilient development given firstly, almost 11% of the global population – 896 million people – lived within the Low Elevation Coastal Zone in 2020, potentially increasing to beyond 1 billion people by 2050, and these people, and associated development and coastal ecosystems, face escalating climate compounded risks, including sea level rise.

What does this have to do with an organization that is neither in a coastal city nor has any direct relations with minority and vulnerable groups in these locations? The point is that out of sight should not be out of mind, because the decisions and activities of organizations contribute to greenhouse emission collectively. The cataclysmic events caused by global warming will affect everyone. The UN Global Compact Principle Eight encourages greater environmental responsibility by business organizations regardless of size. The 1992 Rio Earth Summit Declaration summed up the roles businesses play in sustainable development in Chapter 30 of Agenda 21:

> Business and industry, including transnational corporations, should ensure responsible and ethical management of products and processes from the point of view of health, safety and environmental aspects. Towards this end, business and industry should increase self-regulation, guided by appropriate codes, charters and initiatives integrated into all elements of business planning and decision-making, and fostering openness and dialogue with employees and the public.

The Declaration reinforced the responsibility of a business not to cause harm to the environment due to its activities because society depends on it to be a good actor. Society, as a stakeholder of interest, demands that businesses adopt environmentally sustainable practices which should logically be applicable to all people regardless of color, gender, or economic status. As more and more organizations venture into social responsibility discourse, examining how their environment-related decisions and activities impact minority and vulnerable groups and their communities or societies—near and far—should also be part of the holistic education process.

Precautionary Approach: How does a socially responsible organization develop and implement cost-effective environmental management measures without identifying and engaging minority and vulnerable groups in the process? This intentional or unintentional decision and practices happens quite frequently, because these groups are already marginalized and the concepts of threats of serious or irreversible damage done to them or their environment are less valued or thought of, especially when they are not consulted about environmental management decisions. Examples of "see no evil, hear no evil, and respond to no evil" about the organizational environmental decisions and activities that have marred minority and vulnerable groups and their communities are a dime a dozen. From the lead in water piped to the homes of these groups in Flint, Michigan to miners around the world putting their lives in danger and causing irreversible ecological damage just to produce minerals that fuel or support our modern-day necessities. Learning from past wrongs of other organizations provide teachable moments for those at the table of environmental management decisions.

The UN Global Compact Principle 7 admonishes that *"Businesses should support a precautionary approach to environmental challenges."* This approach was introduced in the 1992 Rio Declaration Principle 15 which states that *"where there are threats of serious or irreversible damage, lack of full scientific certainty shall not be used as a reason for postponing cost-effective measures to prevent environmental degradation"*.

Environmental Risk Management: According to the UN Global Compact Principle 7, precaution includes the systematic application of risk in a trifecta: assessment, management, and communication. Business decisions with a likelihood of causing environmental harm should be guided by precaution rather than pretense wrapped around insufficient scientific data. This can be effectuated through a code of conduct and the establishment of transparent stakeholder communications—principles that are advocated by ISO 26000 and the UN Global Compact.

These principles, had they been in place, would have prevented African Americans living in Cancer Alley in State of Louisiana from falling ill to pollution. Standard Heights is a predominantly African-American neighborhood in downtown Baton Rouge. In 2012, an Exxon plant *"leaked 31,000 pounds of cancer-causing benzene into the air* (Keehan 2018)"—one of eight similar leaks between 2008 and 2012—that went unreported to the EPA despite the fact that reporting such leaks is required by law. These leaks caused many residents to become ill (Keehan 2018).

This is another reason why environmental risk management should consider historical practices that excessively exposed minorities and vulnerable groups to pollutants: environmental health policies did not include them as stakeholders. There has been historically a lack of resources to advocate for their interests, and many other mental models that deters them from participating in organizational risk assessment and mitigation measures. Having environmental policy and social responsibility choruses are insufficient to propel actions and monitoring of those actions. Total disregard for the EPA in reporting pollution leaks and hiding behind deliberately obscured scientific consequences of an event is gaming the system, a system that was supposed to allow for accountability and transparency to reign supreme.

The UN Global Compact Principle 7 offers an exemplary remedy: *"Create a managerial committee or steering group that oversees the company application of precaution, in particular risk management in sensitive issue areas (UN Compact 7 n.d.)."* Environmental Risk Management should not be used to perpetuate inequalities. One study in Canada demonstrated how cumulative hazard indices (CHIs) can be doctored to produce results that accentuates inequality:

> We observe distinct patterns of inequality between the cities, in terms of which marginalized groups consistently experience higher cumulative air pollution burdens (Vancouver: Indigenous residents, Montreal: immigrant residents, Toronto: low-income residents). Results also highlight the importance of using a suite of socio-demographic indicators as patterns can differ between individual racialized/ethnic groups, and between different measures of socio-economic status (Giang & Castellani 2020).

Further, minority and vulnerable communities all over the United States bear the marks of transportation policies that adversely affected their neighborhoods or subjected them to generational economic and environmental damages and disadvantages that are just now been recognized through federal legislation. Furthermore, pollution does not just come from chemical spills like the Bhopal Gas tragedy or Oil spills; it also includes policies that strategically make neighborhoods where minorities and vulnerable groups live the epicenter for environmentally risky experimentations that negatively affect their quality of life.

Polluter Pays: The reason an ounce of prevention is better than a pound of cure is that organizations understand what the cost of mitigation would mean to their economic and social interests if they must actually pay for the adverse impacts due to their activities. In the past, before social media, corporations polluted neighborhoods and communities without batting an eye. Socially responsible organizations, in internalizing the cost of pollution and quantifying the environmental costs of paying for pollution and the financial benefits of its activities, should always choose prevention over mitigation (after the fact). They should also consider doing no harm to minority and vulnerable groups and their communities as part of the prevention strategies. But it is not just minorities and vulnerable groups that are affected by corporate environmental pollution. There are also white cities and towns that are impacted, too.

Pollution anywhere is pollution everywhere, because of the degrading impact to our shared planet. In Spolana, Czech Republic, three decades after the Spolana Neratovice chemical factory closed its doors, high levels of contaminations from benzene, pesticides, chlorine, dioxin, and chloroform remain in all the surrounding areas (Keehan 2018). After changing ownership hands many times over, Spolana in 2016 became 100% owned by UNIPETROL RPA. The question remains whether companies like UNIPETROL RPA who inherit contaminated problems also own 100% of the sins of previous owners and are willing to do the right thing by creating some permanent remediation solutions.

In the 1950s, Pacific Gas and Electric Company (PG&E) operated a natural gas pumping station in a sleepy California Mojave Desert town called Hinkley. PG&E used chromium 6, a chemical that prevented rust, which seeped into the drinking water of the surrounding towns. People in these towns suffered from chronic coughs, nosebleeds, and recurring rashes and bronchitis. It took a single divorced and unemployed mother to turn things around and get PG&E to take full responsibility. Erin Brockovich became an accidental activist whose efforts eventually forced PG&E to accept full responsibility and settle the case for $333 million in 1996 (Dorian, Gorin, Yamada, & Yang 2021). The people in Hinkley were predominantly White rural dwellers and they too needed to be protected from environmental pollution.

Compare these examples to accidents that visibly affect privileged, predominantly White areas. In early 1990, a BP-chartered tanker accidentally ran over its anchor in Huntington Beach in Orange County, California, resulting in 400,000 gallons of crude oil spilling into a pristine surfing enclave. Huntington Beach is an affluent, majority-white county and its pristine beach is one of its crowning ecological glories and selling point. The damage was obvious and BP America's response was swift and instructive. The CEO flew to the site immediately, stood in front of the polluted beach, and told reporters, "Our lawyers tell us it's not our fault. But we feel like it's our fault and we are going to act like its's our own fault." Just imagine this kind of response in Cancer Alley and what it would have done to heal our shared planet's divisive norms. What is good for the goose—in ensuring unbiased dialogue with impacted stakeholders and truthful transparency—should also be good for the gander especially when deciding on which pollution cleanup an organization is willing to own and pay for and which ones it is not.

THE ENVIRONMENT
Creativity-driven equity opportunity/reconciliation/disruption

The decisions and activities of organizations can directly impact vulnerable individuals, groups, and communities, especially when these groups are not represented at the table of decisions at the time environment impacting issues are discussed, planned, and implemented. This creates inequities, especially within minority and vulnerable communities who are left to pay the huge price over multiple generations in health disparities, poverty, lack of upward mobility, etc. These impacts may be associated with the organization's use of living and non-living resources, the location of the organization's manufacturing activities, the generation of pollution and wastes, and the implications of the organization's activities, products and services for natural habitats. Another area of importance for marginalized and vulnerable groups is how health and safety and other environmental hazardous impacts due to organizational activities are communicated to them as workers and to their communities as stakeholders of interest and influence.

EQUITY OPPORTUNITY IN THE ENVIRONMENT

An organization's leadership bears the responsibility for ensuring that DE&I are integrated into its environmental responsibility management. Environmental responsibility that is unjust and unfair to minorities and vulnerable groups is only halfway to the finish line of social responsibility and sustainable development. At the minimum, an organization should look for equity opportunity from a higher-level view. The UN provides the following sustainability guidance:

> Business and industry, including transnational corporations, should ensure responsible and ethical management of products and processes from the point of view of health, safety and environmental aspects. Towards this end, business and industry should increase self-regulation, guided by appropriate codes, charters and initiatives integrated into all elements of business planning and decision-making, and fostering openness and dialogue with employees and the public.

It would be relatively easy for organizations to be socially responsible in their environmental management approach by including minorities and vulnerable groups in their awareness and promotion strategies and communication plans about the environmental impacts of their decisions and activities. Where possible, these efforts should go beyond the organization and include others within its sphere of influence. Taking a life-cycle approach also allows an organization to look deep and wide into its processes and practices for the products and services it produces, utilizes, or markets. In considering the environmental implications of its decisions and activities, an organization should consider their economic and social impacts across a wide spectrum of society, not just the ones to which the organizational leadership belongs.

Organizations should look for opportunities to make new technologies that reduce or eliminate pollution and waste available to minority and vulnerable groups at accessible costs. In employing persons for high-risk jobs with known environmental health and safety hazards, such jobs should not be designated only for minorities and vulnerable groups, especially knowing they have fewer resources and access to healthcare when they fall ill or are injured on the job.

Organizations committed to environmental social justice should at the very least be aware of the historical environmental burdens minority and vulnerable groups bear because of unfair practices and ensure they are not repeating or perpetuating them. ISO 26000 provides the following guidance that should help frame the equity opportunity on the environment:

> **ISO**
>
> In its environmental management activities, an organization should assess the relevance of, and employ as appropriate, the following approaches and strategies:
>
> ☐ **learning and awareness raising** An organization should create awareness and promote appropriate learning to support the

environmental efforts within the organization and its sphere of influence.

☐ **life cycle approach** The main objectives of a life cycle approach are to reduce the environmental impacts of products and services as well as to improve their socio-economic performance throughout their life cycle, that is, from extraction of raw materials and energy generation, through production and use, to end-of-life disposal or recovery. An organization should focus on innovations, not only on compliance, and should commit to continuous improvements in its environmental performance;

☐ **cleaner production and eco-efficiency** These are strategies for satisfying human needs by using resources more efficiently and by generating less pollution and waste. An important focus is on making improvements at the source rather than at the end of a process or activity. Cleaner and safer production and eco-efficiency approaches include: improving maintenance practices; upgrading or introducing new technologies or processes; reducing materials and energy use; using renewable energy; rationalizing the use of water; eliminating or safely managing toxic and hazardous materials and wastes; and improving product and service design.

ISO 26000:2010, page 42.

EQUITY RECONCILIATION IN THE ENVIRONMENT

DE&I and the environment meet at the crossroad of economic and social justice because unjust and unfair environmental practices have historically consigned minority and vulnerable communities to poverty and unhealthy life prospects. Hence, the leadership of an organization should have a comprehensive knowledge about how its environmental decisions and activities impact minorities and vulnerable groups throughout its products and services life cycles and within its ecosystem. This knowledge should be deliberately sought to ensure that the information presented to the leadership does not hide any disproportionate impacts on minorities and vulnerable groups. One way to ensure this is the case is to know the level of involvement by all stakeholder groups in the development of its assessments, processes, decisions, and practices. ISO 26000 provides the following guidance that could assist an organization reconcile its policies and commitments with its environmental decisions and practices:

ISO In its environmental management activities, an organization should assess the relevance of, and employ as appropriate, the following approaches and strategies:

- ☐ **environmental impact assessment**   An organization should assess environmental impacts before starting a new activity or project and use the results of the assessment as part of the decision-making process;
- ☐ **a product-service system approach**   This can be used to shift the focus of market interactions from selling or providing products (that is, transfer of ownership through one-time sale or lease/rental) to selling or providing a system of products and services that jointly fulfil customer needs (by a variety of service and delivery mechanisms). Product-service systems include product lease, product renting or sharing, product pooling and pay-for-service. Such systems can reduce material use, decouple revenues from material flows, and involve stakeholders in promoting extended producer responsibility through the life cycle of the product and accompanying service;
- ☐ **use of environmentally sound technologies and practices**   An organization should seek to adopt and, where appropriate, promote the development and diffusion of environmentally sound technologies and services...

ISO 26000:2010, page 42.

EQUITY DISRUPTION IN THE ENVIRONMENT

Organizations should ensure that any awareness-raising activities and emergency response procedures include marginalized and vulnerable groups in their communication plans. Effective communication with these groups should include use of mental models that counter historically biased ones and social networks where messaging can be amplified for good instead of promoting social divisive norms. Where gaps exist between commitments and practice, organizational leaders should reconcile their talk with the walk on environmental justice.

As ISO 26000 indicates, the survival and prosperity of all human beings begins with environmental responsibility and innately linked to other core subjects and issues within the social responsibility realm. Any organizational behavior that relegates the environment to a see no evil, hear no evil or plan for no evil must be stopped because our humankind and shared planet demands it. The UN added this spice to sustainability reasoning:

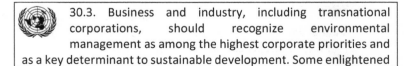

30.3. Business and industry, including transnational corporations, should recognize environmental management as among the highest corporate priorities and as a key determinant to sustainable development. Some enlightened

> leaders of enterprises are already implementing "responsible care" and product stewardship policies and programmes, fostering openness and dialogue with employees and the public and carrying out environmental audits and assessments of compliance. These leaders in business and industry, including transnational corporations, are increasingly taking voluntary initiatives, promoting and implementing self-regulations and greater responsibilities in ensuring their activities have minimal impacts on human health and the environment (United Nations 1992).

Where an organization has not committed to a formal environmental justice policy, the leadership should consider developing one. Having an environmental and social justice policy or ordinance should be used as moderator for both the integration and adoption of DE&I as integral to an organization's environmental decisions and activities. DE&I should not be decisions or activities buried in the bowels of human capital or human resources department but should be intricately tied to an organization's entire ecosystem of decisions and activities—the bottom-lines of profit, people and planet or the value-added proposition. The planet or environmental management part becomes the encircling mechanism for bringing profit and people into the mix and stopping the artificial bifurcation of environmental matters from DE&I matters. One quick way to disrupt the status quo of environmental malpractices that marginalizes people groups is to utilize the procurement life cycle as a catalyst for change. ISO 26000 provides the following guidance:

> **ISO** In its environmental management activities, an organization should assess the relevance of, and employ as appropriate, the following approaches and strategies:
>
> **sustainable procurement** In its purchasing decisions, an organization should take into account the environmental, social and ethical performance of the products or services being procured, over their entire life cycles. Where possible, it should give preference to products or services with minimized impacts, making use of reliable and effective independently verified labelling schemes or other verification schemes, such as eco-labelling or auditing activities...
>
> *ISO 26000:2010, page 42.*

THE ENVIRONMENT
Governance-centered inclusion actionable steps

In reviewing its environmental management and activities, a DE&I lens provides the best moderator for an integrated and inclusive organizational social responsibility framework. Both the UN Global Compact (addressing sustainability) and ISO 26000 (addressing social responsibility) provide systemic and complimentary approaches. As an organization reviews its decisions and activities through the lens of DE&I, such assessment and measurements should consider as added value guide the 3-Step Inclusion principles of redemption, restoration, and responsibility.

Governance-centered inclusion actionable steps in THE ENVIRONMENT

1. In reviewing your organization's policies and procedures around the environment, how do they align with your DE&I policy, commitments, and corporate proclamations on the matter?
2. If there are gaps, what are the actionable steps and timelines you have identified to narrow or eliminate them based on the 3-Step Equity Lens model?
3. Were all relevant stakeholders identified and engaged in the review, modification or development of your policies and procedures around your DE&I moderated by the environment practices?

ISO The 4 Environmental Issues

ENVIRONMENTAL ISSUE 1: DE&I AS MODERATOR FOR POLLUTION PREVENTION

Does your organization address real and potential environmental impacts on minority and vulnerable groups and their communities as part of an overall **pollution prevention** social responsibility construct?

Pollution Prevention
Knowledge-informed diversity call to action

When a transportation agency locates a freeway through or near vulnerable communities, the people in these communities become overexposed to emissions to air pollutants such as mercury, lead, Sulphur dioxide ($SO2$), and other volatile organic compounds (VOCs) compared to other locations within the same city. These legacy freeways and corridors not only divided communities by design but they were also specifically designed to go through low-income neighborhoods where people of color lived, limiting their economic and environmental prosperity and vitality.

This affects the quality of life in these neighborhoods even today, including life expectancies, economic sustainability, etc. The same can also be said for discharges to water from an organization's facilities or a result of the products and services they use, all of which could impact vulnerable communities disproportionately when drinking water becomes polluted. This is particularly true in oil or chemical facilities where the environmental impacts can be disastrous.

Waste is a common byproduct of an organization's activities and how and where it is mitigated is also important in the DE&I continuum. An organization's activities may lead to the generation of solid or liquid waste, which may contaminate water, land, and air. When managed correctly, ISO 26000 recommends that an organization follow the waste reduction hierarchy of "source reduction, reuse, recycle and reprocess, waste treatment and waste disposal."

DE&I comes into play also when an organization releases toxic or hazardous chemicals through its activities or generates other forms of pollution such as odor, noise, infectious agents, radiation, etc. The decisions and activities of organizations can have impacts on vulnerable individuals, groups and communities, especially when they cannot participate when environmental pollution issues are discussed, planned and implemented. When located in vulnerable communities, social justice and equity requires that these communities negotiate or get other in-kind mitigation values or financial renumerations to compensate for the value of the impacts.

All the above environmental issues may impact human health—acutely (immediately) or chronically (long-term)—and the environment with short and long-term economic and social ramifications. When the impacts are disproportionately felt in vulnerable neighborhoods and communities, the issue of equity and shared burden is a factor. ISO 26000 provides the following guidance on pollution prevention:

ISO An organization can improve its environmental performance by preventing pollution, including:

☐ **emissions to air** An organization's emissions to air of pollutants such as lead, mercury, volatile organic compounds (VOCs), sulphur oxides (SOx), nitrogen oxides (NOx), dioxins, particulates and ozone-depleting substances can cause environmental and health impacts that affect individuals differently. These emissions may come directly from an organization's facilities and activities, or be caused indirectly by the use or end-of-life handling of its products and services or the generation of the energy it consumes;

☐ **discharges to water** An organization may cause water to become polluted through direct, intentional or accidental discharges into surface water bodies, including the marine environment, unintentional runoff to surface water or infiltration to ground water. These discharges may come directly from an organization's facilities, or be caused indirectly by the use of its products and services;

☐ **waste management** An organization's activities may lead to the generation of liquid or solid waste that, if improperly managed, may cause contamination of air, water, land, soils and outer space. Responsible waste management seeks avoidance of waste. It follows the waste reduction hierarchy, that is: source reduction, reuse, recycling and reprocessing, waste treatment and waste disposal. The waste reduction hierarchy should be used in a flexible manner based on the life cycle approach. Hazardous waste, including radioactive waste, should be managed in an appropriate and transparent manner;

☐ **use and disposal of toxic and hazardous chemicals** An organization utilizing or producing toxic and hazardous chemicals (both naturally occurring and man-made) can adversely affect ecosystems and human health through acute (immediate) or chronic (long-term) impacts resulting from emissions or releases. These can affect individuals differently, depending on age and gender; and

☐ **other identifiable forms of pollution** An organization's activities, products and services may cause other forms of pollution that negatively affect the health and well being of communities and that can affect individuals differently. These include noise, odour, visual impressions, light pollution, vibration, electromagnetic emissions,

> radiation, infectious agents (for example, viral or bacterial), emissions from diffused or dispersed sources and biological hazards (for example, invasive species).

ISO 26000:2010, pages 42-43.

Why Pollution Prevention should be moderated by DE&I

From emissions to air, discharges to water, waste management, use and disposal of toxic and hazardous chemicals, or any other forms of pollution, people of color in the United States and minorities and vulnerable groups around the world are disproportionately overexposed to pollutants. Poverty and race have long been shown to be interconnected in a wealth of research findings. Pollution and race are now becoming known as interconnected. A body of research findings support the fact that people of color are more exposed to pollution than their white neighbors.

A recent EPA-funded study published in Science Advances in April 2021 reveal that environmental and health impacts on people of color—regardless of income level or region—is disproportionately higher than white racial group in every emitter type:

> *Racial-ethnic minorities in the United States are exposed to disproportionately high levels of ambient fine particulate air pollution (PM2.5), the largest environmental cause of human mortality. However, it is unknown which emission sources drive this disparity and whether differences exist by emission sector, geography, or demographics. Quantifying the PM2.5 exposure caused by each emitter type, we show that nearly all major emission categories—consistently across states, urban and rural areas, income levels, and exposure levels—contribute to the systemic PM2.5 exposure disparity experienced by people of color (Tessum et al 2021).*

This makes pollution prevention a DE&I matter; the above report is just a reflection of far deeper policy drivers with economic and sociological impacts that have spanned generations. In the United States, systemic and structural racism guided decisions that exposed black and brown communities to higher levels of air pollution. While racism and systemic discrimination go back 400 years, it was not until the 1930s that the government used redlining policies to establish segregation in neighborhoods sponsored by the federal government. This federally funded Home Owners' Loan Corporation (HOLC) enabled white Americans—poor and rich—to come out of the Great Depression with the golden opportunity to buy homes backed by federally guaranteed loans. This allowed white American families to establish sustainable wealth portfolios through home ownership, which increased in value over time and enabled many to transfer their wealth to future generations. Nothing was wrong with this policy, in theory, which helped many families achieve the American dream.

The problem was that the HOLC was also a vehicle of promise reengineered that disadvantaged black and brown racial groups, creating a tapestry of unjust home lending policies that limited the ability of black and brown people to create their own wealth through home ownership. It also made it impossible for black and brown people to use home ownership as a means for generational wealth transfers so each succeeding generation would not have to start from scratch.

An even more sinister impact of the HOLC promise was that it deliberately ensured that black and brown neighborhoods would be perpetually hazardous zones, ensuring that they are overrepresented in all the unwanted indicators such as health disparities courtesy of disproportional exposure to pollutants.

HOLC used neighborhood maps during the Great Depression for emergency home lending but by its development was intended to screen out black and brown people from mainstream American success stories. Neighborhoods were sorted into four categories: A was for the most desirable, B was for still desirable, C was for definitely declining, and D was for hazardous neighborhoods. White neighborhoods were generally "A" listed and black and brown neighborhoods were "D" listed which meant that white racial groups did everything to protect their home values by ensuring that black and brown people were not allowed to own homes in their neighborhoods. Not surprisingly, local governments disproportionately located industries, railroads, highways and other known industrial polluters in C and D neighborhoods. A study that explored the links between redlining and present-day air pollution disparities in U.S. cities concluded that there was definitely a correlation:

> HOLC security maps were drawn on the basis of the demographic makeup of neighborhoods, reflecting preexisting racial residential segregation. However, redlining further solidified and accelerated those patterns that exist today. In addition, areas graded as C or D often hosted industrial facilities, railroads, and other pollution sources. We find that, within HOLC-mapped areas, D-grade neighborhoods are more likely to be near industrial sources and that the average number of sources nearby increases from A to D. Additionally, the portion of people living near railroads and primary roadways increases monotonically by HOLC grade from A to D. While U.S. rail infrastructure was largely constructed before the 1930s, limited-access highways were constructed almost entirely after the 1930s and were preferentially constructed through Black and brown communities in U.S. cities. This comparison using rail lines and highways emphasizes that racial

As an organization assesses its pollution prevention or impacts whether caused directly from its facilities and activities or indirectly from other sources, representatives from minority and vulnerable groups should be at the table of these decisions. These groups have earned the rights to be at the table because they have lived experiences that were imposed on them without their consent. Their lived experiences can provide invaluable information on the best ways to create just and fair strategies in reducing or eliminating the pollution inequities. While these findings are based on the American experience, other minority and vulnerable groups around the world are also disproportionally exposed to pollutants even though there may not be as much publicly available data or research to support the correlation. But the connection is clear wherever data is available, and organizations worldwide tend to locate polluting activities in communities that lack the power to prevent it.

POLLUTION PREVENTION
Creativity-driven equity opportunity/reconciliation/disruption

As more and more organizations adopt social responsibility as their chosen path to sustainable development, they can improve their environmental performance by preventing pollution to the extent possible from their activities, services and products. An organization should assess its environmental impacts—potential and actual—to ensure that it addresses all the different forms of pollution generated by its operations and assure that minority and vulnerable groups and their communities are not more adversely impacted by their decisions and activities in this space.

EQUITY OPPORTUNITY IN POLLUTION PREVENTION

An Equity Opportunity lens applied for the prevention of pollution should also include how minority and vulnerable groups have been disproportionately impacted because of societal and organizational biased practices. In seeking opportunities to prevent pollution in general and its impacts on minority and vulnerable groups in particular, an organization should consider the following ISO 26000 guidance to change the discourse towards fair and equitable pollution prevention:

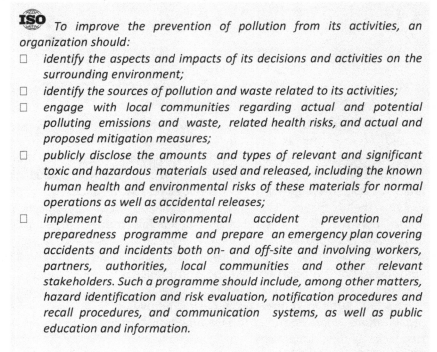

To improve the prevention of pollution from its activities, an organization should:

☐ *identify the aspects and impacts of its decisions and activities on the surrounding environment;*

☐ *identify the sources of pollution and waste related to its activities;*

☐ *engage with local communities regarding actual and potential polluting emissions and waste, related health risks, and actual and proposed mitigation measures;*

☐ *publicly disclose the amounts and types of relevant and significant toxic and hazardous materials used and released, including the known human health and environmental risks of these materials for normal operations as well as accidental releases;*

☐ *implement an environmental accident prevention and preparedness programme and prepare an emergency plan covering accidents and incidents both on- and off-site and involving workers, partners, authorities, local communities and other relevant stakeholders. Such a programme should include, among other matters, hazard identification and risk evaluation, notification procedures and recall procedures, and communication systems, as well as public education and information.*

ISO 26000:2010, pages 43-44.

EQUITY RECONCILIATION IN POLLUTION PREVENTION

An organization's pollution prevention strategies and plans should consider systemic discriminatory norms that accentuated disparities in exposure based on race or other vulnerable groups' status. Equity Reconciliation (ER) in pollution prevention should focus on addressing an organization's pollution prevention strategies and plans against the backdrop of the disproportionate exposure of minorities and vulnerable groups. Organizations should reconcile their commitments to the principles and core subjects of social responsibility and their pollution prevention strategies to include impacts on minorities and vulnerable groups. ISO 26000 provides the following guidance which should be addressed through an equity reconciliation lens that seeks fairness and justice for all:

To improve the prevention of pollution from its activities, an organization should:

- *measure, record and report on its significant sources of pollution and reduction of pollution, water consumption, waste generation and energy consumption;*
- *implement measures aimed at preventing pollution and waste, using the waste management hierarchy, and ensuring proper management of unavoidable pollution and waste;*
- *implement measures to progressively reduce and minimize direct and indirect pollution within its control or influence, in particular through development and promotion of fast uptake of more environmentally friendly products and services;*

ISO 26000:2010, pages 43-44.

EQUITY DISRUPTION IN POLLUTION PREVENTION

An Equity Disruption lens for the prevention of pollution where banned chemicals are identified; its use should not be allowed, justified or ignored in minority and vulnerable groups' communities. Social contracts that devalued these groups and used banned chemicals that disproportionately exposed them to pollution must be stopped in any socially responsible equity framework (racial, gender and others) to develop sustainable roots. ISO 26000 provides the following guidance for chemicals that should not be used, particularly in communities where minority and vulnerable groups could be exposed:

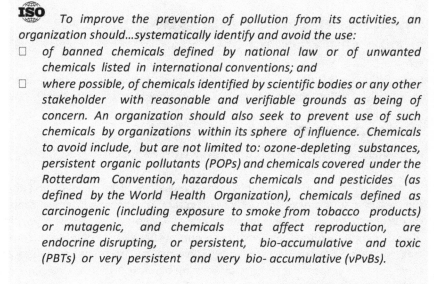

ISO *To improve the prevention of pollution from its activities, an organization should...systematically identify and avoid the use:*
- *of banned chemicals defined by national law or of unwanted chemicals listed in international conventions; and*
- *where possible, of chemicals identified by scientific bodies or any other stakeholder with reasonable and verifiable grounds as being of concern. An organization should also seek to prevent use of such chemicals by organizations within its sphere of influence. Chemicals to avoid include, but are not limited to: ozone-depleting substances, persistent organic pollutants (POPs) and chemicals covered under the Rotterdam Convention, hazardous chemicals and pesticides (as defined by the World Health Organization), chemicals defined as carcinogenic (including exposure to smoke from tobacco products) or mutagenic, and chemicals that affect reproduction, are endocrine disrupting, or persistent, bio-accumulative and toxic (PBTs) or very persistent and very bio- accumulative (vPvBs).*

ISO 26000:2010, pages 43-44.

POLLUTION PREVENTION
Governance-centered inclusion actionable steps

As an organization assesses its environmental management decisions and activities to ensure that it addresses all the different forms of pollution generated by its operations, it should also ensure that minority and vulnerable groups and their communities are involved in the discussion. Where opportunities exist to make amends for past unfair and unjust decisions, an organization should not allow profits to prevent them from doing the right thing.

Governance-centered inclusion actionable steps in Pollution Prevention

1. In reviewing your organization's policies and procedures around Pollution Prevention, how do they align with your DE&I policy, commitments, and corporate proclamations on the matter?
2. If there are gaps, what are the actionable steps and timelines you have identified to narrow or eliminate them based on the 3-Step Equity Lens model?
3. Were all relevant stakeholders identified and engaged in the review, modification or development of your policies and procedures around your DE&I moderated Pollution Prevention practices?

ENVIRONMENTAL ISSUE 2: DE&I AS MODERATOR FOR SUSTAINABLE RESOURCE USE

Does your organization involve minority and vulnerable groups and their communities in its sustainable resource use decisions and activities?

SUSTAINABLE RESOURCE USE
Knowledge-informed diversity call to action

When we think about sustainable resource use, we often do not think about the entire eco-system—from the extraction of the material or mineral resources to actual finished products. Yet, we cannot address the problem of depleting natural resources without comprehensive involvement from all stakeholders. Energy efficiency, water conservation, and access to water and efficiency are important factors in sustainable resource use decisions and activities. Our shared planet has limited resources—renewable and non-renewable:

1. Renewable resources include solar energy, hydroelectricity, wind power, geothermal energy, biomass, tidal and wave energy. Renewable resources are ideal because they can be used sustainably by balancing their usage with their rate of natural recovery.
2. Non-renewable resources include minerals, fossil fuels, metals, etc. Non-renewable resources are limited and irreplaceable once they are exhausted, denying future generations of their need for them. Hence, the need to balance non-renewable usage by supplementing or substituting them with renewable resources at a rate that uses less of them.

As advocated in ISO 26000, an organization can be innovative in its practices and in the use of innovative technologies on its journey to sustainable resource use. ISO 26000 provides the following guidance:

ISO An organization can progress towards sustainable resource use by using electricity, fuels, raw and processed materials, land and water more responsibly, and by combining or replacing non-renewable resources with sustainable, renewable resources, for example, by using innovative technologies.

Four key areas for efficiency improvements are:
☐ **energy efficiency** An organization should implement energy efficiency programmes to reduce the energy demand of buildings, transportation, production processes, appliances and electronic equipment, the provision of services or other purposes. Efficiency improvements in energy use should also complement efforts to advance sustainable use of renewable resources such as solar energy, geothermal energy, hydroelectricity, tidal and wave energy, wind power and biomass;
☐ **water conservation, use and access to water** Access to safe, reliable supplies of drinking water and sanitation services is a fundamental human need and a basic human right. The Millennium Development Goals (see Box 13) include the provision of sustainable access to safe drinking water. An organization should conserve, reduce use of and reuse water in its own operations and stimulate water conservation within its sphere of influence;
☐ **efficiency in the use of materials** An organization should implement materials efficiency programmes to reduce the environmental impact caused by the use of raw materials for production processes or for finished products used in its activities or in the delivery of its services. Materials efficiency programmes are based on identification of ways to increase the efficiency of raw material use within the sphere of influence of the organization. Use of materials causes numerous direct and indirect environmental

impacts, associated, for example, with the impact on ecosystems of mining and forestry, and the emissions resulting from the use, transport and processing of materials; and

☐ **minimized resource requirements of a product** Consideration should be given to the resource requirements of the finished product during use.

ISO 26000:2010, page 44.

There's been progress in consciously linking our everyday products to sustainable resource use. What we have not adequately done is link mineral extractions and sustainable resource use. This gap in thinking leaves opportunities that could help eradicate poverty worldwide and still preserve non-renewable resources for future generations.

Energy efficiency, water conservation, and access to water are familiar and quantifiable measures to socially responsible organizations, but they are not necessarily so in rural communities around the world where mining of minerals take place. It's in these communities where minorities and vulnerable groups engage in practices that undermine their water sources, damage the environment, and contribute to climate change. Mining contributes to climate change whether the community is working for a Large-Scale Extractor company or an Artisanal Small-Scale Mining (ASM) operation.

Sustainable resource use should be as much a part of the process of mineral mining as well as in the strategies we develop to combine or replace non-renewable resources with sustainable renewable ones. What is also salient is making the linkage between efficiency in the use of materials—minerals—and the manner in which they are obtained or mined from the earth. This is akin to kids growing up in urban cities where they cannot mentally make the connection between the chicken in the refrigerator (from live to processed meat) and those at the petting zoo. For most of these kids, making that connection requires a significant mental shift.

Why Sustainable Resource Use should be moderated by DE&I

Much of the developing world has leapfrogged into the twenty-first century without contributing to the use of natural resources to the same degree as the developed countries did on their path to advanced development. However, it is also true that much of the mining of non-renewable minerals does not follow sustainable consumption and production (SCP) practices.

Today, about 100 million people around the world are engaged in Artisanal and Small-Scale Mining—using tools from bygone eras as well as modern day extractive technologies—all trying to make a living and feed their families. Globally, industrial mining only accounts for 7 million people. If no person is an Island, then what is good for the goose is also good for the gander. We can achieve holistic energy efficiency, water conservation, access to water and efficient use of materials when it is a humankind endeavor, not when it's just a rich-people effort. Together, we can also enjoy the benefits of our shared efforts in the pursuit of sustainable resource use when minorities and vulnerable groups around the world are gainfully employed to extract minerals right, understand their role, advocate for themselves, and are compensated fairly.

In pursuing sustainable consumption and production for its activities, an organization should also consider using its influence and resources to cause others in its network to do the same. We live in a shared planet and organizations are a key part of society. While addressing global sustainable resource use is primarily the domain of nation-states, the products and services produced and/or used by organizations also impact the sustenance of the planet. The role organizations play in sustainable resource use, both directly within their activities and indirectly through their sphere of influence, is very important.

Every organization, regardless of size, can contribute to overall sustainable consumption and production goals. Individuals also have a role to play in sustainable resource use by understanding the environmental and social ramifications of clamoring for cheap innovative electronic products like large TV screens, cell phones and other gadgets. It's easy to forget that these devices drive the need for more mineral extractions from the earth. Individuals also have a key role to play in moderating manufacturers' decisions and activities. Understanding the life circle of everyday products that we have come to take for granted in the last 25 years can help inform the decisions we make in reducing our own waste and that of our organizations.

The UN takes a more holistic approach to Sustainable Consumption and Production by first defining it as follows:

> Sustainable consumption and production refers to "the use of services and related products, which respond to basic needs and bring a better quality of life while minimizing the use of natural resources and toxic materials as well as the emissions of waste and pollutants over the life cycle of the service or product so as not to jeopardize the needs of future generations (United Nations 2020e)".

SCP is a holistic approach and is about systemic change. It is built around three main objectives:

Decoupling environmental degradation from economic growth. This is about doing more and better with less, increasing net welfare gains from economic activities by reducing resource use, degradation and pollution along the whole life cycle, while increasing quality of life. 'More' is delivered in terms of goods and services, with 'less' impact in terms of resource use, environmental degradation, waste and pollution.

Applying life cycle thinking. This is about increasing the sustainable management of resources and achieving resource efficiency along both production and consumption phases of the lifecycle, including resource extraction, the production of intermediate inputs, distribution, marketing, use, waste disposal and re-use of products and services.
Sizing opportunities for developing countries and "leapfrogging". SCP contributes to poverty eradication and to the achievement of the UN Millennium Development Goals (MDGs). For developing countries, SCP offers opportunities such as the creation of new markets, green and decent jobs as well as more efficient, welfare-generating natural resource management. It is an opportunity to "leapfrog" to more resource efficient, environmentally sound and competitive technologies, bypassing the inefficient, polluting, and ultimately costly phases of development followed by most developed countries (United Nations 2020e).

SUSTAINABLE RESOURCE USE
Creativity-driven equity opportunity/reconciliation/disruption

In developing and implementing any of the above efficiency improvements categories, organizations should make efforts to ensure the participation of minority and vulnerable groups in their plans. Such considerations should include but not be limited to: involving representatives of these groups in the planning, implementing and reporting processes; ensuring that the communication means are understandable by them (preferably in their primary spoken language); and that enough resources are dedicated to ensure their meaningful participation.

Utilizing a lifecycle thinking approach in energy efficiency, water conservation, and access to water and efficiency are important factors in an organization's sustainable resource use decisions and activities. Organizations should consider two frameworks in addressing sustainable resource use from a home and away perspective. Like in sports, home is your homebase and away is when you are playing outside of your homebase. This is important because in sustainable resource use, we are addressing sustainable consumption and production, and both require us to consider how we use natural resources now and, in the future, so now and in the future, we may have the resources we need. However, ignoring minority and vulnerable groups as partners in the pursuit of sustainable resource use is a mistake, because it can also accentuate systemic divisive norms and undermine the overall goal. Parents for whom mining is the only means for providing food for their family will naturally be tone deaf to platitudes about saving the planet for another generation when they are barely making it from day to day.

EQUITY OPPORTUNITY IN SUSTAINABLE RESOURCE USE

Home perspective:

Sustainable resource use decisions and activities can be a low-hanging fruit for organizations to make a tremendous difference in the closing of the divisive norms gap that has plagued humankind for so long. An organization should identify its own resource consumption as a first step and then identify its procurement and consumption sources and patterns. These identification processes should assist the organization in identifying the unjust and unfair norms within its decisions and activities' eco-system and correct them.

Equity opportunities exist in sustainable resource use. When minority and vulnerable groups remain heavily dependent on fossil fuels because they cannot afford the technological innovations that supports renewable resource use, we have not fully addressed sustainable resource use from a social responsibility holistic framework. Such thinking can be likened to what Dr. Martin Luther King called *"a fantasy of self-deception and comfortable vanity"* in his book: "Where Do We Go from Here: Chaos or Community?" Any life cycle thinking about consumption and production should also consider impacts to minority and vulnerable groups from their perspectives as stakeholders in our shared planet. Quite often, these groups have solutions that are innovative and contribute to sustainability goals and a social responsibility framework. Whatever they help design, they are likely to be more enthused about implementing, monitoring and providing meaningful feedbacks/reports.

When organizations use potable drinking water for their activities and minority and vulnerable groups are left with nothing but polluted water, obviously this is not in the spirit of sustainable resource use. When organizations choose to buy products and services from only organizations that have documented renewable resource use life circles, such decisions should be balanced to ensure that minority and vulnerable groups are not unduly penalized. Where these groups lack the competitive edge in sustainable resource use in their production or consumption life cycles, organizations should not accentuate discriminatory divisive norms but look for opportunities to provide assistance—financial, technical or any other form. ISO 26000 provides the following guidance:

ISO In relation to all its activities an organization should:

☐ *identify the sources of energy, water and other resources used;*
☐ *promote sustainable procurement;*
☐ *promote sustainable consumption.*

ISO 26000:2010, pages 44-45.

In the spirit of our shared humanity, these activities become wholesome when they include the input and participation of minority and vulnerable groups and serve as opportunities for increasing equity and righting unjust and unfair practices.

EQUITY RECONCILIATION IN SUSTAINABLE RESOURCE USE

When the earth is scratched to extract mineral resources the whole planet itches, and little itches become part of a big climate change and global warming debacle. This is where the scientists and designers as social responsibility champions can ask and answer the questions about whose ox is gored in the life circle blueprint of their technological innovations. How can organizations use less material to produce their technologies? How can an organization's experts contribute to the body of knowledge to assist mining communities where indigenous people are slaving away for a pittance while sacrificing their health and wellbeing? How can well-endowed organizations provide technical assistance to the mining communities around the world from whence they get the material that go into their innovations?

Away perspective

In pursuing sustainable resource use goals, organizations should consider the impact on minority and vulnerable groups around the world who are engaged in mining the minerals that make our technologies work—tools we also deploy to assist in sustainable resource use. To produce the minerals that go into our cell phones, computers, and batteries, to mention a few luxuries, these communities—majority poor—scratch the earth and often destroy their environments for subsidence living that further their deep dive into more poverty for themselves and their posterity. Above all, such practices make these groups even more susceptible to harsher climate change episodes with fewer opportunities to rebuild from these disasters—continuing the cycle of poverty for most.

Imagine the impact on these peoples' lives if just a few high-tech organizations endowed 1-10% of their stocks for sustainable resource use funding in developing countries where the materials that support their innovations are mined.

On the other hand, specifying that material be purchased only from industrial miners to avoid the use or abuse of cheap labor will only sustain the rise and perpetuation of poverty—an unintended consequence of this procurement decision would adversely affect vulnerable groups from around the world. There are different solutions for each situation, and the responses that organizations make may vary widely depending on the context.

For some organizations, it may be as simple as organizing annual bring your used electronics to workday in partnership with recycling companies in parking lots. It is not unusual for people to have several used computers, cellphones and other equipment with circuit boards filled with minerals laying around their homes. While it may be a low priority for an individual to take these used gadgets to recycling facilities, if it were a corporate priority, perhaps it could increase the number of recycled equipment. The reuse of these components and valuable minerals could have a measurable impact on the mineral supply chain. Reductions in the extraction of minerals leads to sustainable consumption and sustainable natural resources for future generations. These are not religious sustainable resources use dogmas, just a demonstration of how organizations and individuals can all be part of the solution. ISO provided the guidance below, which can also be extended to reconcile an organization's DE&I policy and commitments with its decisions and practices:

ISO In relation to all its activities an organization should:

☐ *measure, record and report on its significant uses of energy, water and other resources;*

☐ *implement resource efficiency measures to reduce its use of energy, water and other resources, considering best practice indicators and other benchmarks;*

☐ *complement or replace non-renewable resources where possible with alternative sustainable, renewable and low-impact sources;*

☐ *manage water resources to ensure fair access for all users within a watershed;*

☐ *consider adopting extended producer responsibility.*

ISO 26000:2010, pages 44-45.

EQUITY DISRUPTION IN SUSTAINABLE RESOURCE USE

A key equity disruptor in sustainable resource use is identifying and engaging all stakeholders in an organization's products and services' use and their accompanying decisions and activities that envelop such use—consumption and production. This means where an organization's decisions and activities are identified to adversely impact minority and vulnerable group's energy, water and other resources use, such discovery must be acknowledged, and mitigating actions taken to remedy the situation. Nothing is more responsibility-challenged than to report on sustainable resource use metrics at the expense of groups that are impacted that are not treated as stakeholders. By definition, if they are impacted, they are stakeholders and should be treated as such. ISO 26000 suggests that organizations "use recycled materials and reuse water as much as possible." An even more significant gamechanger and equity disruptor is when organizations engage minority and vulnerable groups in the shared benefits of recycling materials and water management best practices.

SUSTAINABLE RESOURCE USE
Governance-centered inclusion actionable steps

Governance-centered inclusion should resolve the equity issues raised in sustainable resource use by addressing them in actionable steps that move the organization forward in its social responsibility commitments. As an organization considers, reviews or implements Sustainable Resource Use strategies, policies and practices through DE&I as moderator, it should utilize the 3-Step Inclusion principles as a framework for action items adapted from ISO 26000.

Governance-centered inclusion actionable steps in SUSTAINABLE RESOURCE USE

1. In reviewing your organization's policies and procedures around sustainable resource use, how do they align with your DE&I policy, commitments, and corporate proclamations on the matter?
2. If there are gaps, what are the actionable steps and timelines you have identified to narrow or eliminate them based on the 3-Step Equity Lens model?
3. Were all relevant stakeholders identified and engaged in the review, modification or development of your policies and procedures around your DE&I moderated sustainable resource use practices?

ENVIRONMENTAL ISSUE 3: DE&I AS MODERATOR FOR CLIMATE CHANGE MITIGATION AND ADAPTATION

Does your organization involve minority, vulnerable groups and their communities as well as address the needs of future generations in its **climate change mitigation and adaptation plans**?

Climate Change has dominated our public scientific discourse for quite some time now and organizations are at the center of it. Scientific evidence abounds indicating that our planet has become hotter since the dawn of the industrial revolution, a trend that continues to be a perennial problem for humankind. Despite a determined denialism by those too profit-driven or short-sighted to acknowledge it, cataclysmic impacts are already manifesting in increasingly aberrant weather patterns. Droughts, flooding, wildfires, and hurricanes are becoming more frequent, widespread, and intense. The collective cost is significant and has dire implications for humankind if we cannot find a way to reduce our planet's home temperature within the next 18 years (2040).

CLIMATE CHANGE MITIGATION AND ADAPTATION
Knowledge-informed diversity call to action

Climate change occurs because the heat from the sun to the earth which normally would just pass through now gets trapped by greenhouse gasses. Greenhouse gasses such as methane and nitrous oxide (from grass-fed livestock and growing crops) and carbon dioxide (from plants, deforestation and burning fossil fuels) all contribute to the problem (World Bank 2015). Communicating the risks to planet earth from humankind's global warming activities has become difficult to decipher by the average person. This is due to several factors, including the deliberate denialism of those with a vested interest in preserving the industrial status quo, the reluctance of people to make sacrifices for long-term goals, and the complexity of the issue. Hence, climate change episodes or events are typically processed by individuals through existing memories or newly created ones.

Some experts refer to this as "availability heuristic" (World Bank 2015) an opined theory that people generally use cognitive stored memories to understand climate change storylines. This is where cognitive reliance alone can be bad for climate change narratives, which tend to be presented in forecasting language and statistical probabilities not used or understood by the average person. In this model, risk behaviors that contribute to global warming are far removed from the minds of those making the direct contributions. As a World Bank report attested:

> *People typically do not systematically update their views over months and years but rather express views based on what they have experienced recently. Eventually, memories of personal experiences could become a reliable indicator that the climate has changed, but this adjustment may be slow, given the inertia of the climate system and the nature of people's beliefs (World Bank 2015).*

The impacts of climate change can be difficult to address because the generation that created most of the problems may not be alive to face them. It is also true that because radical changes in weather patterns take time to manifest, they are often not associated with the activities that led to them. Sometimes, too, impacts do not manifest directly in the place where the activities that caused them occurred. When indigenous people groups burn down forests just to survive, the impact of this deforestation could contribute to the ice in the Glaciers melting and draught in places where rainfall never was a problem. This makes climate change a complex and global problem. An even more salient climate change problem is how the risk is communicated for organizations and individuals to understand enough to want to do something about it.

We can make headway into solving climate change risk behaviors through contextually tailored social, cultural, and psychological messaging that are emotionally connecting narratives. Organizations should consider work-related and work-sponsored initiatives that engages stakeholders of interest and of influence within its internal and external eco-systems when addressing climate change mitigation and adaptation through its products and services. Going beyond statistical probabilities and forecasting potential realities that may come to pass in the distant future requires the reconstruction of the messaging into a narrative that is easily accessible to the baseline experience of the audience. The World Bank report suggested as much:

> Communication about climate change can draw on local narratives. In parts of Brazil, India, Melanesia, and the Sahel, some residents believe that weather is a reward for good human behavior or a punishment for bad human behavior. While these rewards and punishments are believed to be channeled through a deity, other groups, like the Kalahari San, the Inuit, and the indigenous Siberian, share similar beliefs without a religious connection. These narratives of human influence on the weather may provide foundations for presenting contemporary accounts of anthropogenic climate change and informing dialogues among citizens and scientists in different settings (Rudiak-Gould 2013)— (World Bank 2015).

Organizations may also consider using social norms as a means of mitigating climate change risk behaviors. Appropriately designed and strategically deplored, social norms are known key drivers for effective social change, especially when neighbors play influencing roles in the decisions that individuals make. This makes organizational leaders ideally positioned to push both their workers, partners, and society to adapt behaviors favorable to mitigating climate change.

As recent consternations over COVID-19 remedies reminds us, when issues with dire consequences are politicized, reason and rational knowledge give way to emotionally driven beliefs. COVID-19, like climate change's dangers, is harder to communicate across the board when it is politicized, and conclusions are drawn based on fear, distrust and resistance to any form of egalitarian control.

Why Climate Change Mitigation and Adaptation should be moderated by DE&I

Climate change is a humankind-threatening problem, though its immediate effects may not be apparent to many around the world. It is like the frog in the kettle metaphor, where the frog pays no attention to the rising temperature until it is boiled to death. In our case the problem is known to the rich and educated, but the effects are felt by all. Organizations can play a key role in reducing their greenhouse gas contributions while also assisting the rest of the world come to terms with needed changes to protect our planet. Climate change mitigations and adaptations are like the rising tide that should raise all boats with opportunities for job creations through new sustainable infrastructures that can stimulate global prosperity and reduce poverty (United Nations 2022).

Climate Change Mitigation and Adaptation and the risk behaviors that cause it affect us all because we all experience the effects of the abnormal weather patterns, the rise in sea levels, the melting ice in the glaciers, and the acidity in seawater. The World Bank report attested this much:

> *The likelihood and severity of these risks will depend on the amount of additional greenhouse gases added to the atmosphere and on the extent to which individuals and organizations take steps to mitigate and adapt to the risks. While climate change is a global threat, it is of most danger to developing countries, which are both more exposed to its impact and less well equipped to deal with it (World Bank 2015).*

Developing countries are where the world's poor and marginalized people groups call home even though they are also represented in developed countries. It is also true that poor, marginalized and vulnerable groups bear the fullest impacts of *"the effects of climate disruption and also bear significant costs during a transition to a low-carbon economy."*

While there are ways to distribute the burdens of climate change fairly, organizations should consider stepping up and doing their part. In addressing climate change, an organization may deal with three different worldviews in its ecosystem and how it engages and communicates with each group will be different:

1. The individualists are those who do not want to be told what to do on climate change by "big brother"—government or organization. What they believe about climate change is derived solely from their social networks and the norms they hold.
2. The egalitarians are those who would want their organizations to go all out to save the planet no matter the costs to the organization or the boundaries of its contribution to the problem. Organizational egalitarians want their organizations to do more than even governments in solving climate change challenges, regardless of costs or benefit to the organization.
3. The followers are those who would follow whatever directions the organizational leaders present and go along with whatever decision or lack thereof that their organizations make towards climate change mitigation and adaptation.

The United Nations has set forth as Goal 13 some directions and commitments that, while designed for countries, can also be used by other organizations. The UN recommends that strengthening the resilience and adaptive capacity of countries is paramount to addressing climate-related hazards and natural disasters. While nation-states are directly responsible for translating climate change measures into policies, planning and strategies, organizations also have a social responsibility. UN Goal 13 addresses the urgent actions humankind must take now to avoid more costly alternatives when the situation gets out of control than it already is today.

Where an organization is able to assist in addressing climate change and adaptation through education, awareness raising or capacity building for other organizations that may not be where it is in the pursuit of carbon neutrality, it should not hesitate. Our shared planet and humankind demands it. The UN Goal 13.3 encourages the promotion mechanisms for raising climate change effectiveness in both planning and management to also focus on *"women, youth and local and marginalized communities."* This is especially needed in minority and vulnerable communities in all countries, from developed nations to the smallest developing states.

Organizations produce products and services that contribute to greenhouse gasses and conducting an awareness inventory of their contributions to these emissions are a good start. Hence, it is imperative that as organizations address the mitigation of climate change impacts, that they also consider the DE&I ramifications. Climate Change and Adaptations should be addressed from a holistic and inclusive framework—a mission accomplished when DE&I serves as moderator. DE&I is a shared concern for all of humanity. When organizations pursue strategies that reduce their GHG footprint, they help all humanity—both present and future—by mitigating the impacts of global climate change, which has social ramifications on health, human rights and human prosperity on planet Earth.

Organizations can also go beyond reducing their own carbon emission footprint by actively recruiting and engaging minority and vulnerable groups and their communities as part of their own solutions to mitigating GHG emissions. Some vulnerable groups may still be stuck with an ancestral understanding of climate change and using this obsolete framework to adapt. Yet, the potential impacts of climate change on these communities may be even more dire than in communities which have, for example, more updated flood control and water supply infrastructures in place.

CLIMATE CHANGE MITIGATION AND ADAPTATION
Creativity-driven equity opportunity/reconciliation/disruption

Minority and vulnerable groups around the world are stakeholders of interest and of influence when it comes to climate change mitigation and adaptation. Any organizational climate change mitigation and adaptation should include all groups for humankind to realize the fullness of carbon neutrality. It begins by acknowledging that minority and vulnerable groups are relevant to the conversation, are also contributors to the problem and can contribute unique perspectives to the solutions. It continues into how climate change risk behaviors are communicated. If social networks and cultural worldviews play key roles in people's motivation to embrace social change, an organization can become a key ally for climate change programming. This alliance may include not just raising its own internal capacity for climate change planning and management, but also empowering marginalized communities to be part of the conversation in their local land use and other related planning and management actions.

EQUITY OPPORTUNITY IN CLIMATE CHANGE MITIGATION AND ADAPTATION

Climate change is a complex subject and how individuals relate or understand it is even more nuanced based on individual and societal proclivities. People in general tend to evaluate climate risks based on what they have experienced recently in weather patterns and changes. However, climate change is more than personal experiences and requires the analytical and deliberate analysis of quantifiable long-term datasets. This analysis by itself, stuffed in presentations and reports, does not effectively communicate the urgency of the need to change practices around the world that contribute to climate change. We need more interactive real-life situational contexts, and this becomes a challenge for the millennials and the generations following them to help solve. The previous generations have been successful in quantifying the magnitude of global warming and what could become of our planet for this and future generations.

Organizations should consider addressing climate change mitigation and adaption through their decisions and activities that includes the pursuit of carbon neutrality—a net-zero carbon dioxide emissions state. To achieve carbon neutrality, an organization offsets its greenhouse emissions with reductions elsewhere in its eco-system. For example, an organization can plant trees to offset its carbon monoxide emissions. For starters, ISO 26000 provides the following guidance when an organization seeks immediate opportunities to reduce its carbon neutral footprint through fair practices:

ISO *To mitigate climate change impacts related to its activities an organization should:*
- ☐ *identify the sources of direct and indirect accumulated GHG emissions and define the boundaries (scope) of its responsibility;*
- ☐ *realize energy savings wherever possible in the organization, including purchasing of energy efficient goods and development of energy efficient products and services; and*

Climate change adaptation
To reduce vulnerability to climate change, an organization should:
- ☐ *consider future global and local climate projections to identify risks and integrate climate change adaptation into its decision making.*

ISO 26000:2010, pages 45-46.

EQUITY RECONCILIATION IN CLIMATE CHANGE MITIGATION AND ADAPTATION

In reconciling its decisions and activities with its climate change mitigation and adaptation strategies, an organization, where practical, should take a lifecycle approach. Any risk conjures up an emotional response, and this is one of the challenges in promoting climate change strategies because the impacts of the decisions and activities take time to manifest. When climate change is viewed as a global problem, it is difficult for leaders to take on the challenge as an urgent organizational matter, because organizations are always local to some extent, even when they have a presence in multiple locations and countries. Yet, without organizational leadership on climate change challenges, the problem worsens. On climate change adaptations, studies suggest that organizations, like people, may limit how many problems they take on at the same time. Consider how Argentina, facing severe political problems, confronted global warming issues. According to the World Bank report:

> Argentine farmers who were worried about global warming were more likely to change some aspect of their production practices (such as insurance or irrigation) but hardly ever undertook more than one change. It was as if the farmers were eager to dismiss climate change worries in their own minds, believing that with one action they had addressed their problems (Weber 1997)— (World Bank 2015).

Organizations may also choose to remain non-committal when the risks surrounding climate change are ambiguously difficult to fathom. But according to the World Bank, ambiguity can also cause people to take precautionary steps that they would otherwise not take:

> A recent framed field experiment documented high levels of risk aversion among coffee farmers in Costa Rica. The study also found that, among farmers with clearly identifiable preferences regarding ambiguity, twice as many chose to adapt to the risk than not to adapt when confronting ambiguous climate change risks (Alpizar, Carlsson, and Naranjo 2011). In other words, the fact that the risk was unknown induced more adaptation than the corresponding situation with known risk (World Bank 2015).

While ISO 26000 provided the following guide that is applicable to equity reconciliation if DE&I serves as moderator:

ISO   *To mitigate climate change impacts related to its activities an organization should:*

- □   *measure, record and report on its significant GHG emissions, preferably using methods well defined in internationally agreed standards...;*
- □   *implement optimized measures to progressively reduce and minimize the direct and indirect GHG emissions within its control and encourage similar actions within its sphere of influence;*
- □   *review the quantity and type of significant fuels usage within the organization and implement programmes to improve efficiency and effectiveness. A life cycle approach should be undertaken to ensure net reduction in GHG emissions, even when low-emissions technologies and renewable energies are considered;*
- □   *consider aiming for carbon neutrality by implementing measures to offset remaining GHG emissions, for example through supporting reliable emissions reduction programmes that operate in a transparent way, carbon capture and storage or carbon sequestration.*

Climate change adaptation
To reduce vulnerability to climate change, an organization should:

☐   *implement measures to respond to existing or anticipated impacts and within its sphere of influence, contribute to building capacity of stakeholders to adapt.*

ISO 26000:2010, pages 45-46.

EQUITY DISRUPTION IN CLIMATE CHANGE MITIGATION AND ADAPTATION

There is a compelling business case to be made for why we need to improve communication about climate change risk behaviors and impacts. Detailed scientific reports, however valuable, are not compelling to the general public. To avoid the apathy on climate change messaging, organizations should consider using a narrative flow tailored to address social norms, social networks, and cultural worldviews. Since climate change is a humankind problem, organizations, like people, should find ways to engage directly or through worker-empowered engagement to stop practices that perpetuate divisive norms, even if they are geared towards solving a global problem. Including youth, women and local marginalized groups as stakeholders in addressing climate change risk behaviors and its related messaging is important because they too are stakeholders. ISO 26000 provided the following broad guidance:

ISO   *To mitigate climate change impacts related to its activities an organization should:*

☐   *prevent or reduce the release of GHG emissions (particularly those also causing ozone depletion) from land use and land use change, processes or equipment, including but not limited to heating, ventilation and air conditioning units;*

Climate change adaptation
To reduce vulnerability to climate change, an organization should:
☐   *identify opportunities to avoid or minimize damage associated with climate change and where possible take advantage of opportunities, to adjust to changing conditions.*

ISO 26000:2010, pages 45-46.

Social networks and cultural worldviews play key roles on how climate change is perceived based on the social networks where people identify and derive their worldviews. Often, political, religious, or ethnic affinities tend to govern how climate change messaging is received. This makes climate change a difficult issue for organizations to address directly and even more so when it is far removed from the sources causing the climate to change. The Baby Boomer generation has articulated the problem of climate change well. The Millennial and other generations after them must now carry the baton and reimagine how best to communicate the urgency of climate change risk behaviors and their impacts.

Organizations today are filling up with a younger workforce and work-partners who want meaning out of their work-life balance continuum. These are ready-made ambassadors for climate change mitigation and adaptation visioning, decisions and activities. If unleashed, they can tackle this humankind problem through more creative means. ISO 26000 provides the following examples for climate change adaption actions:

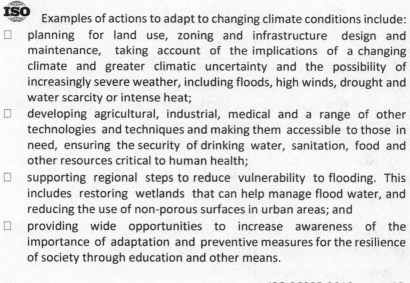

ISO Examples of actions to adapt to changing climate conditions include:
- [ ] planning for land use, zoning and infrastructure design and maintenance, taking account of the implications of a changing climate and greater climatic uncertainty and the possibility of increasingly severe weather, including floods, high winds, drought and water scarcity or intense heat;
- [ ] developing agricultural, industrial, medical and a range of other technologies and techniques and making them accessible to those in need, ensuring the security of drinking water, sanitation, food and other resources critical to human health;
- [ ] supporting regional steps to reduce vulnerability to flooding. This includes restoring wetlands that can help manage flood water, and reducing the use of non-porous surfaces in urban areas; and
- [ ] providing wide opportunities to increase awareness of the importance of adaptation and preventive measures for the resilience of society through education and other means.

ISO 26000:2010, page 46.

CLIMATE CHANGE MITIGATION AND ADAPTATION
Governance-centered inclusion actionable steps

Governance-centered inclusion in addressing climate change mitigation and adaptation should take a holistic and lifecycle approach where minority and marginalized groups' interests and influence are integral in the discussion. The correlation between organizations' actions, direct and indirect, and their impacts on climate change and sustainability of our planet is not in question. What's in question is whether we are bringing our Team Humanity to the game.

1. In reviewing your organization's policies and procedures around climate change mitigation and adaptation, how do they align with your DE&I policy, commitments, and corporate proclamations on the matter?
2. If there are gaps, what are the actionable steps and timelines you have identified to narrow or eliminate them based on the 3-Step Equity Lens model?
3. Were all relevant stakeholders identified and engaged in the review, modification or development of your policies and procedures around your DE&I moderated climate change mitigation and adaptation practices?

ENVIRONMENTAL ISSUE 4: DE&I AS MODERATOR FOR PROTECTION OF THE ENVIRONMENT, BIODIVERSITY AND RESTORATION OF NATURAL HABITATS

Has your organization linked its protection of the environment and restoration of natural habitats to equity considerations in its social responsibility framework?

PROTECTION OF THE ENVIRONMENT, BIODIVERSITY AND RESTORATION OF NATURAL HABITATS
Knowledge-informed diversity call to action

One way to protect the environment, biodiversity and restoration of natural habitats is to reduce or eliminate the greenhouse gasses that an organization produces without any mitigating provisions. According to the UN Climate Change 2022 report, this step is a desirable one because climate change is a threat to the safeguard of biodiversity and ecosystems, necessitating the need for climate resilient mitigations. According to the report:

> Recent analyses, drawing on a range of lines of evidence, suggest that maintaining the resilience of biodiversity and ecosystem services at a global scale depends on effective and equitable conservation of approximately 30% to 50% of Earth's land, freshwater and ocean areas, including currently near-natural ecosystems (high confidence) (IPCC 2022).

Marginalized groups and their communities pay a disproportionately high price for land use and ecological and social planning that does not include them or their interests. This contributes to the perpetuation of disparities in health, well-being, upward mobility, land-use development and adaptation gaps. The Climate Change 2022 report attests that, *"[t]he greatest gains in well-being can be achieved by prioritizing finance to reduce climate risk for low-income and marginalized residents including people living in informal settlements (IPCC 2022)."*

The fact that human activities in urban and rural areas have changed our global ecosystems since the 1960s, more so than at any other time in history, is not in question because we have been able to document the magnitude of the losses of habitat and diversity of life (ISO 26000 2010). While governments continue to do their part in addressing this degradation of ecosystems due to humankind's activities, organizations can play a key role in the solutions. According to ISO 26000:

ISO An organization can become more socially responsible by acting to protect the environment and restore natural habitats and the various functions and services that ecosystems provide (such as food and water, climate regulation, soil formation and recreational opportunities). Key aspects of this issue include:

- **valuing and protecting biodiversity** Biodiversity is the variety of life in all its forms, levels and combinations; it includes ecosystem diversity, species diversity and genetic diversity. Protecting biodiversity aims to ensure the survival of terrestrial and aquatic species, genetic diversity and natural ecosystems;

- **valuing, protecting and restoring ecosystem services** Ecosystems contribute to the well-being of society by providing services such as food, water, fuel, flood control, soil, pollinators, natural fibres, recreation and the absorption of pollution and waste. As ecosystems are degraded or destroyed, they lose the ability to provide these services;

- **using land and natural resource sustainably** An organization's land-use projects may protect or degrade habitat, water, soils and ecosystems; and

- **advancing environmentally sound urban and rural development** Decisions and activities of organizations can have significant impacts on the urban or rural environment and their related ecosystems. These impacts can be associated with, for example, urban planning, building and construction, transport systems, waste and sewage management, and agricultural techniques.

ISO 26000:2010, pages 46-47.

Why Protection of the Environment, Biodiversity and Restoration of Natural Habitats should be moderated by DE&I

Valuing and protecting biodiversity:

Since biodiversity is inclusive of all the variety of life—the whole ecosystems—supporting its integrity while protecting and building its resilience is philosophically consistent with social responsibility. The benefits of this responsibility have far-reaching impact on our humankind including, *"...livelihoods, human health and well-being and the provision of food, fibre and water, as well as contributing to disaster risk reduction and climate change adaptation and mitigation (IPCC 2022)."* This makes it a DE&I matter. As the UN Climate Change 2022 attested:

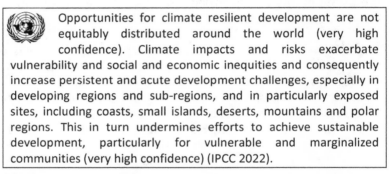 Opportunities for climate resilient development are not equitably distributed around the world (very high confidence). Climate impacts and risks exacerbate vulnerability and social and economic inequities and consequently increase persistent and acute development challenges, especially in developing regions and sub-regions, and in particularly exposed sites, including coasts, small islands, deserts, mountains and polar regions. This in turn undermines efforts to achieve sustainable development, particularly for vulnerable and marginalized communities (very high confidence) (IPCC 2022).

Valuing, protecting and restoring ecosystem services

Since the protection of biodiversity ensures the survival of ecosystems, their degradation or destruction regardless of location or region diminishes our shared planet and our shared humankind's experiences with that ecosystem. Sometimes, the solutions to valuing, protecting and restoring ecosystem services can also become part of the problem when they perpetuate age-old systemic and structural inequities. This makes it a DE&I matter. As the UN Climate Change 2022 attested:

Actions that focus on sectors and risks in isolation and on short-term gains often lead to maladaptation if long-term impacts of the adaptation option and long-term adaptation commitment are not taken into account (high confidence). The implementation of these maladaptive actions can result in infrastructure and institutions that are inflexible and/or expensive to change (high confidence) ···Maladaptation especially affects marginalised and vulnerable groups adversely (e.g., Indigenous Peoples, ethnic minorities, low-income households, informal settlements), reinforcing and entrenching existing inequities. Adaptation planning and implementation that do not consider adverse outcomes for different groups can lead to

The environment, biodiversity and restoration of natural habitats are DE&I matters because they present systemic issues, challenges and opportunities that require systemic responses not ad hoc or maladaptation approaches. We are all in planet earth together and all its ecosystems have direct or indirect impact on us all when they are diminished—the very essence of quality of life or lack thereof.

PROTECTION OF THE ENVIRONMENT, BIODIVERSITY AND RESTORATION OF NATURAL HABITATS
Creativity-driven equity opportunity/reconciliation/disruption

The United Nations in its Climate Change 2022 asserts that about 3.3 to 3.6 billion people live in locations around the world that are highly vulnerable to climate change impacts, with a significant number of species in the same boat. An organization's decisions and activities contribute to global warming which heats up our shared planet creating cataclysmic disasters all over the world with minority and vulnerable groups and where they call home most affected. Creativity-driven equity opportunity/reconciliation/disruption solutions around the protection of the environment, biodiversity and restoration of natural resources as DE&I-related matter enables an organization to examine its decisions and activities from a holistic framework.

Equity opportunity in protection of the environment, biodiversity and restoration of natural habitats

Advancing environmentally sound urban and rural development
When an organization's decisions and activities impact urban or rural environment and their related ecosystems, they generally also touch local communities, minority and vulnerable groups, who often are not at the table. Yet, the impacts can cut across all the ecosystems that keeps the community and our humankind at-large thriving. This calls for what the UN Climate Change 2022 report calls the "Enabling Climate Resilient Development."

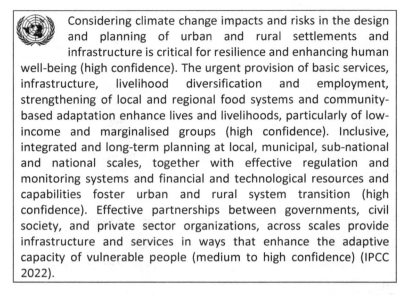

Considering climate change impacts and risks in the design and planning of urban and rural settlements and infrastructure is critical for resilience and enhancing human well-being (high confidence). The urgent provision of basic services, infrastructure, livelihood diversification and employment, strengthening of local and regional food systems and community-based adaptation enhance lives and livelihoods, particularly of low-income and marginalised groups (high confidence). Inclusive, integrated and long-term planning at local, municipal, sub-national and national scales, together with effective regulation and monitoring systems and financial and technological resources and capabilities foster urban and rural system transition (high confidence). Effective partnerships between governments, civil society, and private sector organizations, across scales provide infrastructure and services in ways that enhance the adaptive capacity of vulnerable people (medium to high confidence) (IPCC 2022).

Sustainable climate change mitigation efforts are only feasible when they are designed and implemented with truly inclusive partnerships. A solution that leaves some people out of the discussion is likely to be no solution at all. Equity Opportunities exist in adjusting or correcting current inequitable or biased practices in the protection of the environment, biodiversity and restoration of natural habitats.

☐ *identify potential adverse impacts on biodiversity and ecosystem services and take measures to eliminate or minimize these impacts;*
☐ *take measures to preserve any endemic, threatened or endangered species or habitat that may be adversely affected;*
☐ *adopt sustainable agricultural, fishing, and forestry practices including aspects related to animal welfare, for example, as defined in leading standards and certification schemes.*

ISO 26000:2010, page 47.

Organizations should consider urban greening as part of their climate change mitigation and adaptation plans to eliminate or minimize their contributions to global warming. Organizations should also consider learning and awareness campaigns that educate their workforce and work-partners on how they can get involved in reducing greenhouse gasses at work and in their respective communities. The UN Climate Change 2022 report offers the following:

Effective Ecosystem-based Adaptation reduces a range of climate change risks to people, biodiversity and ecosystem services with multiple co-benefits (high confidence). Ecosystem-based Adaptation is vulnerable to climate change impacts, with effectiveness declining with increasing global warming (high confidence). Urban greening using trees and other vegetation can provide local cooling (very high confidence). Natural river systems, wetlands and upstream forest ecosystems reduce flood risk by storing water and slowing water flow, in most circumstances (high confidence). Coastal wetlands protect against coastal erosion and flooding associated with storms and sea level rise where sufficient space and adequate habitats are available until rates of sea level rise exceeds natural adaptive capacity to build sediment (very high confidence) (IPCC 2022)

Equity reconciliation in protection of the environment, biodiversity and restoration of natural habitats

Using land and natural resource sustainably

An organization's land-use projects offer opportunities for integrated actions that address structural inequities, incorporate local and indigenous knowledge, and reduce risks and lack of resources to deal with climate change impacts—all DE&I matters. There is correlating evidence in support of the effectiveness, legitimacy and relevancy when climate resilient development processes are integrated with *"scientific, Indigenous, local, practitioner and other forms of knowledge* (IPCC 2022)."* This calls for what the UN Climate Change 2022 report described as the "Enabling Climate Resilient Development":

 Climate resilient development is advanced when actors work in equitable, just and enabling ways to reconcile divergent interests, values and worldviews, toward equitable and just outcomes (high confidence). These practices build on diverse knowledges about climate risk and chosen development pathways account for local, regional and global climate impacts, risks, barriers and opportunities (high confidence). Structural vulnerabilities to climate change can be reduced through carefully designed and implemented legal, policy, and process interventions from the local to global that address inequities based on gender, ethnicity, disability, age, location and income (very high confidence). This includes rights-based approaches that focus on capacity-building, meaningful participation of the most vulnerable groups, and their access to key resources, including financing, to reduce risk and adapt (high confidence).

> Evidence shows that climate resilient development processes link scientific, Indigenous, local, practitioner and other forms of knowledge, and are more effective and sustainable because they are locally appropriate and lead to more legitimate, relevant and effective actions (high confidence). Pathways towards climate resilient development overcome jurisdictional and organizational barriers, and are founded on societal choices that accelerate and deepen key system transitions (very high confidence). Planning processes and decision analysis tools can help identify 'low regrets' options that enable mitigation and adaptation in the face of change, complexity, deep uncertainty and divergent views (medium confidence) (IPCC 2022).

This calls for comprehensive stakeholder identification and engagement that includes equitable partnerships with government, organizations, indigenous and minority people groups, civil society and local communities. The UN Climate Change 2022 offers the following guidance:

> Interactions between changing urban form, exposure and vulnerability can create climate change induced risks and losses for cities and settlements. However, the global trend of urbanisation also offers a critical opportunity in the near-term, to advance climate resilient development (high confidence). Integrated, inclusive planning and investment in everyday decision-making about urban infrastructure, including social, ecological and grey/physical infrastructures, can significantly increase the adaptive capacity of urban and rural settlements. Equitable outcomes contributes to multiple benefits for health and well-being and ecosystem services, including for Indigenous Peoples, marginalised and vulnerable communities (high confidence). Climate resilient development in urban areas also supports adaptive capacity in more rural places through maintaining peri-urban supply chains of goods and services and financial flows (medium confidence). Coastal cities and settlements play an especially important role in advancing climate resilient development (high confidence) (IPCC 2022).

An organization's land-use projects may protect or degrade habitat, water, soils and ecosystems. The approach they take towards understanding and managing the projects can either be an opportunity to apply the principles of DE&I, working towards a management protocol that is truly inclusive and forward-thinking, or an opportunity to support the divisive, profit-driven status quo, in which some people remain marginalized and inequities are perpetuated.

Organizations should consider where feasible and appropriate partnering with other organizations, civil society, and governmental bodies to address climate change as a collective whole as opposed to creating just individual mitigating and adaptive solutions for themselves. This makes it more likely that they will value, protect and restore ecosystem services in an effective way that incorporates DE&I principles. ISO 26000 provides the following guide:

☐ *where feasible and appropriate, participate in market mechanisms to internalize the cost of its environmental impacts and create economic value in protecting ecosystem services;*

☐ *establish and implement an integrated strategy for the administration of land, water and ecosystems that promotes conservation and sustainable use in a socially equitable way;*

☐ *implement planning, design and operating practices as a way to minimize the possible environmental impacts resulting from its decisions on land use, including decisions related to agricultural and urban development;*

☐ *incorporate the protection of natural habitat, wetlands, forest, wildlife corridors, protected areas and agricultural lands into the development of buildings and construction works;*

☐ *progressively use a greater proportion of products from suppliers using more sustainable technologies and processes.*

ISO 26000:2010, page 47.

Equity disruption in protection of the environment, biodiversity and restoration of natural habitats

Climate change has exacerbated the vulnerability of our shared planet to serve its life-giving purpose for all of us, both humankind and all the varieties of life within its ecosystems. This means that there are decisions and activities we must stop where feasible and accept the value of other ecosystems, including but not limited to the following guidance from ISO 26000:

☐ *give highest priority to avoiding the loss of natural ecosystems, second to restoring ecosystems, and finally, if the former two actions are not possible or fully effective, to compensating for losses through actions that will lead to a net gain in ecosystem services over time;*

☐ *consider that wild animals and their habitats are part of our natural ecosystems and should therefore be valued and protected and their welfare taken into account.*

PROTECTION OF THE ENVIRONMENT AND RESTORATION OF NATURAL HABITATS
Governance-centered inclusion actionable steps

A socially responsible organization is one that seeks to protect the environment, biodiversity, and natural habitats, to the extent possible, from its activities, services and products. With the rapid growth of human activities in the last century, a great deal of demand has been placed on our natural resources. Using the ISO 26000 guidance discussed above, an organization should consider developing its actionable steps from an inclusive framework guided by the 3-Step Inclusion principles. With the tremendous wealth accumulated by global corporations today, many of the ecosystems destroyed by previous generations could be significantly restored by the concerted efforts of employers, employees, and their contracting communities – if they applied themselves and the necessary resources. Whether an organization is directly responsible for this ecosystem destruction or not is immaterial—the fact is we are all in this together. Economic assistance to minority and vulnerable groups in changing ancestral practices that destroy or contribute to the carbon footprint should be key aspects in addressing protection of the environment and the restoration of natural habitats.

Governance-centered inclusion actionable steps in PROTECTION OF THE ENVIRONMENT AND RESTORATION OF NATURAL HABITATS

1. In reviewing your organization's policies and procedures around protection of the environment and restoration of natural habitats, how do they align with your DE&I policy, commitments, and corporate proclamations on the matter?
2. If there are gaps, what are the actionable steps and timelines you have identified to narrow or eliminate them based on the 3-Step Equity Lens model?
3. Were all relevant stakeholders identified and engaged in the review, modification or development of your policies and procedures around your DE&I moderated protection of the environment and restoration of natural habitats practices?

Chapter Nine

DE&I AS MODERATOR FOR FAIR OPERATING PRACTICES

F air Operating Practices involve the expectations that organizations would act ethically and responsibly in all of their relationships, internally and externally. This is society's expectations set against the backdrop of pressures from the board of directors and shareholders, who demand results and profits at any cost. These shareholders' interests, while very important, must also be balanced against the organization's sustainability and social responsibility pursuits, which runs through people and planet. Some have called this stakeholder capitalism. As Larry Fink, the CEO of Blackrock, ably stated in his 2022 Letter to CEOS:

> At the foundation of capitalism is the process of constant reinvention – how companies must continually evolve as the world around them changes or risk being replaced by new competitors. The pandemic has turbocharged an evolution in the operating environment for virtually every company. It's changing how people work and how consumers buy. It's creating new businesses and destroying others. Most notably, it's dramatically accelerating how technology is reshaping life and business. Innovative companies looking to adapt to this environment have easier access to capital to realize their visions than ever before. And the relationship between a company, its employees, and society is being redefined (Fink 2022).

Fair operating practices are the walking pathways as an organization's social responsibility focuses on anti-corruption, responsible political involvement, fair competition, promotion of social responsibility in the value chain, and respect for property rights. Both sustainability and social responsibility frameworks address why organizational values, principles and behavior should go beyond satisfying just shareholders' interests and more towards meeting the needs of all stakeholders (which also includes shareholders). This new dispensation of organizational thought—sustainability and social responsibility—is far more likely to create a shared prosperity—shared planet continuum because it pulls our humankind toward closing the gaps on our divisive norms that have long been fed by corruption, stratified politics, winner-takes-it-all competition, value chain that disenfranchises and unjust property rights that creates hopelessness.

Sustainability and Social responsibility also involve the expectation that, through ethical and responsible decisions and activities, an organization can assist other organizations within its sphere of influence to act likewise. The clarion call that initially launched the age of sustainability in the early 2000s is slowly gaining steam and pulling organizations into choosing a more purposeful integration of the UN Global Compact's Ten Principles housed in four ecosystems: human rights, labor, environment, and anti-corruption. For a broad working model of fair operating practices, ISO 26000 provides the following guidance:

> **ISO** *Fair operating practices concern ethical conduct in an organization's dealings with other organizations. These include relationships between organizations and government agencies, as well as between organizations and their partners, suppliers, contractors, customers, competitors, and the associations of which they are members...In the area of social responsibility, fair operating practices concern the way an organization uses its relationships with other organizations to promote positive outcomes. Positive outcomes can be achieved by providing leadership and promoting the adoption of social responsibility more broadly throughout the organization's sphere of influence.*
>
> *ISO 26000:2010, page 48.*

Humankind's divisive norms manifests in inequalities and inequities—the results of organizations not dealing fairly and justly with all stakeholders even when their policies, procedures and public proclamations claim otherwise. Sometimes, organizations take the quick-fix route when confronted with these inconsistencies in their fair operating practices, especially as it relates to non-majority groups:

ISO *Behaving ethically is fundamental to establishing and sustaining legitimate and productive relationships between organizations. Therefore, observance, promotion and encouragement of standards of ethical behaviour underlie all fair operating practices. Preventing corruption and practising responsible political involvement depend on respect for the rule of law, adherence to ethical standards, accountability and transparency. Fair competition and respect for property rights cannot be achieved if organizations do not deal with each other honestly, equitably and with integrity.*

ISO 26000:2010, page 48.

Using fair operating practices do not mean lower returns for profit-oriented organizations. In fact, it can be the difference between competing firms as they are judged by their holistic social responsibility values. Fair operating practices contribute to shared prosperity, and it can become a sustainable development secret weapon when moderated by DE&I, prioritizing stakeholder interests not just for the good of the investor, but for consumer, employees, employer and society in general. As Mr. Fink of BlackRock surmised wisely:

> *Stakeholder capitalism is not about politics. It is not a social or ideological agenda. It is not "woke." It is capitalism, driven by mutually beneficial relationships between you and the employees, customers, suppliers, and communities your company relies on to prosper. This is the power of capitalism (Fink 2022).*

When DE&I moderates fair operating practices, it accounts for all stakeholders' interests, including minority and vulnerable groups and their respective communities and concerns. Fair operating practices begin at the top of an organization. Leadership sets both the tone and the direction as to whether an organization will be ethical and socially responsible in its relationship with employees, the contracting community, and the communities where its decisions and activities have direct and indirect impacts. This tone and direction are demonstrated by the values and behavior exhibited by the leadership in its decisions and routine activities. When guided by knowledge-based fair operating practices, an organization's influence on its social responsibility commitments can become far-reaching. One place where an organization can establish a broad walking pathway for its fair operating practices to become normalized is in its code of conduct/ethics, which should constructively inform its response to the interests of all stakeholders:

Figure 9.1: Generic organization's stakeholders

AN ORGANIZATION'S STAKEHOLDERS		
1. Investors	4. Customers	7. Partners/Associations
2. Employees	5. Suppliers	8. Government agencies
3. Contractors	6. Competitors	9. Society

 Fair Operating Practices

FAIR OPERATING PRACTICE ISSUE 1: DE&I AS MODERATOR FOR ANTI-CORRUPTION

Does your organization consider diversity, equity, and inclusion concerns in its anti-corruption operating practices? If yes, how? If no, why not?

Corruption and bribery are regrettably common around the world. These practices lead to civil rights and human rights abuses, cause damage to neighborhoods, redraw electoral maps for political expediencies (resulting in the inequitable distribution of political power, resources, wealth and economic sustainability for minority and vulnerable groups).

ANTI CORRUTION
Knowledge-informed diversity call to action

The death of George Floyd—besides being horrific—was also a transformative event for many reasons, one of which was the demonstration of the cellphone as a powerful medium for capturing real-time events as they happen for everyone in the world to see and become judges as stakeholders of interest and influence. One can only imagine how many hundreds or even thousands of Police brutalities against minority and vulnerable groups in particular and majority groups in general have gone unnoticed and reports fabricated in support of existing social norms. Yet, a cellphone recorder can bring down the high and mighty by exposing behaviors that are corrupt. This can expose an organization to unwanted damning public scrutiny. Organizations that do not have anti-corruption policies, procedures and actionable disciplinary measures are more vulnerable to bad public relations exposure since the age of social media than at any time before. One employee recorded asking for or taking bribes or extorting for it can overnight damage an organization's sustainability and social responsibility successes.

What then is corruption in the face of a globalization effort where cultures have allowances for behaviors that have long been normalized in one area, but smell like injustice of the bribery and extortion kind in another? For example, gift giving and entertainment of public officials including government workers are benign customs in some cultures that have been used to secure unfair favors and unearned advantages.

Transparency International, a global civil society organization leading the fight against corruption with over 90 chapters around the world provides the following definition of **bribery** in its Business Principles for Countering Bribery: *"An offer or receipt of any gift, loan, fee, reward or other advantage to or from any person as an inducement to do something which is dishonest, illegal or a breach of trust, in the conduct of enterprise's business."*

On **extortion**, OECD in its Guidelines for Multinational Enterprises offers the following definition: *"The solicitation of bribes is the act of asking or enticing another to commit bribery. It becomes extortion when this demand is accompanied by threats that endanger the personal integrity or the life of the private actors involved."* ISO 26000 provides the following broad guidance:

ISO *Corruption is the abuse of entrusted power for private gain. Corruption can take many forms. Examples of corruption include bribery (soliciting, offering or accepting a bribe in money or in kind) involving public officials or people in the private sector, conflict of interest, fraud, money laundering, embezzlement, concealment and obstruction of justice, and trading in influence. Corruption undermines an organization's effectiveness and ethical reputation, and can make it liable to criminal prosecution, as well as civil and administrative sanctions. Corruption can result in the violation of human rights, the erosion of political processes, impoverishment of societies and damage to the environment. It can also distort competition, distribution of wealth and economic growth.*

ISO 26000:2010, page 48.

Why is corruption the elephant in the room for organizations? The ramifications of one incident of publicized corrupt act(s) by one organization's representative damages all persons associated with the organization and all its intentional social responsibility goodwill the organization may have garnered over the years. As the UN Global Compact articulated well:

 Corruption negatively impacts social and economic development as well as environmental sustainability. Ineffective implementation of anti-corruption policies contributes to illegal logging, water and air pollution, exploitation of mineral resources, and unsustainable bio-fuel use. Corruption undermines the gains and positive effects generated by sustainable corporate practices (UN Global Compact Principle 10 n.d.).

As the dominant source for derailing an organization's sustainability and social responsibility journey, corruption thrives when there is a lack of identification or silence, especially since it is generally underreported. While there are good reporting tools to assist organizations, the secretive nature of the crime makes it elusive and easily glossed over. The following business case provides more reason for organizations to pursue anti-corruption mechanisms:

 The Business Case for reporting on the 10th Principle:

1. Increased internal integrity and transparency: Formalized and consistent reporting on anti-corruption activities, integrated into already established reporting processes (e.g., accounting), ensures reliable and measurable internal operations. It shows to employees that the fight against corruption is taken very seriously ("What gets measured gets done"). This results in the following benefits:
    -   strengthening anti-corruption behaviour, including better risk management and compliance;
    -   encouraging and supporting employees in resisting corruption;
    -   providing management with a foundation for analysis of progress, planning and continuous improvement; and
    -   motivating employees to be proud of the organization's integrity and reputation.
2. Enhanced reputation: An organization's reputation is a major success factor in today's globalized world. It has a considerable impact on purchasing and contracting capabilities, marketing and recruitment competitiveness. Proactively reporting on anti-

corruption efforts can positively influence public awareness and perception, resulting in the following concrete and indirect benefits for your organization:

- obtaining a competitive advantage as a preferred choice of ethically concerned customers, suppliers and other stakeholders;
- attracting highly skilled and motivated people;
- supporting and encouraging business partners and challenging competitors to resist corruption by setting standards of excellence;
- reducing your cost of financing by helping external financing institutions to assess risk premium through enhanced information; and
- increasing the credibility of voluntary initiatives such as the Global Compact by demonstrating commitment to their values and principles through reporting on progress.

3. Common information basis: Finally, reporting on anti-corruption activities based on a consistent reporting guidance enables different stakeholders to share information, raise awareness, learn from each other and improve practices. Stakeholders, as well as each individual organization, can benefit from this in multiple ways:

- sharing experience and procedures with other organizations;
- stimulating multi-stakeholder dialogues;
- increasing importance of disclosure on anti-corruption activities in overall sustainability agendas; and
- driving media coverage of good anti-corruption practices through provision of comparable progress reports.

Sources: UN Global Compact Principle 10.

ANTI CORRUPTION
Creativity-driven equity opportunity/reconciliation/disruption

A socially responsible organization desiring to act sustainably should seek to prevent corruption and bribery, both internally within its ranks and externally within the networks in which it exerts influence. While corruption takes many forms, in DE&I, it may even involve the falsification or manipulation of data to hide the effects of economic, social and environmental injustices on individuals, groups, and vulnerable communities. Corruption and bribery can be far more devastating when it adversely affects minority and vulnerable groups, because these groups often do not have the resources to seek legal redress and their complaints are generally not believed or dismissed by organizations and/or law enforcement.

The UN Global Compact provides the following three steps an organization can take to fight corruption: (1) **Internally** *"introduce anti-corruption policies and programmes within their organizations and their business operations,"* (2) **externally** *"[r]eport on the work against corruption in the annual Communication on Progress; and share experiences and best practices through the submission of examples and case studies,"* and (3) **collectively** *"[j]oin forces with industry peers and with other stakeholders to scale up anti-corruption efforts, level the playing field and create fair competition for all UN Global Compact Principle 10 n.d.)."*

EQUITY OPPORTUNITY IN ANTI CORRUPTION

Equity opportunity in corruption prevention begins with **internal** introspection. Corruption is an equal opportunity menace that can damage any organization—small or large—which is the reason why organizational leaders must pay close attention to eradicating it. Organizational leaders must set the tone for anti-corruption messaging, policies, and procedures. Corruption is a societal problem that did not begin with organizations, but it is facilitated and enhanced by them if there are no counter-balancing commitments to identify and address them head-on—ethically, transparently, and structurally. ISO 26000 provides the following guidance:

ISO   *To prevent corruption an organization should:*
- ☐ *ensure its leadership sets an example for anti-corruption and provides commitment, encouragement and oversight for implementation of the anti-corruption policies;*
- ☐ *identify the risks of corruption and implement and maintain policies and practices that counter corruption and extortion;*
- ☐ *raise the awareness of its employees, representatives, contractors and suppliers about corruption and how to counter it;*

ISO 26000:2010, pages 48-49.

EQUITY RECONCILIATION IN ANTI CORRUPTION

Corruption has tentacles that pull an organization's vulnerabilities into the limelight, undermining its integrity and social responsibility claims and **externally** eroding its trust and confidence in the eyes of investors and other stakeholders while over-exposing its risks with severe financial, legal, reputational, and other related costs. In other words, while it often works to the benefit of some people within an organization – or even the organization overall – it can also lead to substantial costs, both directly in the form of fines or penalties, and indirectly in the form of a damaged reputation. To shine the light on corruption before it takes the limelight in dooming all the good social responsibility work an organization has done and continues to do, systemic actionable decisions and mechanism should be put in place. This means reconciling the organization's anticorruption commitment with actions that demonstrate it has reviewed all the ways in which it is or could be vulnerable and implementing and monitoring solutions that effectively eradicate or minimize the risk exposures. ISO 26000 provides the following guidance:

ISO *To prevent corruption an organization should:*

☐ *support and train its employees and representatives in their efforts to eradicate bribery and corruption, and provide incentives for progress;*

☐ *ensure that the remuneration of its employees and representatives is appropriate and for legitimate services only;*

☐ *establish and maintain an effective system to counter corruption;*

☐ *encourage its employees, partners, representatives and suppliers to report violations of the organization's policies and unethical and unfair treatment by adopting mechanisms that enable reporting and follow-up action without fear of reprisal;*

ISO 26000:2010, pages 48-49.

Through the lens of DE&I, corruption is not just taking monetary payments and other forms discussed above but for minority and vulnerable groups; it goes further. Corruption can also be embedded in discriminatory practices long accepted as social norms.

EQUITY DISRUPTION IN ANTI CORRUPTION

An organization cannot end corruption in society all by itself, but it can join global **collective actions** to eradicate it. It is a global problem that can be most effectively addressed through each organization doing its part to help solve the gargantuan problem. While large multinational corporations have done a good job of highlighting and addressing corruption head-on, smaller firms have not joined the efforts with the same vigor. As the UN Compact report attests:

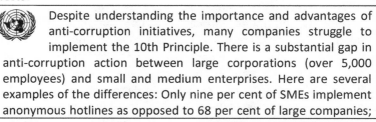

Despite understanding the importance and advantages of anti-corruption initiatives, many companies struggle to implement the 10th Principle. There is a substantial gap in anti-corruption action between large corporations (over 5,000 employees) and small and medium enterprises. Here are several examples of the differences: Only nine per cent of SMEs implement anonymous hotlines as opposed to 68 per cent of large companies;

> less than 12 per cent of SMEs record corruption as opposed to 57 per cent of large companies; less than 23 per cent of SMEs integrate anti-corruption into their management system as opposed to 65 per cent of large companies UN Global Compact Principle 10 n.d.).

If all organizations committed to ending corruption either as participants (givers of bribe) or perpetrators (requestors or extortioners of bribes), the major divisive norms that it exacerbates would be narrowed or even closed. ISO 26000 provides the following guide to help with this endeavor:

 To prevent corruption an organization should:

☐ *bring violations of the criminal law to the attention of appropriate law enforcement authorities; and*

☐ *work to oppose corruption by encouraging others with which the organization has operating relationships to adopt similar anti-corruption practices.*

ISO 26000:2010, pages 48-49.

ANTI CORRUPTION
Governance-centered inclusion actionable steps

Governance-centered inclusion in addressing anti-corruption measures should be guided by the 10th Principle of the UN Compact. Where feasible, organizations should sign the "Anti-corruption Call to Action" pledge located on the UN Global Compact website. A global transparent economy is dependent on individual organizations joining forces with governments and the UN to eradicate issues with global scope such as corruption.

Table 9.1: UN global compact: anti-corruption

Principle 10:	Businesses should work against corruption in all its forms, including extortion and bribery.

Proactive policies and programs designed to address corruption internally, externally and through collective actions (civil society, governments, and United Nations) should be clear, precise, measurable, and actionable—where there is a violation. A code of ethics or conduct is a good way to get everyone on the same page and to articulate the organization's position on corruption and its anti-corruption pursuits. These pursuits should aim at eliminating questionable relationships such as business entertainment or gift-giving – activities that serve as inducements for favors – and prohibiting bribery of government or public officials, foreign and domestic. Organizations should also consider framing their actionable steps through the 3-Step Inclusion Principle: they should be redemption-driven, restoration-focused, and responsibility-centered. Organizations should use these measures to help heal the divisive norms that have marginalized and disadvantaged minority and vulnerable groups for far too long.

Governance-centered inclusion actionable steps in ANTI-CORRUPTION

1. In reviewing your organization's policies and procedures around anti-corruption, how do they align with your DE&I policy, commitments, and corporate proclamations on the matter?
2. If there are gaps, what are the actionable steps and timelines you have identified to narrow or eliminate them based on the 3-Step Equity Lens model?
3. Were all relevant stakeholders identified and engaged in the review, modification or development of your policies and procedures around your DE&I moderated anti-corruption practices?

FAIR OPERATING PRACTICE ISSUE 2: DE&I AS MODERATOR FOR RESPONSIBLE POLITICAL INVOLVEMENT

Does your organization actively participate and engage in DE&I-related public policy discussions as part of its political involvement responsibility? If yes, how? If no, why not?

RESPONSIBLE POLITICAL INVOLVEMENT
Knowledge-informed diversity call to action

Our shared planet continues to be divided by political norms that have made responsible political involvement by organizations tenuous, especially for those consciously pursuing social responsibility. Yet, organizations hold the key today to help break societal gridlocks over divisive norms. They can choose to use their bully pulpits to address these challenges through strategic and respectful involvement in political, governmental, and societal issues. Public policy advocacy is a necessary role that socially responsible organizations play within the communities and societies in which they have influence, and they should be guided by a goal of benefiting society overall, not just individuals that represent the majority. The adage that "politics is business and business is politics" rings true here, but it should be guided by a high ethical standard that does not deprive minority and vulnerable groups of their rights.

ISO *Organizations can support public political processes and encourage the development of public policy that benefits society at large. Organizations should prohibit use of undue influence and avoid behaviour, such as manipulation, intimidation and coercion, that can undermine the public political process.*

ISO 26000:2010, page 49.

Knowledge demands that organizational leaders be aware of the political tapestry that framed the societal norms within the jurisdictions where they operate, as well as those jurisdictions which they impact. DE&I as moderator for responsible political involvement widens the organizational lens and enables it to embrace far more society-benefiting initiatives, initiatives that also enrich its three bottom lines of profit (prosperity), people and planet. The historical marginalization of minority and vulnerable groups should be of concern; actionable decisions should be taken to narrow the divisive societal gaps that disenfranchised them. This applies to the formulation and implementation of DE&I policies and initiatives. For example, even if a society devalues women and puts them at a disadvantage in every strata of its economic, social and political spheres, a socially responsible organization operating in this environment should not amplify these divisive norms through its own practices. The organization cannot play victim or be coerced to play along while it maintains policy and procedures in its own ecosystem about gender equality. The twenty-first century is not the age of gradualism on racial or gender equality. It's an age when bold action is needed to make meaningful change.

In public policy advocacy, an organization should use its influence to avoid complicity by supporting civil and human rights issues that complement its overall DE&I commitments. Responsible political involvement is a tool that organizations can use to bridge gaps in societal norms that are amplified by divisive political rhetoric. For too long, corporate political involvement in American politics—as in other parts of the world— has often favored the majority group, whatever that may be, to secure the most advantageous rights to local resources and labor. Although motivated by the bottom line rather than overtly unfair practices, the reality is that this has sustained divisive norms and discriminatory racial, gender and ethnic political constructs.

Compromise in the name of political expediency has been a part of our political framework used to kick the can down the road for another generation to address. This is what led to the unstable bifurcation of the United States at its founding. During the Constitutional Convention of 1787, when the Founders were trying to craft a governmental framework that could accommodate all the diverse states, the Northerners faced a political dilemma because the Southerners wanted to count the slaves as human beings on a one-to-one basis. As they were designing a representative system correlated with population levels, this benefited the South as it gave them four million African Americans in the Census count (although of course those people weren't actually meant to vote or participate in government). This meant more seats in the US Congress, more tax revenues allocated to them, and more political power and influence in crafting the laws of the land for the wealthy slaveowners in the South. The result of this impasse was the Three-fifths compromise agreement that counted a slave as three-fifth of a person for purposes of calculating representation – a solution that may seem ludicrous to us today, but which at the time seemed reasonable.

The Northerners who participated in the Constitutional Convention and whose descendants led the nation after the Civil War knew that slavery and racism were morally wrong, and that the Three-Fifths Compromise contradicted the Constitution's own assertion that stated all men were created equal. Some scholars assert that the phrase *"all men are created equal"* did not really mean individual equality for its citizens, but rather that the United States was asking to be accepted as an equal state among other nations. Yet, it is not difficult to also accept the natural reality that men are not born as a nation but as individuals, in the same way as one tree does not make a forest. While nations are the creations of men, people are created by God with unalienable rights to life, liberty and the pursuit of happiness. This means that *"all men are created equal"* is a living phrase, a beacon for the journey towards a more perfect union.

When Melissa De Witte of Stanford News Service asked Stanford University historian Jack Rakove about how research into the country's founding history can inform our understanding of American history today, he eloquently replied:

> *Two things. First, the toughest question we face in thinking about the nation's founding pivots on whether the slaveholding South should have been part of it or not. If you think it should have been, it is difficult to imagine how the framers of the Constitution could have attained that end without making some set of "compromises" accepting the legal existence of slavery. When we discuss the Constitutional Convention, we often praise the compromise giving each state an equal vote in the Senate and condemn the Three Fifths Clause allowing the southern states to count their slaves for purposes of political representation. But where the quarrel between large and small states had nothing to do with the lasting interests of citizens – you never vote on the basis of the size of the state in which you live – slavery was a real*

and persisting interest that one had to accommodate for the Union to survive.

Second, the greatest tragedy of American constitutional history was not the failure of the framers to eliminate slavery in 1787. That option was simply not available to them. The real tragedy was the failure of Reconstruction and the ensuing emergence of Jim Crow segregation in the late 19th century that took many decades to overturn. That was the great constitutional opportunity that Americans failed to grasp, perhaps because four years of Civil War and a decade of the military occupation of the South simply exhausted Northern public opinion. Even now, if you look at issues of voter suppression, we are still wrestling with its consequences (Witte 2020, July).

As the new nation grew up, organizations—corporations, institutions, businesses—became the fait accompli instruments of dissensions, which remains the case today. Northern Founders hoped and assumed that slavery would eventually diminish, but they did not account for the influence of individuals and corporations with a vested economic interest in sustaining white supremacy ideals. They institutionalized them in corporate ethics, behavior, values, and practices. If this were not so, we might not have systemic and structural racism thriving in corporate America today, where decisions are still made based on skin color or gender resulting in employment, access to capital, food insecurity, inequities of all types in healthcare, education, and more. That compromise may seem obsolete, a question superseded by the Civil War, but its legacy remains unfortunately significant even today.

To solve a problem, sometimes we must go back in time to the root causes. While the US has struggled with its original slavery sin, it has done more work in positively pushing forward than most countries that have similarly unjust DNA in their national birth history—the bedrock of politics. Since the end of Reconstruction, the majority white racial group has ruled society and organizations with a resulting unequal and unjust America mirrored through a generally complicit corporate America. However, without the intervention of President Lyndon Johnson in forcing the enactment of the 1965 Civil Rights Laws, the workforce today would be consistent with the then practices where most job searches produced only white candidates and most supply chain contracts to white vendors.

Interestingly, the same majority rule that fueled white prosperity at the exclusion of black and brown racial groups is finding itself fading demographically. Every day, America is shifting further towards a majority-minority state, with no one racial group topping the fifty percent mark. Corporate silence and complicity to the unjust treatments of minority and vulnerable groups in today's social media driven world-of-optics are no longer sustainable options, nor are they consistent with the drive to save the planet for another generation. What good is saving the planet for future generations while many in this generation aren't able to fulfill their higher purpose because of white supremacy-driven politics, sheltered by complicit corporate donations?

What these corporations should weigh now is a reality that challenges the political framework that was once controlled by White men, who once had the power to cause them economic harm by legislation and by steering up boycotts from their base. Sustainability-driven and social responsibility focused businesses and organizations can no longer afford to support unfair and unjust decisions by elected officials who have chosen to maintain a White majority culture in a multi-ethnic America and world that has moved beyond this practice and the organizations that support them implicitly or explicitly.

While some politicians continue to feed their base with the "red meat" that perpetuates a divided America, the corporate workforce and supply chain vendors now have significant numbers of Millennials and Generation Z whose values are more in tune with social justice than keeping white supremacist power alive. Interestingly, the Millennials and Generation Zs together are the largest demographic in America, and will remain so for the foreseeable future as the Baby Boomer generation and those before it sunsets. These two generations share a global worldview with their contemporaries around the world, having grown up together on the American MTV phenom and other social media influencers.

When George Floyd was sacrificed on the street of Minnesota, these two generations outnumbered all other demographics in coming out to register their dissatisfaction with the systemic and structural racism that had enabled the crime. Whites stood alongside their black and brown brothers and sisters—fed up by what their fathers and mothers ignored or perpetuated and crying out for justice everywhere. Hence, it is not only a practical necessity but stakeholders' imperative for corporations to get involved in racial equity matters, because the market for talent is fierce, the employee quest for meaning is real, and the potential for consumer boycott of a white supremacist leaning organization is financially significant.

The battle lines within the country have shifted. Ironically, the Republican Party, Lincoln's party that once fought for racial equity, has long ago shifted its values, and the prospect of resurrecting its ideals is near impossible; there are new factions of Republicans who are overtly seeking a White America or no America. The Democratic Party, which for centuries opposed racial equity, even leading and instituting Jim Crow policies, is now the home of minority politicians who exploit the racist vulnerabilities of Republican Party politicians. This explains why the past must inform where we are now and why nothing is new under the sun is an appropriate adage for where we find ourselves in 2022.

In a sense, the role that organizations must now play in a divided society fueled by divisive political rhetoric is a bit like the political and social role the federal forces played when the entire country was struggling to protect the right of African American electorates against southern social norms. The issues preventing what I call the "America's Mission Accomplished Generation" from taking its place are both political and social, and require organizations as stakeholders of interests and of influence to get involved. A rollback in time to how we got where we are today becomes instructive both for America and the rest of the world; as another adage states, "As America goes, so does the world." This is true for good and for ill.

RESPONSIBLE POLITICAL INVOLVEMENT
Creativity-driven equity opportunity/reconciliation/disruption

Organizations today should consider the impact of their political decisions that adversely affect their workforce and their consumer base. To be complicit with non-DE&I compliant standards by staying neutral, silent, or inactive is a recipe for avoidable backlash from within their own ranks and from financial impacts on their pocketbooks. Worst off, it creates sustainability problems down the years, as the available workforce continues to gravitate towards employers with an inclusive workforce and a record for more responsible political involvement.

EQUITY OPPORTUNITY IN RESPONSIBLE POLITICAL INVOLVEMENT

Responsible political involvement doesn't consist just of donations to political parties. It includes influence through public positions taken in opposition to divisive societal norms and political agendas. Recently, organizations have been caught napping when a member of their leadership team is found to be publicly endorsing or advocating for a political position that is contrary to their stated social responsibility stance. In these situations, an organization's responsible political involvement policies and activities need to be transparent if they hope to salvage their reputation and not seem like hypocrites. ISO 26000 offers the following guide:

 An organization should:
☐ *be transparent regarding its policies and activities related to lobbying, political contributions and political involvement;*

ISO 26000:2010, page 49.

EQUITY RECONCILIATION IN RESPONSIBLE POLITICAL INVOLVEMENT

An organization at the very minimum should assess the awareness levels of its leadership and workforce and work partners on what constitutes responsible political involvement. When moderated by DE&I, the assessment results should be used to design effective trainings, policies, and procedures that create an inclusive response which is politically neutral but still engages in righting societal wrongs through political advocacy and support for sustainability. In reconciling its political involvement story with its DE&I commitments, an organization should strive to make such involvement beneficial both to its own interests and to those of society. ISO 26000 offers the following guide:

 An organization should:

☐ *train its employees and representatives and raise their awareness regarding responsible political involvement and contributions, and how to deal with conflicts of interest;*

☐ *establish and implement policies and guidelines to manage the activities of people retained to advocate on the organization's behalf[.]*

ISO 26000:2010, page 49.

What has become ironic in today's political discourse especially in the US is the clamor by some to preserve their privileged status on the basis of race by any means necessary, particularly through political involvement. Socially responsible organizations should reconcile their values and DE&I commitments with the fact that the labor pool demographic cannot sustain a whites-only social thinking norm. In fact, White Millennials and Gen Zs are more inclined to be on board with inclusive policies and guidelines that embraces minority and vulnerable groups than previous generations. This younger workforce is driven by a more progressive set of values, rather than the preservation of white supremacy. While there are exceptions in any demographic, the preponderance of this shift among younger workers does suggest that Millennials and Gen Zs will become a generation of senior citizens accustomed to a majority-minority confluence, in which shared values and behaviors would be inclusive as at no other time in American history.

EQUITY DISRUPTION IN RESPONSIBLE POLITICAL INVOLVEMENT

An organization, in assessing its political involvement, should always avoid questionable contributions and messaging and take a neutral stance on both political parties and politicians to the extent possible. Contributions to political parties should be in concert with what the law requires and not participate in political activities and contributions that are prohibited by law. ISO 26000 offers the following guide:

ISO *An organization should:*
- [ ] *avoid political contributions that amount to an attempt to control or could be perceived as exerting undue influence on politicians or policymakers in favour of specific causes; and*
- [ ] *prohibit activities that involve misinformation, misrepresentation, threat or compulsion.*

ISO 26000:2010, page 49.

RESPONSIBLE POLITICAL INVOLVEMENT
Governance-centered inclusion actionable steps

Governance-centered inclusion in addressing responsible political involvement should be driven by proactive policies and practices revamped or designed to be inclusive of the interests of all stakeholders. The 3-Step Inclusion Principles are worthy guides in ensuring that an organization's responsible political involvement activities are redemption-driven, restoration-focused, and responsibility-centered. Organizations should use responsible political involvement to advocate for and support their interests as well as the interests that benefit all of society. Where appropriate, support measures aimed at closing the divisive gaps that have marginalized and disadvantaged minority and vulnerable groups for far too long.

FAIR OPERATING PRACTICE ISSUE 3: DE&I AS MODERATOR FOR FAIR COMPETITION

Does your organization incorporate DE&I issues in its fair competition operating practices? If yes, how? If no, why not?

Humanity entered the twenty-first century riding the internet revolution in its early years. While the US invented the internet and still controls much of its infrastructure, its population's use of the technological development would not have created a united world connected solely by bits and bytes. Unsurprisingly, in 2000, most plans for internet-related business and access concentrated on the US frontiers, with a sprinkling of users around the world included as an afterthought. This inward focus would have deprived American companies the global market share that they deserve for sharing its innovations with the world. As with the vision that President Kennedy had articulated about why America should seek to dominate Space for the good of humankind, the internet represented a transformational technology that transcends borders. This is where fair competition becomes crucial in an organization's social responsibility and sustainable development journey.

FAIR COMPETITION
Knowledge-informed diversity call to action

An organization whose sights are set on creating organizational wholeness in its ecosystem embraces and promotes fair competition in its activities, products and services. DE&I becomes the means for achieving organizational wholeness through fair competition practices, and this has the potential to take an organization beyond the rudiments of sustainable development. Just as a rising tide lifts all boats, fair competition—devoid of discriminatory practices—benefits all stakeholders, including society at large, by enhancing the economic and living standards of all. Following the guidance provided by ISO 26000,

ISO *Fair and widespread competition stimulates innovation and efficiency, reduces the costs of products and services, ensures all organizations have equal opportunities, encourages the development of new or improved products or processes and, in the long run, enhances economic growth and living standards. Anti-competitive behaviour risks harming the reputation of an organization with its stakeholders and may create legal problems. When organizations refuse to engage in anti-competitive behaviour they help to build a climate in which such behaviour is not tolerated, and this benefits everyone.*

There are many forms of anti-competitive behaviour. Some examples are: price fixing, where parties collude to sell the same product or service at the same price; bid rigging, where parties collude to manipulate a competitive bid; and predatory pricing, which is selling a product or service at a very low price with the intent of driving competitors out of the market and imposing unfair sanctions on competitors.

ISO 26000:2010, pages 49-50.

When DE&I moderates an organization's fair-competition initiatives, it opens the door for all regardless of the divisive norms that marginalize and disadvantage minority groups in favor of the majority. In addition to the forms of anti-competitive behavior identified above, the impact on minority and vulnerable groups is significant and should be part of the discussion.

Large corporations in general already have at least some anti-competition policies and procedures in place, and they cover compliance with competition legislation, support for anti-trust and anti-dumping practices, etc. Where minority and vulnerable groups are most adversely affected by anti-competition practices are in areas like delayed payments to subcontractors, bid rigging, price fixing and cartel activities. Lack of access to capital exacerbates this problem further; when an organization fails to pay its minority subcontractors on time, it sets the stage for their eventual demise.

Fair competition should give minority-owned organizations or individuals an opportunity to participate in the economic engine by creating, selling or participating in the delivery and consumption of products and services on a fair footing with everyone else. De jure or de facto segregation practices, while pervasive, are anathema to these just virtues and behaviors and they exacerbate our divisive norms. One example of salient anti-competitive behavior is discriminating against individuals from minority and vulnerable groups by stereotyping their abilities, demanding that they provide products or services at a quality and price level that other groups are not required to meet—all done sanctimoniously, so the victims self-disqualify. It's a practice that preserves the illusion of fairness, while actually reinforcing discriminatory practices. These practices have their roots in societal norms that are rarely addressed in awareness trainings on fair competition or in policy and procedures. The US provides a good case study for this.

Historically, white supremacists have used businesses as tools to acquire and sustain political power. In the 1874 midterm elections, when the Federal and Alabama state governments were complicit with the whims of KKK intimidation and violence against African Americans, racial harmony gave way to white agitation and acrimonious politics. It was during these election circles that a deeply divided Republican Party succumbed to the aggressive wishes of a segregated America promoted by the then-racist Democratic Party.

The Southern Democrats launched *"… a campaign of economic coercion: Major business owners refused to hire black men or anyone who swore allegiance to the Republican Party…"* which up till that time had led the fight for political and social equality in America. Never mind the fact that at this point in America's socio-economic and political development, the African Americans were more skilled, more workforce-ready and more likely to be independent contractors—all of which should have given them an advantage in a fair market. But their poor White counterparts were keenly aware of this and used unfair competition practices to derail the Black economic engine. The story has not changed much in the years since.

The false narratives today about racial characteristics are a continued propagation of white supremacy messaging from long ago that freed slaves were stupid, illiterate and unable to live or contribute to an Anglo-Saxon civilization. This social mental model flies in the face of the fact that the plantation capitalist economy was built on the backs of black and brown people who ran the plantations, built the highways and railroads, and developed and fixed the technological farming or construction tools of the day.

The White population that lived post-Civil War—from President Andrew Johnson down to the poor White farmer in the Southern States—was threatened by what it considered black supremacy/advantage in the labor market. This in turn led to the unfair competition—systemic unfair practices—that mushroomed into what we call systemic and structural racism today—a whack-a-mole stronghold that makes a mockery of the greatest democratic system in the world. Although explicit racism is no longer an acceptable in-your-face practiced norm (usually), the inequities still manifest in lack of access to capital, employment, health disparities, home ownership, unacceptable incarceration practices, etc. for black and brown people groups. While COVID-19 exposed all these and organizations large and small paid attention, their roots still run deep and their adverse impacts deeper still.

Richard Harvey Cain, an African American Congressman who served in the 43rd (1873-1875) and 45th (1877-1879) Congresses described the state of the labor market: *"…the carpenters, the machinists, the engineers—nearly all the mechanics (Congressional Record 1874)"* who lived in the south during this period were black. Therefore, when the Southern Democrats launched an economic coercion campaign against major businesses who hired African Americans or patronized businesses owned by them, they not only brought the entire black community to its knees—economically—but the movement also became the fertile-ground optic upon which Jim Crow Laws were successfully and sustainably based and driven. This type of economic coercion became the game plan for Jim Crow type socio-political segregations as well. The unofficial campaign of intimidation and closed-access proved effective, and so it was codified into law. In those days, the white demographic controlled the marketplace and the spending dollars and continues today.

However, in the twenty-first century, the market forces have changed; stakeholders are more varied and better educated about their rights and power, and corporations are more vulnerable to non-white controlling internal and external dynamics and forces. Yet, white supremacists remain afraid that when black and brown racial groups, women and immigrants succeed in society, it is at their expense. The chant that rang in Charlottesville *"Jews will not replace us"* was borne out of this related sentiment. Consider this, that on January 10, 1873, Congressman Cain made this observation, and it still rings true today:

> Now I am at a loss to see how the friendship of our white friends can be lost to us by simply saying we should be permitted to enjoy the rights enjoyed by other citizens…We do not want any discrimination. I do not ask for any legislation for colored people of this country that is not applied to the white people. All that we ask is equal laws, equal legislation, and equal rights ⋯.

The above quote was from 1873 and it is just as applicable today. Fair competition is about giving everyone a chance based on their individual and business qualifications regardless of society's discriminatory divisive norms. Fair competition intertwines with life in so many ways because it is the life blood of capitalism.

But old habits die hard. After the 2020 US Elections, when minorities voted in historic numbers in Georgia, Georgia State Legislators passed sweeping reforms to make it difficult for black and brown racial groups to vote in future elections. When corporations began to object, exercising a degree of social responsibility (however limited in many cases), it was not a surprise that one of the most highly skilled lawmakers of our time and a politically astute former speaker of the U.S. Senate—Mitch McConnell—quipped:

> *It's quite stupid to jump in the middle of a highly controversial issue…Republicans drink Coca-Cola too, and we fly and we like baseball…It's irritating one hell of a lot of Republican fans.*

In other words, while corporations are making progress towards more responsible behavior, this movement is facing pushback from entrenched interests uninterested in seeing broader enfranchisement of the people. Senator McConnell blew the "foul" dog whistle here against Coca-Cola ("Republicans drink…"), Delta Airlines ("…we fly") and Major League Baseball ("…we like") because they got involved responsibly in a political matter—yes—but one that also had societal equity ramifications. Massive election turnouts by minority groups would force white racial group candidates to reach out to their black and brown fellow citizens for their votes as opposed to relying on their white racial demographic alone to win elections. While Mr. McConnell wished corporations stayed out of politics, he did acknowledge their rights *"…to participate in the political process."* What some white Republicans who long for the good old days when they were in the majority are grappling with is a demographic shift that puts the white racial group at less than 50% of the U.S. population by 2045 for the first time.

However, on the economic front, even if all Republicans drank Coca-Cola, it will still be only a drop in the bucket of the global revenues the company earns from consumers around the world. The same is true for Delta and MLB as well as for all corporations especially those with global footprints. So, the economic argument today in support of white supremacist norms is not as strong as it may have been in the past, although politicians such as McConnell would like people to believe otherwise. What if countries in which these businesses also have economic interests boycott them for their complicity during anti-democratic political racially motivated divisive norms?

The US Census predicts that by 2028, the foreign-born share of the U.S. population is expected to be higher than at any time since 1850, when over 90% of the new immigrants were White. Behaviors and values in the age of social media are not easily erased or brushed aside. U.S. Corporations and organizations of varying sizes will be dependent on workforces and businesses from black and brown people groups and women than ever before as the population demographic continues to dance toward a majority-minority spectrum. Therefore, fair competition moderated by DE&I becomes crucial for organizations that want to attract the best workforces and work-partners, both now and in the near future.

Figure 9.1: Foreign-born people living in the United States

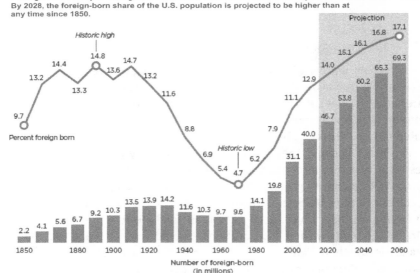

Figure 4.

Foreign-Born People Living in the United States: 1850 to 2010, Projected 2020 to 2060

By 2028, the foreign-born share of the U.S. population is projected to be higher than at any time since 1850.

Number of foreign-born
(in millions)

Source: U.S. Census Bureau, 1850-2000 Decennial Censuses, American Community Survey 2010, 2017 National Population Projections for 2020-2060.

FAIR COMPETITION

Creativity-driven equity opportunity/reconciliation/disruption

The COVID-19 pandemic demonstrated how capitalism and its systems are entrenched globally. For example, when people world-wide could no longer go to restaurants, restaurants came to the people by delivering food to them—facilitated by technological innovations. In the past, this would have been largely restricted to developed countries. But because our world is intertwined socio-culturally, many innovations are easily replicated elsewhere. This is just as true for education or not-for-profit services as it is for a factory producing widgets. For example, people with cellphones in Africa called or used apps to order food and have them delivered by other innovative entrepreneurs who found a way to pick up the food (through automobile, motorcycles or donkey-mobile) and deliver them. The phenomenon began mostly in the advanced countries but was quickly adopted and replicated by entrepreneurs around the world, servicing the needs of their own stakeholder base. The cellphone providers, the equipment manufacturers and installers, their employees, partners, customers, government regulators, etc., are all part of the stakeholder continuum. As Mr. Fink of BlackRock attested:

> *In today's globally interconnected world, a company must create value for and be valued by its full range of stakeholders in order to*

deliver long-term value for its shareholders. It is through effective stakeholder capitalism that capital is efficiently allocated, companies achieve durable profitability, and value is created and sustained over the long-term. Make no mistake, the fair pursuit of profit is still what animates markets; and long-term profitability is the measure by which markets will ultimately determine your company's success (Fink 2022).

With over seven billion people in the world today, more and more business opportunities are waiting to be reimagined or born, and in contrast to the past, the founders and owners of many of these businesses will not be White men. Take Gen Zs, for example. They are just as innovative in Africa or South America or Asia as they are in the United States, because they were literally born with cellphones in their hands. Today, entrepreneurs include black and brown men and women of all races—all stakeholders in the capitalism dance party. Capital markets and those who control them should see access to capital to fund these entrepreneurs worldwide as part of fair competition decisions and practice. They, too, belong in the stakeholder matrix. More than all of these, those who control the financial markets should consider innovative ways to grow their shareholders' funds within socially responsible frameworks that lead to sustainable development—the kind that sees poverty and its eradication as part of the mission.

For much of history, businesses owned by minority and vulnerable groups have not been allowed to compete fairly, restricted by the moderating societal norms that disadvantaged them. While bid rigging, price fixing, cartel activities, and delayed payments to subcontractors are some of the anti-competition practices that organizations address in their policies, these practices are much more pervasive against minority and vulnerable groups in every country, and they are often swept under the carpet. These practices also manifest for these groups through a lack of access to capital to fund projects for months, delays in getting paid, and proposals evaluated based on race, gender, or other social norms that have nothing to do with qualifications.

EQUITY OPPORTUNITY IN FAIR COMPETITION

In stakeholder capitalism, organizations should consider DE&I as a contributing lens for fair competition as it evolves its business models and reimagines its sustainability purpose in a post-pandemic world. At the very least, employee awareness of the impacts of its decisions and activities on businesses owned by minority and vulnerable groups, who are also stakeholders, should be part of the discussion. For many large companies, the solution is to make sure those laws are rewritten to benefit them, rather than to modify a profitable business practice to conform to rules they don't like. ISO 26000 offers the following guide:

ISO
To promote fair competition, an organization should:
☐ *promote employee awareness of the importance of compliance with competition legislation and fair competition;*
☐ *support anti-trust and anti-dumping practices, as well as public policies that encourage competition[.]*

ISO 26000:2010, page 49.

EQUITY RECONCILIATION IN FAIR COMPETITION

Even in situations where fair competition legislation does not directly address issues such as anti-competition activities that adversely impact minority and vulnerable groups, socially responsible organizations should not ignore or fail to address them. Socially responsible organizations can be more proactive than local legal or cultural frameworks require; if they have the foresight and the willpower to enforce their principles globally, they can be trailblazers in establishing standards for fair competition, a progressive approach which will benefit them and society.

ISO
To promote fair competition, an organization should:
☐ *establish procedures and other safeguards to prevent engaging in or being complicit in anti-competitive behaviour;*
☐ *be mindful of the social context in which it operates and not take advantage of social conditions, such as poverty, to achieve unfair competitive advantage.*

ISO 26000:2010, page 49.

EQUITY DISRUPTION IN FAIR COMPETITION

A good means for a socially responsible organization to disrupt unfair competition practices is to enforce existing anti-competition laws and regulations within its own ecosystem. Working with legislative bodies to ensure that minority and vulnerable groups protections and interests are included in legislations is another way to validate and reinforce responsible political involvement. ISO 26000 offers the following guidelines:

ISO
To promote fair competition, an organization should:
☐ *conduct its activities in a manner consistent with competition laws and regulations, and co-operate with the appropriate authorities;*

FAIR COMPETITION

Governance-centered inclusion actionable steps

Governance-centered inclusion through DE&I-moderated fair competition norms and practices should go beyond the traditional focus on anti-competition legislation. It needs to examine how minority and vulnerable groups are impacted by social norms that marginalize them. Proactive policies and programs designed to address fair competition should be guided by the 3-Step Inclusion Principle. Organizations should use these measures to help heal the divisive norms that have marginalized and disadvantaged minority and vulnerable groups for far too long.

Governance-centered inclusion actionable steps in FAIR COMPETITION

1. In reviewing your organization's policies and procedures around fair competition, how do they align with your DE&I policy, commitments, and corporate proclamations on the matter?
2. If there are gaps, what are the actionable steps and timelines you have identified to narrow or eliminate them based on the 3-Step Equity Lens model?
3. Were all relevant stakeholders identified and engaged in the review, modification or development of your policies and procedures around your DE&I moderated fair competition practices?

FAIR OPERATING PRACTICE ISSUE 4: DE&I AS MODERATOR FOR PROMOTING SOCIAL RESPONSIBILITY IN THE VALUE CHAIN

In promoting social responsibility in its sphere of influence, does your organization integrate DE&I as a form of currency for value-added decisions and performance of routine activities? If yes, how? If no, why not?

The application of a DE&I lens to the overall value chain is a good way to ensure comprehensive application of ethical and inclusive principles, both inside and outside an organization. Any organization can influence other organizations through its procurement and purchasing decisions. Using DE&I-conscious leadership and mentorship along the value chain, it can promote adoption and support of the principles and practices of social responsibility and sustainable development.

PROMOTING SOCIAL RESPONSIBILITY IN THE VALUE CHAIN
Knowledge-informed diversity call to action

Organizations have tremendous opportunities to promote social responsibility within their spheres of influence. One such opportunity is through their purchasing and procurement decisions and activities. This "buying power" has the potential to cause social change in other organizations faster than any legislative mandate, because it hits at the core of these organizations' economic survival. If a large company such as Coca-Cola, for example, requires its subcontractors to adhere to standards of DE&I, you can be sure that local contractors, whatever the culture and context, will do all they can to ensure that they meet Coca-Cola's standards in order to get their business. And Coca-Cola could do this immediately through unilateral policy decisions, without having to navigate the often-slow process of changing a regulatory environment.

By incorporating its DE&I policies and practices into its purchasing and procurement requirements, organizations operating in all sectors can help drive the economic growth of vulnerable or disadvantaged communities and promote environmental and social justices in these communities. ISO 26000 provided the following broad guidance:

ISO
> An organization can influence other organizations through its procurement and purchasing decisions. Through leadership and mentorship along the value chain, it can promote adoption and support of the principles and practices of social responsibility. An organization should consider the potential impacts or unintended consequences of its procurement and purchasing decisions on other organizations, and take due care to avoid or minimize any negative impacts. It can also stimulate demand for socially responsible products and services. These actions should not be viewed as replacing the role of authorities to implement and enforce laws and regulations. Every organization in the value chain is responsible for complying with applicable laws and regulations and for its own impacts on society and the environment.
>
> *ISO 26000:2010, page 50.*

There are many more opportunities where an organization can exercise its influence beyond purchasing and procurement. In such opportunity, organizations should use their influence to promote and support social responsibility principles and practices that are aligned with its DE&I policies and practices. Social responsibility in the value chain should not be seen as a profit-buster, because this discounts the value that consumer goodwill (and expanded market share) bring to the table. In essence, promoting social responsibility can actually be a competitive advantage.

PROMOTING SOCIAL RESPONSIBILITY IN THE VALUE CHAIN
Creativity-driven equity opportunity/reconciliation/disruption

Socially responsible organizations pursue an intentional inclusive procurement agenda that seeks to uplift all people groups throughout its entire value chain ecosystem – from raw material procurement to manufacturing and sales; even the recycling of finished products that have completed their lifecycles. When all stakeholders are properly included in discussions of practices and procedures, including minority and disadvantaged groups, they are provided with greater opportunities to participate in and benefit from every stage of the process. The organization also benefits in the triple bottom line of profits, people and planet. It's important to recognize here that stakeholders may include people not in the traditional scope of an organization's priorities, such as external organizations.

EQUITY OPPORTUNITY IN PROMOTING SOCIAL RESPONSIBILITY IN THE VALUE CHAIN

Equity opportunities abound in the value chain when an organization's procurement officers and employees are cognizant of the need to be inclusive in their purchasing activities. People generally prefer to do business with those they know, even when doing so is unfair and unjust to others. A low-hanging fruit in this case is to train all employees with procurement responsibilities to ensure they are aware of the impacts to minority and vulnerable groups when those groups are left out of the supplier chain ecosystem. It does not matter whether the decision to exclude minority and vulnerable groups is biased or not; the fact that they are excluded from participating in the supplier chain is neither equitable nor sustainable.

Procurement employee training should include on-time payments for work performed by vendors, suppliers, contractors, and subcontractors. Delayed or deferred payments, which have historically sometimes been born out of implicit or even explicit bias, place an undue burden on suppliers belonging to minority and vulnerable groups, who are often operating from a position of less capital flexibility. Effective training involves exposure to how humans make decisions through automatic thinking, social thinking, and mental models. While these are just a few examples, the overarching message is that procurement decision makers are at the forefront of an organization's just and fair supplier identification and engagement. ISO 26000 offers the following guidance:

ISO *To promote social responsibility in its value chain, an organization should:*

☐ *consider providing support to SMOs, including awareness raising on issues of social responsibility and best practice and additional assistance (for example, technical, capacity building or other resources) to meet socially responsible objectives;*

☐ *actively participate in raising the awareness of organizations with which it has relationships about principles and issues of social responsibility[.]*

ISO 26000:2010, page 50.

EQUITY RECONCILIATION IN PROMOTING SOCIAL RESPONSIBILITY IN THE VALUE CHAIN

A comprehensive assessment of the value chain also allows an organization to ensure that its practices and procedures are internally consistent at every level, reconciling inequity gaps between systems or aspects of the system which may bear the legacies of multiple historical injustices.

ISO *To promote social responsibility in its value chain, an organization should:*

☐ *integrate ethical, social, environmental and gender equality criteria, and health and safety, in its purchasing, distribution and contracting policies and practices to improve consistency with social responsibility objectives;*

☐ *encourage other organizations to adopt similar policies, without indulging in anti-competitive behaviour in so doing;*

☐ *promote fair and practical treatment of the costs and benefits of implementing socially responsible practices throughout the value chain, including, where possible, enhancing the capacity of organizations in the value chain to meet socially responsible objectives. This includes adequate purchasing practices, such as ensuring that fair prices are paid and that there are adequate delivery times and stable contracts.*

ISO 26000:2010, pages 50-51.

Some socially responsible organizations utilize surveys given to suppliers to assess their ecosystem to ensure they are behaving sustainably and in a socially responsible manner. When the results reveal deficiencies in their management systems, corrective measures can be developed to address them. When a company wants to do the right thing but lacks the financial means or the managerial capacity to implement social responsibility management systems, this should not mean there's nothing to be done. This is where a mentor-mentee relationship comes in handy. This is especially true for suppliers who belong to historically marginalized and discriminated against groups.

EQUITY DISRUPTION IN PROMOTING SOCIAL RESPONSIBILITY IN THE VALUE CHAIN

Companies that refuse to be socially responsible in their management systems and refuse to comply with any corrective measures have already disqualified themselves. In these situations, the socially responsible organization should consider discontinuing any relationship with such companies. But just as an organization can induce others to behave more responsibly, it should consider the potential impacts or unintended consequences of its procurement and purchasing decisions and take care to avoid or minimize any negative impacts. These actions should not be viewed as replacing the role of authorities to implement and enforce laws and regulations, of course, but as a parallel effort that's part of an overall socially responsible environment.

Engaging minority and vulnerable populations in an organization's processes, moderated through the lens of DE&I, will also likely disrupt existing models and norms built on historical injustice and inequities. In many cases, the simple fact of considering DE&I will be considered disruptive to local norms, and organizations need to be ready for the possibility of pushback from entrenched interests. It also means that monitoring of partners is required to ensure compliance. ISO 26000 suggests:

ISO *To promote social responsibility in its value chain, an organization should:*

☐ *carry out appropriate due diligence and monitoring of the organizations with which it has relationships, with a view to preventing compromise of the organization's commitments to social responsibility;*

ISO 26000:2010, page 50.

PROMOTING SOCIAL RESPONSIBILITY IN THE VALUE CHAIN
Governance-centered inclusion actionable steps

Governance-centered inclusion should resolve the equity issues raised in promoting social responsibility in the sphere of influence by addressing them in actionable steps that move the organization forward in its social responsibility commitments. Where feasible, as noted above, organizations should consider signing the "Anti-corruption Call to Action" pledge located on the UN Global Compact website or a similar pledge. A global transparent economy is dependent on individual organizations joining forces with governments and the UN to eradicate a global systemic issue such as corruption. Promoting social responsibility involves setting ethical standards and then abiding by them, requiring similar commitments from those with which an organization does business.

Governance-centered inclusion actionable steps in
PROMOTING SOCIAL RESPONSIBILITY IN THE VALUE CHAIN

1. In reviewing your organization's policies and procedures around promoting social responsibility in the value chain, how do they align with your DE&I policy, commitments, and corporate proclamations on the matter?

2. If there are gaps, what are the actionable steps and timelines you have identified to narrow or eliminate them based on the 3-Step Equity Lens model?

3. Were all relevant stakeholders identified and engaged in the review, modification or development of your policies and procedures around your DE&I moderated promoting social responsibility in the value chain practices?

FAIR OPERATING PRACTICE ISSUE 5: DE&I AS MODERATOR FOR RESPECT FOR PROPERTY RIGHTS

In addressing respect for property rights in your fair operating practices, does your organization also intentionally consider the rights of minority and vulnerable groups? If yes, how? If no, why not?

Property rights are some of the areas where minorities and vulnerable groups have historically been most acutely disenfranchised.

RESPECT FOR PROPERTY RIGHTS
Knowledge-informed diversity call to action

Property rights cover a myriad of rights including home ownership and intellectual property (patents, copyrights, designs, counterfeit product, and brand identity). These rights open doors of opportunity and serve as a foundation of life, liberty and the pursuit of happiness. They ensure the enjoyment and endowment of their economic and innovative achievements across generations. Respecting property rights and property claims are important DE&I issues because historically they represent areas where minority and vulnerable groups' rights have been significantly compromised or abused. There are major social responsibility consequences in this area because the loss of historic land claims or the denial of intellectual property claims has had significant economic, environmental and social ramifications on many communities. To clarify, based on ISO 26000,

> **ISO** *The right to own property is a human right recognized in the Universal Declaration of Human Rights. Property rights cover both physical property and intellectual property and include interest in land and other physical assets, copyrights, patents, geographical indicator rights, funds, moral rights and other rights. They may also encompass a consideration of broader property claims, such as traditional knowledge of specific groups, such as indigenous peoples, or the intellectual property of employees or others. Recognition of property rights promotes investment and economic and physical security, as well as encouraging creativity and innovation.*
>
> *ISO 26000:2010, page 51.*

The right to own property (physical and intellectual) is a human right recognized in the Universal Declaration of Human Rights. When these rights are tampered with through policy or social contracts, they can have generational impacts on multiple fronts. Both Intellectual and physical property rights feature prominently in the American Exceptionalism story, for good and ill.

INTELLECTUAL PROPERTY RIGHTS:
Humankind exists at the crossroads of reproduction, creativity and innovations. Every generation of humankind is born pregnant with new possibilities, new horizons to unleash and higher heights to climb than the previous generation. At the heart of it all is intellectual property rights—how we address challenges, opportunities, threats, and other global problems in all fields but especially in the life sciences, information technology, creative arts, and material sciences, to name a few. Intellectual property rights sustain prosperity (profit), people and planet. They are DE&I matters

because they involve the creation and distribution of a form of wealth, which has moral, economic and socio-cultural values and implications. These values transform the livelihood of the inventor, and society benefits from it directly and indirectly. The rapid development of the COVID-19 and Ebola vaccines is a testament to this. Intellectual property rights are also human rights, because artificial barriers have historically existed to disenfranchise those already marginalized by social contracts and divisive norms from meaningful participation in the economy, including the economy of ideas.

The world looks to the United States for best practices, even though it has not always set a good example. The U.S. Constitution gives the nation the means to reimagine and reinvent itself from generation to generation. When it comes to intellectual property rights, the U.S. has a preponderance of data from which lessons can be learned and social responsibility framework established. While patent laws existed before the United States was formed, its quick rise as a leader amongst industrialized nations was driven by its patent system—a system that from its inception was designed to be colorblind, but as with so much of American society, became color-built.

The Constitution stated: *"To promote the Progress of Science and useful Arts, by securing for limited Times to Authors and Inventors the exclusive Right to their respective Writings and Discoveries (United States n.d.)."* Referred to as the Copyright and Patent Clause, this provision in the Constitution was adopted without discussion and Congress was authorized to promulgate the provisions to implement it without the authority to override the Clause. In the Federalist Papers, James Madison, one of the founding fathers, further described the Copyright Patent Clause and its utility:

> *The utility of this power will scarcely be questioned. The copyright of authors has been solemnly adjudged, in Great Britain, to be a right of common law. The right to useful inventions seems with equal reason to belong to the inventors. The public good fully coincides in both cases with the claims of individuals. The States cannot separately make effectual provision for either of the cases, and most of them have anticipated the decision of this point, by laws passed at the instance of Congress (Madison n.d.).*

The utility of the intellectual property clause settled any future debate by Congress on its merits because it addressed the very lifeblood and sustainability of the nation—a climate for sustainable innovations and commerce to develop and thrive. Yet, because the founders made concessions to slaveholding states, allowing slavery to continue, the Clause simply continued the inequalities inherent in class systems–the same sorts of inequalities that had driven the Americans to start the Revolutionary War. From the outset, the reimagined intellectual property rights only favored

White men. America presented a new problem as it related to societal class systems. The multi-racial truths of America, which embodied the spirit of the Constitution that "All men were created equal," clashed with the traditional implicit mindset that such privileges were really meant for White men only.

Some experts contend that while the Constitution was intentionally protective of property rights, it predominantly favored the interests of the elites while preserving human slavery. Hence, the contention that this worldview ensured intellectual property rights became a vehicle for creating and sustaining income inequality in America. Income inequality is a function of both inequality from capital and inequality from labor. As Brenda Reddix-Smalls ably contended in her seminal work on the issue:

> *What has not been adequately addressed is that these intellectual property statutes were drafted in an environment which supported slavery, oppression, and discrimination against a group of people. Slaves were considered the property of the master, borrower, lessor, or any other person with a possessory interest. The master owned any profits from the slaves' labor; the master owned any rents and proceeds from any developments by the slave. As such, the master, the gatherer of capital, began to amass the profits and rents from the enslaved. The laws were written for his benefit. The laws were designed to encourage the proliferation of capital and capital rents to the elites, the slave owners, and the colonial gentry. Today, intellectual property laws that support the protection of data information as intellectual property serve to provide capital and capital rents to the new owners in the connected global economy (Reddix-Smalls 2018).*

Human labor and human capital intersect at the very essence of who a person is—their identity. Human labor is what a person does to contribute to society and earn a living. Human capital, as expert Charles Wheelan rightly described, *"is the sum total of skills embodied within an individual: education, intelligence, charisma, creativity, work experience, entrepreneurial vigor (Musgrave 2011). "*

Ironically, slavery gave the slave owner more than the physical human labor "person" enslaved by also controlling his or her intellectual property rights (human capital). This is ironic because the very people group who had the products of the mind that facilitated the technology of that day and expanded the economic power of the new nation were the slaves. Freed and enslaved Africans before and after Emancipation could be found both in the North and South performing tasks and roles that gave them real life experiences pregnant with the potential for new inventions and innovative and better ways of doing things. Before America was a nation, these enslaved Africans became masters in their trades and found new ways to modernize and transform the plantation economy whether they were in Jamaica, Surinam or America:

> *Slave work involved much more than mere laboring in the fields. Indeed, slaves undertook the most varied of working tasks, from the simplest of labours through to the most skilled of crafts, everywhere in the Americas. Each of the major American export crops required its own particular skills, in cultivation, cropping, processing and transportation. And each slave settlement required that range of artisans whose abilities made possible the functioning of local economic and social life. Carpenters and masons, factory foremen, distillers, nurses and transport slaves all added their skills and working experiences to the well being of local slave society (Shepherd 2000).*

However, because they were considered property, slaves could not own rights to their innovations. Human labor and human capital are the engine for sustainable economic and social prosperity, but it's an engine that for a long while was firmly placed in the hands of a few. Two U.S. Supreme Court decisions aided in keeping blacks from achieving parity with whites, by preventing them from creating wealth that could have been transferred generationally: the Dred Scott v. Sanford and Plessy v. Ferguson. These decisions and segregation laws, combined with lynching, race riots and state-sponsored terrorism against black and brown people groups, had tremendous impact on patenting that continues in part to this day.

Dred Scott v. Sanford (1856): Dred Scott was born a slave in Virginia. In 1820, he was purchased by John Emerson. Emerson took Scott to two states that prohibited slavery: Illinois and Wisconsin. Scott married and remained in Wisconsin when Emerson returned to Missouri. Before leaving Wisconsin, Emerson leased Scott (considered property) to other White people—which was a violation of the Missouri Compromise which opposed slavery within that region. Emerson was compensated for Scott's slave labor. Later, Emerson relocated to Louisiana where Scott and his wife joined him and had a baby girl born into freedom on the Mississippi River. When Emerson returned to Wisconsin, his wife went back to Missouri and took with her Scott and his wife and daughter. When Emerson died in Iowa, his wife inherited Scott and leased him out to other White people, against the request of Scott to buy his freedom.

Scott and his wife sued Emerson's widow and a jury found in their favor. Emerson's widow filed an appeal after she had moved to Massachusetts and had leased or given Scott and his wife to her brother, John F.A. Sandford. The case went to the Missouri Supreme Court where the decision was reversed because the court agreed that Scott and his wife should have filed for their freedom when they lived in a free state. Sandford later moved to New York and there, Scott resumed his legal action in federal court because diversity jurisdiction was applicable. But the Supreme Court ruled that because slaves—even after they were freed—were not U.S. citizens, they had no standing in federal courts. Justice Roger Brooke Taney who wrote the majority opinion even suggested that the founding fathers regarded blacks as inferior to Whites and therefore could not possibly have granted them citizenship. The opinion went further to assert that Congress did not even have the authority to outlaw slavery in federal territory (Justia n.d.).

Demonstrating that not all White people agreed with this outlook, Justice Benjamin Robbins Curtis dissented on the ground that Taney's belief about what the founders intended was questionable. Justice John McLean agreed with Curtis and argued that because five states already allowed blacks to vote, they could indeed become citizens (Justia n.d.). Even one of the sons of Emerson refused to remain complicit and took action by purchasing freedom for Scott and his wife after the Supreme Court decision was handed down (Justia n.d.). This ruling had broader implications, because it meant that slaves could not patent or copyright their creative works and innovations because an oath of citizenship was required to be taken to complete a patent application. Scott as a freedman worked in a hotel in St. Louis until his death; his wife however lived to see the Supreme Court decision overturned by the passage of the Fourteenth Amendments (Justia n.d.).

The U.S. Congress passed the Thirteenth and Fourteenth Amendments to permanently answer the slavery and citizenship questions. The Thirteenth Amendment (ratified in 1865) ended slavery in the United States (superseding the Emancipation Proclamation, an Executive Order that allowed slaves in some states), which meant former slaves were no longer property to be owned or leased out. The Fourteenth Amendment (ratified in 1868) guaranteed that all persons born or naturalized in the U. S. are citizens, equal under the laws, and cannot be deprived of life, liberty, or property without due process.

Plessy v. Ferguson (1896): The end of slavery and the granting of citizenship to everyone born in the United States did not end the drive to keep African Americans as second-class citizens and thereby marginalize their participation in the economic engine of the nation—capitalism. Plessy v. Ferguson caused lasting damage to the rights of African Americans to hold patents, and the impacts of this decision are still reverberating even in the twenty-first century.

Homer Plessy was a black man in Louisiana who could easily pass for a White man (he was one-eight African descent and seven-eighths White). Plessy was chosen to defy this law by a Committee of Citizens (Comite des Citoyens)—a New Orleans residents mixed ethnic group. The railroad company owned and operated by Whites also agreed to participate in the challenge of the law because it required them to purchase more rail cars to comply with the law requiring separate cars for Whites and Blacks. The Comite also engaged a White detective to arrest Plessy for violating the Act. Plessy was convicted and fined by Honorable John H. Ferguson who was the judge for the criminal District Court for the Parish of Orleans. The case eventually went before the Supreme Court, where Plessy's attorneys argued that the law violated the thirteenth and Fourteenth Amendments.

The U.S. Supreme Court Justice Henry Billings Brown, who authored the now infamous majority opinion, contended that the Louisiana law was not discriminatory because he argued that separate but equal did not mean African Americans were inferior. If African Americans felt inferior by the law, Brown ruled, it was their own interpretation not the law itself that made them feel that way. Justice John Marshall Harlan, the lone dissenter, wrote the now-famous dissent that the Constitution was color-blind, the nation had no class system, and all citizens had equal access to civil rights. This was a transformative declaration by a judge whose thinking about civil rights for freed slaves and even the emancipation declaration had evolved—he had opposed both in the past. But when Harlan witnessed the brutality of white supremacist groups such as the Ku Klux Klan, he refused to continue to be complicit. His dissent read in part:

> I am of the opinion that the statute of Louisiana is inconsistent with the personal liberties of citizens, white and black, in that State, and hostile to both the spirit and the letter of the Constitution of the United States. If laws of like character should be enacted in the several States of the Union, the effect would be in the highest degree mischievous. Slavery as an institution tolerated by law would, it is true, have disappeared from our country, but there would remain a power in the States, by sinister legislation, to interfere with the blessings of freedom; to regulate civil rights common to all citizens, upon the basis of race; and to place in a condition of legal inferiority a large body of American citizens, now constituting a part of the political community, called the people of the United States, for whom and by whom, through representatives, our government is administrated. Such a system is inconsistent with the guarantee given by the Constitution to each State of a republican form of government, and may be stricken down by congressional action, or by the courts in the discharge of their solemn duty to maintain the supreme law of the land, anything in the Constitution or laws of any State to the contrary notwithstanding (Plessy 1896).

Regrettably, Harlan did make some derogatory comments about Asians in his dissent, referring to them as "Chinaman," when he made the point that even foreigners had privileges that the blacks who fought for the country did not. But this derogatory term should not take away from the monumental leap he made in his social thinking over time. Unfortunately, Plessy v. Ferguson created the freeway upon which "separate but equal" legislations and Jim Crow laws were driven through the highways of state legislatures, marginalizing black and brown people group and making it impossible for them to participate freely in American Capitalism for half a century. For a people group to lose half a century when America was moving past the industrial revolution into a new economic dispensation where technological creativity and new innovations were taking root, meant that they were left out of the capitalism mainstream entirely. It was no surprise that their patenting rates dropped almost instantly after 1896. It took another generation of Supreme Court Justices for justice to reign again for the black and brown racial groups, while the disparities and disadvantages as compared with the white racial group continued to increase exponentially.

In Brown v. Board of Education, the Court finally ruled that segregation of schools on the basis of race violated the Equal Protection Clause of the Fourteenth Amendment when the benefits and opportunities accorded white student was higher and better than those for black and brown students, putting the nail in the coffin of Plessy v. Ferguson's legacy.

In her seminar work on "Violence and Economic Activity: Evidence from African American Patents, 1870 to 1940," economist Lisa D. Cook made a compelling case for the relationships. Ms. Cook showed the correlation between the escalating violence, race riots, segregation laws, lynching, state-sponsored or supported violence against African Americans impacted their patenting. Ms. Cook demonstrated through data that from 1870 to 1940, the patenting rates of African Americans declined.

Figure 9.2 How systemic racism destroyed black innovation in the U.S.

How Systemic Racism Destroyed Black Innovation in the U.S.

Violence and segregation undermined African American inventors throughout the 20th century

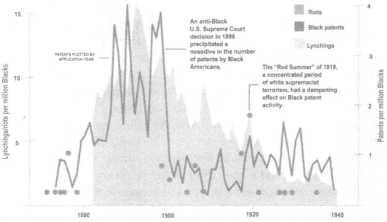

Source: "Violence and Economic Growth: Evidence From African American Patents, 1870-1940, Lisa D. Cook," Journal of Economic Growth, Volume 19 Issue 2 (June 2014), PP.221-257

What Ms. Cook's data revealed is the lost opportunities of black and brown people to fully participate in capitalism and its institutions. Too many barriers were placed in their way, with systemic and structural racism baked into the financial institutions that supported the endeavor and made it possible (patents, lending, investments, insurance, bonding, etc.). The ecosystem of capital financing creativity and innovation to produce products and services are as much a part of the ethos of capitalism as apple pie is to American cuisine.

Access to capital to finance creativity and innovation should be color-blind in a just and fair capitalist system. America and the world will never know how many African Americans went to their graves with skills and innovations that never saw the light of day because they were murdered, marginalized or were simply afraid to unleash their creativity for fear of being lynched. Yet, consider the fact that in the very pivotal movement of America's Space quest, Astronaut John Glenn could not have gone into space and given America a leg up over all countries unless a black woman mathematician he trusted—Katherine Johnson—said the calculations made by computers were correct. This is how NASA told her story:

In 1962, as NASA prepared for the orbital mission of John Glenn, Johnson was called upon to do the work that she would become most known for. The complexity of the orbital flight had required the construction of a worldwide communications network, linking tracking stations around the world to IBM computers in Washington, Cape Canaveral in Florida, and Bermuda. The computers had been programmed with the orbital equations that would control the trajectory of the capsule in Glenn's Friendship 7 mission from liftoff to splashdown, but the astronauts were wary of putting their lives in the care of the electronic calculating machines, which were prone to hiccups and blackouts. As a part of the preflight checklist, Glenn asked engineers to "get the girl"— Johnson—to run the same numbers through the same equations that had been programmed into the computer, but by hand, on her desktop mechanical calculating machine. "If she says they're good,'" Katherine Johnson remembers the astronaut saying, "then I'm ready to go." Glenn's flight was a success, and marked a turning point in the competition between the United States and the Soviet Union in space (NASA 2020).

America's space dominance allowed it to create the internet technology that made the information revolution possible, and Ms. Johnson had a lot to do with it. Every organization on earth has benefited from this revolution because a black woman got the opportunity to play a key role – not because of her color but for her intellectual worthiness, despite all the daunting obstacles placed on her journey to that moment in time. This is a moment indeed when talent and opportunity regardless of color or gender made America great!

In today's digital economy, inventors create wealth through organizations that allow technology to be used to create customers or consumers where the individual user cedes their data willingly, enriching the inventors in the process. Historically, for example, to benefit from the invention of electricity, the user did not have to give up their identity. But to use many digital services today, the user gives up his or her identity and provides a snapshot of themselves by the click of a button to total strangers. The process itself at the core is race and gender neutral. In essence, the individual consumer pays for an all-inclusive view of themselves when they buy or use an app which gathers data on them and sells that data to others, who use it to provide more products and services curated for them. Every producer of apps and contents wants to grow their profit margins or viewership for their shareholders; they are less likely to dictate customer preference based on race unless it serves a different purpose.

When a white person exchanges digital or physical currency, they rarely ask if a minority person touched it. The same is true for blood transfusions; no white person at the point of illness or death demands that the blood transfusion he or she receives should only be from another white person. The point is that the good old dollar knows no race in commerce and financial institutions and financiers can play a key role in dismantling the capital barriers placed in the path of black and brown people groups. As Rayvon Fouche noted in the "the black inventors in the age of segregation:"

> Historians have ignored technology as an institutionalized force that marginalizes black people within American society and culture. Many scholars have overlooked technology because of the perception that it is just "stuff" and therefore value-neutral, non-gendered and non-racist. This perception allows the unproblematic acceptance of technology as a simple black box, which, in turn, supports the assumption that technology can be fully understood by its most simple material form and function. The belief in the uncomplicated meanings of technology promotes the misperception that technologies have one real meaning. Yet this is far from true. In American society, the automobile's dominant meaning is most closely understood as a device that transports people from one location to another. But automobiles have many more complicated meanings within our culture, from a status symbol to a weapon that can kill. When human actors interact with technology, they reinforce, redefine, or subvert the technology's dominant meaning or function. Since technologies traditionally do not design and build themselves, they usually do not exhibit biases on their own. Thus, in a built technological world, human agents must not ignore their place in the construction of the forms and the production of the meanings of the technology. Technology in American society is one of the most efficient systems for transmitting asset of ideological beliefs (Fouche 2003).

With societal acknowledgement that racism and gender inequalities are divisive norms that can no longer be accepted, these customs and practices have gone underground where they are much more difficult to root out and much more potent in their adverse impacts. This runs counter to the social responsibility norms where human creativity and innovation and human labor knows no color, especially as it relates to wealth creation and transfer.

There are inventions today that are designed to multiply, also known as self-replicating technologies (SRT). SRTs include seeds for agriculture, computer codes and vaccines. Seed breeding seeds are generally modified to produce abundantly and withstand climatic conditions that have traditionally doomed many a harvest. The developers of these seeds are protected by patent laws. The same is true for computer codes and vaccines for preventing or curing diseases. While the capital to develop these innovative products come from investors and public funding through governmental structures, the benefits favor the investor and society-at-large becomes an afterthought after the profit margins.

Therefore, intellectual property protection and human rights tussle in the arena of patented food products, educational materials, access to medicine and even protection of the knowledge long in the domain of indigenous groups. The question for our time is whether capital should be driven by shareholders' interests alone at the price of human lives. Should black and brown people in the U.S. continue to die unnecessarily because of the impacts of systemic and structural racism in the entire capitalism ecosystem? Should poor people around the world be denied access to innovative medical treatments so the rich investors who funded the innovations get astronomically richer?

PHYSICAL PROPERTY RIGHTS:

Property ownership in America has never been fair and just for black and brown people groups. When slavery was legal, black slaves lived in shanty homes in the land of the slaveowner. They were responsible for building and maintaining all of the physical infrastructure—homes, plantation facilities, etc—on the plantation. A cursory historical review of some of these plantations show palatial slaveowner homes that were lavishly built and well landscaped—all the works of slaves. Slaves also maintained the domestic affairs of the slaveowner homes, including cleaning and maintaining the welfare and wellbeing of the master's household.

Once freed, many former slaves continued to work for the plantations and maintain the household of the former masters. But a new undercurrent began to brew that was consistent with all the other discriminatory practices that followed Emancipation and the Thirteenth, Fourteenth Amendments. While blacks were sought after for their uncanny skills and knowhow in building homes and in maintaining these homes, they were increasingly branded as detrimental to property values in the very neighborhoods they built and maintained. This new worldview became a self-fulfilling prophecy through systemic and structural racist policies and practices that continue to be true even today. Several federal policies and societal norms (segregations laws, lynching, race riots, etc) cemented the marginalization of black and brown people groups from home ownership in America. The following discussion will look at three key trends that denied the black and brown groups of their rights to home ownership, and four trends that show how the federal government attempted to cure the historical damages:

Three Trends Established America's Systemic Housing discrimination

1. **The National Housing Act of 1934:** By 1934, the U.S. housing market was in crisis: 2 million workers in the construction industry had lost their jobs,

terms for securing mortgages were difficult to obtain, and mortgage loans were limited to 50% of the property's market value (including a balloon payment after five years of spread-out repayment plan). Only 1 in 10 Americans owned homes, which meant that the vast majority of the citizenry were renters. In response, the U.S. Congress created the Federal Housing Administration (FHA) in 1934 (US HUD 2022). The FHA–through the Home Owners' Loan Corporation (HOLC)-began taking over foreclosed property loans from banks by exchanging them for government-guaranteed bonds and refinancing them directly.

This Act formalized the systemic discrimination against minorities in American homeownership. The HPLC began mapping residential neighborhoods by associating risk factors to them from A to D. The D classification as discussed earlier was coded for black and brown neighborhoods. In essence, the HOLC began the practice of creating residential security maps that zoned off black and brown communities as hazardous neighborhoods which were disqualified from any federal home loan guarantees. Known as "Redlining," these maps classified high-risk areas in 239 cities around the country. These neighborhoods were home to minority groups and were denied loans for either repairing their existing homes or for buying new homes. The net result of these policies and practices was that they made minority neighborhoods even less attractive for capital investments, and set them on a trajectory for blight, crime and other neighborhood decay problems–typical of disinvestments in a community.

Figure 9.3: US federal housing authority timeline

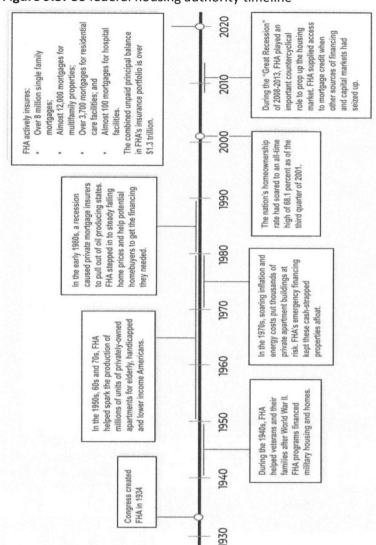

FHA actively insures:
- Over 8 million single family mortgages;
- Almost 12,000 mortgages for multifamily properties;
- Over 3,700 mortgages for residential care facilities; and
- Almost 100 mortgages for hospital facilities.

The combined unpaid principal balance in FHA's insurance portfolio is over $1.3 trillion.

During the "Great Recession" of 2008-2013, FHA played an important countercyclical role to prop up the housing market. FHA supplied access to mortgage credit when other sources of financing and capital markets had seized up.

In the early 1980s, a recession caused private mortgage insurers to pull out of oil producing states. FHA stepped in to steady falling home prices and help potential homebuyers to get the financing they needed.

The nation's homeownership rate had soared to an all-time high of 68.1 percent as of the third quarter of 2001.

In the 1950s, 60s and 70s, FHA helped spark the production of millions of units of privately-owned apartments for elderly, handicapped and lower income Americans.

In the 1970s, soaring inflation and energy costs put thousands of private apartment buildings at risk. FHA's emergency financing kept these cash-strapped properties afloat.

Congress created FHA in 1934

During the 1940s, FHA helped veterans and their families after World War II. FHA programs financed military housing and homes.

Source: FHA history 2022.

2. **The Housing Act of 1937**: The Housing Act of 1937 was the next large step in the government's New Deal approach to the housing crisis. It stated in Section 1:

> It is the policy of the United States to promote the general welfare of the Nation by employing the funds and credit of the Nation, as provided in this chapter–to assist States and political subdivisions of States to remedy the unsafe housing conditions and the acute shortage of decent and safe dwellings for low-income families; to

With the affirmation and expansion of the redlining system, structural racism took root in public housing initiatives produced even more homeownership, public housing, wealth creation, healthcare, income, education and other disparities in the United States. This even though the government was trying to do the right thing, as the Act clearly stated:

··· that our Nation should promote the goal of providing decent and affordable housing for all citizens through the efforts and encouragement of Federal, State, and local governments, and by the independent and collective actions of private citizens, organizations, and the private sector.

The question of citizenship had of course long been settled and so the above stated goal should have included black and brown Americans. However, without first addressing the root of the problem, the solutions often fail even if they are well-intended. In this Housing Act, the federal intent was right and just, but it allocated monies to states already well on their way to establishing a class system reminiscent of the days of slavery through policy and police actions. Segregation laws, lynching, and police brutality were all deliberate attempts to reimagine the vicissitudes of slavery where the benefits were not free labor but reinforcement of white privilege. This is the whack-a-mole game the black and brown people group in America have long endured. Once the federal or state government takes its slow steps towards righting the wrongs of the past (as the nation continues to do so well), other actors within the ecosystem continue to hunger for past divisive glories and act on these yearnings—slowing or working to counter the changes.

3. **The GI Bill (1944):** The "Servicemen's Readjustment Act" or GI Bill was signed into law by President Franklin D. Roosevelt in 1944 and it began the idealism of the American dream. As WWII was ending, the U.S. Government recognized that 15 million men and women were coming back home as veterans, and rising unemployment was sending the economy into a depression. Working with a stakeholder group—the American Legion—the National Resources Planning Board (a White House agency) developed a plan that included healthcare, education and training

as its core programming (Servicemen 1944). The program offered Federal aid that allowed veterans to get free healthcare, purchase homes and businesses, and provided *"tuition, subsistence, books and supplies, equipment, and counseling services for veterans to continue their education in school or college* (Servicemen 1944). *"* When veterans could not find employment, they received up to 52 weeks of unemployment benefits. The government summarized the success of the program as follows:

Within the following seven years, approximately eight million veterans received educational benefits. Under the act, approximately 2,300,000 attended colleges and universities, 3,500,000 received school training, and 3,400,000 received on-the-job training. The number of degrees awarded by U.S. colleges and universities more than doubled between 1940 and 1950, and the percentage of Americans with bachelor degrees, or advanced degrees, rose from 4.6 percent in 1945 to 25 percent a half-century later.

Unfortunately, not all veterans were able to take advantage of the benefits of the G.I. Bill. Black vets were often unable to get bank loans for mortgages in Black neighborhoods, and they faced prejudice and discrimination that overwhelming excluded them from buying homes in "white" suburban neighborhoods (Servicemen 1944).

The economy expanded dramatically and facilitated the creation of new products and services which enabled the rise of both suburbs and suburban ecosystem. Unfortunately for the African American veterans, the seeds of redlining that had produced the roots of segregated public housing and other economic bifurcations gave rise to a new slate of inequities. When it was all said and done, poor and rich whites entered a new era of prosperity; many today have benefited from generational wealth transfers resulting from the G.I. bill. The US Government summed up the success of the G.I. Bill in economic terms:

By 1956, when the G.I. Bill expired, the education-and-training portion had disbursed $14.5 billion to veterans—but the Veterans Administration estimated the increase in Federal income taxes alone would pay for the cost of the bill several times over. By 1955, 4.3 million home loans had been granted, with a total face value of $33 billion. In addition, veterans were responsible for buying 20 percent of all new homes built after the war. The results rippled through the rest of the economy; there would be no new depression—just unparalleled prosperity for a generation. The G.I. Bill has been extended several times. Nearly 2.3 million veterans

African American veterans who looked forward to a new America, however, found out that systemic and structural racism never dies on its own accord. The ecosystem bred by segregation dishonored their service by marginalizing their benefits, denying them rights to own property in nicer neighborhoods on the basis of race despite the new program. African American veterans still could not get loans for property in redlined communities and still could not buy homes in the new suburbs. Realtors dissuaded them from such pursuits; white realtors who attempted to do the right thing were blacklisted. The African American hope of a just nation acting justly once again was shattered across the board. White neighborhoods, flush with the infusion of capital, built a promising future for their inhabitants, with homes building wealth for families and good schools funded by local property taxes.

By way of contrast, redlining kept capital out of black neighborhoods, leaving a significant number crowded in public housing that subjected generations to lead poisoning from dilapidated buildings, lack of access to gainful employment, generational poverty, crime, mass incarceration-the list of negative indicators goes on and on. These are the fruits of the tree of segregation. They are systemic and remain a stronghold in property rights matters today.

The U.S. Government's Response to Systemic Housing Discriminations

That the U.S. Government has been working at eliminating housing discrimination in the country is not in question; most scholars will agree with the preponderance of the evidence. But although the *"goal of providing decent and affordable housing for all citizens through the efforts and encouragement of Federal, State, and local governments, and by the independent and collective actions of private citizens, organizations, and the private sector"* was enacted into law in 1937, the promise has still not been realized, even in 2022. Some have pointed out that this is not impressive for a nation that managed to send a man to the moon with a program that spanned less than a decade. To its credit, the federal government has been actively pursuing innovative ways to address problems rooted in the three trends discussed above. Here are some of the ways the government has tried to deal with the housing segregation stronghold:

- *The Fair Housing Act (1968)*: This was the federal government's attempt to address the blatant systemic housing discrimination practices. The Act outlawed housing discrimination based on race, color, national origin, sex or religion. The Act provided a mechanism for filing a housing discrimination complaint and authorized the

Department of Housing and Urban Development to mediate, though not to prosecute. HUD unfortunately could not file lawsuits or take legal actions on behalf of the victims. Some experts believe that the lack of enforcement powers weakened this Act and allowed segregation and separate but equal social norms to fester.

- *Fair Housing in the Nixon Administration (1971)*: A few years into the implementation of the Fair housing Act, there were known problems that segregated housing policies produced. But to secure the votes of suburban new voters, President Nixon took a backseat to strengthening the fair housing agenda within a deeply segregated nation. President Nixon's administration did not pursue any policy changes that weighed on integration in ever-entrenching suburban vistas where the nation's wealth remained bifurcated.

- *The Equal Credit Opportunity Act of 1974*: This Act addressed one of the loopholes in the Fair Housing Act. It barred discrimination against credit applicants based on "race, color, religion, national origin, sex, marital status, age." It also barred discrimination against an individual loan applicant who received income from a public assistance program, or filed a complaint under the Consumer Credit Protection Act. Where patterns of discrimination existed in home improvement loans or home mortgage loan applications, the Department of Justice was authorized to file a lawsuit under ECOA (US DOJ n.d.).

- *The Home Mortgage Disclosure Act of 1975*: This Act addressed another loophole in the Fair Housing Act that emanated from redlining which led to credit shortages in certain urban neighborhoods. The HMDA provided the public with information that showed whether financial institutions were "serving the housing credit needs of the neighborhoods and communities in which they are located (Home Mortgage n.d.)." It also provided information to public officials *"in targeting public investments from the private sector to areas where they are needed* (Home Mortgage n.d.)*."* Later amendments required the *"collection and disclosure of data about applicant and borrower characteristics to assist in identifying possible discriminatory lending patterns and enforcing antidiscrimination statutes (Home Mortgage n.d.). "*

- *The Community Reinvestment Act of 1977*: This Act addressed banking institutions' discriminatory practices where the credit memorandum or guidelines used were bifurcated—one for white people and the other for black and brown people groups. The Act required the *"Federal Reserve and other federal banking regulators to encourage financial institutions to help meet the credit needs of the communities in which they do business, including low- and moderate-income (LMI) neighborhoods (Community Reinvestment 2022)."* Some experts contend that while this was a well-intentioned directive, it simply moved systemic housing discrimination practices underground. African American borrowers were sometimes given misinformation or lured into outlandish high-interest rate loan products that made them more susceptible to default and thereby lose their homes.

While these Acts have been modified several times over, the presentation here is to show the correlation between the impacts of redlining and other segregation practices in the housing sector and the government's responses over time.

RESPECT FOR PROPERTY RIGHTS
Creativity-driven equity opportunity/reconciliation/disruption

It is precisely because property rights are so valuable for human dignity and generational wealth transfer that they have historically been subject to significant abuse by the majority. It is as much an American phenomenon as it is around the world—same problem, different permutations. This is particularly true as developed countries established presences, political and/or economic, in other nations; when local communities posed an obstacle of any sort towards economic exploitation, organizations have ruthlessly schemed with or manipulated local politics to get what they wanted, or even just seized property and materials. This is, in fact, the core dynamic in colonialism, the inequitable legacy of which is still felt today.

Nations who were once colonized have conjured up new lines of similar discriminatory practices that the colonial masters were accused of. They are branded differently but follow the societal fault lines that were established long ago. The British, for instance, created nations by bringing people groups together that have had historical differences and used these differences to govern them under the divide-and-conquer mantra. Under these regimes, property rights were a function of the will of the colonialists, who used direct and indirect rules to govern their domains. Respecting property rights in today's dispensation calls for understanding how these rights were traditionally abused in the local setting before devising creative ways to ensure they are not perpetuated. The 3-Step Equity Lens can assist in these efforts.

EQUITY OPPORTUNITY IN RESPECT FOR PROPERTY RIGHTS

The U.S. Government has been actively pursuing new innovative ways to address intellectual and property rights of its citizens, and it has been an uphill battle. This is not a uniquely American problem. Every country in the world today has varying degrees of discriminatory property rights issues to address. Respecting property rights is no different than respecting other people as part of our shared humankind. Everyone, including minorities and disadvantaged communities, deserves the opportunity to own and profit from their property, whatever its form. That is why ISO 26000 provided the following broad guidance:

 pay fair compensation for property that it acquires or uses

ISO 26000:2010, page 51.

EQUITY RECONCILIATION IN RESPECT FOR PROPERTY RIGHTS

Reconciling different standards for property rights at home and abroad is an essential component of any organization's global strategy when a DE&I lens is applied to its policies, procedures, and practices. But it is as much an institutional problem as it is an individual one. Segregation laws, lynching, and arson were acts carried out by individuals as lone actors and individuals within groups. For organizations on a path towards social responsibility and sustainable development, ISO 26000 provided the following broad guidance:

☐ *implement policies and practices that promote respect for property rights and traditional knowledge;*
☐ *consider the expectations of society, human rights and basic needs of the individual when exercising and protecting its intellectual and physical property rights.*

ISO 26000:2010, page 51.

EQUITY DISRUPTION IN RESPECT FOR PROPERTY RIGHTS

It's important in asserting and validating property rights of others that organizations make sure that they are not just paying lip service to the ideal, and just as importantly, that those with whom they are doing business are also operating in good faith and holding to the same standards as the organization. ISO 26000 provided the following broad guidance:

□   *conduct proper investigations to be confident it has lawful title permitting use or disposal of property;*

□   *not engage in activities that violate property rights, including misuse of a dominant position, counterfeiting and piracy;*

ISO 26000:2010, page 51.

RESPECT FOR PROPERTY RIGHTS
Governance-centered inclusion actionable steps

Property rights are an essential part of business and intricately involved with the fairness, or inequity (depending on the situation), of resource distribution and allocation. Systemic discrimination has led to the longstanding economic disenfranchisement of minority communities both in the United States and abroad. To help heal the divisive norms that have economically marginalized and disadvantaged minority and vulnerable groups for far too long, organizations should consider its respect for property rights practices to ensure they are not reinforcing these divisive norms.

Governance-centered inclusion actionable steps in
RESPECT FOR PROPERTY RIGHTS

1. In reviewing your organization's policies and procedures around respect for property rights, how do they align with your DE&I policy, commitments, and corporate proclamations on the matter?

2. If there are gaps, what are the actionable steps and timelines you have identified to narrow or eliminate them based on the 3-Step Equity Lens model?

3. Were all relevant stakeholders identified and engaged in the review, modification or development of your policies and procedures around your DE&I moderated respect for property rights practices?

Chapter Ten

DE&I AS MODERATOR FOR CONSUMER ISSUES

C onsumer issues vary by organization. Concerns such as decisions and activities of organizations who produce, manufacture, sell or distribute products and services and consumer wellbeing as a continuum are enhanced from such use. In the previous chapter we focused on commercial customers. The focus in this chapter will be on end-use consumers. All users of products and services, whether corporate or individual, have a social relationship contract with the manufacturers, service providers, and everyone in the value chain that brings the products or services to them. This is in addition to both the economic and environmental contracts innate in the relationship between producer and consumer.

Why Consumer Issues are DE&I matters

States and organizations—to varying degrees—share social responsibility to protect and enhance the public's use of everyday products and services. In the information age, this has become increasingly necessary, even sacrosanct. Necessary because consumers interface with products and services for private use, which sometimes makes them prime candidates for abuse. Sacrosanct because the monetary values of consumer data turned into information may cross the line between commerce and individual privacy rights. This makes both the State and organizations responsible in varying degrees for ensuring that consumer issues are addressed. ISO 26000 provided the following clarifications on types of responsibilities:

ISO *Responsibilities include providing education and accurate information, using fair, transparent and helpful marketing information and contractual processes, promoting sustainable consumption and designing products and services that provide access to all and cater, where appropriate, for the vulnerable and disadvantaged. The term consumer refers to those individuals or groups that make use of the output of the organizations' decisions and activities and does not necessarily mean that consumers pay money for products and services. Responsibilities also involve minimizing risks from the use of products and services, through design, manufacture, distribution, information provision, support services and withdrawal and recall procedures. Many organizations collect or handle personal information and have a responsibility to protect the security of such information and the privacy of consumers.*

ISO 26000:2010, page 51.

Organizations have a key role to play in respecting, promoting, and protecting consumers' rights. When these rights are moderated by DE&I, they can become another avenue by which society corrects its divisive norms. A DE&I framework assists organizations to act responsibly even when the state is struggling to catch up with rapid developments in products and services. ISO provides the following considerations:

ISO *Particularly in areas where the state does not adequately satisfy people's basic needs, an organization should be sensitive to the impact of its activities on people's ability to satisfy those needs. It should also avoid actions that would jeopardize this ability. Vulnerable groups have different abilities and, in their role as consumers, vulnerable groups have particular needs to be addressed and can, in some cases, require specially tailored products and services. They have special needs because they may not know their rights and responsibilities or may be unable to act on their knowledge. They may also be unaware of or unable to assess potential risks associated with products or services and thus to make balanced judgements.*

ISO 26000:2010, page 53.

Before the Great Recession hit and led to the global financial crisis of 2007-2008, the subprime mortgage sector had already imploded. Subprime lending was popular with predatory lenders because they operated outside of federal regulatory oversight, charged exorbitant fees with prepayment penalties, and often imposed premium credit life insurance to the loans. Predatory lending activities had severe consequences for uninformed borrowers who stood to lose the equity they had built in their homes or even lose the homes altogether. Subprime loans targeted historically underserved communities, in particular the African American community.

The Subprime market did not come out of nowhere. As the national homeownership rate peaked around 2005, it created a void that the subprime lenders rumbustiously exploited.

Figure 10.1: The national homeownership rate peaked before subprime lending took off

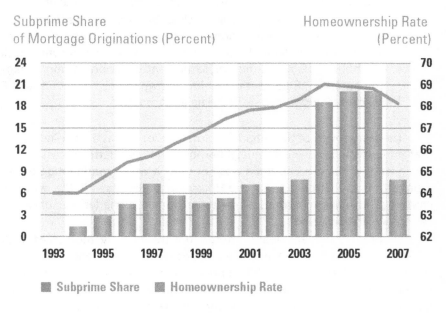

The National Homeownership Rate Peaked Before Subprime Lending Took Off

Note: Subprime share is of the dollar volume of all originations.
Sources: US Census Bureau, Housing Vacancy Survey; Inside Mortgage Finance, *2008 Mortgage Market Statistical Annual.*

A 1998 report by the U.S. Department of Housing and Urban Development titled, "Unequal burden: income & racial disparities in subprime lending in America" found a disproportionate concentration of subprime lending in minority and low-income neighborhoods (US HUD

2009). HUD's analysis of almost 1 million mortgages under the Home Mortgage Disclosure Act (HMDA) revealed the following (US HUD 2009):

1. The number of Subprime loans increased ten-fold between 1993 and 1998, ballooning to 790,000 and $150 billion.

2. Subprime loans in low-income neighborhoods were three times as common as they were in high-income neighborhoods. In 1993, 1 percent of these loans were in each of the moderate and upper-income neighborhoods while 3 percent was in low-income neighborhoods. But by 1998, 26 percent of these loans were in low-income neighborhoods compared to 7 percent in upper-income neighborhoods and 11 percent in moderate income neighborhoods.

3. Compared to white neighborhoods, subprime loans were five times as likely in black neighborhoods. In 1993, 8 percent of these loans were in black neighborhoods while 1 percent were in white neighborhood but by 1998, 51 percent of these home loans were in black neighborhoods compared to just 9 percent in white areas.

4. High-income homeowners in black neighborhoods were twice as likely to have subprime home loans when compared with low-income white neighborhoods. Homeowners in upper-income black neighborhoods accounted for 39 percent of subprime home loans compared to 18 percent in low-income white neighborhoods and 6 percent in upper-income white neighborhoods.

The fast growth of the subprime mortgage loans was a clear indication that minority and low-income neighborhoods needed better access to the prime lending market. This need was not new; it was a continuation of the disinvestments that began with the Housing Acts discussed in the previous chapter. This made minorities a ripe target for subprime lenders once the service became available.

Subprime mortgage loans offered borrowers risky mortgages with initially low interest rates which were expected to be refinanced at a later set date in concert with rising home prices. Then came 2006-2007 when the housing prices began to go down and interest rates rose, and refinancing became impossible. When the low interest loans matured and borrowers could not afford to refinance, defaults and foreclosures followed in quick succession. Hedge funds and global investors whose securities were backed by mortgage values experienced vast losses (US HUD 2009).

While no one was spared losses during the Great Recession, many black and brown people who lost their homes or the equity they had accumulated experienced a disproportionately higher impact than other populations. Since homeownership is one of the key wealth and income builders, the Great Recession and the impact of subprime mortgage loans was starkly apparent in the United States along racial and ethnic lines, and the inequity continues. PEW research published in 2014 (based on Federal Reserve data) reported that since the end of the Great Recession, white household net worth has grown 13 times greater than Black households and 10 times that of Hispanic households (Kochhar & Fry 2014):

Figure 10.2: Racial, ethnic wealth gaps since the great recession

Racial, Ethnic Wealth Gaps Have Grown Since Great Recession

Median net worth of households, in 2013 dollars

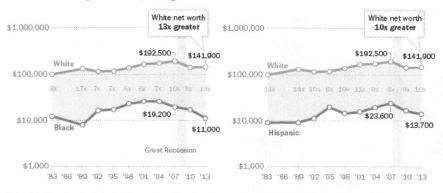

Notes: Blacks and whites include only non-Hispanics. Hispanics are of any race. Chart scale is logarithmic; each gridline is ten times greater than the gridline below it. Great Recession began Dec. '07 and ended June '09.
Source: Pew Research Center tabulations of Survey of Consumer Finances public-use data.

This shows what could happen when demand or need for a product or service by consumers makes them susceptible to predatory practices. The subprime lenders met a need for the historically underserved communities by giving loans to borrowers who did not meet the credit standards in the prime market (US HUD 2009). The loans were driven by opportunism, not any form of DE&I consideration. The chance for financing a home was welcome to this underserved community, but the loans came with a price that many failed to read in the fine print and the associated risks—risks that were often minimized and the benefits glorified. Even when the language was in plain English (or the language of the borrower's choosing) the exuberance of wealth and income possibilities that accompanied the subprime watershed intoxicated even the best of economists. Even the banks were also caught in risky exposures that they did not anticipate. Of course, when things go badly, banks and hedge funds seek shelter in the form of government relief. The subprime borrowers, on the other hand, have no such options.

Social responsibility principles and core subjects provide a holistic systemic tool for organizations to avoid these kinds of consequences. For a broader definition of the needs consumers around the world may have in common, the UN Guidelines for Consumer Protection offered:

 The legitimate needs which the guidelines are intended to meet are the following:

a) Access by consumers to essential goods and services;
b) The protection of vulnerable and disadvantaged consumers;
c) The protection of consumers from hazards to their health and safety;
d) The promotion and protection of the economic interests of consumers;
e) Access by consumers to adequate information to enable them to make informed choices according to individual wishes and needs;
f) Consumer education, including education on the environmental, social and economic consequences of consumer choice;
g) Availability of effective consumer dispute resolution and redress;
h) Freedom to form consumer and other relevant groups or organizations and the opportunity of such organizations to present their views in decision -making processes affecting them;
i) The promotion of sustainable consumption patterns;
j) A level of protection for consumers using electronic commerce that is not less than that afforded in other forms of commerce;
k) The protection of consumer privacy and the global free flow of information.

Source: UNCTAD 2016.

In a global marketplace where states and businesses are playing catchup with what constitutes fair and just new online and offline commercial activities, the UN Guidance for Consumer Protection offers a basic set of best practices for business:

 Principles for good business practices - The principles that establish benchmarks for good business practices for conducting online and offline commercial activities with consumers are as follows:

a) **Fair and equitable treatment**. Businesses should deal fairly and honestly with consumers at all stages of their relationship, so that it is an integral part of the business culture. Businesses should avoid practices that harm consumers, particularly with respect to vulnerable and disadvantaged consumers;

b) **Commercial behaviour**. Businesses should not subject consumers to illegal, unethical, discriminatory or deceptive practices, such as abusive marketing tactics, abusive debt collection or other improper behaviour that may pose unnecessary risks or harm consumers. Businesses and their authorized agents should have due regard for the interests of consumers and responsibility for upholding consumer protection as an objective;

c) **Disclosure and transparency.** Businesses should provide complete, accurate and not misleading information regarding the goods and services, terms, conditions, applicable fees and final costs to enable consumers to take informed decisions. Businesses should ensure easy access to this information, especially to the key terms and conditions, regardless of the means of technology used;

d) **Education and awareness-raising.** Businesses should, as appropriate, develop programmes and mechanisms to assist consumers to develop the knowledge and skills necessary to understand risks, including financial risks, to take informed decisions and to access competent and professional advice and assistance, preferably from an independent third party, when needed;

e) **Protection of privacy.** Businesses should protect consumers' privacy through a combination of appropriate control, security, transparency and consent mechanisms relating to the collection and use of their personal data;

f) **Consumer complaints and disputes.** Businesses should make available complaints-handling mechanisms that provide consumers with expeditious, fair, transparent, inexpensive, accessible, speedy and effective dispute resolution without unnecessary cost or burden. Businesses should consider subscribing to domestic and international standards pertaining to internal complaints handling, alternative dispute resolution services and customer satisfaction codes.

Source: UNCTAD 2016.

Combining elements of the principles above with those from the International Covenant on Economic, Social and Cultural Rights, ISO 26000 provided a set of comprehensive, socially responsible practices about the legitimate needs of consumers that include but are not limited to *"the right of everyone to an adequate standard of living, including adequate food, clothing and housing, and to the continuous improvement of living conditions and availability of essential products and services, including financial."*

ISO *These legitimate needs include:*

☐ *safety   The right of access to non-hazardous products and protection of consumers from hazards to their health and safety stemming from production processes, products and services;*

☐ *being informed   Access of consumers to adequate information to enable them to make informed choices according to individual wishes and needs and to be protected against dishonest or misleading advertising or labelling;*

- ☐ **making choices**   The promotion and protection of the economic interests of consumers, including the ability to select from a range of products and services, offered at competitive prices with an assurance of satisfactory quality;
- ☐ **being heard**   Freedom to form consumer and other relevant groups or organizations and the opportunity of such organizations to present their views in decision-making processes affecting them, especially in the making and execution of government policy, and in the development of products and services;
- ☐ **redress**   Availability of effective consumer redress, in particular in the form of fair settlement of just claims, including compensation for misrepresentation, badly made products or unsatisfactory services;
- ☐ **education**   Consumer education, including education on the environmental, social and economic impacts of consumer choice, enables consumers to make informed, independent choices about products and services while being aware of their rights and responsibilities and how to act on them; and
- ☐ **healthy environment**   This is an environment that is not threatening to the well-being of present and future generations. Sustainable consumption includes meeting the needs of present and future generations for products and services in ways that are economically, socially and environmentally sustainable.

Additional principles include:
- ☐ **respect for the right to privacy**   This is drawn from the Universal Declaration of Human Rights, Article 12, which provides that no one be subjected to arbitrary interference with their privacy, family, home or correspondence, or to attacks upon their honour and reputation, and that everyone has the right to the protection of the law against such interference or attacks;
- ☐ **the precautionary approach**   This is drawn from the Rio Declaration on Environment and Development [158] and subsequent declarations and agreements, which advance the concept that where there are threats of serious or irreversible damage to the environment or human health, lack of full scientific certainty should not be used as a reason for postponing cost-effective measures to prevent environmental degradation or damage to human health. When considering cost-effectiveness of a measure, an organization should consider the long-term costs and benefits of that measure, not only the short-term economic costs to the organization;
- ☐ **promotion of gender equality and empowerment of women**   This is drawn from the Universal Declaration of Human Rights and the Millennium Development Goals. It provides an additional basis on

which to analyse consumer issues and prevent perpetuation of gender stereotypes; and

☐ **promotion of universal design** *This is the design of products and environments to be usable by all people, to the greatest extent possible, without the need for adaptation or specialized design. There are seven principles to universal design: equitable use, flexibility in use, simple and intuitive use, perceptible information, tolerance for error, low physical effort and size and space for approach and use.*

ISO 26000:2010, pages 52-53 (references deleted).

ISO The Seven Consumer Issues

CONSUMER ISSUE 1: DE&I AS MODERATOR FOR FAIR MARKETING, FACTUAL AND UNBIASED INFORMATION AND FAIR CONTRACTUAL PRACTICES

Does your organization consider diversity, equity, and inclusion as currency in its marketing? Does it present factual and unbiased information and follow fair contractual practices?

What consumers understand about products and services is generally limited by the information they are given through word of mouth, pamphlets, product label description or wrap-around product or service marketing materials, etc. How a product or service is marketed or promoted can take on a whole new meaning when it also becomes a moderating avenue for extending an organization's DE&I commitments. As such it can act as an incentivized means to reward behaviors—decisions and activities—that are moderated by fairness and justice. Using fair and just norms as a value-added mechanism for driving an organization's messaging can be a powerful means of bridging the gaps in societal divisive norms.

For example, a socially responsible organization that practices gender pay equality can mention this in its recruitment messaging as well as in other product messaging. This demonstrates an integrative ecosystem where walking the DE&I talk is part of its DNA storyline. This type of deliberate socio-marketing paradigm shift gives a socially responsible organization a canvas to tell its story by showcasing its DE&I decisions and activities as an integrative whole. This can have a positive impact not only on their sales, but on society and other organizations, just as unfair and unjust practices became divisive norms one decision or activity or agenda or film at a time. ISO 26000 provided the following broad definition and understanding:

> **ISO** *Fair marketing, factual and unbiased information and fair contractual practices provide information about products and services in a manner that can be understood by consumers. This allows consumers to make informed decisions about consumption and purchases and to compare the characteristics of different products and services.*

> *ISO 26000:2010, pages 54-55 (references deleted).*

FAIR MARKETING, FACTUAL AND UNBIASED INFORMATION AND FAIR CONTRACTUAL PRACTICES
Knowledge-informed diversity call to action

The information age has revolutionized how we think of advertising and product or service marketing, factual and unbiased information, and fair contracting practices. While unfair marketing and unfair contractual practices have been around forever, they are becoming even more sophisticated and subversive. A growing understanding of consumer behaviors and psychology has allowed the fine-tuning of advertising strategies that lure consumers into making decisions without the full understanding of the entire lifecycle of the product and services. They are subversive because consumers and the way they are aggregated using computer models for marketing, disclosure of information and offered contracts can be divisive and accentuate old systemic norms which marginalize and disadvantage minority and vulnerable groups. Exploiting inequities works, and these practices perpetuate the inequities themselves. This makes fair marketing, factual and unbiased information, and fair contractual practices DE&I issues.

With fair marketing, factual and unbiased information and fair contractual practices the consumer can make an informed choice about an organization's products or services. Of course, this assumes that the organization is interested in being honest. Situations where dishonesty is rewarded need to be better controlled by a regulatory and social framework that disincentivizes such practices.

But human behavior is just one piece of the puzzle. Aside from decisions made by people in an organization, we need to address the automated processes when algorithmic decision-making is driven by artificial intelligence. This often creates models that accentuate the old prejudices in employment processes, access to healthcare, capital, essential services, and many more contractual practices that goes beyond products for personal use. As discussed earlier, humans make decisions using three models: automatic, social, and mental model thinking. This applies also to how the organizations and the consumers make decisions and the activities that come or follow that decision. ISO 26000 provides the following broad definition and understanding:

> **ISO** *Fair contractual processes aim to protect the legitimate interests of both suppliers and consumers by mitigating imbalances in negotiating power between the parties. Responsible marketing may involve provision of information on the social, economic and environmental impacts across the whole life cycle and value chain. Details of products and services provided by suppliers play an important role in purchasing decisions because this information may provide the only data readily available to consumers.*
>
> *ISO 26000:2010, pages 54-55 (references deleted).*

New products and services are coming into the mainstream today that the world has never seen before; how they are marketed and contracted for has also transformed traditional practices. At this crossroad are two main counterbalancing issues: grandfathering the old marketing and contractual practices into the new era of globalization or using DE&I as a framework to examine, develop, and implement practices that convey the social, economic and environmental impact across products and services' life cycle and value chain. At the core is how we ensure that these marketing and informational practices are inclusive not exclusive and that they are targeted appropriately, without discrimination based on protected classifications.

Biased presentation of information wrongfully exacerbates old divisive norms; but when it's done right, with marketing and other information processed through a DE&I framework, it exasperates old divisive norms and offers organizations new ways to implement their DE&I commitments.

The game changer for all of this is artificial intelligence (AI), which is used to aggregate consumer information and can generate strategies to influence, discriminate, or injure minority and vulnerable groups. Today, AI's algorithms can be utilized to source through massive data and programmed step-by-step instructions for the computer to isolate or include different groups. Banks use this information to market their products to different groups of consumers, social media platforms use them to identify demographics and sell this information to marketers and others seeking to influence consumer behaviors and healthcare providers use them to determine care—just to name a few.

Before AI, people made these decisions manually—good and bad—all governed by federal, state or local laws and all judged based on equity, fairness and justice. But when computers take over the decision-making processes as in the case of AI, the rules of engagement on fair marketing, factual and unbiased information and fair contractual practices are altered. While the decisions made or recommended by AI may be efficient and quantitatively sound, they are not necessarily the best indicators of equity, fairness, and transparency. This is partly because they are designed to optimize systems as they currently function, and our current system is full of inequities. Only humans can solve our divisive norms, because we created them as a species. Computers are always based on input-output continuum: garbage in, garbage out – which in this case equates to divisive norms in, divisive outcomes out.

Algorithms depend on machine learning of datasets from existing sources. This reality is ripe for the continuation of divisive norms hidden behind computational rigor and statistical probabilities driven through the highway of prejudice. While a programmer may not have intended for the results produced from his or her programming to be biased, that is often what happens. This is why AI-driven processes must be mitigated as part of a DE&I framework.

As Oxford University researcher Dr. Sandra Wachter noted, *"AI in general can actually reinforce existing stereotypes that we have in our society ···Especially when it comes to employment, you should have some statistical evidence that your system isn't biased. And if you can't provide that, maybe you shouldn't use [the system] for making important decisions (Hamilton 2018)."*

Nonetheless, AI has the potential to produce fair and just results if the input is fair and just and humans as stakeholders of interest and of influence are involved in the design of the training data—not just the programmers. When done right using DE&I as a framework, algorithmic decision-making can be a useful DE&I tool because it is neutral unable to be enticed, forced to act or lie to about the organization's desired DE&I outcome (Hamilton 2018). While AI-generated output can often be flawed, the systems cannot be blamed for biased outcomes when the computers were fed biased input. It can also be a powerful force for good if all stakeholders impacted by the outcome contribute to the input data.

Overall, the importance of unbiased and effective communication is so broad and essential that attempting to cover all the ways in which minority and vulnerable groups have been wronged would take several books. Products and services known to harm people, targeted to vulnerable populations, are part of a broader discussion on fair marketing, factual and unbiased information and fair contractual practices.

FAIR MARKETING, FACTUAL AND UNBIASED INFORMATION AND FAIR CONTRACTUAL PRACTICES
Creativity-driven equity opportunity/reconciliation/disruption

We live in a divisive world where there is an imbalance in negotiating power between parties – suppliers have most of the power and consumers often make purchasing decisions without enough information or any recourse for bad faith or even illegal activities. The behavior we want to change requires incentivization sometimes for such change to take root. Nowhere is this more so than in requiring and incentivizing fair marketing, factual and unbiased information and contractual practices. Every divisive norm in our shared planet is supported by misinformation. We cannot make sustainable changes in these areas where there have been unfairness and unjust practices without addressing the contribution of societal social contracts and divisive mental models—the supply line.

Organizations should pay attention to all stakeholders who may consume or utilize their products and services, not just those they prefer to consider. Organizations can acquire considerable reach into the global community with very little investment in marketing when their products and services tap into and even become global trends. The more diverse an organization, the better the products and services they will produce and market. Inclusive marketing and contractual practices sustainably enhance profit, people and the planet. Conversely, when organizations ignore the needs of minority and vulnerable groups, they may create inequities – intentionally or not – that enable systemic and structural racism and other societal dysfunctions to fester.

By understanding the needs of all its stakeholders, an organization can utilize creativity-driven equity considerations to evaluate (1) where opportunities exist for quick and meaningful changes, (2) where it needs to reconcile its principles and practices in dealing with consumer issues and (3) where practices that run contrary to its DE&I values can be eliminated.

Fair and unbiased marketing, information, and contracting allows consumers to make the right choice of products or services to meet their needs, and also provides a canvas for the socially responsible organization to use its DE&I accomplishments as part of its humankind story.

Unfair, incomplete, misleading or deceptive marketing and information can result in purchase of products and services that do not meet consumer needs, and result in a waste of money, resources and time, and may even be hazardous to the consumer or the environment. It can also lead to a decline in consumer confidence, with consumers not knowing whom or what to believe. This can adversely affect the growth of markets for more sustainable products and services.

ISO 26000:2010, pages 54-55 (references deleted).

EQUITY OPPORTUNITY IN FAIR MARKETING, FACTUAL AND UNBIASED INFORMATION AND FAIR CONTRACTUAL PRACTICES

At a minimum, a socially responsible organization should make it a policy to provide accurate information concerning its products and services to its customers in its advertising. This decision making and activities should also consider how advertising and promotions of products and services target minority and vulnerable groups. ISO 26000 provided a broader guidance:

![ISO] *When communicating with consumers, an organization should:*

☐ *not engage in any practice that is deceptive, misleading, fraudulent or unfair, unclear or ambiguous, including omission of critical information;*

☐ *consent to sharing relevant information in a transparent manner which allows for easy access and comparisons as the basis for an informed choice by the consumer;*

☐ *give primary consideration in advertising and marketing to the best interests of vulnerable groups, including children, and not engage in activities that are detrimental to their interests;*

ISO 26000:2010, page 54.

Dark ads are a good example of exclusionary practices enabled by data mining. Advertisers crave targeted data because they can use them to create dark ads and effectively target the specific demographic that they are looking to reach. While in and of themselves, dark ads are not wrong, when they use sex, race, sexual orientation, or similar characteristics to curate the preferred consumers, they may cross an ethical line.

In 2018, Facebook was accused of violating the Fair Housing Act by the U.S. Department of Housing and Urban Development. According to the complaint, as of July 24, 2018, Facebook enabled advertisers of housing and housing-related services to discriminate by the information it provided them based on (Facebook Business 2018):

- sex by showing ads only to men or only to women.
- disability by not showing ads to users whom Facebook categorizes as interested in "assistance dog," "mobility scooter," "accessibility" or "deaf culture."
- familial status by not showing ads to users whom Facebook categorizes as interested in "child care" or "parenting," or by showing ads only to users with children above a specified age.
- religion by showing ads only to users whom Facebook categorizes as interested in the "Christian Church," "Jesus," "Christ" or the "Bible."
- national origin by not showing ads to users whom Facebook categorizes as interested in "Latin America," "Southeast Asia," "China," "Honduras," "Somalia," the "Hispanic National Bar Association" or "Mundo Hispanico."
- race and color by drawing a red line around majority-minority zip codes and not showing ads to users who live in those zip codes.

In response to the filing, Facebook removed 5,000 ad targeting options and issued the following statement: *"While these options have been used in legitimate ways to reach people interested in a certain product or service, we think minimizing the risk of abuse is more important. This includes limiting the ability for advertisers to exclude audiences that relate to attributes such as ethnicity or religion (Facebook Business 2018). "*

Online giant Amazon in 2018 admitted that its internal AI recruitment tool was biased against women and stopped using the application altogether. The algorithmic decision-making by AI was fed 10 years' worth of data from resumes submitted to Amazon from majority male applicants. (Amazon's global workforce is 60 percent male and men represent 74% of its management team.) Words like "women's" automatically downgraded the resumes of women, giving the men undue advantage (Hamilton 2022). Amazon claimed that its decision-makers looked at these biased recommendations but did not use them for making actual hiring decisions.

COMPAS, a computer application for assessing the risks of reoffending potential by criminals was also found in 2016 by ProPublica to be discriminatory and biased against African Americans. The AI model asked social and environment questions that fed the old social and mental model thinking data into the computer. It produced results that were far removed from the "person" and defined their behavior within the context of their social and environmental background (Hamilton 2022).

EQUITY RECONCILIATION IN FAIR MARKETING, FACTUAL AND UNBIASED INFORMATION AND FAIR CONTRACTUAL PRACTICES

When socially responsible decisions are incentivized by giving them highlight reel time, other parts of the organization are likely to follow suit. Highlight reels are what sports recruitment or performance are built on and athletes at every level covet these exposures. Sports highlight reels have been used to market products and services that have the faintest of affinity but when done correctly can move consumers to purchase or use the products or services.

Reconciling an organization's social responsibility rhetoric with its advertising and promotions as it relates to DE&I is critical to ensure consistency in DE&I commitments with fair marketing, factual and unbiased information and fair contractual practices. When a housing development commits to fair and just practices in selling to those who can afford it without considering race as a factor for such decisions, but marketing strategies target only a particular race, there is a disconnect. When banks use one racial group to advertise and promote their lending facilities while another non-bank institution uses another racial group to advertise payday loan products within the same community, such practices accentuate divisive societal values. But more importantly, these communication strategies demonstrate what population the business prefers doing business with based on discriminatory unfair and unjust precepts. ISO 26000 provides the following broad guidance:

ISO *When communicating with consumers, an organization should: provide complete, accurate, and understandable information that can be compared in official or commonly used languages at the point of sale and according to applicable regulations on:*

☐ *all important aspects of products and services, including financial and investment products, ideally taking into account the full life cycle;*

☐ *the key quality aspects of products and services as determined using standardized test procedures, and compared, when possible, to average performance or best practice. Provision of such information should be limited to circumstances where it is appropriate and practical and would assist consumers;*

☐ *health and safety aspects of products and services, such as potentially hazardous use, hazardous materials and hazardous chemicals contained in or released by products during their life cycle;*

☐ *information regarding accessibility of products and services; and*

An organization can also use its informational practices to bridge the racial divide as a form of reckoning. We have previously documented unfair and unjust divisive norms that have adversely impacted minority and vulnerable groups generationally. A socially responsible organization can use its consumer engagement as an extension of touting its own work on making a difference in the areas that have divided much of society. Depending on the divisive norm, racial, gender, religious, etc., an organization can develop themes and messaging in its marketing that paints a picture of what fair and just decisions and practices should look like in its ecosystem, giving a representative sample of a just and fair world. In essence, socially responsible organizations should use their DE&I commitments to showcase to the world of consumers, through their marketing endeavors, what a beautiful world can be reimagined when profits, people and planet are wholesomely integrated.

EQUITY DISRUPTION IN FAIR MARKETING, FACTUAL AND UNBIASED INFORMATION AND FAIR CONTRACTUAL PRACTICES

In a globalized economic, social and environmental ecosystem, it is easier to flag unfair marketing, untruthful, biased information and skewed contractual practices. These practices are easier to acknowledge today because of the sensitivity to unjust and unfair systemic and structural divisive norms and the increased power of the consumer to demand equitable treatments for all. Consumers are demanding fair contracts that are understandable; they want to know the positives and negatives of the products and services they're buying or using and they want the imagery and tone of advertisements and marketing to be representative of all groups likely to be stakeholders of interest. ISO 26000 provided a broader guideline:

ISO *When communicating with consumers, an organization should:*
□ *clearly identify advertising and marketing;*
□ *substantiate claims or assertions by providing underlying facts and information upon request;*

□ not use text, audio or images that perpetuate stereotyping in regard to, for example, gender, religion, race, disability or personal relationships;

□ use contracts that:

○ are written in clear, legible and understandable language;

○ do not include unfair contract terms, such as the unfair exclusion of liability, the right to unilaterally change prices and conditions, the transfer of risk of insolvency to consumers or unduly long contract periods, and avoid predatory lending practices including unreasonable credit rates; and

○ provide clear and sufficient information about prices, features, terms, conditions, costs, the duration of the contract and cancellation periods.

ISO 26000:2010, page 54.

Some of the practices that affect minority and vulnerable groups include high-pressure tactics, communication disconnects, and branding that perpetuates systemic racial and gender biases, to name a few. These practices must be stopped for true equity to take root. High-pressure marketing to minority and vulnerable groups are practices that adversely affect them. The subprime loan ecosystem is an example of this; institutions aggressively pushed loans that they would not market to white neighborhoods.

A socially responsible organization should review its contracting practices to ensure they do not deliberately segregate consumers by race or other discriminatory norms. They need to be sure that their practices do not gouge minority and vulnerable groups, intentionally or unintentionally, by charging higher prices to them for its products and services. Where such practices exist within its ecosystem, the organization should discontinue it immediately. Policies should also consider artificial inflation of prices for products and services during and after natural disasters, practices that favor the rich and majority groups who can afford them while disadvantaging the poor or minority and vulnerable groups who are most likely to need them and even more likely to be financially ruined or setback because of them.

On a positive note, shortly after the murder of George Floyd, organizations began paying attention to how their marketing perpetuated stereotypes. Below are some examples:

PepsiCo and the Aunt Jemima brand: Aunt Jemima was a portrayal of a black woman on the packaging of products from the Pearl Milling Company that began using this branding in 1933 for its pancake mixes and syrups. The Aunt

Jemima brand had long been condemned as perpetuating the racist stereotypical "mammy," a depiction of a submissive and devoted African American servant woman responsible for the care and feeding of the master's household while neglecting her own (Associated Press 2020). After purchasing the Quaker Oats Company and its brands, PepsiCo in 2001 initially classified the Aunt Jemima brand as portraying *"loving moms from diverse backgrounds who want the best for their families* (Associated Press 2020)." But in 2020 Quaker Foods North America issued a statement through its Vice President and Chief Marketing Officer, Kristin Kroepfl announced that it was finally ending the use of Aunt Jemima:

> As we work to make progress toward racial equality through several initiatives, we also must take a hard look at our portfolio of brands and ensure they reflect our values and meet our consumers' expectations...We recognize Aunt Jemima's origins are based on a racial stereotype. While work has been done over the years to update the brand in a manner intended to be appropriate and respectful, we realize those changes are not enough (Associated Press 2020).

Washington Redskins Football and the Indian moniker brand: For 87 years of its history, this D.C.-based American football team heard from activists and Native American groups that its moniker was offensive to Native Americans but did nothing about it. But after George Floyd's death, the team was forced to consider renaming itself thanks to pressure from other socially responsible organizations. In particular, FedEx, which paid $205 million naming rights to the stadium where the team played, stated that it had *"communicated to the team in Washington our request that they change the team's name."* Others had also pressured the team to change its name including some *"87 investment firms and shareholders worth a combined $620 billion (Booker 2020)"* who pressured FedEX, PepsiCo and Nike to do the same. This was all happening even as Walmart, Target, and Amazon announced their intentions to stop selling the team's products. The pressure worked and today, the Washington Redskins have been rebranded as the Washington Commanders.

Conagra and its Mrs. Butterworth's brand: According to Conagra, the Mrs. Butterworth brand was intended to project images of loving grandmother. But after George Floyd's murder, the imagery was reconsidered. Acknowledging its social responsibility to all its consumers, the company stated:

> We stand in solidarity with our Black and Brown communities and we can see that our packaging may be interpreted in a way that is wholly inconsistent with our values...We understand that our

actions help play an important role in eliminating racial bias and as a result, we have begun a complete brand and packaging review on Mrs. Butterworth's...It's heartbreaking and unacceptable that racism and racial injustices exist around the world. We will be part of the solution. Let's work together to progress toward change (Conagra 2020)."

Mars, Inc. and its Uncle Ben's Rice brand: Uncle Ben's Rice has been around for a long time and since the 1940s has featured a white-haired African American, often depicted wearing a bow-tie. Some critics contended that the imagery connoted servitude. Mars rebranded the product line in 2021 to Ben's Original, issuing the following statement when it began the transition in 2020:

As a global brand, we know we have a responsibility to take a stand in helping to put an end to racial bias and injustices. As we listen to the voices of consumers, especially in the Black community, and to the voices of our Associates worldwide, we recognize that now is the right time to evolve the Uncle Ben's brand, including its visual brand identity, which we will do...Racism has no place in society. We stand in solidarity with the Black community, our Associates and our partners in the fight for social justice. We know to make the systemic change needed, it's going to take a collective effort from all of us – individuals, communities and organizations of all sizes around the world (Sherman 2020).

NASA and its non-scientific planetary bodies naming practices: The National Aeronautics and Space Administration (NASA) also announced about the same time that it too would stop using nicknames for celestial bodies that could be considered offensive.

As the scientific community works to identify and address systemic discrimination and inequality in all aspects of the field, it has become clear that certain cosmic nicknames are not only insensitive, but can be actively harmful. NASA is examining its use of unofficial terminology for cosmic objects as part of its commitment to diversity, equity, and inclusion. As an initial step, NASA will no longer refer to planetary nebula NGC 2392, the glowing remains of a Sun-like star that is blowing off its outer layers at the end of its life, as the "Eskimo Nebula." "Eskimo" is widely viewed as a colonial term with a racist history, imposed on the indigenous people of Arctic regions. Most official documents have moved away from its use. NASA will also no longer use the term "Siamese Twins Galaxy" to refer to NGC 4567 and NGC 4568, a pair of spiral galaxies found in the Virgo Galaxy Cluster. Moving forward, NASA will use only the official, International Astronomical Union designations in cases where nicknames are inappropriate (NASA 2022).

FAIR MARKETING, FACTUAL AND UNBIASED INFORMATION AND FAIR CONTRACTUAL PRACTICES
Governance-centered inclusion actionable steps

When DE&I moderates fair marketing, factual and unbiased information and fair contractual practices, it allows an organization to ensure that its policies and practices are in alignment with its DE&I commitments. For example, a travel advocacy group in a major city that is known for its historical diversity and inclusiveness produced a video inviting people and groups from around the world to come and visit its city. The problem was that the video only presented one group and one culture in a multicultural city.

While the need to separate advertising from marketing is essential, when dealing with social responsibility, images and textual presentations that represent diverse peoples is the beginning on the road to inclusiveness. The adage that a person's name is the sweetest sound they ever hear is also applicable here: a person's sense of belonging is enhanced when they see images and people like themselves included in the organization's decisions and activities as well as in staffing and vendors.

Further, discriminatory practices when offering consumers credit are not new. To avoid this form of abuse, an organization should provide details of the credit including the actual annual interest rate, the average percentage rate (APR), amount to be paid, due dates of installment payments and the number of payments. As part of its pursuit of a sustainable DE&I strategy, an organization should seek to educate all its employees and others in its sphere of influence about implicit and explicit bias. Explicit bias is easily identifiable, while implicit bias can be harder to spot. This makes implicit bias far harder to root out than explicit bias. Implicit bias cannot be easily identified and unlearned from an academic or executive proclamation alone as it requires social dialogue, where people describe and confront the issues of implicit and explicit bias head-on.

In reviewing its operating documents, an organization should consider using the 3-Step Equity Lens and 3-Step Inclusion Principles models to drive the process to identify policies, processes, and practices which are in concert with the pursuit of fair and just actions within an activated DE&I ecosystem.

Governance-centered inclusion actionable steps: fair marketing, factual and unbiased information and fair contractual practices

1. In reviewing your organization's policies and procedures around fair marketing, factual and unbiased information, how do they align with your DE&I policy, commitments, and corporate proclamations on the matter?
2. If there are gaps, what are the actionable steps and timelines you have identified to narrow or eliminate them based on the 3-Step Equity Lens model and guided by the 3-Step Inclusion model?
3. Were all relevant stakeholders identified and engaged in the review, modification or development of your policies and procedures around your DE&I moderated fair marketing, factual and unbiased information, and fair contractual practices?

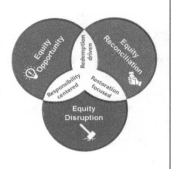

CONSUMER ISSUE 2: DE&I AS MODERATOR FOR PROTECTING CONSUMERS' HEALTH AND SAFETY

Does your organization consider DE&I as currency in protecting consumers' health and safety?

PROTECTING CONSUMERS' HEALTH AND SAFETY
Knowledge-informed diversity call to action

The protection of consumer health and safety is a shared social responsibility between the state and the "distributors" which the UN defines as retailers, importers, exporters and suppliers (manufacturers)—(UNCTAD 2016). The UN contends that the state should promulgate and adopt appropriate consumer health and safety regulations, legal system, standards (national, international, and voluntary), and promote the need for the maintenance of safety records to ensure that products and services meet the safety requirements expected from normal and foreseeable use or as intended (UN Guidelines 2016).

Manufacturers have a responsibility to ensure that their products are safe when used for their intended purpose. Distributors, the UN also contends, own the responsibility of bringing safe products and services to the market by ensuring that they are not rendered unsafe while in their care due to storage or mishandling. Further, the UN contends that consumers should be informed about any risks involved in the normal foreseeable use of the product or service and that they are provided appropriate instructions on the best way to use them. In communicating vital safety information to consumers, the ideal practice, wherever possible, is to use understandable symbols that are internationally recognized (UN Guidelines 2016). ISO 26000 provided the following overall guidance:

> **ISO** *Protection of consumers' health and safety involves the provision of products and services that are safe and that do not carry unacceptable risk of harm when used or consumed. The protection should cover both the intended use and foreseeable misuse. Clear instructions for safe use, including assembly and maintenance, are also an important part of the protection of health and safety. An organization's reputation may be directly affected by the impact on consumers' health and safety of its products and services. Products and services should be safe, regardless of whether or not legal safety requirements are in place. Safety includes anticipation of potential risks to avoid harm or danger. As all risks cannot be foreseen or eliminated, measures to protect safety should include mechanisms for product withdrawal and recall.*
>
> *ISO 26000:2010, page 57 (references deleted).*

Products and services should be safe, regardless of who the consumer is or what race or gender they belong to or even whether there are existing safety obligatory requirements. The protection of consumers' health and safety is a DE&I matter because in addition to covering *"intended use and foreseeable misuse,"* distributors need to consider how vital information about the product and service is communicated to minority and vulnerable groups. This is where stakeholder identification and engagement can act as a crucial value-added equity mechanism to the lifecycle of a product or service, because it gives a socially responsible organization the impetus or tools to do the right thing by consumers. This also allows distributors another opportunity to counter societal norms that segregate groups on artificial differentiators—favoring one over the other even in product and service lifecycle.

In the information age, conducting product safety surveys, focus groups and outreaches are far easier and less costly to administer than in the past. These are potential gold mines of information to help ensure that consumer health and safety are not compromised because they purchased or used a product or service. When an organization becomes aware that a product or service is hazardous, it should consider taking it off the market; when not immediately possible, they should consider adequate compensation for users. When considering any such measures, all consumers known to have purchased or used the product or service should be considered, not just one racial or gender group. Fair and just consumer health and safety protection programs or initiatives should be universal.

PROTECTING CONSUMERS' HEALTH AND SAFETY
Creativity-driven equity opportunity/reconciliation/disruption

DE&I as moderator for consumer health and safety protections allows an organization to proactively integrate social responsibility principles into its product and service ecosystems (design, manufacture, and distribution). Using the 3-Step Equity Lens provides a deeper and richer context from both producer and user frames that could help improve the safety of consumer products and services in a fair and equitable way. As a bonus, this approach could also create greater consumer loyalties that might translate to economic returns.

EQUITY OPPORTUNITY IN PROTECTING CONSUMERS' HEALTH AND SAFETY

Minority and disadvantaged groups and their concerns as consumers should not be discounted or ignored or buried in a do-nothing filing system. Distributors should also have equity opportunity mechanisms for ensuring that at the very least, the information provided on safe use is not discriminatory (intentionally or not). ISO 26000 provided the following broad guidance:

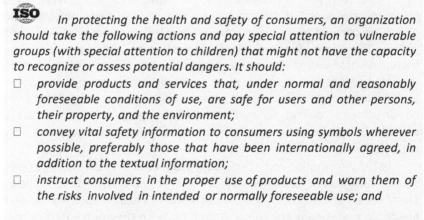

In protecting the health and safety of consumers, an organization should take the following actions and pay special attention to vulnerable groups (with special attention to children) that might not have the capacity to recognize or assess potential dangers. It should:

☐ *provide products and services that, under normal and reasonably foreseeable conditions of use, are safe for users and other persons, their property, and the environment;*

☐ *convey vital safety information to consumers using symbols wherever possible, preferably those that have been internationally agreed, in addition to the textual information;*

☐ *instruct consumers in the proper use of products and warn them of the risks involved in intended or normally foreseeable use; and*

ISO 26000:2010, pages 55-56.

EQUITY RECONCILIATION IN PROTECTING CONSUMERS' HEALTH AND SAFETY

Historically, because minority and disadvantaged groups are sometimes not represented in the organization's product and service creation and delivery ecosystem, their contributions, which could add diverse and enhancing perspective, are not heard. Diverse perspectives from different representatives of people groups could enhance relevant information on the use, repair and disposal of these products and services. This reconciling assessment should be driven by the organization's DE&I policy and commitments. More importantly, this approach could also serve as a marketing and promotional tool touting the inclusive and belonging values of the creators of the products and services and distributors, with stakeholder interest and consumer influence as central drivers. ISO 26000 provided the following broad guidance:

ISO

In protecting the health and safety of consumers, an organization should take the following actions and pay special attention to vulnerable groups (with special attention to children)....:

☐ *assess the adequacy of health and safety laws, regulations, standards and other specifications to address all health and safety aspects. An organization should go beyond minimum safety requirements where there is evidence that higher requirements would achieve significantly better protection, as indicated by the occurrence of accidents involving products or services that conform to the minimum requirements, or the availability of products or product designs that can reduce the number or severity of accidents;*

☐ *minimize risks in the design of products by:*

    o *identifying the likely user group(s), the intended use and the reasonably foreseeable misuse of the process, product or service, as well as hazards arising in all the stages and conditions of use of the product or service and, in some cases, provide specially tailored products and services for vulnerable groups;*

    o *estimating and evaluating the risk to each identified user or contact group, including pregnant women, arising from the hazards identified; and*

    o *reducing the risk by using the following order of priority: inherently safe design, protective devices and information for users;*

☐ *assure the appropriate design of information on products and services by taking into account different consumer needs and respecting differing or limited capacities of consumers, especially in terms of time allocated to the information process;*

☐ *as appropriate, perform a human health risk assessment of products and services before the introduction of new materials, technologies or production methods, and, when appropriate, make documentation available to consumers;*

ISO 26000:2010, pages 55-56.

EQUITY DISRUPTION IN PROTECTING CONSUMERS' HEALTH AND SAFETY

Sometimes companies need to pull products or services from the market for various reasons. It happens and doesn't always reflect willful neglect. But some cases, minority and vulnerable groups don't get the same access to information presented in a form that effectively communicates to them, and consequently face greater hazards from such products. It is important to note that these principles apply to all organizations providing products and services to consumers even though not all issues may apply to all circumstances. ISO 26000 provided the following broad guidance:

ISO *In protecting the health and safety of consumers, an organization should take the following actions and pay special attention to vulnerable groups (with special attention to children)....:*

☐ *when a product, after having been placed on the market, presents an unforeseen hazard, has a serious defect or contains misleading or false information, stop the services or withdraw all products that are still in the distribution chain. An organization should recall products using appropriate measures and media to reach people who purchased the product or made use of the services and compensate consumers for losses suffered. Measures for traceability in its value chain may be pertinent and useful;*

☐ *in product development, avoid the use of harmful chemicals, including but not limited to those that are carcinogenic, mutagenic, toxic for reproduction, or persistent and bio-accumulative. If products containing such chemicals are offered for sale, they should be clearly labelled;*

☐ *adopt measures that prevent products from becoming unsafe through improper handling or storage while in the care of consumers.*

ISO 26000:2010, pages 55-56.

PROTECTING CONSUMERS' HEALTH AND SAFETY
Governance-centered inclusion actionable steps

Social responsibility in consumer health and safety challenges organizations to provide goods and services that are safe and do not come with high levels of risks to the consumer. This is particularly true for minority and vulnerable groups who as consumers may be adversely impacted by unclear instructions due to language or other barriers.

1. Are your product(s) and service(s), under normal and reasonably foreseeable conditions of use, safe for users, and other persons, their property, and the environment? Is this true for all users regardless of color of skin, gender, or other protected class identifiers under the law?

2. Are the vital safety information and the user instructions provided to consumers reflective of the diversity of the known or expected user base and provided in such a way that they can be understood?

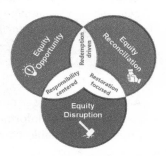

3. Has your organization assessed whether it is abiding by the health and safety laws, regulations and other specifications in its product(s) and service(s) offerings and where necessary exceed the minimum safety requirements?

4. Has your organization taken both a stakeholder (identification and engagement) and lifecycle approaches to its product(s) and service(s) offerings and reconciled its current decisions and practices with its DE&I framework?

5. Are there product recall or discontinuance mechanisms in place to pull out of the market, products and services that have been deemed hazardous to consumer health and safety?

CONSUMER ISSUE 3: DE&I AS MODERATOR FOR SUSTAINABLE CONSUMPTION

Does your organization consider DE&I as currency in formulating its sustainable consumption practices?

SUSTAINABLE CONSUMPTION
Knowledge-informed diversity call to action

Sustainable consumption is a DE&I matter because it encompasses the impacts consumers' current behavior have on future generations. When consumer behavior is informed, they contribute to the sustainability of profit, people and planet alike. As covered in the chapter dealing with the environment, our current consumption of natural resources is not sustainable. ISO 26000 frames it this way:

> **ISO** *Sustainable consumption is consumption of products and resources at rates consistent with sustainable development. The concept was promoted by Principle 8 of the Rio Declaration on Environment and Development, which states that to achieve sustainable development and*

a higher quality of life for all people, states should reduce and eliminate unsustainable patterns of production and consumption. The concept of sustainable consumption also encompasses a concern for animal welfare, respecting the physical integrity of animals and avoiding cruelty...Current rates of consumption are clearly unsustainable, contributing to environmental damage and resource depletion. Consumers play an important role in sustainable development by taking ethical, social, economic and environmental factors into account based on accurate information in making their choices and purchasing decisions.

ISO 26000:2010, page 56 (references removed).

An organization's products and services, its value chain and life cycle, and the content of the information it provides to the consumer all contribute to its role in sustainable consumption (ISO 26000 2010). This means that everyone has a role to play—states, businesses, advocacy and support groups, etc. The UN Guidelines for Consumer Protection considers sustainable consumption as a shared responsibility:

1. States have responsibility to enact and implement sustainable consumption policies that are integrated with other public policies and that are developed through a consultative process that engages stakeholders of interests and of influence
2. Businesses have a responsibility to produce and market sustainable products and services and promote sustainable consumption of them
3. Informed consumers can influence the development and marketing of economically, socially and environmentally sustainable products and services by their patronage. If consumers fail to patronize a particular product or service, the producers will cease to produce them
4. Consumer and environmental organizations have the duo responsibility of informing and promoting public participation and debate on sustainable consumption and engaging both the state and businesses on these matters (UNTAD 2016).

SUSTAINABLE CONSUMPTION PRACTICES
Creativity-driven equity opportunity/reconciliation/disruption

While it is generally agreed that the state is responsible for enacting consumer protection laws and ordinances, organizations can commit to not only abiding by these laws but going beyond them when they don't go far enough to promote sustainable consumption. For example, to reduce pollution and the depletion of natural resources, socially responsible organizations develop environmentally sound products and services through new technologies, dissemination of clear sustainable consumption information, and innovative communication mechanisms. Further, when states and organizations develop land use, housing, transportation, and energy policies, they should also consider how these policies address historical divisive norms that have long marginalized minority and vulnerable consumers.

Ignoring minority and vulnerable groups in any organizational sustainable consumption decisions and activities is not a plan that looks to future generations. To be effective, all of current humankind must be engaged as part of the solution. Likewise, state-sponsored subsidies that do not incentivize sustainable patterns of production and consumption or fail to promote awareness of the impacts of consumption (UN Guidelines 2016) behaviors limit the influence they would otherwise have on producers of products and services. Incentivizing sustainable consumption is a way of ensuring future generations can also meet their needs. As the UN wisely admonished, promoting sustainable consumption is a task in which states, international organizations and businesses must work together to at the very least commit to doing something about it:

> To promote sustainable consumption, Member States, international bodies and business should work together to develop, transfer and disseminate environmentally sound technologies, including through appropriate financial support from developed countries, and to devise new and innovative mechanisms for financing their transfer among all countries, in particular to and among developing countries and countries with economies in transition. Member States and international organizations, as appropriate, should promote and facilitate capacity-building in the area of sustainable consumption, particularly in developing countries and countries with economies in transition. In particular, Member States should also facilitate cooperation among consumer groups and other relevant organizations of civil society, with the aim of strengthening capacity in this area (UNTAD 2016).

As discussed previously, organizations have a role to play in educating consumers on the impacts of their choices on the environment and on their well-being. The impacts considered should also include those that fall in the realm of social justice; these could be assessed through the 3-Step Equity lens of opportunity, reconciliation, and disruption.

EQUITY OPPORTUNITY IN SUSTAINABLE CONSUMPTION

Organizations should not only work to inform and educate consumers about sustainable consumption practices, but also seek new ways to be inclusive, especially where these consumers belong to minority and vulnerable groups.

Some of these strategies could be as simple as involving members of these groups in developing the messaging for how to avoid harm or incur unnecessary risks from use of their products and services.

There's equity opportunity in informing consumers about the health and safety benefits of products and services in the market today because such awareness enables consumers to make the right choices in their own consumption patterns. This awareness information should include, though not be limited to, potential adverse impacts to themselves and to the environment. ISO 26000 offered the following broad guidance:

ISO *To contribute to sustainable consumption, an organization, where appropriate, should:*

☐ *promote effective education empowering consumers to understand the impacts of their choices of products and services on their well being and on the environment. Practical advice can be provided on how to modify consumption patterns and to make necessary changes;*

☐ *offer consumers socially and environmentally beneficial products and services considering the full life cycle, and reduce adverse impacts on society and the environment by:*

    o *preferring supplies that can contribute to sustainable development;*

    o *offering high quality products with longer product life, at affordable prices;*

ISO 26000:2010, pages 56-57.

Minority and vulnerable groups need to be consulted to find out the best ways they receive information on these matters. Organizations can't assume that a one-size-fits-all education strategy will equally empower all consumers. Part of considering full life cycle of products and services should include how to effectively engage minority and vulnerable groups. Further, companies should not implement policies and decision-making mechanisms for *"preferring supplies that can contribute to sustainable development"* as a pretext to screen out minority and vulnerable group suppliers. The same is true for screening out these suppliers on terms such as "best high quality" offerings. When it is a mere screen for perpetuating privilege that advantages one group over another, organizations need to face the facts and adjust their strategies accordingly. Where minority and vulnerable groups have supplies that do not contribute to sustainable development, it should not exclude them entirely, but serve as an opportunity for socially responsible organizations to step up and assist these firms improve their products and services offerings to be competitive and increase the diversity of the supply pipeline.

EQUITY RECONCILIATION IN SUSTAINABLE CONSUMPTION

By considering a product or service lifecycle, an organization can gain valuable insights into its impacts and use this knowledge to make it safe and both resource and energy efficient. Organizations can also implement recycling schemes *"that encourage consumers to both recycle wastes and purchase recycled products (UNTAD 2016)."* especially those that use natural resources that cannot easily be replaced. Some Cellphones manufacturers already incorporate schemes that enable consumers to exchange old cellphones for new ones. These types of social responsibility activities have socio-economic impacts and their social values converted into economic terms.

ISO *To contribute to sustainable consumption, an organization, where appropriate, should: offer consumers socially and environmentally beneficial products and services considering the full life cycle, and reduce adverse impacts on society and the environment by:*

☐ *designing products and packaging so that they can be easily used, reused, repaired or recycled and, if possible, offering or suggesting recycling and disposal services;*

☐ *providing consumers with scientifically reliable, consistent, truthful, accurate, comparable and verifiable information about the environmental and social factors related to production and delivery of its products or services, including, where appropriate, information on resource efficiency, taking the value chain into account;*

☐ *providing consumers with information about products and services, including on: performance, impacts on health, country of origin, energy efficiency (where applicable), contents or ingredients (including, where appropriate, use of genetically modified organisms and nanoparticles), aspects related to animal welfare (including, where appropriate, use of animal testing) and safe use, maintenance, storage and disposal of the products and their packaging.*

ISO 26000:2010, pages 56-57.

In reconciling its decisions and practices with the above stated best practices, an organization should also extend these full cycle reviews to include historical impacts on minority and vulnerable groups and clearly state how it plans to ensure that it is not contributing to the perpetuation of these divisive norms. It should also use this review and reconciliation process to report where there had been untruthful and misleading information provided in the past and what the organization is doing now to ensure that is no longer the case going forward. This a good way to establish or reestablish trust.

EQUITY DISRUPTION IN SUSTAINABLE CONSUMPTION PRACTICES

Organizations that already produce products and services that contain environmentally harmful substances should seek to develop new sound alternatives as quickly as possible and not continue to milk the economic benefits at the expense of the wellbeing of people and the planet. ISO 26000 provided the following broad guidance:

ISO *To contribute to sustainable consumption, an organization, where appropriate, should: offer consumers socially and environmentally beneficial products and services considering the full life cycle, and reduce adverse impacts on society and the environment by:*

☐ *eliminating, where possible, or minimizing any negative health and environmental impact of products and services, and where less harmful and more efficient alternatives exist, providing the choice of products or services that have less adverse effects on the society and the environment; and*

☐ *making use of reliable and effective, independently verified labelling schemes or other verification schemes, such as eco-labelling or auditing activities, to communicate positive environmental aspects, energy efficiencies, and other socially and environmentally beneficial characteristics of products and services.*

ISO 26000:2010, pages 56-57.

Where historically, an organization has used minority and vulnerable groups as testing labs for new products and services that are potentially harmful to people and the environment, such practices must stop, and adequate compensatory actions taken. When potential environmentally harmful products and services must be tested, minority and vulnerable groups should be represented where feasible in the decision-making process either as stakeholders of interest or of influence.

SUSTAINABLE CONSUMPTION
Governance-centered inclusion actionable steps:

Governance-centered inclusion assist organizations resolve the equity issues raised in sustainable consumption practices by addressing them in actionable steps that move the organization forward in its social responsibility commitments. An organization's products and services, its value chain and life cycle, and the content of the information it provides to the consumer all contribute to its sustainable consumption role. Using ISO 26000's broad guidance, consumers can also play a key role in promoting sustainable development, as they decide on which products to buy (conscious consumerism).

Organizations have a role to play in educating consumers who use their products and services on the impacts of their choices on the environment and on their well-being. The impacts considered should be encircled by social justice. DE&I policies and practices are very important to minority, vulnerable and disadvantaged groups, especially when they go beyond mere words and are actually acted upon in decision-making processes. To the extent that organizations can tie their whole lifecycle for their products and services on how they address the concerns of these groups, the more they would become informed consumers of these products and services and the better off economically for everyone. For example, in seeking to court minority and vulnerable groups because of its DE&I commitments and policy, an organization can integrate this into a broader storytelling wraparound for its products and services. This would address not just the required sustainable consumption ideals, but also demonstrate how the organization is proactively closing the divisive gaps in our shared planet—an important aspect of ESG performance monitoring.

Governance-centered inclusion actionable steps: sustainable consumption

1. In reviewing the equity issues, opportunities discussed in this section, how has your organization implemented policies and practices that promote an inclusive sustainable consumption culture that is DE&I moderated within the organization and with your external partners?
2. Are these policies and practices aligned with your DE&I policy and commitments?
3. Where there are gaps between DE&I policy and commitments with the organization's existing policies and procedures, are there plans to remediate or close the gaps?
4. In promoting the contributions of your organization's products and services and in touting their contributions to the consumer's wellbeing and the environment, are minority and vulnerable groups seen and addressed as part of the consumers targeted?

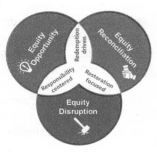

5. When a minority or vulnerable groups supplies fail to contribute to sustainable development, are there mitigating technical or resource assistance that your organization can offer so they can become complaint?
6. Has your organization in the past or currently engaged in practices where environmentally harmful uses of substances were tested or promoted within minority and vulnerable groups' communities? If yes, what are current plans to remediate or make this right by these communities?

CONSUMER ISSUE 4: DE&I AS MODERATOR FOR CONSUMER SERVICE, SUPPORT, AND COMPLAINT AND DISPUTE RESOLUTION

Does your organization consider diversity, equity, and inclusion as currency in its consumer service, support, and complaint and dispute resolution processes?

CONSUMER SERVICE, SUPPORT, AND COMPLAINT AND DISPUTE RESOLUTION
Knowledge-informed diversity call to action

Organizations that produce products or deliver services have consumers that are both stakeholders of interests and of influence. An organization can increase the satisfaction and reduce the numbers of complaints it receives by committing to offering products and services that are of high quality where consumers are given clear instructions on how to use them and where to get remedies for faulty products and services. ISO 26000 provided this guidance:

> **ISO** *Consumer service, support, and complaint and dispute resolution are the mechanisms an organization uses to address the needs of consumers after products and services are bought or provided. Such mechanisms include proper installation, warranties and guarantees, technical support regarding use, as well as provisions for return, repair and maintenance. Products and services that do not provide satisfactory performance, either because of flaws or breakdowns or as a result of misuse, may result in a violation of consumer rights as well as a waste of money, resources and time. Providers of products and services can increase consumer satisfaction and reduce levels of complaints by offering high quality products and services. They should provide clear advice to consumers on appropriate use and on recourse or remedies for faulty performance. They can also monitor the effectiveness of their after- sales service, support and dispute resolution procedures by surveys of their users.*
>
> *ISO 26000:2010, page 57 (references deleted).*

DE&I as moderator for consumer service, support, and complaint and dispute resolution provides the framework for an organization to look at the entire life cycle of its delivery and post delivery mechanism. This approach allows the organization to consider the minority and vulnerable groups who as stakeholders need their concerns and interests addressed. Both the internal and external staff or third-party partners who handle consumer service, support, and complaint and dispute resolution should be familiar with the organization's DE&I policy, commitments and drive and ensure that as the face to the consumers, these values, beliefs and behaviors are in sync in their interactions.

In seeking informed knowledge from a diverse base of consumers, an organization will do well in ensuring that survey or focus group questionnaires are understandable, culturally relevant, and applicable to the respective groups. Historical societal discriminatory practices placed little value on inputs from minority and vulnerable groups, but socially responsible organizations can seize on this knowledge and purposefully take action that addresses these divisive norms.

CONSUMER SERVICE, SUPPORT, AND COMPLAINT AND DISPUTE RESOLUTION
Creativity-driven equity opportunity/reconciliation/disruption

Organizations should consider a wider tent for its consumer service, support, and complaint and dispute resolution beyond the traditional registered user's approach. There may be limitations or other barriers for why minority and vulnerable groups may not register their ownership and use of an organization's products and services, but it should not limit their access to service, support, and complaint and dispute resolution. Where support services and complaint and dispute resolution are outsourced whether in-country or abroad, the quality of service and support rendered or made available should not discriminate by what race, gender, national origin, sexual orientation, or other protected class differentiators. A consumer is a stakeholder of interest and of influence when they purchase or use an organization's products or services. ISO provides three standards that can help organizations address customer complaints prevention and handling and dispute resolution from a systemic approach. Depending on needs, circumstances and feasibility, a combination of any or all three can provide structured guidance in hearing from consumers and addressing their concerns. These standards are:

☐ *ISO 10001, Quality management — Customer satisfaction — Guidelines for codes of conduct for organizations. This International Standard assists organizations in developing and implementing effective, fair and accurate codes of conduct.*

☐ *ISO 10002, Quality management — Customer satisfaction — Guidelines for complaints handling in organizations. This International Standard provides guidance on how organizations can fairly and effectively address complaints about their products and services.*

☐ *ISO 10003, Quality management — Customer satisfaction — Guidelines for dispute resolution external to organizations. This International Standard addresses situations where organizations have been unable to resolve complaints through their internal complaints handling mechanisms.*

ISO 26000:2010, page 58.

Using the 3-Step Equity Lens presented throughout this book, an organization should consider the following guidelines provided in ISO 26000 in framing its consumer service, support, and complaint and dispute resolution practices moderated by DE&I.

EQUITY OPPORTUNITY IN CONSUMER SERVICE, SUPPORT, AND COMPLAINT AND DISPUTE RESOLUTION

ISO *An organization should:*

☐ *if appropriate, offer warranties that exceed periods guaranteed by law and are suitable for the expected length of product life;*

☐ *offer adequate and efficient support and advice systems;*

ISO 26000:2010, page 57.

EQUITY RECONCILIATION IN CONSUMER SERVICE, SUPPORT, AND COMPLAINT AND DISPUTE RESOLUTION

ISO *An organization should:*

☐ *review complaints and improve practices in response to complaints;*

☐ *offer maintenance and repair at a reasonable price and at accessible locations and make information readily accessible on the expected availability of spare parts for products; and*

☐ *make use of alternative dispute resolution, conflict resolution and redress procedures that are based on national or international standards, are free of charge or are at minimal cost to consumers, and that do not require consumers to waive their rights to seek legal recourse.*

ISO 26000:2010, pages 57-58.

EQUITY DISRUPTION IN CONSUMER SERVICE, SUPPORT, AND COMPLAINT AND DISPUTE RESOLUTION

CONSUMER SERVICE, SUPPORT, AND COMPLAINT AND DISPUTE RESOLUTION

Governance-centered inclusion actionable steps:

When DE&I moderates consumer service, support, and complaint and dispute resolution, minority and vulnerable groups' issues and interests are more effectively represented. Ensuring that all stakeholders regardless of color or gender are treated fairly as consumers is a triple bottom line matter—economic, social and environmental.

Governance-centered inclusion actionable steps: consumer service, support, and complaint and dispute resolution

1. Are your current policies and procedures on consumer service, support, and complaint and dispute resolution aligned with your DE&I policy and commitments?
2. If not, are there plans and timeline to align your DE&I walk with the organization's decision making and practices talk?
3. Were all relevant stakeholders identified and engaged in the review, modification or development of your policies and procedures around your DE&I moderated consumer service, support, and complaint and dispute resolution practices?

CONSUMER ISSUE 5: DE&I AS MODERATOR FOR CONSUMER DATA PROTECTION AND PRIVACY

Does your organization consider DE&I as currency in its consumer data protection and privacy practices?

CONSUMER DATA PROTECTION AND PRIVACY
Knowledge-informed diversity call to action

Data has become the new gold and it continues to transform humankind's daily experiences, with the potential to also leave poor people and poor nations behind, exacerbating our divisive norms. But that should not be how the storyline ends. Consumer data protection and privacy practices is not only a necessity but should also be implemented in a way that does not further marginalize historical poor and disenfranchised people groups. ISO 26000 provides the following broad guidance:

ISO *Consumer data protection and privacy are intended to safeguard consumers' rights of privacy by limiting the types of information gathered and the ways in which such information is obtained, used and secured. Increasing use of electronic communication (including for financial transactions) and genetic testing, as well as growth in large-scale databases, raise concerns about how consumer privacy can be protected, particularly with regard to personally identifiable information...Organizations can help to maintain their credibility and the confidence of consumers through the use of rigorous systems for obtaining, using and protecting consumer data.*

ISO 26000:2010, page 58 (references deleted).

The possibilities for the creative uses of data have been nothing short of revolutionary. They can be used to expeditiously close the gaps in our divisive norms if access to the fruits of this data is inclusive. This makes the collection and use of consumer data a DE&I matter. All organizations touch consumer data protection and privacy either directly or indirectly, and this makes them vital institutions to institute fair and just practices in data management and governance.

The perpetuality of data make it invaluable as a means for building sustainable development by informing policy makers and organizational leaders of fair and just applications that close the gaps in our divisive norms. A 2021 World Development Report 2021 by the World Bank Group titled "Data for Better Lives" explored how data can be used to improve the lives of poor people living in poor countries, and by extension minorities and vulnerable groups living in more advanced economies.

Figure 10.3: How data can support development: a theory of change

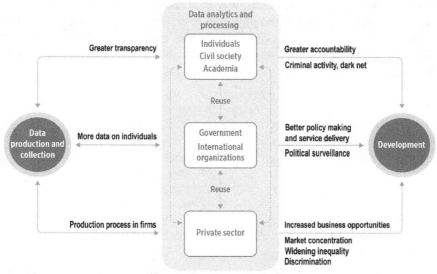

Source: World Bank 2021.

The possibilities of consumer data, collected for one purpose and then repurposed for other uses, can in theory lead to providing consumers better products and services. The data can also be used to improve the quality of life for marginalized and vulnerable groups by exposing the inequities inherent in existing systems. The above diagram shows how the flow of data collected from one source can benefit another group through the two-way arrows. These arrows also suggest that data should be collected, used and repurposed for broader missions including the information they provide and the disparities they expose.

It is true that consumer data within these three pathways could be used for good or bad, depending on the actors and their motivations. On the individual pathway, there is potential for using the data collected to provide streamlined information that enhances the consumer's quality of life experiences – or could open them up to cyberattacks and compromise their privacy. And cybercriminals are not the only ones phishing for individual data to cause harm; other actors including governments sometimes abuse sensitive consumer data for reasons other than those that benefit the consumer.

Data collected at the government pathway, for example, could be used to provide essential services – or used to discriminate against people based on race, gender, sexual orientation, religion, etc., or even abused for political reasons. Private pathway data can be aggregated to inform product and service providers about consumer behavior leading to better marketing strategies to reach them – or they can be used for microtargeting consumers through unjust marketing strategies that continue the old exploitations through the new medium. If consumer data can be used to improve the lives of humankind, but also has the potential to be used to disenfranchise a large body of the human population, how can we create an inclusive "trusted" data infrastructure ecosystem that raises all boats equally? The World Development Report 2021 summed this up well:

> *Whether the focus is on the collection, use, transfer, or processing of data between businesses, or among citizens, businesses, and governments, each of these interactions is a data transaction with the potential to create value—as long as both parties trust the over-all process sufficiently. However, a variety of factors can undermine trust. These may include the absence, weakness, or uneven application of the legal frame-work; weak institutions and law enforcement or lack of effective ways for parties to enforce their rights; practices that unfairly benefit certain actors; skewed or lopsided incentives...and poor or insecure infrastructure (World Bank 2021).*

A data infrastructure ecosystem, whether corporate, national, or international in scope, is essentially a new form of social contract to be negotiated for fairness and justice for all. Generally, when data is collected, it has a potentially wide range of social and economic values. This is where the issue of trust comes into the picture. There must be safeguards to protect the data from misuse or abuse and from continuing the historic divisions that marginalizes people groups unfairly and unjustly. Finally, the issue of equity comes to play in how data is shared. As with any resource, it must be applied to benefit all stakeholders on a level playing field that does not continue the divisive norms that society historically endorsed.

Figure 10.4: The social contract

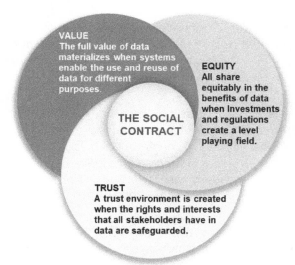

VALUE
The full value of data materializes when systems enable the use and reuse of data for different purposes.

EQUITY
All share equitably in the benefits of data when investments and regulations create a level playing field.

THE SOCIAL CONTRACT

TRUST
A trust environment is created when the rights and interests that all stakeholders have in data are safeguarded.

Source: World Bank 2021.

On September 4. 2019, the US Federal Trade Commission and the New York Attorney General filed a lawsuit in the US District Court for the District of Columbia against Google and YouTube for violating the Children's Online Privacy Protection Act (COPPA). YouTube, owned by Google collected personal information across its channels and used identifiers or cookies to aggregate data on children without getting parental consent as required by the COPPA rule. The lawsuit alleged that the defendants used this collected personal information to curate ads geared towards kids. They also sold the information to product and service providers who did the same. According to the lawsuit, Google and YouTube had actual knowledge that they were *"collecting personal information directly from users of these child-directed channels"* and failed to obtain parental consent. Google and YouTube settled the lawsuit for $170 million.

Since 2013, when Edward Snowden leaked classified documents that revealed how western governments were using data collected by private companies such as Amazon, Google, Twitter, Apple and Facebook for global surveillance purposes, considerable legal and organizational frameworks have been put in place to address the gaps in consumer data abuse and misuse. But experts agree that a great deal of work remains to ensure adequate consumer data protection. To create an inclusive data infrastructure ecosystem that meet the needs of those who collect, process and utilize consumer data while still protecting the interests of consumers, the World Development Report 2021 suggested that a trust framework should be employed in which collected data is safeguarded first before it is used:

- Safeguards are *"···those norms and legal frameworks that ensure and promote trust in the data governance and data management ecosystem by avoiding and limiting harm arising from the misuse of data or breaches affecting their security and integrity (World Bank 2021). "*
- Enablers are *"···those policies, laws, regulations, and standards that facilitate the use, reuse, and sharing of data within and between stakeholder groups through open- ness, interoperability, and portability. Whereas the approach to safeguards differs markedly for personal and nonpersonal data, a common set of enablers is relevant to both categories (World Bank 2021). "*

Data governance refers to the entire ecosystem of policies, systems, platforms, and standards in which digital data exist. When organizations collect data and use them as they see fit for their own interests with no guidelines, it does not serve the interests of consumers and society in the long run. This is why governmental policy makers need to protect the interests of minority and vulnerable groups and weigh in on unfair and unjust practices facilitated through big data.

For example, in 2018 the U.S. Department of Housing and Urban Development (HUD) alleged that Facebook was engaged in discriminatory practices that disadvantaged minority and vulnerable groups. Specifically, the complaint stated that:

> *Facebook unlawfully discriminates by enabling advertisers to restrict which Facebook users receive housing-related ads based on race, color, religion, sex, familial status, national origin and disability. Facebook mines extensive user data and classifies its users based on protected characteristics. Facebook's ad targeting tools then invite advertisers to express unlawful preferences by suggesting discriminatory options, and Facebook effectuates the delivery of housing-related ads to certain users and not others based on those users' actual or imputed protected traits (Park 2019).*

At issue was the way in which Facebook created, used, reused and repurposed its data for advertisers to target and exclude people based on *"attributes that the users who will be shown the ad must have and attributes that users who will be shown the ad must not have."* This option gave advertisers the ability to include or exclude people based on stereotypes, not individual capabilities. Facebook also dished out the data based on *"sex and close proxies for the other protected classes."*

Data, like statistics, can be used descriptively to summarize the characteristics of a data set, it can also be used to draw conclusions and make predictions. Using its data, Facebook also decided which users would see what ads based *"...in large part on the inferences and predictions it draws about each user's likelihood to respond to an ad based on the data it has about that user, the data it has about other users whom it considers to resemble that user, and the data it has about 'friends' and other associates of that user (World Bank 2021)."*

In response to the complaint, Facebook said that there was "no place for discrimination in its decisions and practices" and proceeded to remove 5,000 ad target options, stating that "While these options have been used in legitimate ways to reach people interested in a certain product or service, we think minimizing the risk of abuse is more important..." The problem is that Facebook knew perfectly well that these practices were adversarial to the benefits and interests of minority and vulnerable groups. They just didn't care until they were caught. This is why a stronger framework needs to be put into place to incentivize fair and equitable practices, one that will work proactively, not just reactively.

Data that gives organizations the power to target groups and customers based on characteristics like age, gender, address, race, or sex provides a new avenue for old discriminatory norms to manifest. In drawing on the literature and global knowledge and drive for a systemic approach to corporate data governance, the World Bank's World Development Report, 2021 offered four data governance functions that are needed:

1. Strategic planning: The rapid growth of data landscape and the need for endless data collection from a plethora of entities necessitates some level of strategic planning at both the governmental and organizational levels so data use is not abused. As the report indicated, *"The overall objective of data institutions and governance frameworks is to safely realize greater social value from data. Finding the appropriate balance between encouraging greater use of data while maintaining safeguards against misuse is ultimately the role played by each country's social contract for data. Achieving this balance in practice requires that institutions and actors work together to transform the general principles of the social contract into strategies, policies, and integrated data systems (World Bank 2021)."*

2. Rule making and implementation: Regulatory bodies must come up to speed with the rapidly increasing demand for data by setting standards for interoperability, data quality and improvement in the usability and integrity of data while also providing guidance and clarification through laws and regulations that reduce barriers to compliance. The report opined that rule-making functions should

include, *"...creating new public sector data governance institutions whose mandate, criteria for appointing managers, and funding arrangements are stipulated by regulation or decree...[and] [t]he more complex the data and the actors involved, the greater may be the need to clarify and guide participants to ensure a shared understanding of how the data are governed (World Bank 2021)."*

3. Compliance: Four areas in compliance: (1) enforcement or the day-to-day activities that ensures compliance with laws and regulatory norms and standards, (2) remediation of faults to compensate or correct for damage or breaches from the use of data, (3) arbitration needed when there are unanswered questions from the regulations or standards, such as handling specific minority or vulnerable groups' sensitive data that may not be covered by law but are known to have been used historically for discriminatory norms like in the justice system, and (4) audits used to supplement enforcements by identifying noncompliance requiring improvements or remedies in the rules (World Bank 2021).

4. Learning and evidence: three areas of focus: (1) backward-looking monitoring and evaluation (M&E) serve as performance tracking of staff and organizations and an assessment mechanism for how the *"program and policy delivers on identified objectives."*, (2) forward-looking learning and risk management provide tools and approaches that may require policy makers before any misuse of data occurs to adapt existing data governance regimes by identifying and responding to *"emerging or unforeseen issues before they become acute societal challenges and to inform planning and policy-making activities"* and (3) innovation in the rapidly changing data technology landscape poses M&E and risk management challenges and gives institutions the *"...important role in facilitating timely assessments of what works in the newly evolving data environment and offer guidance on how to quickly adapt to change and promote knowledge sharing (World Bank 2021)."*

Data management encompasses the creation, processing, storing, transferring, analyzing, archiving or use of previously created data. Once data is collected or created, it can be processed, stored, transferred or shared, analyzed and used, archived and preserved, destroyed or reborn into another data life cycle:

Figure 10.5: The data life cycle

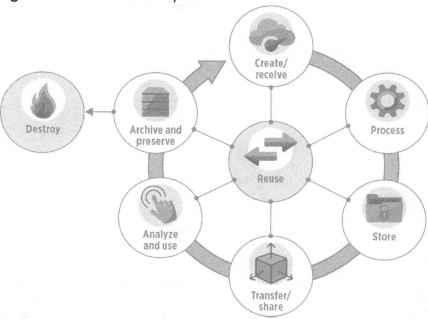

Source: World Bank 2021.

The infrastructure is the necessary digital framework that enables the collection, exchange, storage, processing, and distribution of both personal and nonpersonal data. Personal data include those provided by the individual and nonpersonal are those that can be associated with the individual through machine-generated information—for example, from mobile phone data or public surveys, etc.

For DE&I to moderate consumer data protection, two key issues are important: trust and fair and just practices. Trust can be achieved through safeguards and enablers anchored by good governance and the rule of law, if they align with social responsibility principles of *"...transparency, accountability, nondiscrimination, fairness, inclusiveness, and openness. They are subject to due process limitations such as necessity and proportionality* (World Bank 2021)*."*

Fair and just practices speak to both the organizational and global responsibility to ensure that consumer data are not used to exacerbate our already existing divisive norms. This is the new social contract that will ensure fair and just data practices that go beyond the benefits of the advanced countries or organizations; it should also consider benefits for developing countries and the organizations. The World Development Report contended that:

Many stakeholders around the world have concluded that some sort of global charter or convention is now required to realize the benefits of data in a safe and secure way and to avoid destructive beggar-thy-neighbor strategies...A global consensus would give individuals and enterprises confidence that data relevant to them carry similar protections and obligations no matter where they are collected or used. It would effectively establish a social contract that would strike a balance between the use of data for development and the protection of data in terms of security, privacy, and human rights of the individual. It would also establish ground rules for the exchange of data between commercial use and the public good. The consensus would constitute an integrated set of data values, principles, and standards that define the elements of responsible and ethical handling and sharing of data and that unite national governments, public institutions, the private sector, civil society organizations, and academia. A global mechanism is needed to provide incentives for applying these principles and overseeing their consistent application across different communities (World Bank 2021).

This is where organizational leaders can ask questions about the state of their consumer data enterprise considering data life cycle and provide leadership and guidance beyond the technical. They need to provide guidance on the socially responsible collection, sharing and use of data. However, even before a global charter or convention comes to fruition, organizations can still use existing best practice mechanisms to create an inclusive data infrastructure ecosystem where consumer data and privacy is protected. One such mechanism is the role data governance and data management play in the organizational data infrastructure ecosystem, and it is within this framework that a socially responsible organization can address DE&I questions about its consumer data decisions and practices.

Figure 10.6: Data governance and data management in support of the social contract

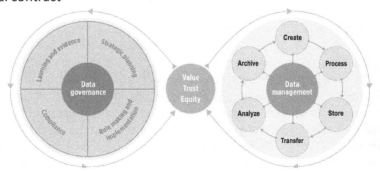

Source: World Bank 2021.

CONSUMER DATA PROTECTION AND PRIVACY
Creativity-driven equity opportunity/reconciliation/disruption

Consumer data protection and privacy is a DE&I matter because it requires accountability and certainty in rulemaking and transparency governed by good regulatory practices developed through fair and just laws and regulations. These regulations should be evidence-based and supported by consultative rulemaking that is also stakeholder-driven and informed input from minority and vulnerable groups. As the World Development Report affirmed, *"…recent developments in regulatory design have included efforts to adapt regulations to the digital age. Mechanisms such as regulatory sandboxes and laboratories help make regulations more agile and readily adaptable to evolving circumstances. By drafting principle-based and technologically neutral laws and regulations, policy makers help them remain relevant as technologies evolve and reduce compliance burdens (World Bank 2021)."*

Strengthening data safeguards and enablers using DE&I as a moderator can help guide the development, implementation and enforcement of a data protection and privacy regimen that is fair and just for consumers. I am adapting the following recommendations from the World Development Report 2021 for principle-based and technologically neutral DE&I organizational policies and procedures:

For safeguards,

- Adopting and implementing personal data protection policy (for organizational actors) and legislation (for government actors) that are DE&I moderated for and influenced by fairness and social justice.
- Introducing inclusive meaningful models of consent where all stakeholders are identified and engaged based on their literacy levels and ability to understand and take responsibility for the permission they give to collectors to use and reuse their data. This is important because legal checkboxes that organizations unfairly use to shift responsibility to individuals, who often waive their rights to personal data and privacy without realizing it. Few people even in advanced countries with higher levels of education read these disclosure statements; and with the billions that have come online from around the world, we need new DE&I driven models that puts the responsibility on collectors and users of data to protect them and not on the individuals.
- Expanding protection to mixed data and group privacy that does not marginalize or disenfranchise minority or vulnerable groups by association and by DE&I identification and linkages. Today, the lines of demarcation between personal and nonpersonal data has been compromised by the advent of the Internet of Things and other technologies like algorithm-based

data mining (big data). Mixed data can easily be identified and linked as new datasets back to personal data thanks to these technologies and as the World Development Report attested: *"...current provisions for personal data protection, which focus on the individual, do not preclude the identification and potential misuse of data attributes pertaining to homogeneous groups (including those defined by ethnicity, race, religion, or sexual orientation). These protections are particularly important in complex or fragile sociopolitical environments or emergency contexts because of the increased risk of misuse of such data for targeting or surveillance (World Bank 2021).*

- Adopting data protection both by design and default within privacy-enhancing technologies (PET) that initially embeds DE&I moderated data protection practices into the design phase of data-driven products and services (World Bank 2021).

- This approach can be used to safeguard *"...fundamental data rights in contexts in which weak institutional capacity diminishes the legal enforceability of those rights. However, for technical mechanisms to have teeth, they must be underpinned by a robust legal frame-work that creates the rights and limits on use that privacy-enhancing technologies reinforce (World Bank 2021)."*

- Prioritizing cybersecurity practices is a DE&I matter because individuals and organizations can be held hostage by criminals who take advantage of weak data infrastructure systems. The weakest link is where the cybercriminals would generally attack; when the infrastructure and system are not protected, the data in them can be exposed. While governmental bodies may enact legislation that balances fundamental rights with security concerns, organizations can and should do the same with policy and procedures (World Bank 2021).

For enablers,

- Building both a robust and flexible platform for electronic commerce that is fair and just, especially when it comes to digital authentication and verification for minority and vulnerable groups. For example, it is estimated that 1 billion people today do not have a government-verified proof of identity (World Bank 2021). This marginalizes people groups who cannot participate either as vendors or consumers in the digital payment system and is reminiscent of how banks kept minorities marginalized through qualifications for credit card issuance schemes. Creating technology-neutral digital identity laws and programs would allow for *"...a wide range of technical solutions and avoid requiring specific authentication technologies to the exclusion of others (World Bank 2021)."*

- Making data both easy to access and open by default requires legislation across the board in support of open-by-default public sector data approaches where published datasets are organized based on end user input and where the end user do not have to pay for it (World Bank 2021).

This is another approach to leveling the playing field where end users are not demarcated, disadvantaged, and marginalized by affordability schemes.

- Applying consistent fair and just norms for data classification is a DE&I matter because data laws and policies should be consistently applied within clear and socially responsible data classification policies (World Bank 2021).
- Adopting both friendly license sharing and open standards are good socially responsible practices because they allow policy makers and organizational leaders to pursue an *"...open access to public intent data (World Bank 2021)"* especially when they address and narrow divisive norms.
- Strengthening access to information provisions especially for those that are non-sensitive should be prioritized through legislation that organizations can support and advocate for through personal or corporate lobbying efforts (World Bank 2021).
- Promoting the interoperability of data and systems should be supported by organizations when feasible as they can lead to common standards in machine-readable format (World Bank 2021) where DE&I moderates what is classified and processed as fair and just in the collection and use of data.
- Supporting data portability as rights require data to be collected in *"structured, commonly used, and machine-readable format...[and] address the lack of clear understanding of these rights by data subjects, as well as the implementation challenges faced by micro, small, and medium enterprises (World Bank 2021)."*
- Promoting sharing of private intent data that increases the reusability of data and reduces the push for hoarding data. The World Development Report 2021 contended that to enhance intellectual property rights and promote data sharing, governments should consider adding private sector data sharing through incentivized agreements (World Bank 2021).

EQUITY OPPORTUNITY IN CONSUMER DATA PROTECTION AND PRIVACY

Safeguarding consumer data and privacy should be approached both as a matter of substantive and procedural rights. The following definitions are adapted from the 2021 World Development Report:

- **Substantive rights** should be protected from unauthorized disclosure, unwarranted surveillance, "...unfair targeting, exclusion, discrimination, unjust treatment, or persecution. Such substantive rights also require purpose specification, data minimization, and storage limitations."
- **Procedural rights** should be based on social responsibility principles of need to know (necessity), accountability, transparency, due process and proportionality that includes the "...rights to receive notice about and to object to how data are used and rights of access to correct and erase data (including the right to be forgotten), as well as rights to redress and remedy (World Bank 2021)."

Organizational leaders, at the very minimum, should ensure that their consumer data protection and privacy practices are fair and just to minority and vulnerable groups, and that their commitment to DE&I in these practices is internalized in their policy and procedures. They should include provisions that cover the entire data lifecycle—from collection to storage and/or destruction. ISO 26000 provides an even broader guidance:

ISO *To prevent personal data collection and processing from infringing privacy, an organization should:*

- ☐ *limit the collection of personal data to information that is either essential for the provision of products and services or provided with the informed and voluntary consent of the consumer;*
- ☐ *protect personal data by adequate security safeguards; and*
- ☐ *disclose the identity and usual location of the person accountable for data protection in the organization (sometimes called the data controller), and hold this person accountable for complying with the above measures and applicable law.*

ISO 26000:2010, page 55-59.

To ensure that the data it is collecting, using, repurposing or destroying after use is consistent with its social responsibility norms, organizational leaders should do a cursory review of the DE&I implications of its data management and governance practices. Where there are unfair and unjust issues in its data life cycle, these leaders can implement strategic best practices to remedy them. The reason organizational leaders should be involved in reviewing the data life cycle is because everyone within an organization touches data in some form or another, and the practice and enforcement of fair and just practices falls under the purview of leadership. The following table provides a framework for asking DEI-related questions to ensure fair and just practices are implemented or planned to be implemented:

Table 10.1: Data management decisions along the data life cycle with DE&I as moderator

Stage of life cycle	Area in which data management is needed
Create/receive	• Determine lawful use (such as obtaining consent for data collection and sharing). • Collect identifications that allow data to be merged with other datasets.
Process	• Standardize units and categories (such as industry classifications). • Use data formats that are widely compatible and accessible.

	• Validate the quality (accuracy), relevance, and integrity of data.
Store	• Encrypt data; use secure servers; back up and archive data.
Transfer/share	• Verify whether consent allows for data to be shared. • Identify data, if appropriate (reference deleted). • Sign confidentiality agreements for use of identified data. • Publish data via bulk downloads or APIs.
Analyze and use	• Ensure reproducibility; publish code or algorithms. • Do not publish identifiable data. • Visualize and communicate insights from data.
Archive and preserve	• Classify and catalog data systematically so they can be found easily. • Include data dictionaries and notes on how data were created. • Maintain access to data and their security and integrity over time.
Destroy or use	• Keep records of destruction processes. • Verify that consent for use is still valid.
Source: World Bank 2021.	

EQUITY RECONCILIATION IN CONSUMER DATA PROTECTION AND PRIVACY

In a world driven by significant automated acquisition of personal information, an organization can maintain consumer confidence by establishing rigorous protocols for collecting, using and protecting consumer data. These systems should also include provisions to ensure that vulnerable individuals, groups and communities are not taken advantage of, or worse, microtargeted or even abused. In a world that increasingly relies on highly sophisticated data mining and analytics through the use of artificial intelligence, it is far easier to identify and segregate demographic pools. This information can be easily manipulated to isolate vulnerable groups as consumers and use them for experimental purposes or deny them services. Because of this, it is important to limit the collection of personal and vulnerable consumer information to only that which is given voluntarily and with informed consent, or where essential for providing products and services. This can be achieved within an organization's DE&I policies and practices. ISO 26000 proves the following broad guidance:

ISO *To prevent personal data collection and processing from infringing privacy, an organization should:*
- ☐ *specify the purpose for which personal data are collected, either before or at the time of data collection;*
- ☐ *provide consumers with the right to verify whether the organization has data relating to them and to challenge these data, as defined*

The World Development Report advocated for a nonpersonal data ecosystem that is:

[A] balance of interests approach to safeguards and enablers, recognizing that trade-offs typically arise between increasing data access and safeguarding intellectual property rights (IPRs) over nonpersonal data. The focus is thus on a legal framework that enables the (re)use and sharing of data through regulatory predictability, data openness, and portability (the ability to readily transfer data from one service to another based on clear legal and technical standards). Of growing importance are data that blend both personal and nonpersonal sources—so-called mixed data (World Bank 2021).

Table 10.2. Recommendations organized according to a maturity model based on data safeguards and enablers

Stage of country's data system	Safeguards	Enablers
Establishing fundamentals	Conduct a baseline needs assessment. Develop a comprehensive policy framework based on best practices that does the following: • Safeguards personal, nonpersonal, and evolving categories of data and promotes greater equity around data • Enhances the security of systems and infrastructure that protect against misuse of data • Expands individuals' agency and control over their personal data • Promotes certainty and predictability, integrating the	Conduct a baseline needs assessment. Develop a comprehensive policy framework based on best practices that enables the use and sharing of data for development purposes, ensuring access, openness, interoperability, portability, predictability, and transparency, while integrating the fundamental enablers discussed in this chapter, such as electronic transactions.

	fundamental safeguards discussed in this chapter such as data protection and cybersecurity.	
Initiating data flows	Elaborate a legal framework that embodies policy prerogatives that include: • Personal data protection • Promotion of cybersecurity and combating of cybercrime • Regulation of competition • Provisions in the legal framework to provide for establishment of the relevant enforcement institutions.	Elaborate a legal framework that embodies policy prerogatives that include: • Legal recognition of e-transactions • Access to information • Intellectual property rights for nonpersonal data • Openness of public intent data, including the use of licenses that encourage data sharing • Data classification principles.
Optimizing the system	Promote awareness of safeguards: • Domestically, through adoption of data protection by design and default, together with associated cybersecurity measures • Internationally, through cross-border interoperability of data protection standards • Address more complex issues such as mixed data and group rights • Ensure that the capacity of the institutions responsible for overseeing these activities is sufficient • Establish metrics to monitor and evaluate the implementation and enforcement of these policies • and laws.	Consider issues such as data portability and increasing incentives around sharing of private intent data. Ensure that the capacity of the institutions responsible for overseeing these activities is sufficient. Establish metrics to monitor and evaluate the implementation of these policies, laws, and institutions.
Source: World Bank 2021.		

EQUITY DISRUPTION IN CONSUMER DATA PROTECTION AND PRIVACY

The life cycle of consumer data today is far longer than most people realize. Individuals today enter their personal information into data infrastructure that they neither own nor control, and the organization that collects this data for one purpose likely has no control how it may be used by others down the road. For example, an individual orders pizza and gives his or her name, address, phone number or even email. Who owns this individual data, online? An individual may claim right of ownership to personal data, but the legal system is not built to enforce such claims, especially when the personal data has flowed into the ocean of aggregated data. While the prospect of perpetual individual data is out there, there are socially responsible actions that organizations can take to disrupt practices that compromise consumer data and privacy. ISO 26000 provides the following broad guidance:

> **ISO** *To prevent personal data collection and processing from infringing privacy, an organization should:*
> ☐ *refrain from making the use of services or the claim to special offers contingent on agreement by the consumer to the unwanted use of data for marketing purposes;*
> ☐ *specify the purpose for which personal data are collected, either before or at the time of data collection;*
> ☐ *provide consumers with the right to verify whether the organization has data relating to them and to challenge these data, as defined by law. If the challenge is successful, the data should be erased, rectified, completed or amended, as appropriate; [and]*
> ☐ *be open about developments, practices and policies regarding personal data, and provide readily available ways of establishing the existence, nature and main uses of personal data[.]*
>
> *ISO 26000:2010, pages 55-59.*

The data life cycle provides a framework for organizations to establish DE&I policies and procedures that protects the interests of all stakeholders. This is especially true for minority and vulnerable groups who face targeting practices that are adversely consequential. As the World Development Report 2021 attested, data can be extracted and reused perpetually because they are *"...are inexhaustible or "nonrival"—that is, a person's call detail records, location history, internet usage, and medical records, among other things, can be used repeatedly by firms and governments for different purposes without depleting them."*

CONSUMER DATA PROTECTION AND PRIVACY
Governance-centered inclusion actionable steps

Consumer data protection is a big deal for socially responsible organizations because it allows for both the opportunity to ensure fair and just data collection and use practices. In reviewing, developing, or implementing a DE&I-moderated consumer data protection and privacy ecosystem, an organization should look at the data life cycle as a key framework for balancing safeguards and enablers' interests and influences.

Governance-centered inclusion actionable steps: consumer data protection and privacy

1. In review your organization's policies and procedures around consumer data protection and privacy, how do they align with your DE&I policy, commitments, and corporate proclamations on the matter?
2. If there are gaps, what are the actionable steps and timelines you have identified to narrow or eliminate them based on the 3-Step Equity Lens model Lens model guided by the 3-Step Inclusion principles?
3. Were all relevant stakeholders identified and engaged in the review, modification or development of your policies and procedures around your DE&I moderated consumer data protection and privacy?

CONSUMER ISSUE 6: DE&I AS MODERATOR FOR ACCESS TO ESSENTIAL SERVICES

Does your organization consider DE&I as currency in providing and negotiating access to essential services?

ACCESS TO ESSENTIAL SERVICES
Knowledge-informed diversity call to action

Historically, in most jurisdictions around the world, the state is responsible for providing access to essential services. However, what constitutes essential services today has become more complicated. Traditional services such as energy have become intertwined with more nuanced services such as socio-economic and sustainable development. Some contend that the internet should be classified as such a service. There is even a push to make social media a guaranteed public utility essential service and to regulate third-party contents. As Harvard Professor John G. Palfrey suggests, *"We need a regulatory regime today for technology that puts the public interest first, with equity and inclusion as a design principle and not an afterthought (Milano 2021)."* ISO 26000 contended that:

ISO *Although the state is responsible for ensuring that the right to satisfaction of basic needs is respected, there are many locations or conditions in which the state does not ensure that this right is protected. Even where satisfaction of some basic needs, such as health care, is protected, the right to essential utility services, such as electricity, gas, water, wastewater services, drainage, sewage and communication may not be fully achieved. An organization can contribute to the fulfilment of this right.*

ISO 26000:2010, page 59 (references deleted).

Access to power, climate mitigation and adaptative technologies and sustainable jobs are some of the key challenges of our time. Amid so much personal wealth creation, accumulation and distribution necessitated and fueled by the information age, there is a corresponding need to provide access to essential services to billions of our fellow humans who are not sharing in these essential qualities of life benefits.

According to the World Bank's Energy Sector Management Assistance Program (ESMAP): *"There are currently 63 countries that have more than half a million people living without access to electricity (World Bank 2022)."* ESMAP's 2021 Energy Progress Report did indicate that there was some recent global electrification progress, with more than one billion people gaining access to electricity between 2010 and 2019. However, the news is mixed. The report also stated that:

COVID's financial impact has made basic electricity services unaffordable for 30 million more people, the majority located in Africa...Globally, the number of people without access to electricity declined from 1.2 billion in 2010 to 759 million in 2019. Electrification through decentralized renewable-based solutions in particular gained momentum. The number of people connected to mini grids has more than doubled between 2010 and 2019, growing from 5 to 11 million people. However, under current and planned policies and further affected by the COVID-19 crisis, an estimated 660 million people would still lack access in 2030, most of them in Sub-Saharan Africa (World Bank 2022).

Millions lurk in the dark unaware of the human possibilities today because they do not have access to reliable or affordable clean energy—many even still stuck with kerosene and other pollution-centric fossil fuels to light up their homes, businesses, educational and other institutions. This during an age of breakthroughs that has made renewable energy more affordable and *"the cheapest option for new power in more than two-thirds of the world (TRF 2021)."* Access to energy looked like this using 2016 data:

- 40% of the world or 3 billion people have no access to clean fuels for cooking with a high health cost due to indoor pollution.
- Around the world, the per capita consumption of electricity varies by more than 100-fold and of energy by 10-fold.
- 13% of the world or 940 million people have no access to electricity.
- Poor households around the world are more likely to have no energy access because it is tied to affordability which is linked to income *(TRF 2021)*.

It is in these times that we are reminded of the famous "Moon speech" by President John F. Kennedy, in which he made the case for why America should lead the way in space exploration on behalf of humanity:

We set sail on this new sea because there is new knowledge to be gained, and new rights to be won, and they must be won and used for the progress of all people. For space science, like nuclear science and all technology, has no conscience of its own. Whether it will become a force for good or ill depends on man, and only if the United States occupies a position of pre-eminence can we help decide whether this new ocean will be a sea of peace or a new terrifying theater of war.

Today, knowledge acquired from space exploration has given the world the internet and other communications tools that have enabled billions of people to be interconnected in so many different life-altering ways. It has also exposed us to energy applications as a source for good in transforming rural and urban life. In fact, the UN's Sustainable Development Goals (SDGs) identified universal electrification as a key link to modern energy for all that is also affordable, sustainable, and reliable.

The sustainable use of all these technologies for good depends on how inclusively they're implemented. While essential services fall in the domain of the state, organizations should be part of the solution to broader, more equitable access as well. For minority and vulnerable groups around the world, including those that live in developed countries, access to essential services may include:

Transportation systems: these enable people to easily move from place to place connecting them to education, healthcare, jobs, and other opportunities. Historically, these systems have been used to divide communities, establish artificial barriers that marginalizes people groups through lack of access and dwarfed the economic vitality of too many minority and vulnerable groups.

Clean energy – electricity: the current global shift towards clean energy contribute to less dependence on fossil fuels and thus serve as a key remedy for rising temperatures. Provision of clean renewable energy, climate change and the eradication of poverty around the world are related concerns. They are related because solving one problem—lack of electricity or reliable electricity in rural areas—can also help reduce CO_2 emissions and create sustainable clean jobs. According to data from the Global Energy Alliance for People and Planet, energy-poor countries today account for 25% of global CO_2 emissions, though this contribution is expected to rise to 75% by 2050. Interestingly, poor countries' access to energy financing accounts for 13% even though they are home to 50% of the world's population (TRF 2021). Access to clean energy cannot be driven by privilege, but by our shared responsibility to effectively use the resources we need today while ensuring future generations have resources to fulfil theirs.

Highspeed Internet and cellphone connectivity: access to cellphone service is not only essential, but it has also become a lifeline for most, from daily business and trading transactions to familial relationship connections, to educational pursuits. These connectivity possibilities have allowed us to continue business as usual when COVID-19 forced us to transact business in unusual ways. Minority and vulnerable groups especially those in rural areas need highspeed internet connections to bridge the technology gaps that are widening daily between those that have access and those that do not. This makes highspeed internet and cellphone connectivity a DE&I consumer issue and a corporate social responsibility call to action.

Food: food insecurity can be a significant drain that siphons human energy, forcing people to focus on just surviving another day, another blistering winter, another harrowing firestorm, or unjust food supplies for the rich while the poor languish in avoidable hunger spells. In developed countries, it is more policy-driven social norms that keep mainstream food suppliers and distributors out of neighborhoods zoned (in the case of America) as D from the relics of redlining. Ironically, these neighborhoods, essentially "food deserts," generally have easier access to alcoholic beverages than for essential nutritious foods.

Water: an essential necessity for human bodily functions—waste removal, cellular function, and temperature regulation to name a few. Access to clean drinking water is a DE&I issue and a fundamental human right. The need to improve supply and distribution of clean drinking water and the deployment of technologies to restore polluted or convert salt water to quality drinking water are becoming a humankind challenge, needing fresh new ideas and solutions.

Public utilities: universal access to public utilities is a right, especially in those areas where taxes are collected from all constituents to fund the existence of the utility. While the state sets the rules and statutes that govern public utilities, they have been known to respond less to the interests of minorities, vulnerable groups, and the poor in every racial group. This makes policies on collecting *"consumer information, security deposits and advance payment for service, late payment fees, (UN Guidelines 2016)"* and handling *"termination and restoration of service, establishment of payment plans and dispute resolution between consumers and utility service providers (UN Guidelines 2016)"* all DE&I issues.

Pharmaceuticals: Those who invest in the research and development of pharmaceuticals should be able to profit from their investments, or course. But pharmaceuticals can be an essential service and access to lifesaving or life-altering medications needs to be considered a DE&I issue. The accessibility of Covid-19 vaccines around the world is a good example. The entire ecosystem of pharmaceuticals—development, distribution, procurement, distributions, licensing arrangements, and even the availability of pharmaceutical information—are all DE&I matters because each one is an essential or contributor to access to essential pharmaceutical services. I've previously covered patent rights and how they can be deployed for good especially when in the past they were manipulated for accentuating divisive norms. We need to create a win-win system in which pharmaceutical companies can thrive from their investments and still serve our shared humanity by making access to their products and services affordable or available to those who need them.

ACCESS TO ESSENTIAL SERVICES
Creativity-driven equity opportunity/reconciliation/disruption

Access to essential services are DE&I matters. Organizations should look beyond just profits and consider opportunities to use its decisions and activities as vehicles for good either as a stakeholder of interest or of influence in advocating and promoting local and global (where appropriate) initiatives that narrow the digital divide. Experts agree that access to energy spurs economic growth and vitality.

In 2021, a new global initiative was launched by the Global Alliance for People and Planet with the audacious goal of raising $100 billion from public and private entities to:

> *[A]ccelerate investment in green energy transitions and renewable power solutions in developing and emerging economies worldwide. Over the next decade, the Alliance aims to unlock USD100 billion in public and private capital and tackle three profound human problems simultaneously: (1) POWER – reaching one billion people with reliable, renewable energy; (2) CLIMATE – avoiding and averting four billion tons of carbon emissions; and (3) JOBS – building an on-ramp to opportunity by creating, enabling,*

These are the types of initiatives and investment commitments that are transformative and create a platform for making our world much fairer and just. Access to clean energy is a key link to closing the divisive gaps that have made our time on planet earth prosperous for some and tortuous for the vast majority with widespread inequalities that accentuate poverty on a global scale instead of eradicating it. Bridging the gaps can benefit from the utilization of the 3-Step Equity lens to find opportunities and reconcile our shared commitment to how we deploy, distribute, and make access to clean energy affordable to all consumers. We need to disrupt or stop practices that exclude others from contributing their part in solving climate change problems.

EQUITY OPPORTUNITY IN ACCESS TO ESSENTIAL SERVICES

At the minimum, organizations should commit to ensuring that minority and vulnerable groups are not priced out of access to essential services. These organizations should make sure that their decisions and activities do not perpetuate racism and other forms of divisive norms that marginalize people groups. ISO 26000 provides the following broad guidance:

ISO   *An organization that supplies essential services should:*
☐   *in setting prices and charges, offer, wherever permitted, a tariff that will provide a subsidy to those who are in need; [and]*
☐   *operate in a transparent manner, providing information related to the setting of prices and charges[.]*

ISO 26000:2010, page 59.

Organizations that do not provide access to essential services but whose products and services require the use of these services should also consider how they can assist vulnerable communities to enrich their experiences with their products and services. This is part of the global sustainability continuum. For example, a cellphone provider may purchase a mini-grid power system for its activities with enough capacity to distribute lighting and other energy services to a rural community for profit. Alternatively, a local entrepreneur could also purchase a mini-grid and sell power to a cellphone company as its anchor-load customer while providing additional power to local businesses and homes. Organizations with surplus idle capital can use some of it to finance these types of ventures around the world as part of their social responsibility and sustainable development goals.

EQUITY RECONCILIATION IN ACCESS TO ESSENTIAL SERVICES

An organization should assess its products and services and align them where appropriate to the life cycle of essential services to ensure that their decisions and activities are fair and just to all who are dependent on them. This holistic view takes essential services beyond the traditional view of who is responsible for providing them. ISO 26000 provided the following guidance:

> **ISO** *An organization that supplies essential services should:*
> ☐ *expand their coverage and provide the same quality and level of service without discrimination to all groups of consumers; [and]*
> ☐ *manage any curtailment or interruption of supply in an equitable manner, avoiding discrimination against any group of consumers[.]*
>
> *ISO 26000:2010, page 59.*

For example, an information technology company could seek opportunities to invest in building smart grid systems in vulnerable communities so more people from around the world can be included in the utilization of their products and services. As the Rockefeller Foundation put it, *"...providing access to reliable and affordable electricity for productive use can stimulate sustainable economic opportunities and bring a better, healthier quality of life to poor and vulnerable people living in underserved regions in India, Myanmar, and Africa (TRF 2022)."*

EQUITY DISRUPTION IN ACCESS TO ESSENTIAL SERVICES

Consumer behavior is not just a gold mine for marketers; it can help determine their own essential services—what they cannot live without. For some it is the information or news they consume from the internet (real or imagined) while for others it could be as simple as breathing unpolluted air. When an organization discovers that its "access to essential services"' decisions and activities disproportionately discriminates against any group, it should seek quick and decisive remedies. ISO 26000 provided the following broad guidance:

> **ISO** *An organization that supplies essential services should:*
> ☐ *not disconnect essential services for non-payment without providing the consumer or group of consumers with the opportunity to seek*

reasonable time to make the payment. It should not resort to collective disconnection of services that penalize all consumers regardless of payment; [and]

☐ *maintain and upgrade its systems to help prevent disruption of service.*

ISO 26000:2010, page 59.

ACCESS TO ESSENTIAL SERVICES
Governance-centered inclusion actionable steps

Access to essential services should be a part of governance-centered DE&I policy and practices to ensure that services are not used to perpetuate racism or other inequities. This involves dealing with legacy infrastructure inequities, like lead-based pipes still used in poor areas (such as Flint Michigan). Freeway design has been another historic inequity, often placed in less affluent communities with no consideration for the impact of the roads. Disproportionately quick disconnection of services to disenfranchised communities is also a common problem. Sometimes these inequities are deliberate, sometimes they are legacies of past discriminatory practices. Regardless of their provenance, they must be identified and dealt with appropriately.

Governance-centered inclusion actionable steps: access to essential services

1. In review your organization's policies and procedures around access to essential services, how do they align with your DE&I policy, commitments, and corporate proclamations on the matter?
2. If there are gaps, what are the actionable steps and timelines you have identified to narrow or eliminate them based on the 3-Step Equity Lens model guided by the 3-Step Inclusion principles?
3. Were all relevant stakeholders identified and engaged in the review, modification or development of your policies and procedures around your DE&I moderated access to essential services practices?

CONSUMER ISSUE 7: DE&I AS MODERATOR FOR EDUCATION AND AWARENESS PRACTICES

An organization's education and awareness programming are a good way to focus its policies and procedures around its DE&I commitments. ISO 26000 summed it up as follows:

ISO *In Education and awareness initiatives enable consumers to be well informed, conscious of their rights and responsibilities, more likely to assume an active role and to be able to make knowledgeable purchasing decisions and consume responsibly. Disadvantaged consumers in both rural and urban areas, including low- income consumers and those with low literacy levels, have special needs for education and increased awareness. Whenever there is a formal contract between an organization and a consumer, the organization should verify that the consumer is properly informed of all applicable rights and obligations. The aim of consumer education is not only to transfer knowledge, but also to empower consumers to act on this knowledge. This includes developing skills for assessing products and services and for making comparisons. It is also intended to raise awareness about the impact of consumption choices on others and on sustainable development. Education does not exempt an organization from being responsible if a consumer is harmed when using products and services.*

ISO 26000:2010, page 60 (reference deleted).

Chapter eleven

DE&I AS MODERATOR FOR COMMUNITY INVOLVEMENT AND DEVELOPMENT

Community involvement and development are critical to the alleviation of poverty and many of the divisive norms associated with, such as lack of access to education, gender inequalities, curable diseases, and generational poverty transfer, to name a few. Most people agree—experts and nonexperts alike—that the relationship between organizations and the communities in which they operate is important. In the preceding chapters, we discussed divisive norms that marginalize and disenfranchises communities through policies, and social contracts. Our discussion presented the rich landscape from which organizations can participate in addressing social contracts that have adversely divided our humankind. If it takes a village to raise a child, it also takes organizations to change the course of our systemic and structural racism, tribalism, gender, sexual orientation, and other protected class disparities.

In this chapter, the emphasis is on how organizations develop relationships and partnerships with the communities in which they operate. We're going to look at where their decisions and activities have the potential to strengthen civil society through development and implementation of sustainable development goals. Community, as ISO 26000 defines it,

ISO *[R]efers to residential or other social settlements located in a geographic area that is in physical proximity to an organization's sites or within an organization's areas of impact. The area and the community members affected by an organization's impacts will depend upon the*

context and especially upon the size and nature of those impacts. In general, however, the term community can also be understood to mean a group of people having particular characteristics in common, for instance a "virtual" community concerned with a particular issue.

Community involvement and community development are both integral parts of sustainable development. Community involvement goes beyond identifying and engaging stakeholders in regard to the impacts of an organization's activities; it also encompasses support for and building a relationship with the community. Above all, it entails acknowledging the value of the community. An organization's community involvement should arise out of recognition that the organization is a stakeholder in the community, sharing common interests with the community.

ISO 26000:2010, pages 60-61.

Organizations can develop these relationships aimed at the public good through a myriad of ways—working with individuals, associations, or supporting and advocating for their employees to get involved with community activities. ISO 26000 offers additional principles that are more suited for community involvement and development:

ISO *An organization should:*

☐ *consider itself as part of, and not separate from, the community in approaching community involvement and development;*

☐ *recognize and have due regard for the rights of community members to make decisions in relation to their community and thereby pursue, in the manner they choose, ways of maximizing their resources and opportunities;*

☐ *recognize and have due regard for the characteristics, for example, cultures, religions, traditions and history, of the community while interacting with it; and*

☐ *recognize the value of working in partnership, supporting the exchange of experiences, resources and efforts.*

ISO 26000:2010, page 61.

An organization's influence and effectiveness in community development can raise the general well-being of a community and provide both the financial and people resources needed to address perennial neglect. Socially responsible community development should be lifegiving and enrich the quality-of-life experiences of the community. As ISO 26000 correctly affirmed,

Community development is not a linear process; moreover, it is a long-term process in which different and conflicting interests will be present. Historical and cultural characteristics make each community unique and influence the possibilities of its future. Community development is therefore the result of social, political, economic and cultural features and depends on the characteristics of the social forces involved. Stakeholders in the community may have different—even conflicting—interests. Shared responsibility is needed to promote well being of the community as a common objective.

ISO 26000:2010, page 61.

Determining what shared responsibility looks like is the first challenge that we must first engage in. It involves understanding what the community's issues, challenges and opportunities are that can create a healthy relationship and partnership between organizations and communities. Within the social responsibility construct moderated by DE&I, community involvement and development needs to transcend just throwing money at community events. It must be more deliberately inclusive of the following three frameworks:

1. Understand community needs and interests
2. Support public policies that uplift the community interests
3. Contribute to community development through core activities

Understand community needs and interests through a stakeholder identification and engagement planning process that does not presume to know what a community needs or is interested in without first consulting with its members. This is especially true when there is a preexisting majority-minority dichotomy, where social norms established through divisive social contracts are integrated into organizational culture and values. A better approach is for an organization to first research what impacts it hopes to achieve and develop a plan in consultation with stakeholders, along with any mitigation for negative impacts. It goes without saying that in a stakeholder approach, the organization should seek a broad range of people, especially minority and vulnerable groups that have long been marginalized and disadvantaged. ISO 26000 provided the following guidance:

ISO
Issues of community development to which an organization can contribute include creating employment through expanding and diversifying economic activities and technological development. It can also contribute through social investments in wealth and income creation through local economic development initiatives; expanding education and

skills development programmes; promoting and preserving culture and arts; and providing and/or promoting community health services. Community development may include institutional strengthening of the community, its groups and collective forums, cultural, social and environmental programmes and local networks involving multiple institutions.

ISO 26000:2010, page 61.

Support public policies that uplift the community interests by integrating existing public policies that address systemic and structural barriers to life, liberty, and the pursuit of happiness. Organizations cannot remain neutral in public discourses on divisive norms because silence makes them complicit. Where governmental policy makers are divided on doing the right thing for all citizens because of political expediencies, organizations and their leaders are the last vestige of hope for minority and vulnerable groups. This is not only a social responsibility, but a moral one as well. In advocating and supporting legislations that benefits its interests, organizations can also extend these interests to include those ones that help end divisive social contracts on marginalization of people groups on a swathe of discriminatory issues. ISO 26000 provides the following broad guidance:

ISO Organizations often join partnerships and associate with others to defend and advance their own interests. However, these associations should represent their members' interests on the basis of respecting the rights of other groups and individuals to do the same, and they should always operate in a way that increases respect for the rule of law and democratic processes...Community development is usually advanced when the social forces in a community strive to promote public participation and pursue equal rights and dignified standards of living for all citizens, without discrimination. It is a process internal to the community that takes account of existing relations and overcomes barriers to the enjoyment of rights. Community development is enhanced by socially responsible behaviour.

ISO 26000:2010, page 61, 51.

Contribute to community development through core activities, integrating them where feasible into its decisions and activities to maximize their benefits within the communities they impact. ISO 26000 provides the following examples:

ISO Some examples of ways in which an organization's core activities can contribute to community development include:

- an enterprise selling farm equipment could provide training in farming techniques;
- a company planning to build an access road could engage the community at the planning stage to identify how the road could be built to also meet the needs of the community (for example, by providing access for local farmers);
- trade unions could use their membership networks to disseminate information about good health practices to the community;
- a water-intensive industry building a water purification plant for its own needs could also provide clean water to the community;
- an environmental protection association operating in a remote area could buy the supplies needed for its activities from local commerce and producers; and
- a recreational club could allow use of its facilities for educational activities for illiterate adults in the community.

ISO 26000:2010, page 63.

Organizational social responsibility can help energize a community's development, helping them invest time, resources, and staff in cultivating a healthy small business advocacy and support ecosystem. Using the creativity-driven equity opportunity, reconciliation and disruption model, organizations can minimize or avoid negative impacts in their community involvement through a holistic approach that integrates its core DE&I commitments as part of the mission to grow sustainably together. Yet, it should also be noted that not all investments that an organization contributes to community development are channeled through its core operational activities; some are channeled through philanthropy. The **philanthropy approach** supports communities through grants, donations, gifts and endowments.

Philanthropy is important, but the business development and support approach is more potent because it is driven by partnerships that enhance the capacity of the community to be self-supporting over time. As ISO 26000 well noted, *"philanthropic activities alone do not achieve the objective of integrating social responsibility into the organization."* To grow together and build a strong community involvement and development, an organization's strategies should transcend philanthropy and integrate small business advocacy and support because they sustain a community economically, socially, and environmentally. I've developed six steps necessary to holistically support small businesses in marginalized and disadvantaged communities:

1. **Contracting and Employment**: Socially responsible organizations should enable or support the creation of new business and employment

opportunities that includes minority and disadvantaged groups as a matter of DE&I policy, principles and core commitments. Small businesses are the lifeblood of most minority and disadvantaged communities. According to the UN:

> *Micro-, small and medium-sized enterprises represent around 90 per cent of global businesses, more than 60 per cent of employment and half of gross domestic product (GDP) worldwide. They are the economic lifeblood of communities around the world. But, they have also been disproportionately impacted by a host of challenges that are disrupting economies — from climate catastrophe to COVID-19 to the global fallout from the war in Ukraine.*

Contracting opportunities that deliberately include small businesses from minority and vulnerable groups allow both the owners and the community to become self-sustaining and even experience wealth transfer across generations. They can also hire more people within their respective communities. Extending human development and intentional recruitment of minority and vulnerable groups into the organization's workforce and work-partners' networks are all positive, actionable steps that can shift the conversation on systemic and structural divisive norms supported by racist and gender social norms.

2. **Education**: Organizations that have the capacity to provide on-the-job training opportunities to minority and disadvantaged businessowners should not hesitate in doing so. Providing knowledge-transfers teach small businessowners how to fish for themselves in areas where organizations have already established their own prowess and expertise through their workforce. Incentivizing employees to give back to their communities in support of small business creation, development, support and patronage is a winning framework for social responsibility.

3. **Healthcare**: When small businessowners worry about their healthcare or that of their employees—because they cannot afford the costs—they become distracted from the everyday demands of running a small business. Sometimes, these businessowners are forced to ignore health-related work balance and wellbeing habits just to sustain their businesses. Where socially responsible organizations have the means to assist, they should consider funding community healthcare initiatives that leverage healthcare options for minority and vulnerable groups. As we saw in previous chapters, some of the inequalities in healthcare—outcomes associated with minority groups (such as respiratory diseases) are direct results of adverse social engineering policies and politics and as such deserve remediation.

4. **Housing**: Home ownership provides stability for small businessowners, who are more likely to own homes in disadvantaged and underserved

communities. Minority and vulnerable groups, regardless of locale, are more likely to live in substandard housing stocks—testimonials of historic discriminatory investment practices as demonstrated in previous chapters. Affordable housing curated for minority small businessowners and their employees is a community-sustaining action on all fronts—for the businessowner, employees and the various other businesses they patronize and support within their respective communities. Policymakers and organizational leaders should consider utilizing deliberate community affordable housing investments and developments as key pathways to sustaining communities that have long experienced disinvestments. These pathways remain necessary because there are still banks that will not readily provide home loans to minority and vulnerable groups. Organizations should consider using their financial leverage in these situations to increase home ownership in disadvantaged communities as part of their overall social responsibility tapestry—especially for those small businesses in their supply value chain. It is a worthwhile use of resources with a disproportionately high return, and a marginal investment in affordable housing initiatives will neither break a bank nor force a multinational corporation into bankruptcy.

5. **Socio-economic stabilization**: Small businesses in disadvantaged and marginalized communities should not be dealt with primarily by NGOs providing social support services and safety nets. Small businesses within these communities need more than benevolent gifts and donations - they need contracts and other inclusive economic sustaining opportunities (like investments, access to capital, etc.,) to thrive as legitimate business entities within mainstream economies. When small businesses within minority and vulnerable groups' communities are self-sufficient, they can hire more people within their communities and enhance the socio-economic vitality of the entire community. Policymakers and organizational leaders can play a vital role in making these communities sustainable by both investing and providing technical and capacity-building support for minority and vulnerable groups' small businesses (their owners and employees) through a continuum of philanthropic and social investment initiatives.

6. **Demographic stabilization**: Social community reengineering policies have long marginalized people groups and made their communities the targets of disinvestments, leading to blight. This in turn has made minority and vulnerable groups' communities a haven for all the wrong performance metrices, making them vulnerable to outmigration, gentrification and other maladies. Proper community investments can help cure these maladies when they manifest, instead of denying the underlying causes of the retrogressions. Where feasible, organizations

should use their bully pulpits to advocate for and sponsor small business support networks and ethnic chambers of commerce as socially responsible actionable steps. In places where outmigration has significantly impacted traditional minority communities, organizations should also consider including their restoration as part of their overall advocacy and business growth efforts. Growing together economically in the information and green economies should be coupled with restoring, where feasible, some of the character of minority communities which have suffered from unjust and unfair practices.

Figure 11.1 Ajiake 6-Step small business support framework

Ajiake 6-Step Small Business Support Framework

Demographic Stabilization

Advocate and sponsor small business support networks

Socio-economic Stabilization

Provide opportunities to thrive through collective community growth and development

Housing

Where possible, engage in creative solutions for affordable housing for small business owners and employees

Contracting & Employment

Create new opportunities and increase or enhance existing ones for small businesses

Education

Provide educational opportunities for small businesses to develop and build on business best practices that become sustainable over time

Healthcare

Come up with opportunities for small businesses to leverage healthcare options and focus on work balance and wellbeing

Ajiake Small Business Support Framework

CE
ED
DS
HC
HO
SS

COMMUNITY INVOLVEMENT ISSUE 1: DE&I AS MODERATOR FOR COMMUNITY INVOLVEMENT

Does your organization include DE&I in its community involvement activities?

COMMUNITY INVOLVEMENT
Knowledge-informed diversity call to action

An organization's community involvement can be lifeblood to communities that have suffered historical disenfranchisements. Therefore, any community involvement by organizations should be strategic and where necessary, curated to address divisive norms, past and present. By partnering with local organizations and stakeholders, an organization can fulfill its social responsibility as a citizen of the community or as global citizen by the issues, challenges, and opportunities it gets involved in for the betterment of the community and our shared humankind.

This generation of humankind cannot aspire to pursue sustainable development that meets the needs of the present by ignoring the needs of minority and vulnerable groups. As the UN put it:

Sustainable development calls for concerted efforts towards building an inclusive, sustainable and resilient future for people and planet.

For sustainable development to be achieved, it is crucial to harmonize three core elements: economic growth, social inclusion and environmental protection. These elements are interconnected and all are crucial for the well-being of individuals and societies. Eradicating poverty in all its forms and dimensions is an indispensable requirement for sustainable development. To this end, there must be promotion of sustainable, inclusive and equitable economic growth, creating greater opportunities for all, reducing inequalities, raising basic standards of living, fostering equitable social development and inclusion, and promoting integrated and sustainable management of natural resources and ecosystems (United Nations n.d.).

In seeking to be a good citizen, an organization should consider familiarizing itself with the needs and priorities of the community or society so they are strategically aligned together. It should identify stakeholders and engage the community through individuals, focus groups, surveys, civil institutions, and other forms of networks, all important spokes in the wheel of progress, with the following acknowledgement that:

ISO *Some traditional or indigenous communities, neighbourhood associations or Internet networks express themselves without constituting a formal "organization". An organization should be aware that there are many types of groups, formal and informal, that can contribute to development. An organization should respect the cultural, social and political rights of such groups. It is important that actions for community involvement uphold respect for the rule of law and for participatory processes that respect the rights and have due regard for the views of others to express and defend their own interests.*

ISO 26000:2010, page 63.

Since our divisive norms, are generally the same, just dressed differently according to context, an organization can begin its DE&I-driven community involvement plans and engagements by becoming familiar with some of our shared global issues – as well as challenges and opportunities. Table 11.1 presents a list of these issues as adapted from the UN Sustainable Development Goals:

Figure 11.1: Community involvement and development by adapting sustainable development goals

UN Sustainable Development Goals	Some key UN statistics of needs and opportunities for organizational involvement and development
SDG-1: No poverty	• fallout from the global pandemic could increase global poverty by as much as half a billion people, or 8% of the total human population. This would be the first time that poverty has increased globally since 1990. • More than 700 million people, or 10 per cent of the world population, still live in extreme poverty today,

	struggling to fulfil the most basic needs like health, education, and access to water and sanitation, to name a few.
	• The majority of people living on less than $1.90 a day live in sub-Saharan Africa. Worldwide, the poverty rate in rural areas is 17.2 percent—more than three times higher than in urban areas (UN 2021).
SDG-2: Zero hunger	• Current estimates show that nearly 690 million people are hungry, or 8.9 percent of the world population – up by 10 million people in one year and by nearly 60 million in five years.
	• The world is not on track to achieve zero Hunger by 2030. If recent trends continue, the number of people affected by hunger will surpass 840 million by 2030. (UN 2020g).
SDG-3: Good health and well-being	• In 2018 an estimated 6.2 million children and adolescents under the age of 15 years died, mostly from preventable causes. Of these deaths, 5.3 million occurred in the first 5 years, with almost half of these in the first month of life.
	• Every day in 2017, approximately 810 women died from preventable causes related to pregnancy and childbirth.
	• 38 million people globally were living with HIV in 2019. Globally, adolescent girls and young women face gender-based inequalities, exclusion, discrimination and violence, which put them at increased risk of acquiring HIV (UN 2020k).
SDG-4: Quality education	• Before the coronavirus crisis, projections showed that more than 200 million children would be out of school, and only 60 per cent of young people would be completing upper secondary education in 2030.
	• Before the coronavirus crisis, the proportion of children and youth out of primary and secondary school had declined from 26 per cent in 2000 to 19 per cent in 2010 and 17 per cent in 2018.
	• Some 750 million adults – two thirds of them women – remained illiterate in 2016. Half of the global illiterate population lives in South Asia, and a quarter live in sub-Saharan Africa (UN 2020).
SDG-5: Gender equality	• Globally, 750 million women and girls were married before the age of 18 and at least 200 million women and girls in 30 countries have undergone FGM.
	• The rates of girls between 15-19 who are subjected to FGM (female genital mutilation) in the 30 countries where the practice is concentrated have dropped from 1 in 2 girls in 2000 to 1 in 3 girls by 2017.

	• One in five women and girls, including 19 per cent of women and girls aged 15 to 49, have experienced physical and/or sexual violence by an intimate partner within the last 12 months. Yet, 49 countries have no laws that specifically protect women from such violence (UN 2020f).
SDG-6: Clean water and sanitation	• 3 in 10 people lack access to safely managed drinking water services and 6 in 10 people lack access to safely managed sanitation facilities. Each day, nearly 1,000 children die due to preventable water and sanitation-related diarrheal diseases • Water scarcity affects more than 40 per cent of the global population and is projected to rise. Over 1.7 billion people are currently living in river basins where water use exceeds recharge. • 2.4 billion people lack access to basic sanitation services, such as toilets or latrines. At least 892 million people continue to practice open defecation (UN 2020i).
SDG-7: Affordable and clean energy	• 3 billion people rely on wood, coal, charcoal or animal waste for cooking and heating • Energy is the dominant contributor to climate change, accounting for around 60 per cent of total global greenhouse gas emissions. • Indoor air pollution from using combustible fuels for household energy caused 4.3 million deaths in 2012, with women and girls accounting for 6 out of every 10 of these (UN n.d.).
SDG-8: Decent work and economic growth	• Globally, 61 percent of all workers were engaged in informal employment in 2016. Excluding the agricultural sector, 51 percent of all workers fell into this employment category. • Men earn 12.5 percent more than women in 40 out of 45 countries with data. • The global gender pay gap stands at 23 per cent globally; without decisive action, it will take another 68 years to achieve equal pay. The women's labour force participation rate is 63 per cent while that of men is 94 per cent Martin & Dpi 2020).
SDG-9: Industries, innovation and infrastructure	• In 2018, 96 per cent of the world's population lived within reach of a mobile-cellular signal, and 90 per cent of people could access the Internet through a third generation (3G) or higher-quality network. 16 per cent of the global population does not have access to mobile broadband networks. • Least developed countries have immense potential for industrialization in food and beverages (agro-industry),

	and textiles and garments, with good prospects for sustained employment generation and higher productivity
	• Developing countries continued to outpace developed economies in renewables investment. In 2019, they committed $152.2 billion, compared to $130 billion for developed countries (Martin & Dpi 2020).
SDG-10: Reduced inequalities	• Social protection has been significantly extended globally, yet persons with disabilities are up to five times more likely than average to incur catastrophic health expenditures.
	• Up to 30 percent of income inequality is due to inequality within households, including between women and men. Women are also more likely than men to live below 50 percent of the median income
	• Only 28 percent of persons with significant disabilities have access to disability benefits globally, and only 1 percent in low-income countries (UN 2020h).
SDG-11: Sustainable cities and communities	• Half of humanity – 3.5 billion people – lives in cities today and 5 billion people are projected to live in cities by 2030.
	• The world's cities occupy just 3 per cent of the Earth's land, but account for 60-80 per cent of energy consumption and 75 per cent of carbon emissions.
	• By 2050 it's predicted that 70 per cent of the world population will live in urban settlements (UN 2020c).
SDG-12: Responsible consumption and production	• Each year, an estimated one third of all food produced – equivalent to 1.3 billion tonnes, worth around $1 trillion – ends up rotting in the bins of consumers and retailers, or spoiling due to poor transportation and harvesting practices.
	• If people worldwide switched to energy-efficient light bulbs the world would save US$120 billion annually.
	• Should the global population reach 9.6 billion by 2050, the equivalent of almost three planets could be required to provide the natural resources needed to sustain current lifestyles UN 2020e).
SDG-13: Climate action	• From 1880 to 2012, the average global temperature increased by 0.85°C. To put this into perspective, for each 1 degree of temperature increase, grain yields decline by about 5 per cent. Maize, wheat and other major crops have experienced significant yield reductions at the global level of 40 megatons per year between 1981 and 2002 due to a warmer climate.
	• Oceans have warmed, the amounts of snow and ice have diminished and sea level has risen. From 1901 to 2010, the global average sea level rose by 19 cm as

	oceans expanded due to warming and ice melted. The Arctic's sea ice extent has shrunk in every successive decade since 1979, with 1.07 million km² of ice loss every decade
	• Given current concentrations and on-going emissions of greenhouse gases, it is likely that by the end of this century, the increase in global temperature will exceed 1.5°C compared to 1850 to 1900 for all but one scenario. The world's oceans will warm and ice melt will continue. Average sea level rise is predicted as 24 – 30cm by 2065 and 40-63cm by 2100. Most aspects of climate change will persist for many centuries even if emissions are stopped (UN 2020b).
SDG-14: Life below water	• Oceans cover three-quarters of the Earth's surface, contain 97 per cent of the Earth's water, and represent 99 per cent of the living space on the planet by volume. Over three billion people depend on marine and coastal biodiversity for their livelihoods.
	• Around the world, one million plastic drinking bottles are purchased every minute, while up to 5 trillion single-use plastic bags are used worldwide every year
	• Sustainable and climate-resilient transport, including maritime transport, is key to sustainable development. Around 80 per cent of the volume of international trade in goods is carried by sea, and the percentage is even higher for most developing countries (UN 2022).
SDG-15: Life on land	• Human activity has altered almost 75 per cent of the earth's surface, squeezing wildlife and nature into an ever-smaller corner of the planet and increasing risks of zoonotic diseases like COVID-19.
	• Around 1.6 billion people depend on forests for their livelihood, including 70 million indigenous people.
	• Illicit poaching and trafficking of wildlife continues to thwart conservation efforts, with nearly 7,000 species of animals and plants reported in illegal trade involving 120 countries (UN 2020).
SDG-16: Peace, justice and strong institutions	• Conflict, insecurity, weak institutions and limited access to justice remain a great threat to sustainable development.
	• In 2019, the United Nations tracked 357 killings and 30 enforced disappearances of human rights defenders, journalists and trade unionists in 47 countries.
	• And the births of around one in four children under age 5 worldwide are never officially recorded, depriving them of a proof of legal identity crucial for the protection of their rights and for access to justice and social services (UN 2020d).

SDG-17: Partnership for the goals	• 79 percent of imports from developing countries enter developed countries duty-free • Almost half of the world's population is not connected to the internet, particularly in poor countries (UN 2021).

COMMUNITY INVOLVEMENT
Creativity-driven equity opportunity/reconciliation/disruption

The involvement of an organization can go a long way in improving the economic, social and environmental vitality of a community. Any commitment to community development must include the community's own cultural and historical characteristics, as well as the integration of its divergent or conflicting socio-political, economic, and cultural interests. Common goals are achieved when equity considerations lead the dialogue in three areas: equity opportunity, reconciliation and disruption. Together, they provide a structural guide that can assist organizations in making their social responsibility commitments effective. Using the 3-Step Equity Lens presented here, an organization should consider the following guidelines provided in ISO 26000 to frame its community involvement practices, moderated by DE&I.

EQUITY OPPORTUNITY IN COMMUNITY INVOLVEMENT

  An organization should:

☐ *consult representative community groups in determining priorities for social investment and community development activities. Special attention should be given to vulnerable, discriminated, marginalized, unrepresented and under-represented groups, to involve them in a way that helps to expand their options and respect their rights; [and]*

☐ *consult and accommodate communities, including indigenous people, on the terms and conditions of development that affect them. Consultation should occur prior to development and should be based on complete, accurate and accessible information [.]*

ISO 26000:2010, page 64.

EQUITY RECONCILIATION IN COMMUNITY INVOLVEMENT

  An organization should:

- participate in local associations as possible and appropriate, with the objective of contributing to the public good and the development goals of communities;
- maintain transparent relationships with local government officials and political representatives, free from bribery or improper influence; [and]
- contribute to policy formulation and the establishment, implementation, monitoring and evaluation of development programmes. When doing so, an organization should respect the rights and have due regard for the views of others to express and defend their own interests.

ISO 26000:2010, page 64.

EQUITY DISRUPTION IN COMMUNITY INVOLVEMENT

ISO *An organization should:*
- *maintain transparent relationships with local government officials and political representatives, free from bribery or improper influence; [and]*
- *encourage and support people to be volunteers for community service[.]*

ISO 26000:2010, page 64.

COMMUNITY INVOLVEMENT
Governance-centered inclusion actionable steps

A socially responsible organization should employ proactive outreach efforts to engage the community in nurturing partnerships with local stakeholders and organizations. This is a more effective way to not only solve problems, but prevent them before they occur. Community involvement can serve as a good input point for organization's DE&I policy and initiatives, because it helps in identifying community needs and priorities in order to align its own social responsibility efforts with the priorities of the community. Community involvement also allows an organization to identify and work with various community networks, both formal and informal, to develop effective programs that meet the needs of both sides in the organization's products and life cycle whole systems. It also gives vulnerable groups an opportunity to present and defend their interests in a more proactive forum, as long as the organization is genuine in its efforts and respectful of the rights of all participants.

COMMUNITY INVOLVEMENT ISSUE 2: DE&I AS MODERATOR FOR EDUCATION AND CULTURE

In addressing education and culture, does your organization consider DE&I issues?

EDUCATION AND CULTURE
Knowledge-informed diversity call to action

Systemic and structural racism and gender inequalities were firmly entrenched before we began to pursue social responsibility discourses and sustainable development goals to save our planet from climate change. The historic disinvestments in communities of color have social and economic impacts in these communities—adversely shaping their educational attainments and socio-cultural sustainment. Organizations seeking to be involved in solving community challenges should consider the educational and cultural foundations that have shaped them; as ISO 26000 opined, *"[p]reservation and promotion of culture and promotion of education compatible with respect for human rights have positive impacts on social cohesion and development."*

EDUCATION AND CULTURE
Creativity-driven equity opportunity/reconciliation/disruption

There are some fundamental inequities built into public education in the US, particularly the link between educational resources and local property taxes. Basically, most funding is raised and spent locally. Schools in richer districts will always have more resources under this model, and states make few efforts to promote equity in the system. COVID-19 has also left its mark on the school attendance of children around the world. According to the UN, in 2020, almost 1.6 billion children and youth stopped attending school; one of the consequences of this was that nearly 369 million children who relied on subsidized food at school were forced to find alternative sources (UN 2021).

An organization should consider the different systemic inequalities we discuss here as well as the UN SDG goals as a template for developing creative solutions that have marginalized people groups, keeping them from realizing the benefits of a knowledge economy. Using the 3-Step Equity Lens, an organization should consider the following guidelines provided in ISO 26000 in framing education and culture practices that are moderated by DE&I.

EQUITY OPPORTUNITY IN EDUCATION AND CULTURE

ISO *An organization should:*

☐ *promote and support education at all levels, and engage in actions to improve the quality of and access to education, promote local knowledge and help eradicate illiteracy;*

☐ *in particular, promote learning opportunities for vulnerable or discriminated groups;*

☐ *encourage the enrolment of children in formal education and contribute to the elimination of barriers to children obtaining an education (such as child labour); and*

☐ *consider facilitating human rights education and awareness raising[.]*

ISO 26000:2010, pages 64-65.

EQUITY RECONCILIATION IN EDUCATION AND CULTURE

ISO *An organization should:*

☐ *promote cultural activities where appropriate, recognize and value the local cultures and cultural traditions, consistent with the principle of respect for human rights. Actions to support cultural activities that empower historically disadvantaged groups are especially important as a means of combating discrimination;*

☐ *help conserve and protect cultural heritage, especially where the organization's activities have an impact on it; and*

☐ *where appropriate, promote the use of traditional knowledge and technologies of indigenous communities.*

ISO 26000:2010, pages 64-65.

EQUITY DISRUPTION IN EDUCATION AND CULTURE

ISO   *An organization should:*

☐   *help conserve and protect cultural heritage, especially where the organization's activities have an impact on it; and*

☐   *where appropriate, promote the use of traditional knowledge and technologies of indigenous communities.*

ISO 26000:2010, page 64-65.

EDUCATION AND CULTURE
Governance-centered inclusion actionable steps

Social cohesion and development are framed by respect for human rights and the preservation and promotion of relevant education and culture. They play pivotal roles in a community's identity, preservation, inclusion and sustainability. Using the equity opportunity, reconciliation and disruption lens, an organization can assist in shaping or reshaping the social and economic development landscape, by promoting learning opportunities for vulnerable or groups that have been historically excluded. This can include sponsorship of some to return to school so they can gain valuable knowledge that the organization deems necessary for upward mobility within its ranks, especially senior management positions.

Governance-centered inclusion actionable steps: education and culture

1. In reviewing your organization's policies and procedures around education and culture, how do they align with your DE&I policy, commitments, and corporate proclamations on the matter?
2. If there are gaps, what are the actionable steps and timelines you have identified to narrow or eliminate them based on the 3-Step Equity Lens model?
3. Were all relevant stakeholders identified and engaged in the review, modification or development of your policies and procedures around your DE&I moderated education and culture practices?

COMMUNITY INVOLVEMENT ISSUE 3: DE&I AS MODERATOR FOR EMPLOYMENT CREATION AND SKILLS DEVELOPMENT

In its employment creation and skills development practices, does your organization address DE&I concerns?

EMPLOYMENT CREATION AND SKILLS DEVELOPMENT
Knowledge-informed diversity call to action

Poverty is one of the most enduring legacies of systematic marginalization of minority and vulnerable groups. Alleviating it begins with job creation and sustainable gainful employment. Employment, as ISO 26000 articulated, is an internationally recognized goal in economic and social development that contributes to poverty reduction and is an essential component of skills development. Working with communities to improve the skills of its members is vital for economic and social development. As of 2018, the UN stated that 8 percent of employed workers and their families still lived in extreme poverty, and for children that number was one in five. Employment skills development, in combination with social protection for all children, could make a significant difference in reducing poverty, the UN attested.

EMPLOYMENT CREATION AND SKILLS DEVELOPMENT
Creativity-driven equity opportunity/reconciliation/disruption

Using the 3-Step Equity Lens, an organization should consider the following guidelines provided in ISO 26000 in framing its employment creation and skills development practices, moderated by DE&I of course.

EQUITY OPPORTUNITY IN EMPLOYMENT CREATION AND SKILLS DEVELOPMENT

ISO *An organization should:*
- ☐ *consider participating in local and national skills development programmes, including apprenticeship programmes, programmes focused on particular disadvantaged groups, lifelong learning programmes and skills recognition and certification schemes;*
- ☐ *consider helping to develop or improve skills development programmes in the community where these are inadequate, possibly in partnership with others in the community; and*
- ☐ *consider helping to promote the framework conditions necessary to create employment.*

EQUITY RECONCILIATION IN EMPLOYMENT CREATION AND SKILLS DEVELOPMENT

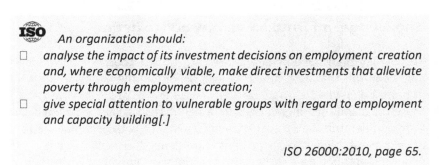

An organization should:

☐ *consider the impact of technology choice on employment and, where economically viable in the longer term, select technologies that maximize employment opportunities;*

☐ *consider the impact of outsourcing decisions on employment creation, both within the organization making the decision and within external organizations affected by such decisions; [and]*

☐ *consider the benefit of creating direct employment rather than using temporary work arrangements[.]*

ISO 26000:2010, page 65.

EQUITY DISRUPTION IN EMPLOYMENT CREATION AND SKILLS DEVELOPMENT

An organization should:

☐ *analyse the impact of its investment decisions on employment creation and, where economically viable, make direct investments that alleviate poverty through employment creation;*

☐ *give special attention to vulnerable groups with regard to employment and capacity building[.]*

ISO 26000:2010, page 65.

EMPLOYMENT CREATION AND SKILLS DEVELOPMENT
Governance-centered inclusion actionable steps

Both large and small organizations should seek to include the voices and participation of vulnerable and discriminated groups and consider issues addressed in human rights and labor practices. Skills development assists vulnerable and discriminated individuals and groups to secure good paying jobs and stimulates their economic and social development individually and as a community.

1. In reviewing your organization's policies and procedures around employment creation and skills development, how do they align with your DE&I policy, commitments, and corporate proclamations on the matter?

2. If there are gaps, what are the actionable steps and timelines you have identified to narrow or eliminate them based on the 3-Step Equity Lens model?

3. Were all relevant stakeholders identified and engaged in the review, modification or development of your policies and procedures around your DE&I moderated employment creation and skills development practices?

COMMUNITY INVOLVEMENT ISSUE 4: DE&I AS MODERATOR FOR TECHNOLOGY DEVELOPMENT AND ACCESS

Does your organization seek DE&I in its technology development and deployment?

TECHNOLOGY DEVELOPMENT AND ACCESS
Knowledge-informed diversity call to action

Technology development and access are potent tools for narrowing the divisive norms that have made the rich richer and the poor poorer. What is in question is whether organizations have the will to get involved and use these tools and their innovations to bridge that social and economic divide. Communities and their members need assistance with economic and social development, which organizations can generally facilitate better than governmental bodies. Yet, because technology companies write their own rules of engagement, governmental oversight is essential for fair and just practices to prevail.

ISO To help advance economic and social development, communities and their members need, among other things, full and safe access to modern technology. Organizations can contribute to the development of the communities in which they operate by applying specialized knowledge, skills and technology in such a way as to promote human resource development and technology diffusion. Information and communication technologies characterize much of contemporary life and are a valuable basis for many economic activities. Access to information is key to

A good data management infrastructure should be seen as one of the best weapons for leveling the economic playing field, a great equalizer just as education overall is considered. Organizations can promote technology diffusion and human resource development by using specialized knowledge, skills, and technology to engage marginalized communities. Improving access to technology and information and providing training, partnerships, and other actions to foster digital inclusion is an essential step in addressing social and economic inequities.

TECHNOLOGY DEVELOPMENT AND ACCESS
Creativity-driven equity opportunity/reconciliation/disruption

Using data analytics and artificial intelligence tools, an organization can help move the needle forward in underprivileged communities by promoting human resource development and technology diffusion. It does so in multiple ways: first, by implementing training, partnerships and other creative solutions in concert with individual and community needs. Second, the technology itself can be used to more accurately document patterns of discrimination and inequity that may be otherwise difficult to spot. Using the 3-Step Equity Lens, an organization should consider the following guidelines provided in ISO 26000 in framing its technology development and access practices moderated by DE&I.

EQUITY OPPORTUNITY IN TECHNOLOGY DEVELOPMENT AND ACCESS

EQUITY RECONCILIATION IN TECHNOLOGY DEVELOPMENT AND ACCESS

An organization should:

☐ *consider contributing to the development of low-cost technologies that are easily replicable and have a high positive impact on poverty and hunger eradication;*

☐ *consider engaging in partnerships with organizations, such as universities or research laboratories, to enhance scientific and technological development with partners from the community, and employ local people in this work[.]*

ISO 26000:2010, page 66.

EQUITY DISRUPTION IN TECHNOLOGY DEVELOPMENT AND ACCESS

An organization should:

☐ *adopt practices that allow technology transfer and diffusion, where economically feasible. Where applicable, an organization should set reasonable terms and conditions for licenses or technology transfer so as to contribute to local development. The capacity of the community to manage the technology should be considered and enhanced.*

ISO 26000:2010, page 66.

TECHNOLOGY DEVELOPMENT AND ACCESS
Governance-centered inclusion actionable steps

Technology development and access are key gamechangers in this, the Information Age. It also provides the best opportunities known to humankind to address the tide of the ever-growing divisive norms that have exacerbated inequalities in every measurable metrics. As the UN Secretary-General Guterres warned: *"The digital divide reinforces social and economic divides, from literacy to healthcare, from urban to rural, from kindergarten to college. In 2019, some 87 per cent of people in developed countries used the internet, compared with just 19 per cent in the least developed countries. We are in danger of a two-speed world."*

Figure 11.2: Internet usage (developed vs least developed countries)

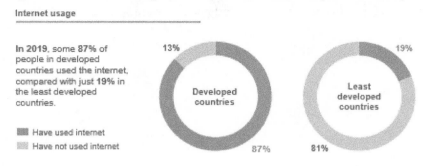

Internet usage

In 2019, some 87% of people in developed countries used the internet, compared with just 19% in the least developed countries.

Have used internet
Have not used internet

Organizations should evaluate their current and desired positions on the technology development and access landscape and where feasible become part of the solution in narrowing the current gaps in internet usage as part of an overall strategy.

Governance-centered inclusion actionable steps: technology development and access

1. In reviewing your organization's policies and procedures around technology development and access, how do they align with your DE&I policy, commitments, and corporate proclamations on the matter?
2. If there are gaps, what are the actionable steps and timelines you have identified to narrow or eliminate them based on the 3-Step Equity Lens model?
3. Were all relevant stakeholders identified and engaged in the review, modification or development of your policies and procedures around your DE&I moderated technology development and access practices?

In addressing the mobilization issue of his day, Dr. King made the following clarion call for all to participate in the Civil Rights activities: *"If you can't fly then run, if you can't run then walk, if you can't walk then crawl, but whatever you do you have to keep moving forward."*

Today, that clarion call is applicable when it comes to the "danger of a two-speed world" and organizations and individuals can play roles in several ways in the technology development and access realm. Whether it is as an advocate, investor, supplier, or supporter, a summary view of what happens in an integrated national data system provides several opportunities to get engaged and do something:

Figure 11.3: Overview of an integrated national data system

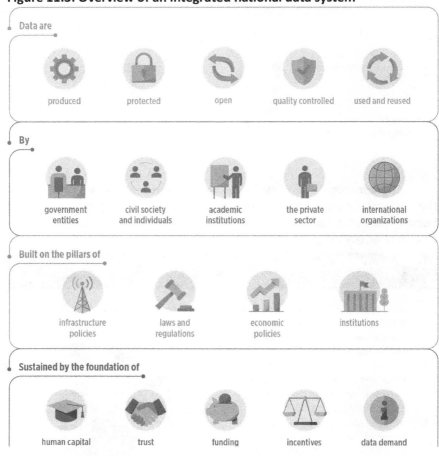

Data are

produced · protected · open · quality controlled · used and reused

By

government entities · civil society and individuals · academic institutions · the private sector · international organizations

Built on the pillars of

infrastructure policies · laws and regulations · economic policies · institutions

Sustained by the foundation of

human capital · trust · funding · incentives · data demand

Source: World Bank 2021.

COMMUNITY INVOLVEMENT AND DEVELOPMENT ISSUE 5: DE&I AS MODERATOR FOR WEALTH AND INCOME CREATION

Does your organization incorporate DE&I in its wealth and income creation continuum—from your organization to communities, especially those historically disadvantaged and marginalized?

WEALTH AND INCOME CREATION
Knowledge-informed diversity call to action

Wealth and income creation are DE&I matters because they reflect the outcome of discriminatory norms. Money is power, and marginalization of any group is usually focused at least in part on diverting money from that group in one way or another. Applying a DE&I filter to the world of resource generation and allocation is essential to achieve true change. If we fail to break the circle of generational wealth and income disparities based on artificial human demarcations, then we won't be able to truly address some of the root causes of inequity today. The UN Secretary-General Guterres painted the bleak prospects:

> More than 70 per cent of the world's people are living with rising income and wealth inequality. The 26 richest people in the world hold as much wealth as half the global population. But income, pay and wealth are not the only measures of inequality. People's chances in life depend on their gender, family and ethnic background, race, whether or not they have a disability, and other factors. Multiple inequalities intersect and reinforce each other across the generations. The lives and expectations of millions of people are largely determined by their circumstances at birth (United Nations 2022).

Poverty elimination is possible if every generation works on narrowing the wealth and income gaps. ISO 26000 provides the following guidance:

ISO Competitive and diverse enterprises and co-operatives are crucial in creating wealth in any community. Organizations can help to create an environment in which entrepreneurship can thrive, bringing lasting benefits to communities. Organizations can contribute positively to wealth and income creation through entrepreneurship programmes, development of local suppliers, and employment of community members, as well as through wider efforts to strengthen economic resources and social relations that facilitate economic and social welfare or generate community benefits. Furthermore, by helping to create wealth and income at the local level and promoting a balanced distribution of the economic benefits among community members, organizations can play a significant role in reducing poverty. Entrepreneurship programmes and co-operatives targeting women are particularly important as it is widely recognized that the empowerment of women contributes greatly to the well being of society.

ISO 26000:2010, page 66.

Sometimes organizations are not able to do more in investing in community development due to lack of proper organizing structures. This is often an economic decision, because such investments cannot be written off in taxes if the community organizations are not recognized by the state as legally constituted entities. Offering tax deductions for work considered to benefit the community (such as that by nonprofit organizations) is an important way that governments can incentivize constructive community development. However, not all groups are able to achieve that tax-deductible status. Rather than allow these regulatory obstacles to impede community investment, an organization can help spur wealth and income creation through them by assisting them to structure themselves properly. ISO 26000 provides the following guidance:

> **ISO** *An organization contributes to development through compliance with laws and regulations. In some circumstances community groups' failure to operate within the intended legal framework is a consequence of poverty or development conditions. In these circumstances, an organization that is involved with groups operating outside the legal framework should aim to alleviate poverty and promote development. An organization should also seek to create opportunities that will enable these groups to achieve greater, and ultimately full, compliance with the law, especially concerning economic relationships.*
>
> *ISO 26000:2010, page 66.*

WEALTH AND INCOME CREATION
Creativity-driven equity opportunity/reconciliation/disruption

We've examined several social engineering practices that have caused minority and vulnerable communities to remain disadvantaged despite the fact that society has undergone some of the greatest economic breakthroughs and booms in human history. Organizations that benefited from these boom times have a social responsibility to assist in creatively engaging with minority and vulnerable groups to addressing wealth and income creation inequities. ISO 26000 provides the following broad guidance:

> **ISO** *Wealth and income creation also depend on a fair distribution of the benefits of economic activity. Governments rely upon organizations meeting their tax obligations to obtain revenues for addressing critical development issues. In many situations the physical, social and economic isolation of communities can be an obstacle to their development. Organizations can play a positive role in the development of communities by integrating the local people, groups and organizations in their activities*

or value chain. In this way, community development considerations can become an integral part of organizations' core activities.

ISO 26000:2010, page 66.

Using the 3-Step Equity Lens, an organization should consider the following guidelines provided in ISO 26000 to help frame its wealth and income creation practices moderated by DE&I.

EQUITY OPPORTUNITY IN WEALTH AND INCOME CREATION

ISO *An organization should:*

☐ *consider supporting appropriate initiatives to stimulate diversification of existing economic activity in the community;*

☐ *consider giving preference to local suppliers of products and services and contributing to local supplier development where possible;*

☐ *engage in economic activities with organizations that, owing to low levels of development, have difficulty meeting the legal requirements only where:*

    ○ *the purpose is to address poverty;*

    ○ *the activities of these organizations respect human rights, and there is a reasonable expectation that these organizations will consistently move towards conducting their activities within the appropriate legal framework;*

☐ *encourage the efficient use of available resources including the good care of domesticated animals;*

☐ *consider supporting organizations and persons that bring needed products and services to the community, which can also generate local employment as well as linkages with local, regional and urban markets where this is beneficial for the welfare of the community; [and]*

☐ *consider appropriate ways to help in the development of community-based associations of entrepreneurs[.]*

ISO 26000:2010, pages 66-67.

EQUITY RECONCILIATION IN WEALTH AND INCOME CREATION

ISO *An organization should:*

- consider the economic and social impact of entering or leaving a community, including impacts on basic resources needed for the sustainable development of the community;
- consider contributing to durable programmes and partnerships that assist community members, especially women and other socially disadvantaged and vulnerable groups to establish businesses and co-operatives, in improving productivity and promoting entrepreneurship. Such programmes could, for example, provide training in business planning, marketing, quality standards required to become suppliers, management and technical assistance, access to finance and facilitation of joint ventures;
- consider appropriate ways to make procurement opportunities more easily accessible to community organizations, including, for example, through capacity-building on meeting technical specifications, and making information about procurement opportunities available[.]

ISO 26000:2010, pages 66-67.

EQUITY DISRUPTION IN WEALTH AND INCOME CREATION

ISO *An organization should:*
- consider undertaking initiatives to strengthen the ability of and opportunities for locally based suppliers to contribute to value chains, giving special attention to disadvantaged groups within the community;
- fulfil its tax responsibilities and provide authorities with the necessary information to correctly determine taxes due; and
- consider contributing to superannuation and pensions for employees.

ISO 26000:2010, pages 66-67.

WEALTH AND INCOME CREATION
Governance-centered inclusion actionable steps

There are many ways an organization can be instrumental in the development of wealth creation in a community. They can facilitate economic and social programs through the development of local suppliers, employment of community members, and promotion of entrepreneurship, among other activities. Wealth and income creation by a large organization at the local level can be one of the most effective ways to alleviate poverty. Using the social responsibility currency of DE&I, organizations can help isolated communities and those economically and socially disadvantaged by including them within their value chain. When organizations play an active role in bridging the gap of wealth and income creation for vulnerable and discriminated individuals and groups, it shows in their employment demographics, their utilization numbers for suppliers, contractors and service providers, and in their entrepreneurial empowerment schemes. This ensures that DE&I is integrated into an organization's whole ecosystem. It also furthers the strengthening of vulnerable and discriminated communities' economic resiliency, expanding their economic resources and empowering a social relationship networking continuum, resulting in reduced inequalities and poverty. All these can be integrated in a social valuation metrics using the 3-Step Equity Lens.

Governance-centered inclusion actionable steps: wealth and income creation

1. In reviewing your organization's policies and procedures around wealth and income creation, how do they align with your DE&I policy, commitments, and corporate proclamations on the matter?

2. If there are gaps, what are the actionable steps and timelines you have identified to narrow or eliminate them based on the 3-Step Equity Lens model?

3. Were all relevant stakeholders identified and engaged in the review, modification or development of your policies and procedures around your DE&I moderated wealth and income creation practices?

COMMUNITY INVOLVEMENT ISSUE 6: DE&I AS MODERATOR FOR HEALTH

Does your organization, in addressing <u>health</u> and health-related matters, consider the impact to DE&I in its overall approach?

HEALTH
Knowledge-informed diversity call to action

The COVID-19 pandemic exposed the disparity of healthcare resources that remain a relic and a legacy of structural racism. Even well-equipped and staffed hospitals struggled to keep pace with the punishing onslaught of the new disease; impoverished and neglected communities had little chance, and the communities they served suffered accordingly. Yet, healthcare is a recognized human right because it is an essential part of our humanity. Neglect of health concerns for minority and vulnerable groups creates an unjust and unfair ecosystem that mocks our shared humanity. There are many diseases that plague minority and vulnerable groups around the world which have long been eradicated in more advanced countries. Organizations can help address these health disparities as part of their DE&I community involvement and development commitments.

Health, the adage goes, is wealth. The two are tied together by nature and opportunity. Organizations should consider where feasible how to engage in the broader discussion and support of community health initiatives in underserved communities. Even when an organization cannot financially invest in community healthcare programs, it can mobilize or encourage its workforce and work-partners to become advocates and supporters in reducing the impacts of healthcare deserts within minority and vulnerable groups' communities. This kind of movement should unite civil society, young people, the private sector, regions, and cities together in support of combating healthcare desert. For publicly traded stock corporations, this could be part of their ESG selling point.

HEALTH
Creativity-driven equity opportunity/reconciliation/disruption

Policy decisions can create environments in which minority and vulnerable groups manifest health predispositions that have nothing to do with their DNA. Health conditions like asthma, high blood pressure, etc. are all correlated with environmental factors. Public policies that redlined neighborhoods, putting transportation hubs and polluting industries in neighborhoods populated by marginalized groups, have had lifelong consequences for millions, generationally.

Minority kids and other kids born into these disinvested neighborhoods are health-disadvantaged from the moment they take their first breath. This makes the health disparities a DE&I matter requiring a broad and concerted effort to address them as both a social responsibility and a sustainable development concern. In general, on health matters as social responsibility, ISO 26000 offered the following broad guidance:

ISO *[A]ll organizations, both large and small, should respect the right to health and should contribute, within their means and as appropriate, to the promotion of health, to the prevention of health threats and diseases and to the mitigation of any damage to the community...This may include participation in public health campaigns. They should also contribute where possible and appropriate to improving access to health services especially by reinforcing and supporting public services. Even in countries where it is a role of the state to provide a public health system, all organizations can consider contributing to health in communities. A* *healthy community reduces the burden on the public sector and contributes to a good economic and social environment for all organizations.*

ISO 26000:2010, page 67.

Using the 3-Step Equity Lens, an organization, where feasible, should consider the following guidelines provided in ISO 26000 in framing its health support and advocacy practices moderated by DE&I.

EQUITY OPPORTUNITY IN HEALTH

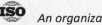 *An organization should:*

☐ *consider raising awareness about health threats and major diseases and their prevention, such as HIV/AIDS, cancer, heart disease, malaria, tuberculosis and obesity; and*

☐ *consider supporting long lasting and universal access to essential health care services and to clean water and appropriate sanitation as a means of preventing illness.*

ISO 26000:2010, page 68.

EQUITY RECONCILIATION IN HEALTH

 An organization should:

☐ *consider promoting good health by, for example, contributing to access to medicines and vaccination and encouraging healthy lifestyles, including exercise and good nutrition, early detection of diseases, raising awareness of contraceptive methods and discouraging the consumption of unhealthy products and substances. Special attention should be given to child nutrition[.]*

ISO 26000:2010, page 68.

EQUITY DISRUPTION IN HEALTH

 An organization should:

☐ *seek to eliminate negative health impacts of any production process, product or service provided by the organization[.]*

ISO 26000:2010, page 68.

HEALTH
Governance-centered inclusion actionable steps

Organizations should consider the broader issues, challenges and opportunities discussed above through the 3-Step Equity Lens to evaluate where they are in both their current practices and their DE&I commitments:

Governance-centered inclusion actionable steps: health

1. In reviewing your organization's policies and procedures around health, how do they align with your DE&I policy, commitments, and corporate proclamations on the matter?
2. If there are gaps, what are the actionable steps and timelines you have identified to narrow or eliminate them based on the 3-Step Equity Lens model?
3. Were all relevant stakeholders identified and engaged in the review, modification or development of your policies and procedures around your DE&I moderated health practices?

COMMUNITY INVOLVEMENT ISSUE 7: DE&I AS MODERATOR FOR SOCIAL INVESTMENT

Does your organization have a social investment plan, and does that plan integrate DE&I as a social responsibility currency?

SOCIAL INVESTMENT
Knowledge-informed diversity call to action

Today's organizations have more resources than ever before, wielding tremendous power and influence in society globally. The magnitude of these organizations, many of which have worldwide reach and access to enormous amounts of technology and information, is unprecedented. The digital age has greatly aided this phenomenon. Ideally, the newly created wealth confers a social responsibility to use some of it to do good works for the benefit of humankind. Unfortunately, a good number of global organizations have not used their power to steer economic growth. There's more wealth than ever, but communities of color continue to lack access to capital.

Interestingly, many of these global corporations have billions, sometimes trillions, of dollars stashed away in financial institutions which are themselves the gatekeepers of oppressive practices. Systemic racism has led to longstanding credit denial and other forms of discriminatory practices.

These organizational assets, rather than providing access to capital for minority and disadvantaged communities around the world, become the final vistas of hope deferred. Even a 1-2% investment of these funds as equity opportunity funds would provide much-needed capitalization for minority and disadvantaged communities around the world. This would be an easy step that would in addition help reconcile an organization's community involvement and development commitments with its social responsibility obligations, disrupting the discriminatory practices that have caused historical disinvestments in these communities. ISO 26000 provides this broad guidance:

ISO *Social investment takes place when organizations invest their resources in initiatives and programmes aimed at improving social aspects of community life. Types of social investments may include projects related to education, training, culture, health care, income generation, infrastructure development, improving access to information or any other activity likely to promote economic or social development. In identifying opportunities for social investment, an organization should align its contribution with the needs and priorities of the communities in which it operates, taking into account priorities set by local and national policymakers. Information sharing, consultation and negotiation are useful tools for a participative approach to identifying and implementing social investments.*

ISO 26000:2010, page 68.

SOCIAL INVESTMENT
Creativity-driven equity opportunity/reconciliation/disruption

An organization can play a key role in the economic and social revitalization of underprivileged communities through its social investment when it deploys DE&I as its currency for moderating good works. A DE&I conscious organization can offer opportunities to communities that do not have them, some of which may have meaningful impacts with long-term ripple effects. Through social investments in these communities' economic development initiatives, expansion of education and skills development initiatives, and providing or funding community health services and cultural preservation, an organization can substantially contribute to the wealth, income creation and sustainability of minority and vulnerable communities. As ISO 26000 articulated well:

ISO *Social investments do not exclude philanthropy (for example, grants, volunteering and donations). Organizations should also encourage community involvement in the design and implementation of projects as* *this can help projects to survive and prosper when the organization is no longer involved. Social investments should prioritize projects that are viable in the long term and contribute to sustainable development.*

ISO 26000:2010, page 68.

Using the 3-Step Equity Lens, an organization should consider the following guidelines provided in ISO 26000 in framing its social investment practices moderated by DE&I.

EQUITY OPPORTUNITY IN SOCIAL INVESTMENT

ISO *An organization should:*

☐ *consider partnering with other organizations, including government, business or NGOs to maximise synergies and make use of complementary resources, knowledge and skills; and*

☐ *consider contributing to programmes that provide access to food and other essential products for vulnerable or discriminated groups and persons with low income, taking into account the importance of contributing to their increased capabilities, resources and opportunities.*

ISO 26000:2010, page 68.

EQUITY RECONCILIATION IN SOCIAL INVESTMENT

ISO *An organization should:*

☐ *take into account the promotion of community development in planning social investment projects. All actions should broaden opportunities for citizens, for example by increasing local procurement and any outsourcing so as to support local development; [and]*

☐ *assess its own existing community-related initiatives and report to the community and to people within the organization and identify where improvements might be made[.]*

ISO 26000:2010, page 68.

EQUITY DISRUPTION IN SOCIAL INVESTMENT

ISO *An organization should:*

☐ *avoid actions that perpetuate a community's dependence on the organization's philanthropic activities, on-going presence or support[.]*

SOCIAL INVESTMENT
Governance-centered inclusion actionable steps

Social investment occurs when organizations invest resources in infrastructure and other programs designed to improve the social aspects of community life. These investments could include training, education, healthcare, culture, infrastructure development, income generation, improved access to information, or other economic or social development activities. ISO 26000 underscored the role organizations play in identifying and investing in priority projects and programs that align with the local and national priorities set by policymakers. It's a more effective way to meet the needs and priorities of the communities in which they operate. Organizations intending to carry out social investments should incorporate tools like participatory approaches, negotiation and consultation, information sharing, etc. when identifying and implementing social investments. While philanthropy can be a part of this mix, it should be aligned with local and national capacity-building goals that focus on developmental programs and projects. Sustainable long-term projects, ISO 26000 positioned, are those with strong community involvement in their design and implementation. When the community is involved from the beginning, programs tend to survive and prosper long after the investing organization is no longer involved.

Governance-centered inclusion actionable steps: social investment

1. In reviewing your organization's policies and procedures around social investment, how do they align with your DE&I policy, commitments, and corporate proclamations on the matter?
2. If there are gaps, what are the actionable steps and timelines you have identified to narrow or eliminate them based on the 3-Step Equity Lens model?
3. Were all relevant stakeholders identified and engaged in the review, modification or development of your policies and procedures around your DE&I moderated social investment practices?

CONCLUSION

We know that the past never dies. As we've seen, it is a living classroom from which we can learn about broken divisive systems that have enabled unjust and unfair practices to thrive. The endurance of these broken systems may seem discouraging, but once we cast the light upon them, we can commit to just and fair practices going forward. Humanity has been torn asunder by divisive norms and biases that pit brother against brother because of skin pigmentations, brother against sister because of gender differences, brothers, and sisters against each other because of national, religious, regional, tribal, and other differences – many other factors that have been invented to divide and conquer, establishing dichotomies in which someone is always superior to someone else. The UN Secretary-General in a July 2020 Nelson Mandela Lecture captured this sentiment well:

> *Even before the COVID-19 pandemic, many people around the globe understood that inequality was undermining their life chances and opportunities. They saw a world out of balance. They felt left behind. They saw economic policies channeling resources upwards to the privileged few...Millions of people from all continents took to the streets to make their voices heard. High and rising inequalities were a common factor. The anger feeding two recent social movements reflects utter disillusionment with the status quo. Women everywhere have called time on one of the most egregious examples of gender inequality: violence perpetrated by powerful men against women who are simply trying to do their jobs. The anti-racism movement that has spread from the United States around the world in the aftermath of*

George Floyd's killing is one more sign that people have had enough: Enough of inequality and discrimination that treats people as criminals on the basis of their skin colour; Enough of the structural racism and systematic injustice that deny people their fundamental human rights (UN 2022).

These artificial norms have kept humankind distracted enough to ignore our social responsibility to each other and to nature. As Nelson Mandela articulated well, *"One of the challenges of our time… is to re-instill in the consciousness of our people that sense of human solidarity, of being in the world for one another and because of and through others (UN 2022)."* According to the UN, seventeen percent of children born in the year 2000 in low human development countries had died by 2020—taking with them cures that were never invented, books that were never written, and uncounted collaborative activities with their contemporaries that would never be realized.

Figure 00.1 Death rate of children born in low human development countries

Death rate of children born in low human development countries

17% of the children born twenty years ago in countries with low human development have already died.

Climate change and other nature-degrading practices and consequences have also become normalized, although their impacts are most felt by the marginalized and vulnerable groups. As the UN Secretary General noted, *"The countries that are most affected by climate disruption did the least to contribute to global heating (UN 2022)."* In all, this means that our human gift of life, liberty and the pursuit of happiness is not available to a vast majority of our contemporaries, and future generations are imperiled as well. Yet, because we are endowed with the ability to reexamine, reimagine, and reinvent ourselves, all hope is not lost.

Our divisive norms continue to fester and grow from generation to generation because we have failed to unleash the full power of our shared human ingenuity to tackle them holistically. We need to adopt a lifecycle and global social responsibility focus with sustainable development implications. We must remember who we are at the elemental level—predominantly water—and why we cannot afford not to live and flow in the pursuit of goodness for ourselves, our posterities and for our shared humankind and shared planet. Like water, humans need to go with the flow, pursuing a level playing field to do what we do best: live for ourselves and for posterity, using fair and just everyday decisions and practices!

Remember that DE&I and all its issues, challenges and opportunities are as much family matters as they are societal and organizational. Many of the models and tools discussed are applicable to at least some of the issues family, society and organizations face in addressing DE&I within their respective ecosystems. Remember, too, that every family, organization, society, community, locale, country, or continent will always have its norms and biases. Every human being alive today, will always have at least one norm or bias. It's part of being human. Working to better ourselves, to overcome our innate limitations and reassess ourselves, is also part of being human.

Norms and biases are housed within the internal recesses of our minds from wherever they were acquired, and they manifest in our decisions without permission, influencing our beliefs, values, and behaviors through the three thinking models: automatic, social and mental models. Yet, norms and biases do not have to be divisive. They can also be nerve connectors to lifegiving sustainable humanity's goodness, exemplified through goodwill to all, practicing deliberate social responsibility. This makes integrating DE&I into every aspect of our human development a necessity, not an abstraction; as an emerging social science it becomes a very important tool and systemic structure for addressing organizational norms that are unfair and unjust.

DR. MARTIN LUTHER KING'S ANATOMY OF SOCIAL CHANGE

As we conclude our journey together, we can draw a global inference from the "I have a dream" speech Dr. Martin Luther King, Jr., gave in 1963. This address captured the very essence of the anatomy of social change using social responsibility framework and the three models I introduced in this book: KCG, the Ajiake 3-Step Equity Lens and the 3-Step Inclusion Principles. I have included the full text of the speech in the appendix, but here, I rearrange them to sum up the parts of the anatomy of social change by examining how one leader called his country to a social responsibility and sustainable development pursuit on race relations driven by the bottom lines of people, prosperity and planet:

Knowledge-informed Diversity Call-to-Action

When we are afraid of learning about how divisive norms and biases became part of our operating racial and gender dialoguing currency of exchange, we are consciously consenting to two realities: (1) desire to continue the divisive norms and (2) denial of our own humanity by erasing the existence of those who came before us, including those who are irrevocably etched into our very DNA. The past never dies, nor can it be ignored, denied, or erased by those who lived or did not live or personally experience it. Our human past is as much alive as those who lived it. It remains forever alive because their blood continues to flow through our veins. Seeking knowledge-informed data on our past gives us the motivation and the drive to seek diversity-framed actions.

<u>Summarize the problem:</u> In seeking to address social change issues, challenges and opportunities, it is important to be first guided by the root causes—the history of the problem and why it continues to be a problem: Dr. King put it this way:

> *Five score years ago, a great American, in whose symbolic shadow we stand today, signed the Emancipation Proclamation. This momentous decree came as a great beacon light of hope to millions of Negro slaves who had been seared in the flames of withering injustice. It came as a joyous daybreak to end the long night of their captivity. But 100 years later, the Negro still is not free. One hundred years later, the life of the Negro is still sadly crippled by the manacles of segregation and the chains of discrimination. One hundred years later, the Negro lives on a lonely island of poverty in the midst of a vast ocean of material prosperity. One hundred years later the Negro is still languished in the corners of American society and finds himself in exile in his own land. And so we've come here today to dramatize a shameful condition. In a sense we've come to our nation's capital to cash a check.*

<u>Redefine human divisive norms as social responsibility problem(s):</u> Dr. King reminded all Americans in every age that the founding fathers envisioned an inclusive country where all were able to experience life, liberty and to pursue happiness together:

> *When the architects of our republic wrote the magnificent words of the Constitution and the Declaration of Independence, they were signing a promissory note to which every American was to fall heir. This note was a promise that all men — yes, Black men as well as white men — would be guaranteed the unalienable rights of life, liberty and the pursuit of happiness. But there is something that I must say to my people who stand on the warm threshold which leads into the palace of justice. In the process of gaining our rightful place, we must not be guilty of wrongful deeds. Let us not seek to satisfy our thirst for freedom by drinking from the cup of bitterness and hatred. We must forever conduct our struggle on the high plane of dignity and discipline. We must not allow our creative protest to degenerate into physical violence. Again and*

again, we must rise to the majestic heights of meeting physical force with soul force.

The marvelous new militancy which has engulfed the Negro community must not lead us to a distrust of all white people, for many of our white brothers, as evidenced by their presence here today, have come to realize that their destiny is tied up with our destiny. And they have come to realize that their freedom is inextricably bound to our freedom. We cannot walk alone. And as we walk, we must make the pledge that we shall always march ahead. We cannot turn back.

Draw undisputable Problem(s) conclusion: Establishing why social change is a problem becomes a way to bring most people to the table of agreement that the problem is real, cannot be denied or wished away and must be addressed face-on. For true prosperity, peace, and happiness to take root from systemic and structural racism and the house it built through white privilege, politics and policies, racial reckoning becomes a necessity, not a benevolence to be gifted by those who benefited from the divisive norms and biases. Dr. King made this observation and clarion call to action:

It is obvious today that America has defaulted on this promissory note insofar as her citizens of color are concerned. Instead of honoring this sacred obligation, America has given the Negro people a bad check, a check which has come back marked insufficient funds.

It would be fatal for the nation to overlook the urgency of the moment. This sweltering summer of the Negro's legitimate discontent will not pass until there is an invigorating autumn of freedom and equality. 1963 is not an end, but a beginning. Those who hope that the Negro needed to blow off steam and will now be content will have a rude awakening if the nation returns to business as usual. There will be neither rest nor tranquility in America until the Negro is granted his citizenship rights. The whirlwinds of revolt will continue to shake the foundations of our nation until the bright day of justice emerges.

The sacrificial slaying of George Floyd in 2020 and the national and global unrest that followed was a poignant reminder that after 57 years of failing to address the problems of systemic and structural racism, the problems did not go away, and Dr. King's words remained eerily true: *"There will be neither rest nor tranquility in America until the Negro is granted his citizenship rights."*

Acknowledge the pain, suffering and triumph of social change contextually and perpetually: Dr. King recognized those who were at the forefront for the social change that Americans were being called upon to embrace—with an optimistic commitment that was integral to what it means to be an American in a democratic ecosystem:

> I am not unmindful that some of you have come here out of great trials and tribulations. Some of you have come fresh from narrow jail cells. Some of you have come from areas where your quest for freedom left you battered by the storms of persecution and staggered by the winds of police brutality. You have been the veterans of creative suffering. Continue to work with the faith that unearned suffering is redemptive. Go back to Mississippi, go back to Alabama, go back to South Carolina, go back to Georgia, go back to Louisiana, go back to the slums and ghettos of our Northern cities, knowing that somehow this situation can and will be changed. Let us not wallow in the valley of despair, I say to you today, my friends.

> So even though we face the difficulties of today and tomorrow, I still have a dream. It is a dream deeply rooted in the American dream. I have a dream that one day this nation will rise up and live out the true meaning of its creed: We hold these truths to be self-evident, that all men are created equal. I have a dream that one day on the red hills of Georgia, the sons of former slaves and the sons of former slave owners will be able to sit down together at the table of brotherhood. I have a dream that one day even the state of Mississippi, a state sweltering with the heat of injustice, sweltering with the heat of oppression will be transformed into an oasis of freedom and justice.

Contextualizing complicity as a nemesis of social change: Dr. King recognized that there will be good people who nonetheless wonder why we cannot just accept the status quo today and let time mediate the social change we seek tomorrow. Dr. King's response was both contextual and transcendental as a mental model to complicit advocates:

> There are those who are asking the devotees of civil rights, when will you be satisfied? We can never be satisfied as long as the Negro is the victim of the unspeakable horrors of police brutality. We can never be satisfied as long as our bodies, heavy with the fatigue of travel, cannot gain lodging in the motels of the highways and the hotels of the cities.

> We cannot be satisfied as long as the Negro's basic mobility is from a smaller ghetto to a larger one. We can never be satisfied as long as our children are stripped of their selfhood and robbed of their dignity by signs stating: for whites only. We cannot be satisfied as long as a Negro in Mississippi cannot vote and a Negro in New York believes he has nothing for which to vote. No, no, we are not

satisfied, and we will not be satisfied until justice rolls down like waters, and righteousness like a mighty stream.

Creativity-driven Equity Opportunity, Reconciliation and Disruption

Throughout this book, I've established the linkage between learned values, behaviors, and thinking models in relation to divisive norms, because we cannot talk about DE&I without first understanding how our history and societal influences contribute to how we process everyday decisions. Once we understand the divisive norms we want to address, creativity-driven equity opportunity, reconciliation and disruption become useful tools and systemic structure for addressing them from a holistic and lifegiving perspective. This is how Dr. King's speech addressed each one:

- Equity Opportunity: I have a dream that my four little children will one day live in a nation where they will not be judged by the color of their skin but by the content of their character. I have a dream today.
- Equity Reconciliation: I have a dream that one day down in Alabama, with its vicious racists, with its governor having his lips dripping with the words of "interposition" and "nullification", one day right there in Alabama little black boys and black girls will be able to join hands with little white boys and white girls as sisters and brothers. I have a dream today.
- Equity Disruption: I have a dream that one day every valley shall be exalted, every hill and mountain shall be made low, the rough places will be made plain, and the crooked places will be made straight, and the glory of the Lord shall be revealed, and all flesh shall see it together.

Governance-centered Inclusion Actionable Steps:

Humankind Shared Planet Divided by Norms has explored our past experiences on DE&I questions and provided tools and structures for addressing them from a social responsibility and sustainable development perspective. Governance-centered inclusion is essential for implementing the solutions that we created using DE&I as a moderator for the seven principles and seven core subjects as presented by International Standards Organization in its ISO 26000 Social Responsibility, reinforced by the United Nations' Sustainable Development Goals.

Since every country has DE&I issues, challenges, and opportunities, governance structures—policies and procedures and DE&I commitment—make them desired organizational and societal values and behaviors in actionable steps. The manner in which we collate these divisive norms and address them from a systemic approach that is applicable across families, organizations, countries, cultures, and societal proclivities will be contextual and culture-driven.

When we focus on what we know about a divisive norm or bias (history, impacts, etc.), we can create and document appropriately fair and just solutions, centered by inclusion and established as uncompromising principles. Guiding principles are easily framed contextual thoughts that help establish broader buy-in, because they are affirming and forward-facing statements of hope that cannot be dashed even when the current reality is far from what is desired. Dr. King phrased America's racial issues within the context of a hopeful future outcome that was inclusive of all Americans:

> *This is our hope. This is the faith that I go back to the South with. With this faith we will be able to hew out of the mountain of despair a stone of hope. With this faith we will be able to transform the jangling discords of our nation into a beautiful symphony of brotherhood. With this faith we will be able to work together, to pray together, to struggle together, to go to jail together, to stand up for freedom together, knowing that we will be free one day.*

As we go about integrating DE&I into every aspect of our decision-making and practices by creating solutions to our divisive norms, we should be guided by the 3-Step Inclusion principles, so we are not unintentionally creating additional norms and biases that are not wholesomely inclusive and accepted. In this example with the *I have a Dream* speech, the 3-Step Inclusion Principles and the 3-Step Equity Lens models aligned contextually on a one-to-one basis, though it is not always a one-to-one relationship because it is context-driven. Dr. King's speech provided a good integrative example:

- Redemption-driven principle allows us to make equity opportunity decisions now because they are low-hanging fruits that do not need to be studied or debated—just dealt with. Dr. King described it this way:

  > *We refuse to believe that there are insufficient funds in the great vaults of opportunity of this nation. And so we've come to cash this check, a check that will give us upon demand the riches of freedom and the security of justice.*

- Restoration-focused principle allows us to make equity reconciliation demands that are guided by examining our current decisions and practices against who we claim to be in our vision, mission statements and in our DE&I commitments. There are times when reconciling our stated DE&I commitments with our policies and procedures also requires some immediate restoration of what was lost or damaged or taken from minority and vulnerable groups. Dr. King described it this way:

We have also come to his [Abraham Lincoln] hallowed spot to remind America of the fierce urgency of now. This is no time to engage in the luxury of cooling off or to take the tranquilizing drug of gradualism. Now is the time to make real the promises of democracy. Now is the time to rise from the dark and desolate valley of segregation to the sunlit path of racial justice. Now is the time to lift our nation from the quick sands of racial injustice to the solid rock of brotherhood. Now is the time to make justice a reality for all of God's children.

- Responsibility-centered principle allows us to disrupt or stop decisions and practices that strengthen our divisive norms by uprooting them responsibly, even if they originated with aspirational goals. Dr. King described it this way:

This will be the day when all of God's children will be able to sing with new meaning: My country, 'tis of thee, sweet land of liberty, of thee I sing. Land where my fathers died, land of the pilgrims' pride, from every mountainside, let freedom ring. And if America is to be a great nation, this must become true. And so let freedom ring from the prodigious hilltops of New Hampshire. Let freedom ring from the mighty mountains of New York. Let freedom ring from the heightening Alleghenies of Pennsylvania. Let freedom ring from the snowcapped Rockies of Colorado. Let freedom ring from the curvaceous slopes of California. But not only that, let freedom ring from Stone Mountain of Georgia. Let freedom ring from Lookout Mountain of Tennessee. Let freedom ring from every hill and molehill of Mississippi. From every mountainside, let freedom ring.

And when this happens, and when we allow freedom ring, when we let it ring from every village and every hamlet, from every state and every city, we will be able to speed up that day when all of God's children, Black men and white men, Jews and Gentiles, Protestants and Catholics, will be able to join hands and sing in the words of the old Negro spiritual: Free at last. Free at last. Thank God almighty, we are free at last.

America is still awaiting the generation(s) that will come together and metaphorically begin to sing this old Negro spiritual, because their organizations and society reflects freedom for all Americans regardless of color of skin. With Juneteenth finally becoming a national holiday, perhaps we are finally on this journey to the end of systemic and structural racism and gender inequalities. When it happens, it will be because organizational leaders led the way in words and deeds!

America's problems are in the spotlight, but the rest of the world cannot rest on its own discriminatory divisive norms while waiting for America to get its racial and gender disparities in order. If anything, the murder of George Floyd brought the whole world together in protest of unfair and unjust treatments of minority and vulnerable groups. The cry for justice for all echoed around the world, and it is a sustainable one because it has such broad implications, including the injustices we visit upon our planet. Together, as we are forced to address climate change impacts because our very lives and future generations of humankind demand actions, our human divisive norms demand our response in tackling them as well. In 1968, the great American musician/songwriter, Louis Armstrong, gave the world a beautiful song that summed up our humankind shared planet possibilities— a song generations of humanity (present and future) would always find meaningful and relevant:

What a Wonderful World Lyrics
I see trees of green, red roses too
I see them bloom for me and you
And I think to myself
What a wonderful world
I see skies of blue and clouds of white
The bright blessed days, the dark sacred nights
And I think to myself
What a wonderful world
The colors of the rainbow
So pretty in the sky
Are also on the faces
Of people going by
I see friends shaking hands, saying, "How do you do?"
They're really saying, "I love you"
I hear babies cry, I watch them grow
They'll learn much more
Than I'll ever know
And I think to myself
What a wonderful world
Yes, I think to myself
What a wonderful world
Oh Yeah

In conclusion, as humans, we have the individual and collective will to reevaluate, reimagine, or reinvent ourselves from engaging in past unfair and unjust societal practices and become the generation that begins to address humankind's divisive norms by seeing them as an individual, societal, national and global pariah. This is in recognition that we will always remain a part of a transcendent tapestry. Even when we have passed on, our decisions and activities will remain part and parcel of the human story on planet Earth. Remember that the past is as much alive as those who lived it remain forever alive because we are humans even when we are no longer alive physically.

What then will you have added to humankind's continuum story when your own human story is fully written, and the final full stop is in place with no opportunity for any do-overs? I hope the issues, challenges and opportunities presented in this book about our divided humanity gave you the impetus to continue to pursue goodness for humankind in your decisions and activities. Even if this is not the case, I hope you found inspiration, motivation, and purpose in the pages of this book and the courage to pursue them.

Going forward, I invite you to continue the journey with me as we explore DE&I stories from around the world beginning with Humankind Shared Planet: Global DE&I Stories Volume II—Brazil, India, Nigeria, and the United States.

REFERENCES

Alpizar, F., Carlsson, F., & Naranjo, M. A. (2011). The effect of ambiguous risk, and coordination on farmers' adaptation to climate change—A framed field experiment. *Ecological Economics*, *70*(12), 2317.

Andrew Johnson, Freedmen's Bureau Bill veto message. (1866, February 19). House Divided: The Civil War Research Engine at Dickinson College, https://hd.housedivided.dickinson.edu/node/45150.

Associated Press. (2020, June17). *After 130 years, Aunt Jemima will vanish from packaging*. PBS News Hour. https://www.pbs.org/newshour/nation/after-130-years-aunt-jemima-will-vanish-from-packaging (Accessed May 3, 2022).

Bellis, M. (2021, January 24). *Biography of Elijah McCoy, American Inventor*. ThoughtCo. https://www.thoughtco.com/elijah-mccoy-profile-1992158

Bennhold, K. (2013). *Britain's Ministry of Nudges*. New York Times. http://www.nytimes.com/2013/12/08/business/international/britainsministry-of-nudges.html?pagewanted=all&_r.

Boffey, P. (1984). *Disaster in India sharpens debate on doing business in third world; modern pesticides aid in insuring more food for poorest countries*. New York Times. https://www.nytimes.com/1984/12/16/world/disaster-india-sharpens-debate-doing-business-third-world-modern-pesticides-aid.html

Bourdieu, P. (1997). *Outline of a Theory of Practice*, Cambridge University Press, UK.

Brakkton, B. (2020, July 13). After Mounting Pressure, Washington's NFL Franchise Drops Its Team Name. NPR.KQED. https://www.npr.org/sections/live-updates-protests-for-racial-justice/2020/07/13/890359987/after-mounting-pressure-washingtons-nfl-franchise-drops-its-team-name (Accessed May 3, 2022).

Britannica, The Editors of Encyclopaedia. (2017). *Land-Grant Universities*. Encyclopedia Britannica. https://www.britannica.com/topic/land-grant-university.

Cambridge Dictionary | English Dictionary, Translations & Thesaurus. (2022, July 20). Cambridge Dictionary. https://dictionary.cambridge.org/

Cassels, J. (1993). *The uncertain promise of law: Lessons from Bhopal* (p. 43). Toronto: University of Toronto Press.

Cohen, G. L., Garcia, J., Purdie-Vaughns, V., Apfel, N., & Brzustoski, P. (2009). Recursive processes in self-affirmation: Intervening to close the minority achievement gap. *science*, *324*(5925), 400-403.

Community Reinvestment Act (CRA). (2022, June 24). *What is the Community Reinvestment Act (CRA)?*. Board Of Governors Of The Federal Reserve System. https://www.federalreserve.gov/consumerscommunities/cra_about.htm.

Conagra Brands. (2020, June 17). *Conagra Brands Announces Mrs. Butterworth's Brand Review*. News Release. https://www.conagrabrands.com/news-room/news-conagra-brands-announces-mrs-butterworths-brand-review-prn-122733 (Accessed May 3, 2022).

Congressional Record. (1874, January 10). House, 43rd Cong., 1st sess, 565–567.

Cragg, W. (Ed.). (2005). *Ethics codes, corporations, and the challenge of globalization.* Edward Elgar Publishing.

Deloitte & United Nations Global Compact. (2010). *UN Global Compact Management Model: Framework for Implementation.* https://www.unglobalcompact.org/library/231.

Devillard, S., Sancier-Sultan, S., Zelicourt, A. D., & Kossoff, C. (2016). Women Matter 2016: Reinventing the workplace to unlock the potential of gender diversity. *McKinsey & Company*, 1-34.

Diamond, S. (1985) *The disaster in Bhopal: lessons for the future.* New York Times. https://www.nytimes.com/1985/01/30/world/the-disaster-in-bhopal-workers-recall-horror.html (Accessed December 25, 2021).

Diamond, S. (1985). *Plant had to be locally designed and operated.* New York Times. https://www.nytimes.com/1984/12/13/world/plant-had-to-be-locally-designed-and-operated.html.

DiMaggio, P. (1997). Culture and cognition. *Annual review of sociology, 23*(1): 263–87. doi: 10.1146/annurev.soc.23.1.263.

Dorian, M., Gorin, T., Yamada, H., & Yang, A. (2021, June 10). *Erin Brockovich: the real story of the town three decades later.* ABC News. https://abcnews.go.com/US/erin-brockovich-real-story-town-decades/story?id=78180219

Earley, P. (1986, February 16). *DESMOND TUTU.* The Washington Post. https://www.washingtonpost.com/archive/lifestyle/magazine/1986/02/16/desmond-tutu/3fc3da7f-4926-44cf-896a-5d1bf7f00206/#comments.

Facebook Business. (2018, August 21). *Keeping Advertising Safe and Civil.* Meta. https://web.facebook.com/business/news/keeping-advertising-safe-and-civil?_rdc=1&_rdr (Accessed May 2, 2022).

Federal Trade Commission. (1980, December 17). FTC Policy Statement on Unfairness. https://www.ftc.gov/legal-library/browse/ftc-policy-statement-unfairness

Feigenberg, B., Field, E., & Pande, R. (2013). The economic returns to social interaction: Experimental evidence from microfinance. *Review of Economic Studies, 80*(4), 1459-1483.

Fink, L. (2022). *Larry Fink's 2022 Letter to CEOS: The Power of Capitalism.* BlackRock. https://www.blackrock.com/corporate/investor-relations/larry-fink-ceo-letter?cid=ppc:CEOLetter:PMS:US:NA&gclid=CjwKCAjwlcaRBhBYEiwAK341jap6a0UEmKs4YwI39TZYGQW03DKVB1JvTk3O0Je6-CLY2O0i_O_q4hoCpFIQAvD_BwE&gclsrc=aw.ds

Ford Foundation. (2022). *Diversity, equity, and inclusion.* https://www.fordfoundation.org/about/people/diversity-equity-and-inclusion/ (Acceed July 22, 2022).

Fouché, R. (2003). *Black Inventors in the Age of Segregation: Granville T. Woods, Lewis H. Latimer, and Shelby J. Davidson.* JHU Press.

Ghosh, I. (2020). *These countries will have the largest populations - by the end of the century.* World Economic Forum. https://www.weforum.org/agenda/2020/09/the-world-population-in-2100-by-country/

Giang, A., & Castellani, K. (2020). Cumulative air pollution indicators highlight unique patterns of injustice in urban Canada. *Environmental Research Letters*, *15*(12), 124063.

Goetzmann, W. N. (2022) Shareholder democracy, meet memocracy, Financial Analysts Journal, 78:3, 5-8, DOI: 10.1080/0015198X.2022.2074773

Gray, C. B. (2021, April 27). *Coca Cola's racially discriminatory outside counsel policy.* Boyden Gray & Associates PLLC. https://mma.prnewswire.com/media/1498756/POFR_COKE_Boyden_Gray__21_4_27_Letter_to_Coca_Cola_FINAL.pdf?p=pdf

Guterres, A. (2017). *Tackling the inequality pandemic: a new social contract for a new era.* The 18th Nelson Mandela annual lecture. United Nations. https://www.un.org/en/coronavirus/tackling-inequality-new-social-contract-new-era.

Guyon, N., & Huillery, E. (2014). The Aspiration-Poverty Trap: Why Do Students from Low Social Background Limit Their Ambition? Evidence from France. *documento de trabajo disponible en https://www. unamur. be/en/eco/eeco/pdf/paper_autocensure_feb2014. pdf.*

Hall, C. C., Zhao, J., & Shafir, E. (2014). Self-affirmation among the poor: Cognitive and behavioral implications. *Psychological science*, *25*(2), 619-625.

Hamilton, I. A. (2018, October 13). *Why It's Totally Unsurprising That Amazon's Recruitment AI Was Biased against Women.* Business Insider. https://www.businessinsider.com/amazon-ai-biased-against-women-no-surprise-sandra-wachter-2018-10 (Accessed May 1, 2022).

Hanly, F. (2020). Dred Scott v Sandford 60 US 393 (1867). *Plassey L. Rev.*, *1*, 56.

History, Art & Archives, U.S. House of Representatives, Office of the Historian (2008). *The Negroes' Temporary Farewell: Jim Crow and the Exclusion of African Americans from Congress, 1887–1929.* https://history.house.gov/Exhibitions-and-Publications/BAIC/Historical-Essays/Temporary-Farewell/Introduction/

History, Art & Archives, U.S. House of Representatives. (2021). *Civil Rights Act of 1875.* https://history.house.gov/Exhibitions-and-Publications/BAIC/Historical-Essays/Fifteenth-Amendment/Civil-Rights-Bill-1875/

History, Art & Archives, U.S. House of Representatives. (2022). The Civil Rights Bill of 1866. https://history.house.gov/Historical-Highlights/1851-1900/The-Civil-Rights-Bill-of-1866/

History.com Editors. (2021, March 23). *Exxon Valdez Oil Spill.* HISTORY. https://www.history.com/topics/1980s/exxon-valdez-oil-spill#section_2

Hoff, K., & Pandey, P. (2006). Discrimination, social identity, and durable inequalities. *American economic review*, *96*(2), 206-211.

Hoff, K., & Pandey, P. (2014). Making up people—The effect of identity on performance in a modernizing society. *Journal of Development Economics*, *106*, 118-131.

Home Mortgage Disclosure Act. (n.d.). *Examination Procedures.* 1-18.

https://kinginstitute.stanford.edu/king-papers/documents/i-have-dream-address-delivered-march-washington-jobs-and-freedom

https://www.hud.gov/program_offices/housing/fhahistory Retrieval date: April 13, 2022.

https://www.hud.gov/sites/dfiles/PIH/documents/HUD_01-18-0323_Complaint.pdf (last accessed May2, 2022).

International Labour Organization. (1998). *ILO declaration on fundamental principles and rights at work and its follow-up*. International Labour Organization.

International Organization for Standardization (ISO). (2018). *Discovering ISO 26000: Guidance on social responsibility*. iso.org. https://www.iso.org/files/live/sites/isoorg/files/store/en/PUB100258.pdf (Accessed September 8, 2021).

ISO 26000 (2010*). International Standard: Guidance on social responsibility*. 1st edition [Reference no: ISO 26000:2010(E)]. https://documentation.lastradainternational.org/lsidocs/3078-ISO%2026000_2010.pdf

JPMorgan Chase & Co. (2022). *Who we are: frequently asked questions.* https://www.jpmorganchase.com/corporate/About-JPMC/diversity.htm

Justia. (n.d.). Dred Scott v. Sandford, 60 U.S. 393 (1856). *Justia Opinion Summary and Annotations, 60.* https://supreme.justia.com/cases/federal/us/60/393/

Kapila, M., Hines, E., & Searby, M. (2016). *Why Diversity, Equity, and Inclusion Matter*. Independent Sector.

Keehan, C. J. (2018). Lessons from cancer alley: How the clean air act has failed to protect public health in Southern Louisiana. *Colo. Nat. Resources Energy & Envtl. L. Rev.*, *29*, 341.

Kleinman, A. (2007). *What really matters: Living a moral life amidst uncertainty and danger*. Oxford University Press.

Kochhar, R., & Fry, R. (2014, December 12). *Wealth inequality has widened along racial, ethnic lines since end of Great Recession*. Pew Research Center. https://www.pewresearch.org/fact-tank/2014/12/12/racial-wealth-gaps-great-recession/.

Kumar, H., & Polgreen, L. (2010). *8 former executives guilty in '84 Bhopal chemical leak*. New York Times. https://www.nytimes.com/2010/06/08/world/asia/08bhopal.html?hp

Lane, H. M., Morello-Frosch, R., Marshall, J. D., & Apte, J. S. (2022). Historical redlining is associated with present-day air pollution disparities in US cities. *Environmental science & technology letters*, *9*(4), 345-350. https://doi.org/10.1021/acs.estlett.1c01012.

Madison. (n.d.). *The Federalist Papers: No. 43*. The Avalon Project, 271-72. https://avalon.law.yale.edu/18th_century/fed43.asp

Martin, & Dpi campaings. (2020c, July 23). *Energy*. United Nations Sustainable Development. https://www.un.org/sustainabledevelopment/energy/

Martin, Blazhevska, V., & Dpi campaigns. (2020, August 11). *Economic Growth*. United Nations Sustainable Development. https://www.un.org/sustainabledevelopment/economic-growth/

Martin, Blazhevska, V., & Dpi campaings. (2020, August 11). *Infrastructure and Industrialization*. United Nations Sustainable Development.

https://www.un.org/sustainabledevelopment/infrastructure-industrialization/

Martin, M., A, R., Blazhevska, V., Dpi Campaings, M., & Intern, D. D. (2020, July 23). *Education*. United Nations Sustainable Development. https://www.un.org/sustainabledevelopment/education/

Martin. (2021, January 5). *Global Partnerships*. United Nations Sustainable Development. https://www.un.org/sustainabledevelopment/globalpartnerships

Milano, B. (2021, April 20). *Should the internet be treated like a public utility?*. Harvard Law Today. https://today.law.harvard.edu/should-the-internet-be-treated-like-a-public-utility/?utm_source=hltTwitter (Accessed July 5, 2022).

Morenoff, D. (2021, June 11). *Open Letter on Behalf of Shareholders to Officers and Directors of Coca-Cola Company*. American Civil Rights Project. https://www.americancivilrightsproject.org/blog/submissions/open-letter-on-behalf-of-shareholders-to-officers-and-directors-of-coca-cola-company/

Musgrave, G. L. (2011). Charles Wheelan, Naked Economics: Undressing the Dismal Science.

NASA. (2020). *NASA to Reexamine Nicknames for Cosmic Objects*. https://www.nasa.gov/feature/nasa-to-reexamine-nicknames-for-cosmic-objects

NASA. (2020, February 25). *Katherine Johnson Biography*. National Aeronautics and Space Administration. https://www.nasa.gov/content/katherine-johnson-biography

National Archives. (2021). *The Freedmen's Bureau*. https://www.archives.gov/research/african-americans/freedmens-bureau (Accessed Janury 5, 2022).

Niiler, E. (2021, July 20). *Why Civil Rights Activists Protested the Moon Landing*. HISTORY. https://www.history.com/news/apollo-11-moon-landing-launch-protests

Nunn, N. (2008). The long-term effects of Africa's slave trades. *The Quarterly Journal of Economics, 123*(1), 139-176.

Nunn, N., & Wantchekon, L. (2011). The slave trade and the origins of mistrust in Africa. *American Economic Review, 101*(7), 3221-52.

Pager, D., & Shepherd, H. (2008). The sociology of discrimination: Racial discrimination in employment, housing, credit, and consumer markets. *Annual review of sociology, 34*, 181-209.

Park, D. (2019, May 24). *HUD v. Facebook* [Compliance Blog]. NAFCU. https://www.nafcu.org/compliance-blog/hud-v-facebook (Accessed April 23, 2022).

Plessy v. Ferguson (1896). *National Archives*. https://www.archives.gov/milestone-documents/plessy-v-ferguson

Pramuk, J. (2016, April 26). *JPMorgan Chase named top US company for diversity*. CNBC. https://www.cnbc.com/2016/04/25/jpmorgan-chase-named-top-us-company-for-diversity.html

Reddix-Smalls, B. (2018). Intellectual Property, Income Inequality, and Societal Interconnectivity in the United States: Social Calculus and the

Historical Distribution of Wealth. *North Carolina Central University Science & Intellectual Property Law Review, 11*(1), 1.

Richter, P. (1989). *$470-Million Settlement for Bhopal OKd : Union Carbide to Pay 500,000 Claimants in India Gas Leak.* New York Times. https://www.latimes.com/archives/la-xpm-1989-02-15-mn-2452-story.html

Robert Wood Johnson Foundation. (n.d.). *What is a Culture of Health?.* Evidence for action. https://www.evidenceforaction.org/about-us/what-culture-health

Safe at Work California. (2020, December 23). *What is Safety Culture?* https://www.safeatworkca.com/safety-articles/what-is-safety-culture/?utm_source=Paid_Search&utm_medium=SafetyAtWork&utm_campaign=Safe_At_Work_California_2021&utm_content=General&gclid=CjwKCAiAvriMBhAuEiwA8Cs5la96-YdIWCep69pirMZIk-uKLyPp3uJaxv3ETrDaQ_1yh1b0zuMmVRoC2DoQAvD_BwE

Section 8 (Enumerated Powers). https://constitution.congress.gov/browse/article-1/section-8/clause-8/

Servicemen's Readjustment Act (1944). National Archives. https://www.archives.gov/milestone-documents/servicemens-readjustment-act.

Shepherd, V. A. (2000). Trade and Exchange in Jamaica in the Period of Slavery. *Caribbean Slavery in the Atlantic World: A Student Reader.*

Sherman, C. (2020, June 17). *Uncle Ben's Brand Evolution.* Press Release. https://www.mars.com/news-and-stories/press-releases/uncle-bens-brand-evolution (Accessed May 3, 2022).

Son, H. (2019, December 13). *Jamie Dimon says he's "disgusted by racism" and progress is needed at JP Morgan after report.* CNBC. https://www.cnbc.com/2019/12/13/jamie-dimon-says-hes-disgusted-by-racism-and-progress-is-needed-at-jp-morgan-after-report.html

Statista. (2022, June 7). *Number of employees of JP Morgan Chase 2008–2021.* https://www.statista.com/statistics/270610/employees-of-jp-morgan-since-2008/

Streitfeld, D. (2021). *How Amazon crushes unions.* The New York Times. https://www.nytimes.com/2021/03/16/technology/amazon-unions-virginia.html

Swidler, A. (1986). Culture in action: Symbols and strategies. *American sociological review*, 273-286.

Swidler, A. (1986). Culture in action: Symbols and strategies. *American sociological review*, 273-286.

Tessum, C. W., Paolella, D. A., Chambliss, S. E., Apte, J. S., Hill, J. D., & Marshall, J. D. (2021). PM2. 5 polluters disproportionately and systemically affect people of color in the United States. *Science Advances*, 7(18), eabf4491. https://doi.org/10.1126/sciadv.abf4491.

The Coca Cola Company. (2022). *Diversity, equity and inclusion.* https://www.coca-colacompany.com/shared-future/diversity-and-inclusion.

The Coca Cola Company. (n.d.) *Commitment to Diversity, Belonging, and Outside Counsel Diversity.* https://www.coca-colacompany.com/media-center/bradley-gayton-on-commitment-to-diversity.

The Nobel Prize. (1964, December 11). *The quest for peace and justice.* Martin
     Luther King Jr. Nobel Lecture.
     https://www.nobelprize.org/prizes/peace/1964/king/lecture/.\
The Rockefeller Foundation. (2021, January 11). *Historic Alliance Launches at*
     COP26 to Accelerate a Transition to Renewable Energy, Access to
     Energy for All, and Jobs. Press Release.
     https://www.rockefellerfoundation.org/news/historic-alliance-launches-
     at-cop26-to-accelerate-renewable-energy-climate-solutions-and-jobs/
     (Accessed April 23, 2022).
The World Bank. (2022). *Integrated electrification strategies and planning.*
     ESMAP.
     https://esmap.org/integrated_electrification_strategies_planning
Tutu, D. [@DesmondTutuPF]. (2015, August 18). *All of our humanity is*
     dependent upon recognizing the humanity in others [Tweet]. Twitter.
     https://twitter.com/DesmondTutuPF/status/633608189288693760/phot
     o/1
U.S. Senate: Freedmen's Bureau Acts of 1865 and 1866. (2017, January 12).
     United States Senate.
     https://www.senate.gov/artandhistory/history/common/generic/Freedm
     ensBureau.htm
 UN Documents. (n.d.). *Our Common Future: Report of the World Commission*
     on Environment and Development. http://www.un-documents.net/ocf-
     02.htm#IV
UNCTAD. (2016). *United Nations Guidelines for Consumer Protection.* United
     Nations, New York and Geneva. 1-35.
     https://unctad.org/system/files/official-
     document/ditccplpmisc2016d1_en.pdf
United Nations Global Compact. (2012). *Global Compact for the 10th*
     Principle: Corporate Sustainability with Integrity.
     https://www.unglobalcompact.org/library/151
United Nations Global Compact. (n.d.). *Principle Four: Labour.*
     https://www.unglobalcompact.org/what-is-
     gc/mission/principles/principle-4
United Nations Global Compact. (n.d.). *Principle Seven: Environment.*
     https://www.unglobalcompact.org/what-is-
     gc/mission/principles/principle-7 ?.
United Nations Global Compact. (n.d.). *Principle Ten: Anti-Corruption.*
     https://www.unglobalcompact.org/what-is-
     gc/mission/principles/principle-10
United Nations. (2020, August 11). *Forests, desertification and biodiversity.*
     United Nations Sustainable Development.
     https://www.un.org/sustainabledevelopment/biodiversity/
United Nations. (2020, July 23). *Education.* United Nations Sustainable
     Development. https://www.un.org/sustainabledevelopment/education/
United Nations. (2020b, August 11). *Climate Change.* United Nations
     Sustainable Development.
     https://www.un.org/sustainabledevelopment/climate-change/

United Nations. (2020c, August 11). *Cities - United Nations Sustainable Development Action 2015*. United Nations Sustainable Development. https://www.un.org/sustainabledevelopment/cities/

United Nations. (2020d, August 11). *Peace, justice and strong institutions*. United Nations Sustainable Development. https://www.un.org/sustainabledevelopment/peace-justice/

United Nations. (2020e, August 11). *Sustainable consumption and production*. United Nations Sustainable Development. https://www.un.org/sustainabledevelopment/sustainable-consumption-production/

United Nations. (2020f, July 23). *Gender equality and women's empowerment*. United Nations Sustainable Development. https://www.un.org/sustainabledevelopment/gender-equality/

United Nations. (2020g, July 23). *Goal 2: Zero Hunger*. United Nations Sustainable Development. https://www.un.org/sustainabledevelopment/hunger/

United Nations. (2020h, July 23). *Reduce inequality within and among countries*. United Nations Sustainable Development. https://www.un.org/sustainabledevelopment/inequality/

United Nations. (2020i, July 23). *Water and Sanitation*. United Nations Sustainable Development. https://www.un.org/sustainabledevelopment/water-and-sanitation/

United Nations. (2020j, July 8). *Equity and Accessibility in Times of Pandemic: Building "Cities For All" Post-COVID19*. UN Department of Economic and Social Affairs. https://www.un.org/development/desa/disabilities/news/news/building-cities-for-all.html

United Nations. (2020k, July 23). *Health*. United Nations Sustainable Development. https://www.un.org/sustainabledevelopment/health/

United Nations. (2021). *COVID-19 Outbreak and Persons with Disabilities*. UN Department of Economic and Social Affairs. https://www.un.org/development/desa/disabilities/covid-19.html

United Nations. (2021, January 5). *Global Partnerships*. United Nations Sustainable Development. https://www.un.org/sustainabledevelopment/globalpartnerships/

United Nations. (2022). *Tackling Inequality: A New Social Contract for a New Era*. https://www.un.org/en/coronavirus/tackling-inequality-new-social-contract-new-era

United Nations. (2022, May 10). *Oceans*. United Nations Sustainable Development. https://www.un.org/sustainabledevelopment/oceans/

United Nations. (n.d.) *Transforming our world: the 2030 Agenda for Sustainable Development*. https://sdgs.un.org/2030agenda.

United Nations. (n.d.). *#Envision2030: 17 goals to transform the world for persons with disabilities*. UN Department of Economic and Social Affairs. https://www.un.org/development/desa/disabilities/envision2030.html

United Nations. (n.d.). *Ensure access to affordable, reliable, sustainable and modern energy*. Sustainable Development.

https://www.un.org/sustainabledevelopment/energy/ (Accessed April 23, 2022).

United Nations. (n.d.). *Goal 9: Build resilient infrastructure, promote sustainable industrialization and foster innovation*. United Nations Sustainable Development. https://www.un.org/sustainabledevelopment/infrastructure-industrialization/

United Nations. (n.d.). *Promote inclusive and sustainable economic growth, employment and decent work for all*. UN Sustainable Development. https://www.un.org/sustainabledevelopment/economic-growth/

United Nations. (n.d.). Strengthening the role of major groups, chapter 30. Agenda 21 from the 1992 Rio Earth Summit. https://www.un.org/esa/dsd/agenda21/res_agenda21_30.shtml.

United States Senate. (n.d.). *Freedmen's Bureau Acts of 1865 and 1866*. https://www.senate.gov/artandhistory/history/common/generic/FreedmensBureau.htm

US Constitution. (n.d.). *Browse the Constitution Annotated Article I Legislative Branch*

US Department of Housing and Urban Development. (2009). Unequal burden: Income and racial disparities in subprime lending in America. https://archives.hud.gov/reports/subprime/subprime.cfm.

US Department of Justice. (n.d.). *The Equal Credit Opportunity Act*. https://www.justice.gov/crt/equal-credit-opportunity-act-3

WCED, S. W. S. (1987). World commission on environment and development. *Our common future, 17*(1), 1-91.

Weber, E. U. (1997). Perception and expectation of climate change: Precondition for economic and technological adaptation In Bazerman M., Messick D., Tenbrunsel A., and Wade-Benzoni K.(Eds.) Psychological perspectives to environmental and ethical issues in management (314–341).

Wiener, E. L. (1988). Cockpit automation. In *Human factors in aviation* (pp. 433-461). Academic Press.

Wikipedia contributors. (2022, June 28). *Howard University*. Wikipedia. https://en.wikipedia.org/wiki/Howard_University#cite_note-official_history-6

Witte, M. D. (2020, July 1). *When Thomas Jefferson penned "all men are created equal," he did not mean individual equality, says Stanford scholar*. Stanford News Service. https://news.stanford.edu/press-releases/2020/07/01/meaning-declaratnce-changed-time/

World Bank. (2012). *Turn Down the Heat: Why a 4°C Warmer World Must Be Avoided*. Washington, DC. https://openknowledge.worldbank.org/handle/10986/11860 License: CC BY-NC-ND 3.0 IGO."

World Bank. (2015). *World development report 2015: Mind, society, and behavior*. The World Bank. https://doi.org/10.1596/978-1-4648-0342-0

World Bank. (2021). *World Development Report 2021: Data for Better Lives*. Washington, DC. doi:10.1596/978-1-4648-1600-0.

World Bank. (2022). *Closing the gender gap*. ESMAP. https://www.esmap.org/closing_the_gender_gap.

Index

9 781600 121098